Guide to

NEW YORK CITY
LANDMARKS
T H I R D   E D I T I O N

Guide to

NEW YORK CITY LANDMARKS

THIRD EDITION

New York City Landmarks
Preservation Commission

Text by
Andrew S. Dolkart
Matthew A. Postal

WILEY

JOHN WILEY & SONS, INC.

Maps © 2004 Protonic, Washington, D.C. All rights reserved.
Maps licensed to the New York City Landmarks Preservation Foundation, Inc.

Page layout and typographical design by Jay Anning, Thumb Print.

Cover photo credits. Front cover, left to right, top to bottom: Jumel Terrace Historic District (Manhattan H.D. 46), Landmarks Preservation Commission collection; Bronx County Courthouse Bronx No. 14), photo by John Barrington Bayley; Trans World Airlines Flight Center at John F. Kennedy International Airport (Queens No. 50), photo by Carl Forster; Solomon R. Guggenheim Museum (Manhattan No. 472), photo by Caroline Kane Levy; Lever House (Manhattan No. 300), photo by Florian Holzherr, Courtesy Skidmore, Owings & Merrill; Parachute Jump (Brooklyn No. 100), photo by Carl Forster; Gould Memorial Library (Bronx No. 26), Landmarks Preservation Commission collection; Municipal Building (Manhattan No. 74), photo by Carl Forster; Alice Austen House (Staten Island No. 26), courtesy Staten Island Historical Society. *Back cover, left to right:* Tweed Courthouse (Manhattan No. 65), photo by Carl Forster; George S. Bowdoin Stable (Manhattan No. 322), photo by Carl Forster; Bartow House (Bronx No. 63), photo by John Barrington Bayley.

Library of Congress Control Number: 2003112635

ISBN: 0471-36900-4

Printed in the United States of America

10 9 8 7 6 5 4 3

Contents

STATEN ISLAND

THE ISLANDS: GOVERNORS, LIBERTY, ELLIS, AND ROOSEVELT 365

OF SPECIAL INTEREST

FOREWORD

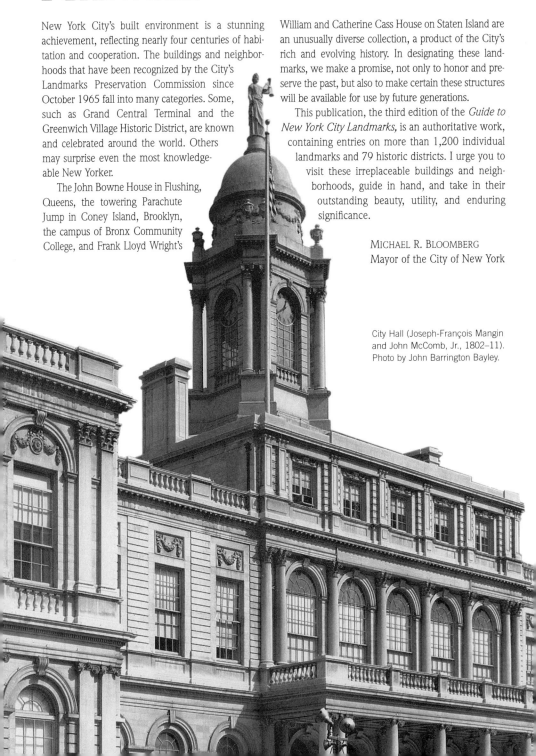

New York City's built environment is a stunning achievement, reflecting nearly four centuries of habitation and cooperation. The buildings and neighborhoods that have been recognized by the City's Landmarks Preservation Commission since October 1965 fall into many categories. Some, such as Grand Central Terminal and the Greenwich Village Historic District, are known and celebrated around the world. Others may surprise even the most knowledgeable New Yorker.

The John Bowne House in Flushing, Queens, the towering Parachute Jump in Coney Island, Brooklyn, the campus of Bronx Community College, and Frank Lloyd Wright's William and Catherine Cass House on Staten Island are an unusually diverse collection, a product of the City's rich and evolving history. In designating these landmarks, we make a promise, not only to honor and preserve the past, but also to make certain these structures will be available for use by future generations.

This publication, the third edition of the *Guide to New York City Landmarks,* is an authoritative work, containing entries on more than 1,200 individual landmarks and 79 historic districts. I urge you to visit these irreplaceable buildings and neighborhoods, guide in hand, and take in their outstanding beauty, utility, and enduring significance.

MICHAEL R. BLOOMBERG
Mayor of the City of New York

City Hall (Joseph-François Mangin and John McComb, Jr., 1802–11). Photo by John Barrington Bayley.

PREFACE

Welcome to the third edition of the *Guide to New York City Landmarks*, an introduction to the historic, architectural, and cultural treasures of New York City's five boroughs by the City's Landmarks Preservation Commission. From the Woolworth Building in Lower Manhattan, to the Bronx Zoo, to the Unisphere in Queens, to Prospect Park in Brooklyn, to the Alice Austen House on Staten Island, the nearly 23,000 landmarks designated by the Landmarks Preservation Commission—individual, interior, historic districts, and scenic—define the culture and character of this great metropolis.

First, a bit of history about how the New York City Landmarks Preservation Commission has come to protect and preserve this legacy. In a sense, this is a tale of two train stations: the loss of one—McKim, Mead & White's Pennsylvania Station—galvanized preservation advocates and led to the passage of the New York City Landmarks Law and the creation of the Landmarks Preservation Commission in 1965. Years later, the Commission's decision to deny permission to build a 55-story tower above a second train station—Grand Central Terminal—was challenged and resulted in a 1978 United States Supreme Court decision that upheld the Landmarks Law and strengthened the historic preservation movement throughout the United States.

This year, 2003, marks the twenty-fifth anniversary of this ruling, and the occasion invites a look back at the Commission's work and its impact. Unquestionably, New York would be a different city had the Landmarks Law not been upheld. Many great buildings would almost certainly have been razed by bulldozers, as was Pennsylvania Station; others would have been altered beyond recognition. In the decision that preserved Grand Central Terminal, Supreme Court Justice William Brennan wrote: "Structures with special historic, cultural, or architectural significance enhance the quality of life for all. Not only do these buildings and their workmanship represent the lessons of the past and embody precious features of our heritage, they serve as examples of quality for today." The recent restoration of Grand Central Terminal is a testament to these ideas.

After the Landmarks Law established the Landmarks Preservation Commission and empowered the City to protect New York's architectural heritage, the Commission turned its attention initially to those neighborhoods, house museums, and civic structures that were the oldest and best known in the City. In its early years, the Commission designated the Pieter Claesen Wyckoff House in Brooklyn, the oldest house in New York; the United States Custom House in Lower Manhattan; the John Bowne House in Queens; the Pierre Billiou House on Staten Island; and the Brooklyn Heights Historic District.

As time passed, however, our definition of a landmark evolved. With the encouragement of architectural historians, preservationists, and local residents, the Commission designated such varied structures as the Brooklyn Clay Retort and Fire Brick Works Storehouse in Brooklyn; the Brown Building, site of the Triangle shirtwaist factory fire; and several significant modern buildings, including Lever House and the Seagram Building.

Once perceived as an obstacle to progress, preservation is now understood to play an integral role in the City's economy. This shift in perception is exemplified by plans for a new Pennsylvania Station within the U.S. General Post Office. The developers who tore down the original station gave little thought to the historical and architectural significance of the building. Today, the landmark U.S. General Post Office, designed by McKim, Mead & White as a companion to the original station, is being adapted for a new use: an expanded Pennsylvania Station transit hub, to be named after the late Senator Daniel Patrick Moynihan, who championed efforts to relocate the station to the post office site.

The Commission takes great pride in preserving the character of our neighborhoods and buildings, in the belief that landmarks anchor community renewal and pride and touch all New Yorkers. Our collective memories of New York's past, and our appreciation of its present, are the templates for its future. I invite you to use this guide to explore all the diverse historical, architectural, and cultural riches New York City has to offer, perhaps to take a moment to reflect upon what might have been lost, and to celebrate all that has endured.

ROBERT B. TIERNEY, Chairman
New York City Landmarks
Preservation Commission

Acknowledgments

This is the third edition of the *Guide to New York City Landmarks*. It is our hope that the new and revised entries, updated maps, and essays will encourage city residents and visitors to discover the abundant treasures described in these pages. A grant from the New York City Landmarks Preservation Foundation provided the crucial financial support that enabled us to update and expand the book's content. The Foundation was also on board and enthusiastically backed the addition of the freshly created "Of Special Interest" essays. Mark Silberman, counsel to the New York City Landmarks Preservation Commission, served as an intrepid organizer in tackling the tasks of the new edition and was joined this time by the devoted researcher and writer, Matthew A. Postal. Matthew, who served as the project's coordinator, wrote the new entries and updated the existing ones. The thematic essays sprinkled throughout the book were Matthew's idea and were developed by him. The contributions Andrew S. Dolkart made to the previous editions were indispensable. His concise and thoughtful entries continue to serve as the foundation for this publication. Mary Beth Betts, director of research, and Brian Hogg, director of preservation, lent their encyclopedic knowledge of New York City and its landmarks, as well as their deep-felt enthusiasm, to the project. Members of the Commission's research department, under Ms. Betts' direction, conducted the research and wrote most of the designation reports on which the entries are based.

The maps, locating all designated landmarks in New York City, were done under the thorough and skilled supervision of Ted Ostindien of Protonic, a Washington, D.C., company specializing in custom maps and real-estate graphics. Most of the photographs were taken by the Commission's staff photographer, Carl Forster. Kate Daly, community associate, and Diane Jackier, director of community and government affairs, both at the Commission, helped with the research and editing. Sherida Paulsen, chairman of the Commission during the initial development of this edition, was essential to its publication. She championed the project and put her total support behind it. Robert Tierney, the current Chairman of the Landmarks Preservation Commission, continued to lend generous additional support through the completion of the guidebook. All important to the revision of this guidebook was the encouragement and advocacy of our editor, Amanda Miller at John Wiley & Sons, Inc. We thank her for spearheading its revision. We continue to be appreciative to the American Express Company, and to Furthermore, the publication program of the J.M. Kaplan Fund, for grants that allowed the publication of the previous edition.

Susan H. Ball, Chairman
New York City Landmarks
Preservation Foundation
May 2003

INTRODUCTION:
HOW TO USE THIS GUIDE

This guide includes information on all individual landmarks, interior landmarks, scenic landmarks, and historic districts designated by the New York City Landmarks Preservation Commission from October 14, 1965 (when the Commission made its first designations) through December 2002. During this time 1,093 individual landmarks, 104 interior landmarks, 9 scenic landmarks, and 79 historic districts—a total of more than 22,000 properties—were designated. The entries briefly explain the architectural and historical significance of these landmark properties. Listings have been divided among New York City's five boroughs: Manhattan, Brooklyn, Queens, the Bronx, and Staten Island. Governors, Liberty, Ellis (in part), and Roosevelt Islands, which are under the jurisdiction of the borough of Manhattan, appear in a chapter of their own for easier reference.

The designer, Protonic, subdivided Manhattan in its entirety into eighteen maps, while it created more geographically specific maps appropriate to Brooklyn, Queens, the Bronx, and Staten Island. Overview maps, located at the beginning of each borough, outline these subdivisions. Within each map or area, historic districts are listed first, followed by entries for individual landmarks.

Each individual, interior, and scenic landmark has been assigned a number. Each number is contained within an oval or circle. Individual entries can encompass more than one landmark structure (see, for example, Staten Island No. 23), or more than one type of landmark within a single building (see, for example, Manhattan No. 235, which has both interior and exterior designations). The scenic landmarks, some containing individual designations within their borders, are identified with a maple leaf (see, for example, Brooklyn No. 79). Historic district boundaries have been drawn where appropriate. These districts (sometimes abbreviated "H.D.") are numbered separately, and the number is contained within a diamond shape that is incorporated into the boundary line (see, for example, Queens H.D. 3). Each borough's landmarks and historic districts have been numbered separately, beginning with "1." Entries on notable buildings that are not individual landmarks but are found within the Greenwich Village or Brooklyn Heights historic districts are identified by a capital letter contained within a square (see, for example, Manhattan H.D. 12, J).

Any guidebook faces the challenge of how to organize information. For ease of reference, each borough's entries are listed in numerical order. With respect to the numbering, it was our goal to group entries in a way that would appear logical to a reader using the book to plan an itinerary. Given that each reader may have their own way of moving through the city we, somewhat arbitrarily, adopted the following rules: numbering generally goes from west to east, and from south to north, in Manhattan and the Bronx, and from north to south in Brooklyn, Queens, and Staten Island. (This corresponds to the general historical develop-

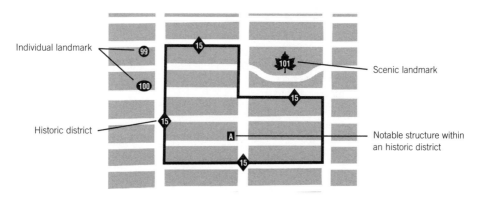

Individual landmark
Historic district
Scenic landmark
Notable structure within an historic district

1

ment pattern of the boroughs.) In Manhattan, where a map covers a large geographic area or contains many landmarks, we have subdivided the map and grouped entries—using these same general rules—within each subdivision. This orientation is not followed on the Upper West Side (maps 12 and 13). There, under the assumption that many readers would be orienting themselves from Central Park, the subdivisions and entries run from east to west.

Entries begin with the number that corresponds to the location of the landmark on the map. The historic name is listed first, followed, where applicable, by other names associated with the property, and then the address. In a few cases where use of a historic name might lead to confusion or where a later name is much better known, the entry begins with the common name (for example, Fordham University, rather than Saint John's College). Architects associated with the original construction and any significant additions to the property, along with the dates indicating the widest determinable span of years associated with the design, construction and completion of the building, are cited next. Interior landmarks are indicated in two ways. Where only the interior is a landmark, the word "interior" is contained in parentheses after the name. Where both the exterior and the interior are landmarks, the interior landmark designation is indicated by the word **interior** in boldface type within the text.

This expanded edition contains several innovations. In response to public inquiries we have added the date that each landmark and historic district was designated, and in most cases, how it was identified at the time of designation. Fifteen brief essays, organized under the title "Of Special Interest," have been inserted throughout the text. These informative essays highlight specific aspects of the Commission's work, for instance, designations from the colonial era, innovative housing complexes, rare and unusual structures, as well as new construction and additions to historic districts. These thematic essays are listed in the table of contents.

Andrew S. Dolkart wrote the entries for the first two editions (1992 and 1997) of the guidebook. Matthew A. Postal has updated these entries and writ-ten the new entries for the individual landmarks and historic districts designated by the Commission from February 1997 through December 2002, as well as the "Of Special Interest" essays. All entries are based on the designation reports researched and written by the Commission's research staff under the supervision of the director of research, although Mr. Dolkart and Mr. Postal did independent research for some entries. The research staff is currently composed of Gale Harris, Virginia Kurshan, Matthew A. Postal, Donald G. Presa, and Jay Shockley; Marjorie Pearson served as the director from 1978 to 1999, Mary Beth Betts has served in the position from 1999 to the present. The Commission continues to designate new landmarks and historic districts. Information on new designations can be obtained by visiting the Commission's web site at www.nyc.gov/landmarks.

Please note that the New York City Landmarks Preservation Commission does not own or operate any landmark properties. In many cases, these properties are private residences, and the reader is asked to respect the privacy of owners and occupants. Viewing a landmark from a street or other public way is, of course, permissible. However, permission must be obtained from the owner or occupant before venturing onto the property. The entries indicate which properties are museums or otherwise open to the public; visitors to these properties are, in many cases, charged a fee. Interior landmarks are customarily open to the public. Depending on the nature and current use of the space, a ticket may be required or a fee charged.

The Commission recognizes that ongoing research on the city's architecture and history will continue to bring new information to light. The Commission would be pleased to receive such information directed to the attention of its research department. Corrections of errors that might inadvertently have crept into this edition of the guide may also be addressed to:

Research Department
The New York City Landmarks
Preservation Commission
1 Centre Street, 9th Floor North
New York, NY 10007

MANHATTAN

MANHATTAN

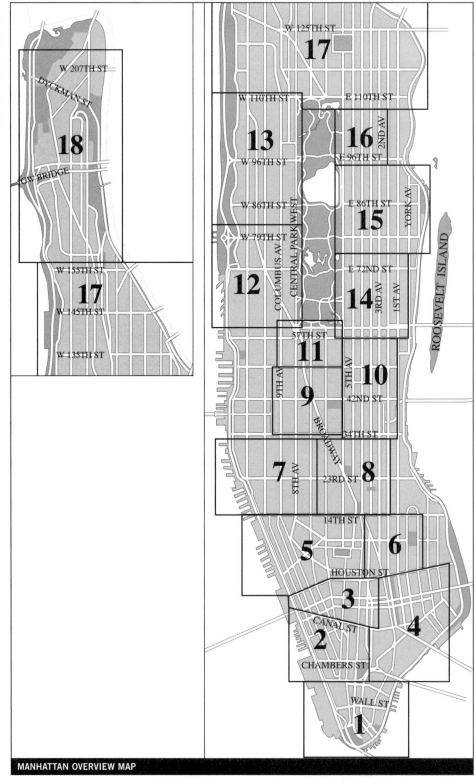

MANHATTAN OVERVIEW MAP

4

HISTORIC DISTRICTS

1 Fraunces Tavern Block Historic District, designated 1978. The low-rise buildings of this square block provide an unusual illustration of the early building history of Lower Manhattan. Dating primarily from the early 19th century, these buildings stand in marked contrast to the surrounding 20th-century skyscrapers. The block escaped the fire of December 1835 that devastated most of Lower Manhattan. Thus the district retains eleven early buildings, erected between 1827 and 1833, including a rare example of a warehouse in the Federal style (62 Pearl Street, 1827) and several Greek Revival countinghouses. Also in the district is Fraunces

Tavern (see No. 46). Much of the block was saved from demolition in 1974.

2 Stone Street Historic District, designated 1996. This small historic district, incorporating a part of the colonial street plan of New Amsterdam (see No. 1), is an extraordinary remnant of New York's small-scale commercial architecture, set amid tall 20th-century skyscrapers. The area, initially built up in the 17th and 18th centuries, was destroyed in the fire of December 1835. Immediately after the fire, Greek Revival–style countinghouses, with granite bases of post-and-lintel construction and brick upper stories, were erected for importers, dry goods dealers, and other merchants. Many of these four-

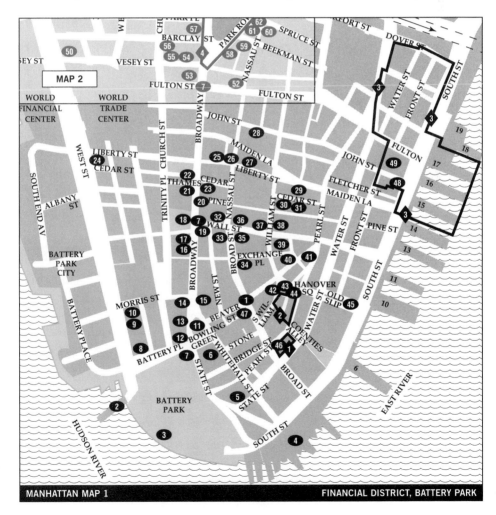

Stone Street Historic District (H.D. 2) looking down South William Street. Nestled among towering skyscrapers, the Stone Street Historic District is a remnant of an earlier period in New York's commercial development. Photo by Caroline Kane Levy.

story commercial structures survive on Stone and Pearl Streets; most extend through the block and thus have two street facades. In the mid-19th century, the austere Greek Revival style was superseded by the Italianate style, as exemplified by the major commercial building from this era in the district, the Hanover Bank (now India House; see No. 44) on Hanover Square. In the first years of the 20th century, major changes began occurring in the district, initiated by the Eno family, which had extensive real-estate holdings in New York. In 1903 Amos F. Eno commissioned the prominent architect C. P. H. Gilbert to design new street facades on the building at 13 South William Street/57 Stone Street for his family's real-estate office. Gilbert's picturesque neo–Dutch Renaissance design (expanded in 1908 with another new front at 15 South William Street), with its stepped gables and strapwork detail, is a nostalgic reminder of the area's colonial heritage. During the next several decades, other facades were redesigned or new buildings constructed in a variety of revival styles, notably the neo-Renaissance front of 17 South William Street (Edward L. Tilton, 1906), the neo-Tudor club at 21–23 South William Street (William Neil Smith, 1927–28), the neo-Renaissance facade with exposed metal lintels designed by Arthur C. Jackson (1919) for marine underwriters Chubb & Son at 54 Stone Street, and the neo-Gothic office building for the marine insurance firm William H. McGee & Co. (William Neil Smith, 1929) at 9–11 South William Street. In 1995 Beyer Blinder Belle prepared a master plan for the upgrading and economic revitalization of the area.

❸ **South Street Seaport Historic District and Extension,** designated 1977 and 1989. This district contains the largest concentration of early 19th-century commercial buildings in New York. It is an unparalleled physical representation of the extraordinary development of trade and commerce in the early decades of the 19th century as New York City became the economic and financial capital of the nation. The streets are lined with the countinghouses where New York's merchants had their offices and warehoused their goods. Among the very early buildings are those of 1811–12 that make up the Georgian-Federal-style Schermerhorn Row on Fulton Street (see No. 49). More common are the Greek Revival countinghouses of the 1830s, most with first stories of granite post-and-lintel construction with

brick above, such as 247 Water Street (1837; restored, Peter Talbot and James D'Auria, 1992–93) and the trio at 207–211 Water Street (1835–37). A few of the countinghouses have stone fronts, such as the granite Hickson W. Field Store (see No. 48) at 170–176 John Street and the brownstone building erected for A. A. Low & Brothers in 1849 at 167–171 John Street (see Schermerhorn Row Block, No. 49; Low Memorial Library at Columbia University is named for Abiel Abbot Low; see No. 525). By the second half of the 19th century, the South Street area had lost its prominence in New York's commercial life. Many buildings were converted for the wholesale Fulton Fish Market, and a few new structures were built. Among the prominent later buildings designed by noted New York architects are 116–119 South Street (John B. Snook, 1873), which became Meyers Hotel in 1881; 142–144 Beekman Street, a Romanesque Revival building designed by George B. Post in 1885 for fish dealers and ornamented with terra-cotta fish keystones and seashell cornice and iron starfish tie-rods; and Richard Morris Hunt's 1873 red brick building with black brick decorative trim at 21–23 Peck Slip. The area deteriorated in the 20th century, but restoration began in the early 1970s with the creation of the South Street Seaport Museum and Marketplace. Notable new construction in the area has included 15–19 Fulton Street (Beyer Blinder Belle, 1977–83), which is faced with steel panels emulating cast iron, and the Seamen's Church Institute (James Stewart Polshek & Partners, 1989–91) at 241 Water Street.

INDIVIDUAL LANDMARKS

❶ **Street Plan of New Amsterdam and Colonial New York,** including all or part of Beaver, Bridge, Broad, Hanover, Marketfield, New, Pearl, South William, Stone, Wall, Whitehall, and William Streets; Exchange Place; Hanover Square; Mill Lane; and Broadway, designated 1983. The financial center of the United States was built on the 17th-century street pattern of colonial New Amsterdam. The Dutch colonial street plan of Lower Manhattan, south of Wall Street, underwent only minor additions and alterations by the British. These narrow streets are the only visible aboveground evidence in Manhattan of the colonial settlement. Streets developed in an organic manner from the original waterfront at Pearl Street. Broadway was the major colonial street, running north along a ridge from the original fort at the Battery. Broad Street ran from the waterfront and contained a canal, which explains its exceptional width.

2 **Pier A,** Battery Park (George Sears Greene, Jr., engineer, 1884–86; addition, 1900), designated 1977. Jutting into New York Bay at the southern end of Manhattan, Pier A was built for the city's Department of Docks and Harbor Police and was designed by the department's chief engineer. It is the last surviving historic pier in Manhattan. Additions include the three-story pier head (1900) and the clock located in the tower at the west end of the pier, which was installed in 1919 as a memorial to servicemen who died in World War I.

3 **Castle Clinton,** now Castle Clinton National Monument, Battery Park (Lt. Col. Jonathan Williams and John McComb, Jr., 1808–11), designated 1965. Originally built on an artificial island off the Battery, and referred to as West Battery, Castle Clinton—so named in 1815—was one of a series of forts, including Castle Williams on Governors Island (see Governors Island Historic District), erected to protect New York Harbor. Although the design of the brownstone fort is often attributed to John McComb, Jr., he was probably responsible only for the entrance. After becoming the property of New York City in 1823, the former fort served as a theater (Castle Garden), an immigrant station, and an aquarium before it was restored by the federal government in the early 1970s.

4 **Whitehall Ferry Terminal,** now the Battery Maritime Building, 11 South Street (Walker & Morris, 1906–09), designated 1967. The ferry terminal with its three slips was designed in a Beaux-Arts style and built with exposed steel reminiscent of French exposition architecture. The only survivor of the many historic ferry terminals that once lined New York's waterfront, it now serves ferries running to Governors Island.

5 **James Watson House,** now the Rectory of the Shrine of Saint Elizabeth Ann Seton, 7 State Street (attributed to John McComb, Jr., 1793; extension, 1806), designated 1965. When this house was erected, Lower Manhattan was still a fashionable residential area. The original Georgian structure has an elegant addition in the Federal style with an Ionic portico conforming to the curve of the street. The building is now a shrine to the first native-born American (and New Yorker) granted sainthood by the Roman Catholic Church.

6 **United States Custom House,** now Alexander Hamilton Custom House (National Museum of the American Indian and Federal Bankruptcy Court), Bowling Green (Cass Gilbert, 1899–1907), designated 1965, interior 1979. In 1899 the Minnesota architect Cass Gilbert won the competition for New York's new customhouse with a masterful essay in Beaux-Arts design. The building has bold three-dimensional massing and an extensive sculptural program on themes related to commerce and trade; the most notable sculptures are Daniel Chester French's *Four Continents,* which flank the grand entrance stairway. The **interiors** on the main floor are as ornate as the exterior. The richly detailed marble entrance hall leads to an oval rotunda embellished with a mural cycle by Reginald Marsh installed in 1936–37 as part of the Treasury Department's Depression-era arts project. Magnificently decorated offices are arranged along the front of the building. After standing empty for many years, most of the landmark spaces have been restored for the National Museum of the American Indian under the direction of Ehrenkrantz & Eckstut Architects.

7 **Interborough Rapid Transit System:** Numerous sites in Manhattan and Brooklyn, including **Control Houses,** Battery Park and West 72nd Street (Heins & La Farge, 1904–05), designated 1973 and 1979; **Manhattan Valley Viaduct,** Broadway from West 122nd to West 135th Streets (William B. Parsons, engineer, 1900–04), designated 1981; **Underground Stations,** Wall Street, Fulton Street, City Hall, Bleecker Street, Astor Place, and 33rd Street, Manhattan, and Borough Hall, Brooklyn, on the Lexington Avenue IRT Line; 59th Street–Columbus Circle, 72nd Street, 79th Street, 110th Street, and 116th Street–Columbia University on the Seventh Avenue IRT Line (Heins & La Farge, architect, and William B. Parsons, engineer, Contract 1, 1899–1904; Contract 2, 1902–08), designated 1979. Following a succession of aborted attempts to build a subway system in Manhattan, a contract was signed in 1899 for the construction of the Interborough Rapid Transit Company's first subway. The original IRT line (Contract 1) ran from City Hall to Grand Central Terminal and then turned west to Times Square and north along Broadway to the Bronx. In 1902 Contract 2 extended the system south from City Hall through Lower Manhattan and into Brooklyn. Chief engineer Parsons and his staff were responsible for the construction of the system. One of the most spectacular engineering features planned by Parsons is the Manhattan Valley Viaduct, which carries the Broadway line over a valley at West 125th Street and which consists of approaches faced with rock-fronted granite blocks, steel viaducts, and a central span with three parabolic arches. Although the engineers sited and planned each subway station, the architecture firm of Heins & La Farge designed the ornamentation. The architects were required to use white tile and light-colored brick except where color was "introduced for architectural effect." Color was used for the mosaic sign panels and for the terra-cotta and faience plaques (provided by the Rookwood Pottery of Cincinnati and the Grueby Faience Company of Boston) that embellish each station. At many stations the plaques were designed with an attribute unique to that stop. These include the beavers at Astor Place (John Jacob Astor made his initial fortune in beaver pelts), a sailing ship at Columbus Circle, and the seal of Columbia University at 116th Street. In addition to the subterranean stations, Heins & La Farge designed the aboveground entrance structures. Although all the original cast-iron entrance canopies have been removed (a canopy has been reconstructed at Astor Place), two of the Flemish-inspired brick and terra-cotta control houses still stand in Manhattan—at Battery Park just south of Bowling Green and at Broadway and West 72nd Street.

8 **Whitehall Building**, 17 Battery Place (Henry J. Hardenbergh, 1902–04; addition, Clinton & Russell, 1908–10), designated 2000. This former office building occupies one of Lower Manhattan's most prominent sites. Named for the mid-17th-century home of Dutch governor Peter Stuyvesant that was located nearby, it was designed with bold Renaissance motifs by Henry J. Hardenbergh, one of the city's premier architects. A 30-story addition, crowned by a rounded pediment, was completed in 1910. The building was converted to apartments in 2000.

United States Custom House (No. 6). The Custom House is an essay in Beaux-Arts design and also has an extensive sculptural program on themes relating to commerce and trade. The park in the foreground is Bowling Green (No. 11). Photo by Carl Forster.

MANHATTAN

❾ Downtown Athletic Club, 19 West Street (Starrett & Van Vleck, 1929–30), designated 2000. A rare example of a skyscraper clubhouse, the Downtown Athletic Club was designed in the Art Deco style by Starret & Van Vleck, the architects of 21 West Street. The irregular massing reflects the configuration of the facilities inside, which originally included a miniature golf course. Mottled orange brick, laid in various patterns, was used to create subtle textural patterns on the facades. Since 1935, the club has sponsored the Heisman Trophy, awarded to each year's outstanding college football player.

❿ 21 West Street Building (Starett & Van Vleck, 1929–31), designated 1998. Faced in patterns of tan, orange, and purple brick, this Art Deco skyscraper was designed to complement the neighboring Downtown Athletic Club. Starett & Van Vleck, who were responsible for several of the city's most famous department stores, gave this speculative office building many stylish features, including a set-back profile, corner windows, and a recessed shopping arcade. In 1998 it was converted to apartments.

⓫ Bowling Green Fence, Bowling Green Park (1771), designated 1970. This simple iron fence was erected in 1771 to protect a statue of King George III. Although the statue was destroyed in 1776, the fence survives as a unique example of pre–Revolutionary War craftsmanship in New York City.

⓬ International Mercantile Marine Company Building, 1 Broadway (Walter B. Chambers, 1919–21), designated 1995. This austere neoclassical office building, a recladding of an 1880s structure, has facades that are appropriately ornamented with symbols of the sea (seashells, ropes, tridents, dolphins, etc.) and mosaic shields representing many of the world's great port cities. The project was commissioned by the International Mercantile Marine Co., a firm organized in 1902 by J. P. Morgan that combined several independent steamship companies into one powerful entity later known as the United States Lines. The Battery Place entrances, marked "First Class" and "Cabin Class," led into an elegant ticketing hall.

⓭ Bowling Green Offices Building, 5–11 Broadway (W. & G. Audsley, 1895–98), designated 1995. This massive office building was designed by British-immigrant architects who described it as a work in the "Hellenic Renaissance" style. The use of Greek, or "Hellenic," forms is evident in the basic tripartite massing (resembling the base-shaft-capital form of a column), in the line of bold pilasters at the base, and in the impressive Grecian entrance enframements. The building initially housed steamship lines and many firms involved with shipping.

⓮ Cunard Building, 25 Broadway (Benjamin Wistar Morris; Carrère & Hastings, consulting architect, 1917–21), designated 1995. Benjamin Wistar Morris worked on the design of this building in 1917–19, experimenting with many massing ideas and a variety of styles before settling on a powerful Renaissance form with subtle nautical detail. The simplicity of the exterior contrasts with the extraordinary richness of the **interior,** which served as the booking hall for the great ocean liners owned by Cunard. The entrance lobby and the Great Hall are two of the finest spaces of their era. The groin-vaulted lobby contains nautical ceiling sculpture carved by Carl Jennewein and painted by Ezra Winter. Gates by master ironworker Samuel Yellin of Philadelphia lead into the spectacular Great Hall (now a post office), with its complex spatial arrangement and superb ceiling frescoes by Winter, wall murals by Barry Faulkner, and rich travertine and marble detail.

⓯ Standard Oil Building, 26 Broadway (Carrère & Hastings; Shreve, Lamb & Blake, associate, 1920–28), designated 1995. Thomas Hastings was largely responsible for the Renaissance-inspired design of this impressive limestone skyscraper, which served as the corporate headquarters and a powerful symbol of Standard Oil, the huge oil company founded by John D. Rockefeller. The complex design takes into consideration the alignment of Broadway and the irregular pentagonal plot, resulting in a curved base and skewed tower capped by a bronze brazier. The tower is a prominent feature of the skyline when viewed from the harbor. The building was constructed in five sections beginning in 1921, so that office tenants, including Standard Oil itself, could be conveniently relocated, and a Childs Restaurant on Beaver Street, which refused to move, could be accommodated until its lease expired in 1928. The facades are ornamented with symbolic lamps, flaming torches, and "SO" ciphers. Standard Oil sold the building in 1956.

16 **American Express Company Building,** 65 Broadway (James L. Aspinwall of Renwick, Aspinwall & Tucker, 1914–17), designated 1995. American Express was established in 1850 to provide reliable transport of packages and valuables. Among the founders were Henry Wells and William Fargo. In the late 19th century, the firm branched into financial services, instituting the money order in 1882 and inventing the traveler's check in 1891. American Express purchased the property on Broadway, stretching through the block to Trinity Place, in 1903 and began planning a towering new home in 1914. Two years later construction began on this 21-story neoclassical-style concrete and steel-framed building faced with white brick and terra cotta over a granite base. American Express retained its headquarters here until 1975.

17 **Empire Building,** 71 Broadway (Kimball & Thompson, 1895–98), designated 1996. The richly decorative classically inspired detail on the Empire Building's three street elevations exemplify the manner in which skyscraper architects in New York adapted traditional architectural styles to the new skyscraper building type. Francis Kimball, a pioneer in the design of steel-skeleton-frame skyscrapers, created a boldly detailed structure with a triumphal-arch entry. It was the headquarters of the United States Steel Corporation from its establishment by J. P. Morgan in 1901 until 1976. The building was converted to apartments in 1997.

18 **Trinity Church (Episcopal) and Graveyard,** Broadway at Wall Street (Richard Upjohn, 1839–46; sacristy, Frederick Clarke Withers, 1876–77; All Saints' Chapel, Thomas Nash, 1911–13; Manning Wing, Adams & Woodbridge, 1966), designated 1966. One of the first Gothic Revival buildings in New York and one of Upjohn's earliest works, Trinity Church was for many years the tallest structure in the city, its spire towering over New York's business district. The present church is the third built on this site for New York's oldest Episcopal congregation. The building was constructed of New Jersey brownstone, whose original light and varied hues were revealed when the exterior was cleaned in 1990–91 by Brisk Waterproofing Co. The church has had several important additions, including the sacristy, the chapel, and Manning Wing at the west end, and the bronze entrance doors (1890–96) donated as a memorial to John Jacob Astor

III, which were designed by Richard Morris Hunt in collaboration with the sculptors Karl Bitter, J. Massey Rhind, and Charles Niehaus. The surrounding graveyard contains the tombs of such famous Americans as Alexander Hamilton, Albert Gallatin, Francis Lewis, William Bradford, and Robert Fulton, as well as many fine 18th-century gravestones.

19 **1 Wall Street,** now the Bank of New York (Ralph Walker of Voorhees, Gmelin & Walker, 1929–31), designated 2001. A superb example of the Art Deco style, this 50-story skyscraper was built as the headquarters of the Irving Trust Company. Walker made skillful use of traditional materials, cladding the steel frame with limestone blocks that suggest a fluted column or draped cloth. The resulting tower is one of the city's most visible and elegant, enhanced by rhythmic setbacks, chamfered corners, and concave windows that conform to the

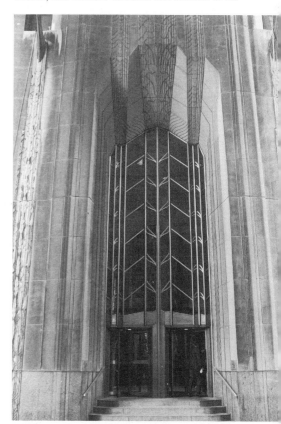

Ralph Walker's 1 Wall Street (No. 19) is a masterpiece of the Art Deco style. Photo by Carl Foster.

shape of the walls. The building was acquired as part of a merger by the Bank of New York in 1988.

20 **American Surety Company Building**, 100 Broadway (Bruce Price, 1894–96; addition, Herman Lee Meader, 1920–22), designated 1997. Among Manhattan's most important and influential early skyscrapers, the American Surety Company Building stands opposite Trinity Church, in what was once the heart of the insurance district. Built as a free-standing tower, it was one of the first buildings in the city to use steel framing and curtain-wall construction techniques. The Renaissance-inspired elevations were designed to suggest a column, divided into a base, shaft, and capital. Price's solution was widely praised, and many subsequent office buildings adopted this model. In 1920–22, Herman Lee Meader designed an L-shaped addition, fronting both Broadway and Pine Streets. Although the original proportions were altered, the new bays were executed with great sensitivity.

21 **Trinity Building and United States Realty Building,** 111 and 115 Broadway (Francis H. Kimball, 1904–07), designated 1988. These two skyscrapers were designed with Gothic detail to harmonize with neighboring Trinity Church (see No. 18) and were dubbed by the *New York Times* "twin examples of Gothic splendor." The construction of these enormous slabs was a major undertaking, entailing the relocation of Thames Street and the construction of caissons 80 feet into the marshy subsoil. The limestone-faced buildings are carefully detailed with towers, gables, and fanciful carved ornament.

22 **United States Realty Building**, see above.

23 **Equitable Building,** 120 Broadway (Ernest Graham & Associates, Peirce Anderson, architect in charge, 1913–15), designated 1996. At its completion in 1915, the Equitable Building was the largest office building in the world in square footage. This massive structure, with its entrances in the form of triumphal arches and its classical ornamental detail, was a speculative venture, largely planned by Thomas Du Pont, that housed the headquarters of Equitable Life, as well as the offices of many small firms. The bulk of the H-shaped building, rising 38 stories with no setbacks, provoked great controversy and was cited by opponents of unregulated growth as an example of

the evils of skyscraper construction. Its presence helped insure the passage of the first zoning law in the United States in 1916. A restoration by Ehrenkrantz, Eckstut & Whitelaw was completed in 1990.

24 **West Street Building**, 90 West Street and 140 Cedar Street (Cass Gilbert, 1905–07), designated 1998. This important midcareer work by Cass Gilbert was significantly damaged in the attack on the World Trade Center. Completed in 1907, the building, with its Gothic-inspired vocabulary, represented a major advance in early skyscraper design. The tripartite elevations, facing West, Albany, and Cedar Streets, have uninterrupted clustered piers that rise to a richly embellished mansard roof. Praised by critics, the building's romantic character anticipates Gilbert's design for the Woolworth Building (see No. 57).

25 **Chamber of Commerce of the State of New York,** now the International Commercial Bank of China, 65 Liberty Street (James B. Baker, 1900–01), designated 1966. This imposing Beaux-Arts building was erected to symbolize the chamber's importance in New York's commercial life. The marble structure, occupied by the chamber until 1980, was restored by the current owner in 1990–91.

26 **Liberty Tower,** 55 Liberty Street (Henry Ives Cobb, 1909–10), designated 1966. This handsome neo-Gothic skyscraper—clad entirely in white terra cotta and enlivened with fanciful ornament, including birds and alligators—is an important antecedent to the Woolworth Building (see No. 57). The freestanding building, which at the time of its construction was known as "the tallest building in the world on so small an area of ground," was also one of the earliest residential conversion projects in Lower Manhattan.

27 **Federal Reserve Bank of New York,** 33 Liberty Street (York & Sawyer, 1919–24), designated 1965. The massive rusticated walls of the Federal Reserve Bank, constructed of stone in two colors, symbolize the strength of the Federal Reserve system and the impregnability of this building, which stores a significant part of the world's gold reserves. The Floren-

West Street Building (No. 24) is an important midcareer work by Cass Gilbert. Photo by Carl Forster.

tine palazzo form was chosen by York & Sawyer for its association with the Medicis and other leading Renaissance families whose fortunes were made, at least in part, from banking. The iron detail was crafted by the master ironworker Samuel Yellin of Philadelphia.

28 John Street Methodist Church, 44 John Street (attributed to Philip Embury, 1841), designated 1965. John Street is the oldest Methodist congregation in North America. Founded in 1766 as the Wesleyan Society in America, the congregation erected its first church in 1768. The well-proportioned Georgian-inspired building with a brownstone facade is the third church on the site.

29 90–94 Maiden Lane (attributed to Charles Wright, 1870–71), designated 1989. One of the few mid-19th-century commercial structures still standing in Lower Manhattan, this small French Second Empire building has an iron front, cast at Daniel D. Badger's Architectural Iron Works, that united three early 19th-century warehouses. The facade was commissioned by Roosevelt & Son, the nation's leading importer of plate glass and mirrors, among whose principals was Theodore Roosevelt, the father of the country's twenty-sixth president.

30 56–58 Pine Street (Oswald Wirz, 1893–94), designated 1997. This 12-story office building, originally called the Wallace Building after its developer James Wallace, was designed by his company's architect, Oswald Wirz, with Romanesque Revival characteristics. Faced with brick, stone, and terra cotta, the building is distinguished by its round-arched openings, deeply set windows, and truncated columns, and embellished by some of the finest Byzantine carving in New York, including intricate foliate panels and fantastic heads.

31 Down Town Association Building, 60 Pine Street (Charles C. Haight, 1886–87; addition, Warren & Wetmore, 1910–11), designated 1997. This elegant Romanesque Revival–style clubhouse was designed by Charles C. Haight for one of New York's earliest private clubs. Faced with Roman brick and highlighted by terra-cotta ornament, the building has a large round-arched entranceway and arched window openings. A two-bay extension to the east of the original building by Warren & Wetmore echoes the Haight building in its materials, fenestration, and details.

32 Bankers Trust Building, 14 Wall Street (Trowbridge & Livingston, 1910–12; addition, Shreve, Lamb & Harmon, 1931–33), designated 1997. The stepped pyramid that crowns this great neoclassical limestone tower is one of the most prominent elements of the Lower Manhattan skyline and was such an icon that it became the corporate logo of Bankers Trust. Bankers Trust was organized in 1903 by a group of commercial banks that wanted to enter the lucrative market of trusts and estates; it became a full-service bank in 1917. This office building, containing space for bank offices as well as offices to produce rental income, is located at one of the most important intersections in the financial district. A major addition with subtle Art Deco detail, erected early in the 1930s, was carefully designed to be subordinate to the original structure. Bankers Trust sold the building in 1987.

33 New York Stock Exchange, 8–18 Broad Street (George B. Post, 1901–03), designated 1985. This marble-fronted building has been the home of America's principal securities market since 1903. The exchange—which dates back to 1792, when stock dealers met under a buttonwood tree on Wall Street—had been housed at a number of sites before it moved into a building at 12 Broad Street (John Kellum, architect), just south of Wall Street, in 1865. That building was enlarged in 1880–81 (James Renwick, Jr., architect) and eventually replaced by the present structure, whose six monumental Corinthian columns support a pediment containing an allegorical sculptural ensemble entitled *Integrity Protecting the Works of Man,* designed by John Quincy Adams Ward and executed by Paul Wayland Bartlett.

34 Broad Exchange Building, 25 Broad Street (Clinton & Russell, 1900–02), designated 2000. Standing opposite the New York Stock Exchange, this Renaissance-inspired skyscraper attracted many bankers and brokers as tenants. The building was converted to residential use in the late 1990s.

35 J. P. Morgan & Company, 23 Wall Street (Trowbridge & Livingston, 1913), designated 1965. At a time when skyscrapers were being erected throughout Lower Manhattan, the Morgan Bank erected this small headquarters building on one of the most valuable pieces of land in New York City,

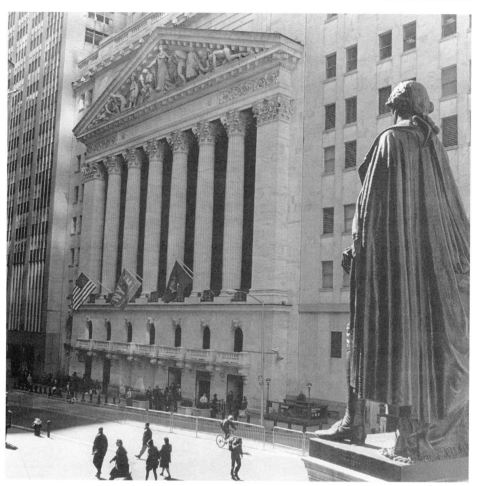

New York Stock Exchange (No. 33). The home, since 1903, of America's principal securities market. The statue of George Washington in the foreground stands on the steps of Federal Hall (No. 36). Photo by Caroline Kane Levy.

the juncture of Wall and Broad Streets. The low-scaled, austere classical building, clad in white marble, symbolized the wealth and power of this banking institution. The importance of the bank was further underscored by the absence of a name on the exterior; for those wealthy enough to bank at Morgan, no introduction was needed.

36 United States Custom House, later the U.S. Sub-Treasury, now Federal Hall National Memorial, 28 Wall Street (Town & Davis, Samuel Thompson, William Ross, and John Frazee, 1833–42), designated 1965, interior 1975. This building at the juncture of Wall, Broad, and Nassau Streets in the heart of New York's financial district occupies one of the most historic locations in New York—the site of the original Federal Hall, where George Washington took the oath of office as the nation's first president (commemorated by John Quincy Adams Ward's 1883 sculpture of Washington on the building's steps). Town & Davis designed the imposing marble Custom House, adapting the form of the Parthenon to the needs of a great 19th-century civic monument. The job of supervising construction went to the builder Samuel Thompson. Thompson and his successors, Ross and Frazee, were responsible for design changes that distressed A. J. Davis. **Interior:** The rotunda is among the finest Greek Revival rooms in New York, especially noteworthy for its Corinthian columns, saucer dome, and elegant iron railings cast in the form of classical maidens and twining vines. In 1862, when the U.S. Custom Service moved to the old Merchants' Exchange (see National City Bank, No. 31), this building became a branch of the Sub-Treasury. The building was designated a National Historic Site in 1939 and a National Memorial in 1955.

37 **Manhattan Company Building,** now the Trump Building, 40 Wall Street (H. Craig Severance; Yasuo Matsui, associate architect; Shreve & Lamb, consulting architect, 1929–30), designated 1995. Among the most visible buildings in Lower Manhattan, this 927-foot-tall skyscraper, capped by a pyramidal roof and French Gothic spire, was planned as the world's tallest building (the Chrysler Building won the battle of height). The tower was a speculative venture built by a syndicate of investors that included the Manhattan Company, parent to the Bank of the Manhattan Company, New York's second-oldest bank. The Bank of Manhattan occupied the previous building on the site; it maintained a bank and office space in this skyscraper until 1960. In an extraordinary construction campaign, builders Starrett Brothers & Eken erected the structure in less than one year.

38 **Bank of New York & Trust Company Building,** 48 Wall Street (Benjamin Wistar Morris, 1927–29), designated 1998. This neo-Georgian skyscraper was built by the Bank of New York & Trust Company, the city's oldest financial institution. As the first bank to build on Wall Street, it helped set a precedent for the street's development as the spine of the financial district. Clad in limestone, the tower rises gracefully from a rusticated base to a Federal-style cupola, crowned by an American eagle.

The elevations of the neo-Georgian Bank of New York & Trust Company Building (No. 38) rise to a four-tier lantern crowned by an American eagle. Photo by Carl Foster.

39 **National City Bank** (incorporating the Merchants' Exchange), now a hotel, 55 Wall Street (Isaiah Rogers, 1836–41; additions, McKim, Mead & White, 1907–10), designated 1965, interior 1999. The National City Bank building appears to be a single unified structure but is actually the result of two

building campaigns begun sixty-eight years apart. The Boston architect Isaiah Rogers designed the original building for the Merchants' Exchange. The three-story Greek Revival structure of Quincy granite with a dome and a colonnade of twelve Ionic columns, each a single block of stone, was one of the most impressive early 19th-century buildings in America. In 1862 the U.S. Custom Service moved from its home at 28 Wall Street (see No. 36) into this building, where it remained until a new custom house (see No. 6) was erected on Bowling Green. In 1907 James Stillman, president of the National City Bank, recognized that this freestanding Wall Street landmark would be a fitting home for his growing bank, and he arranged for its purchase from the government. Charles F. McKim was commissioned to enlarge the building. The dome was removed, the interior was gutted, four floors were added, and a second granite colonnade was carefully proportioned to align with the original. At this time, the **interior** of the main floor was redesigned in the classical Roman style by Charles F. McKim, with assistance from William S. Richardson. Built to serve as a banking hall and offices, the room is decorated with luxurious gray marble walls and floors, monumental Corinthian columns, and other grandly scaled elements inspired by Roman antiquity. At center is an immense dome embellished with astrological symbols. Since 1998 this extraordinary space has been used as a ballroom.

40 City Bank–Farmers Trust Company Building, 20 Exchange Place (Cross & Cross, 1930–31), designated 1996. This tower, designed with a combination of classical and Art Deco forms, in a style often referred to as "Modern Classic," exemplifies the dramatic exploitation of the requirements of the 1916 zoning law. The base of the freestanding building hugs the lot line and rises up through a series of setbacks to a relatively thin tower that soars 685 feet, to create one of the most prominent features of the Lower Manhattan skyline. The building has superb ornament that alludes to the National City Bank, one of the original tenants, including freestanding stylized heroic figures at the first setback, known as the "giants of finance." At the street level are spectacular doors and grilles created in nickel silver (an alloy of nickel, zinc, and copper) by sculptor David Evans.

41 Beaver Building, later the New York Cocoa Exchange Building, 82–92 Beaver Street/1 Wall Street Court (Clinton & Russell, 1903–04), designated 1996. Clinton & Russell was the leading architecture firm active in the design of speculative office buildings in New York at the beginning of the 20th century. This "flatiron"-shaped 15-story office building incorporates the Classical and Renaissance details and tripartite massing that the firm favored. The brick-clad structure was among the first skyscrapers ornamented with polychromatic glazed terra cotta. From 1904 to 1921 this was the headquarters of the Munson Steamship Company, and from 1931 to 1972 the building housed the New York Cocoa Exchange and other businesses involved in the cocoa trade.

42 Delmonico's Building, 56 Beaver Street (James Brown Lord, 1890–91), designated 1996. The legendary Delmonico's Restaurant was established as a modest café on William Street in 1827 by Swiss immigrants John and Peter Delmonico. After that building burned in 1835, the business moved to this Beaver Street location. In 1890 a luxurious new restaurant with offices above was constructed at this irregularly shaped corner site. The elegant Renaissance-inspired building is faced in beautiful orange brick with a brownstone base and terra-cotta trim. The columns that flank the corner entrance, reputedly from Pompeii, were reinstalled from the portico of the 1835 building.

43 J. & W. Seligman & Co. Building, later Lehman Brothers, now Banca Commerciale Italiana, 1 William Street (Francis H. Kimball with Julian C. Levi, 1906–07; alterations, Harry R. Allen, 1929; addition, Gino Valle, 1982–86), designated 1996. Francis Kimball's Beaux-Arts skyscraper, with its crowning *tempietto,* exploits an awkwardly shaped site to create an important focal point on William Street south of Wall Street. The building was erected as the headquarters of the investment banking firm established by the Seligmans, who were leaders of New York's German-Jewish community. In 1929, when the building was sold to Lehman Brothers, the main entrance was relocated to the rounded corner, closer to Wall Street. Italian architect Gino Valle's addition skillfully abstracts and complements Kimball's original design.

44 **Hanover Bank,** now India House, 1 Hanover Square (1852–53), designated 1965. The former Hanover Bank is the only survivor of the many Italianate banks erected in Manhattan's financial district in the 1850s. The sandstone-fronted building was modeled on Italian Renaissance palazzo prototypes, appropriate since many of the Renaissance families made their fortunes in banking. The building served as the Cotton Exchange and as the headquarters of W. R. Grace & Co. before being converted into India House, a private club whose founders were involved in foreign trade. The name was chosen because "India" and "the Indies" suggest exotic (and profitable) trading centers.

45 **First Precinct Police Station,** now the New York City Police Museum, 100 Old Slip (Hunt & Hunt, 1909–11), designated 1977. Hunt & Hunt, the firm established by the sons of the famed Richard Morris Hunt, designed this limestone police station in the form of an Italian Renaissance palazzo. The arched openings, rustication, and imposing cornice have been compared to those of the 15th-century Palazzo Riccardi in Florence. In 1973 the building closed; after standing vacant for many years it was renovated by the New York City Department of General Services. From 1993 to 2001 the offices of the Landmarks Preservation Commission were located here.

46 **Fraunces Tavern,** 54 Pearl Street (1719; reconstruction, William H. Mersereau, 1904–07, designated 1965. The original building on this site was erected in 1719 by Stephen DeLancey. In 1763 the house was converted into a tavern by Samuel Fraunces, and it was here that George Washington gave his famous farewell address to his officers. The building suffered several additions and fires in the 19th century. In 1904 the heavily altered and deteriorated building was purchased by the Sons of the Revolution, which sponsored a somewhat speculative reconstruction that is an important example of Colonial Revival design. Fraunces Tavern is now a museum and restaurant.

47 **American Bank Note Company Office Building**, 70 Broad Street (Kirby, Petit & Green, 1907–08), designated 1997. This neoclassical structure was built to serve as the corporate, administra-

tive, and sales headquarters of the American Bank Note Company. Throughout the late 19th and early 20th centuries, the firm dominated the specialized field of security engraving, producing bank notes, stamps, stock certificates, checks, drafts, and letters of credit. Though small in size, the use of overscaled columns and continuous windows enhances the building's monumental character. In 1995, after several changes of ownership, the building was converted to a restaurant.

48 **Hickson W. Field Stores,** also known as the Baker, Carver & Morrell Building, 170–176 John Street (1840; addition, Buttrick, White & Burtis, 1981–82), designated 1968. Erected for a commission merchant, this building is a rare surviving example of a Greek Revival warehouse with an all-granite front. This building type, characterized by an austere facade and a ground floor articulated by post-and-lintel construction, represents a form first perfected in Boston and introduced to New York in 1826 by Ithiel Town at his Tappan Store (demolished) on Pearl Street. At the time of designation in 1968, the building housed the Baker, Carver & Morrell ship's chandlery. The top story was added in 1981–82 during conversion into a restaurant and apartments.

49 **Schermerhorn Row Block,** 2–18 Fulton Street, 189–195 Front Street, 159–171 John Street, and 91–92 South Street (1811–49), designated 1968. Historically and architecturally, this block is the most important in the South Street Seaport area. All the buildings were erected as warehouses or countinghouses for New York's rapidly expanding mercantile sector. The oldest buildings on the block are 191 and 193 Front Street, both probably erected circa 1793 but redesigned in the 19th century. The principal developer on the block was Peter Schermerhorn, a leading merchant and a member of a prominent New York family. He was responsible for the famous Schermerhorn Row (1811–12), the four-story brick warehouses on Fulton and intersecting streets that were built in the Georgian-Federal style and were originally linked by distinctive sloping roofs with tall chimneys (the mansard on the building at the corner of Fulton and South Streets was added in 1868, when the building was a hotel). Contemporaneous with Schermerhorn Row was a group of six countinghouses on John Street, only one of which (No. 165) survives. In the 1830s Greek Revival buildings began to appear throughout New York's business district. Among the finest of these is A. A. Low & Brothers' stone warehouse at 167–171 John Street (1849), built for one of the most important firms involved in the China trade. Simpler Greek Revival brick warehouses are located at the corner of Front and John Streets (1835–36). In the early 1980s all these buildings were restored (Jan Hird Pokorny, architect) for the South Street Seaport Museum and Marketplace.

Schermerhorn Row Block (No. 49). These buildings were erected as warehouses or countinghouses for New York's rapidly expanding mercantile sector. Photo by Caroline Kane Levy.

19

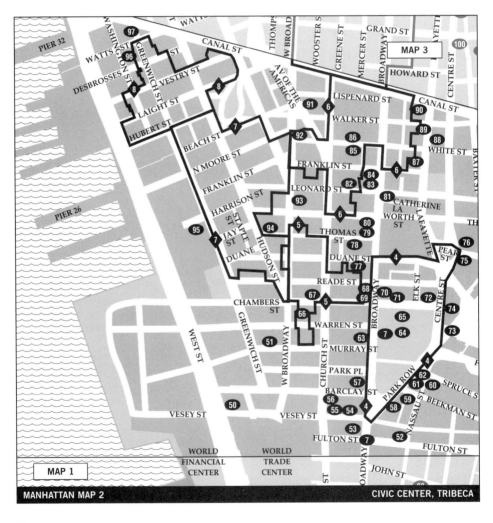
HISTORIC DISTRICTS

◆4 **African Burial Ground and the Commons Historic District**, designated 1993. This archaeological historic district commemorates two important areas that were situated on the periphery of the 17th- and 18th-century colonial settlement. The **African Burial Ground** was located on the slopes leading from the level Commons down to the Collect Pond, which is now approximately the area from Chambers to Duane Streets, and from Broadway to Foley Square. People of African ancestry—both enslaved and free—were denied the privilege of church burial during the colonial era. They used this area for interment, and it was undoubtedly a

center of spiritual and community life. By the early 19th century, the burial ground was subsumed into the city. Miraculously, the fill that was used protected many of the burials from subsequent waves of development. Archaeological investigations conducted in the early 1990s, in connection with the construction of 290 Broadway, rediscovered the burial ground. Once the analysis is complete, new light will be shed upon its important history. One portion of the site, along Duane Street, still contains burials and serves as a memorial to all who were buried here. **The Commons** was located on the current site of City Hall (see No. 64) and the surrounding park. Since the mid-17th century, it has served as a pasturage and parade ground, and as the site of nu-

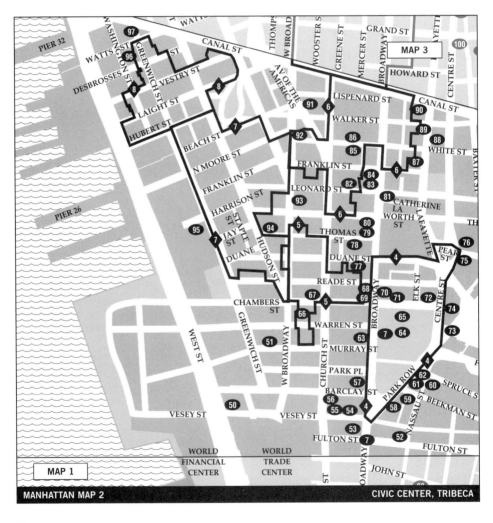

merous public events and celebrations. Archaeological work undertaken in 1999, in connection with the reconstruction of City Hall Park and Tweed Courthouse (see No. 65), uncovered information about the two almshouses that were once on the site, the Gaol (jail), the Bridewell (another penal institution) and British barracks, as well as a number of associated burials. Once the analysis is complete, it should provide important information about groups of early New Yorkers about whom there is little documentation. The current park design provides visitors with an opportunity to learn more about its history—the approximate boundaries of the structures that once stood in the park are outlined in the pavements, along with explanatory text and images.

❺ ❻ ❼ ❽ Tribeca Historic Districts (Tribeca South and Extension, Tribeca East, Tribeca West, and Tribeca North), designated

1992 and 2002, 1992, 1991, 1992. The Tribeca historic districts provide an incomparable history of the development of commercial and industrial architecture in New York City from about 1850 through the early years of the 20th century. In the late 18th century, the Lower West Side area now known as Tribeca (from "triangle below Canal") was largely in the hands of two owners—Trinity Church in the western section and the Lispenard family in the eastern section. As development in the city spread north, these owners laid out separate grids of streets (generally separated by Hudson Street) and then leased or sold plots for residential development. Tribeca became New York City's first residential neighborhood. Several early houses survive, notably at 2 White Street (1808–09; see No. 92). With the opening of the A. T. Stewart Store on the corner of Broadway and Reade Street in 1846 (see No. 70), the transformation of Tribeca into a commercial area

The north side of Leonard Street, between Broadway and Church Street, is part of the Tribeca East Historic District (H.D. 6). The cast-iron store and loft building, at center (see No. 82), was designed by James Bogardus. Photo by Oliver Allen.

began. In the 1850s and 1860s, large numbers of store and loft buildings modeled after Italian Renaissance palazzi were constructed along Broadway and on the nearby side streets, many housing retail and wholesale dry goods stores and other establishments, with storage and manufacturing space above. Most of these buildings are faced with Tuckahoe marble from Westchester County, New York, with a smaller number exhibiting facades of cast iron or Dorchester stone, a yellowish sandstone imported from New Brunswick, Canada. All these buildings had cast-iron storefronts with large plate-glass windows. Excellent examples of this type of commercial design can be seen on the north side of Reade Street between Broadway and Church Street and on the south side of Duane Street between Church Street and West Broadway in the Tribeca South Historic District and on Franklin, White, and Walker Streets between Broadway and Church Street in the Tribeca East Historic District. The architects, including Isaac Duckworth, Henry Fernbach, James H. Giles, John B. Snook, and Samuel Warner, were specialists in this building type. Of special note is the concentration of buildings in the sperm-candle mode, with their slender two-story columns resembling candles made of sperm-whale oil. Examples include the cast-iron Kitchen, Montross & Wilcox Store (1860–61; see No. 82) and the Condict Store, 55 White Street (1861; see No. 85), and the marble buildings at 80–82 (James H. Giles, 1860–62), 83 (1860–65), and 87–89 (1860–63) Leonard Street and 388 (King & Kellum, 1858–59), 392 (1859–60), and 394 (1864–65) Broadway between White and Walker Streets, all in the Tribeca East Historic District. In the late 19th century, development moved west into the area adjoining the Washington Market, the city's major source of fresh produce. Many of the buildings of the 1880s and 1890s, primarily in the Tribeca West Historic District, are Romanesque Revival–style structures with brick facades and stone and cast-iron trim, erected to house produce-related businesses. The development of boldly massed commercial and industrial buildings with Romanesque-inspired round arches began at 173–175 Duane Street, an extraordinary essay in the use of arched openings and subtle brickwork and terra-cotta detail designed by Babb & Cook in 1879. Other exceptional individual buildings from this period include 36–38 Hudson Street (Babcock & Morgan, 1891–92) and the D. S. Walton & Co. printed wrap-

ping paper factory at 1–9 Varick Street at the corner of Franklin Street (Albert Wagner, 1887–88), both with Romanesque Revival brick facades; the picturesque Dutch Renaissance–inspired 168 Duane Street (Stephen Decatur Hatch, 1886–87); and Hatch's Schepp Building at 45–53 Hudson Street, a Romanesque Revival red brick spice warehouse with black brick trim, designed in 1880. On Jay Street between Staple and Greenwich Streets and Franklin Street between Varick and Hudson Streets are examples of the unified blockfronts of five-story brick commercial buildings popular in the late 19th century. At the end of the 19th century and during the first years of the 20th century, huge, often block-square, rectilinear warehouses were erected, primarily in the Tribeca North Historic District, near the Hudson River Railroad freight terminal on Hudson Square. Prime examples of these buildings are 415–427 Greenwich Street (Charles B. Meyers, 1912–13); 443–453 Greenwich Street (Charles C. Haight, 1883–84), erected for the Trinity Church Corporation, which still owned a great deal of land in Tribeca; and 32–54 Hubert Street (William H. Birkmire, 1903–06). With the removal of the Washington Market to Hunt's Point in the Bronx in the early 1960s and the exodus of industry from the city, Tribeca became a backwater with a significant amount of empty space. Artists began to move into the area in the 1970s. Since the 1980s, large-scale conversion has virtually transformed this former commercial neighborhood into a thriving residential district.

INDIVIDUAL LANDMARKS

50 **Barclay-Vesey Building,** 140 West Street (McKenzie, Voorhees & Gmelin, Ralph Walker, architect in charge, 1923–27), designated 1991. The first major design of Ralph Walker, this brick-faced building, whose name derives from its location between Barclay and Vesey Streets, was commissioned by the New York Telephone Company for its headquarters. It is one of the most significant structures in the annals of skyscraper design, since it was the first building in New York City to exploit the requirements of the 1916 zoning code, leading to the tower's dramatic massing. Walker also pioneered in the use of complex, nontraditional, naturalistic, carved ornament. **Interior:** Exterior ornamental motifs are repeated in the lobby, which contains veined marble walls, travertine floors with bronze medallions, and a vaulted ceiling embellished with murals depicting the stages in the evolution of human communication.

51 **Hopkins Store** (1857), designated as 75 Murray Street Building, 1968. The Venetian Renaissance–inspired cast-iron facade of this five-story commercial structure, built to house the glassware business of Francis and John Hopkins, was probably cast in the foundry of James Bogardus. It is among a handful of surviving buildings with iron elements attributed to Bogardus, the self-proclaimed inventor of cast-iron architecture. The building was rehabilitated in 1994–96 when it was converted to residential use.

52 **Bennett Building,** 139 Fulton Street (Arthur D. Gilman, 1872–73; addition, James M. Farnsworth, 1890–92 and 1894), designated 1995. The Bennett Building, with three fully designed, ten-story cast-iron facades, is thought to be the tallest cast-iron building ever erected. It was built in three campaigns, beginning in 1872 when *New York Herald* publisher James Gordon Bennett, Jr., commissioned a seven-story French Second Empire building that would be rented for stores and offices. In 1892–93 the original mansard roof was removed and four stories were added in a design that replicated the original castings. Architect James Farnsworth returned in 1894, adding a 25-foot-wide section on Ann Street that is also indistinguishable from the original.

53 **Saint Paul's Chapel (Episcopal) and Graveyard,** Broadway at Fulton Street (1764–66; porch, 1767–68; tower, James C. Lawrence, 1794), designated 1966. Manhattan's oldest surviving church is also one of the finest Georgian buildings in the United States. Saint Paul's, the "uptown" chapel for Trinity Church, is a simplified version of James Gibbs's London masterpiece, Saint Martin-in-the-Fields on Trafalgar Square. Built of local stone with brownstone trim, the church has a modest portico on its towered front facade, which faces the 18th-century graveyard. The rear elevation on Broadway features an imposing brownstone Ionic porch—part of the original plan, but not built until 1767–68—sheltering a large Palladian window. The design of

the church is often ascribed to Thomas McBean, but no evidence supports this attribution. George Washington worshiped at Saint Paul's during the brief period when New York was the nation's capital.

54 **New York County Lawyers' Association,** 14 Vesey Street (Cass Gilbert, 1929–30), designated 1965. This building, designed in the 18th-century English Georgian style, is a late work by Gilbert. Commissioned by an organization that had been founded in 1908 to serve the public interest and the legal profession, the building handsomely complements the 18th-century Saint Paul's Chapel (see above) across the street.

55 **New York Evening Post Building,** 20 Vesey Street (Robert D. Kohn, 1906–07), designated 1965. Built as the offices and printing plant of the *New York Evening Post,* this 13-story limestone-faced structure is a rare example of a New York City

Saint Paul's Chapel (Episcopal) and Graveyard (No. 53). Built of local stone, Saint Paul's is Manhattan's oldest surviving church. Photo by Carl Forster.

building inspired by the early 20th-century Central European artistic reform movement known as the Vienna Secession. Kohn designed several buildings in the style, notably this structure and the meetinghouse of the New York Society for Ethical Culture (see No. 373). The building's refined classicism, rational expression of structure, and stylized ornament are evocative of Viennese precedents. Of special note are the four statues on the tenth floor known as the *Four Periods of Publicity;* two are by Gutzon Borglum, the sculptor of Mount Rushmore, and two are by Estelle Rumbold Kohn, the architect's wife.

56 Saint Peter's Roman Catholic Church, 22 Barclay Street (John R. Haggerty and Thomas Thomas, 1836–40), designated 1965. Saint Peter's is the oldest Roman Catholic parish in New York City. This imposing Greek Revival granite church, with its six Ionic columns, replaced an earlier building of 1785. Although a pagan Greek temple might seem an unusual model for a Catholic church, this was a popular form for buildings erected by all denominations.

57 Woolworth Building, 233 Broadway (Cass Gilbert, 1910–13), designated 1983. The Woolworth Building was commissioned by F. W. Woolworth, who instructed his architect to design the world's tallest building. Cass Gilbert's neo-Gothic masterpiece, faced almost entirely in terra cotta, rapidly became one of the symbols of New York City. The building's prominence on the skyline was a constant advertisement for Woolworth's stores. When the building was completed, the Woolworth firm occupied only one and one-half stories but profited from the rental of offices on other floors. The F. W. Woolworth Company, which sold the building in 1998, undertook a major rehabilitation of the facade (Ehrenkrantz & Associates, architects) during the 1980s that included the replacement of much of the terra cotta with cast stone. **Interior:** The symmetrically planned lobby is among the most spectacular of the early 20th century in New York City. Its rich decorative treatment includes an Early Christian–inspired mosaic barrel vault; a stained-glass skylight; marble walls; bronze furnishings; murals entitled *Labor* and *Commerce* on the mezzanine balconies; and plaster grotesques depicting some of the men involved with the building's construction, among them Woolworth (counting his nickels and dimes) and Gilbert (cradling a model of the building).

58 Park Row Building, 15 Park Row (R. H. Robertson, 1896–99), designated 1999. For nearly a decade the city's tallest building and one of tallest structures in the world, the Park Row Building rises 30 stories to a height of 391 feet. It is one of several late 19th-century office towers located on what was once known as Newspaper Row. The Renaissance-inspired facade has four large female figures attributed to the sculptor J. Massey Rhind and twin cupola-topped towers. Despite a mixed response in architectural circles, the building was well known, and celebrated by such noted photographers as Alvin Langdon Coburn and Charles Sheeler.

59 Temple Court Building and Annex, 3–9 Beekman Street (Silliman & Farnsworth, 1881–83; annex, James M. Farnsworth, 1889–90), designated 1998. Visible from City Hall Park, this twin-towered structure is one of the city's earliest surviving tall office buildings. Commissioned by Eugene Kelly, an Irish-American millionaire, the red brick and terracotta elevations combine Queen Anne, neo-Grec, and Renaissance Revival motifs. The annex, clad mainly in Irish limestone, was completed in 1890.

60 American Tract Society Building, 150 Nassau Street (R. H. Robertson, 1894–95), designated 1999. R. H. Robertson, an architect known for his churches and institutional structures, designed this richly textured building as a speculative venture for the American Tract Society, a publisher of religious literature. Completed in 1895, it is one of the earliest extant steelframe skyscrapers in Manhattan. Twenty stories tall, the granite, brick, and terra-cotta elevations combine Romanesque and Renaissance-inspired elements, including a picturesque roof tower decorated with winged caryatids.

61 Potter Building, 38 Park Row and 145 Nassau Street (Norris G. Starkweather, 1882–86), designated 1996. Real-estate investor and politician Orlando B. Potter commissioned this picturesque Queen Anne/neo-Grec office building after his previous building on the site burned. He used the most advanced fireproofing then available, employing rolled-iron beams, cast-iron columns, brick walls, and tile arches for structural support, as well as red brick, brownstone-colored terra cotta, and cast iron on the exterior load-bearing walls, which are forty inches thick at the ground level. The extensive terra-cotta detail provided by the Boston Terra Cotta Company so pleased Potter that he established his own firm, the New York Architectural Terra Cotta Company, in Long Island City (see Queens No. 3). The building was converted into apartments in 1979–81.

62 **New York Times Building**, 41 Park Row (George B. Post, 1888–89; enlarged, Robert Maynicke, 1903–05), designated 1999. Designed by George B. Post, one of the period's most celebrated architect-engineers, this impressive Romanesque Revival skyscraper replaced an earlier *New York Times* building on the corner site while maintaining the existing floor framing so that newspaper operations could continue during construction. Originally 12 stories tall, the rusticated granite and limestone elevations are articulated through a series of impressive multistory arcades. *King's Handbook of New York*

(1892) described the building as "the *Times* expressed in stone." When the owner, Adolph Ochs, decided to relocate to Times Square in 1904, the building was sold and 4 stories were added in a complementary style. Pace University acquired the building in 1951.

63 **Home Life Insurance Company Building** (incorporating the **Postal Telegraph Building**), 256–257 and 253 Broadway (Napoleon Le Brun & Sons, Pierre Le Brun, architect in charge, 1892–94; Harding & Gooch, 1892–94), designated 1991. Home Life, founded in Brooklyn in 1860, opened a branch office on this site in 1866. The company held a competition for the design of a new Manhattan office in 1892. The result was Pierre Le Brun's Renaissance-style marble-clad building, an early steel-skeleton-framed skyscraper. The building is a fine

FACTS & FIGURES

Since the establishment of the Landmarks Preservation Commission in 1965, more than 1,093 individual landmarks and 79 historic districts have been designated. The Pieter Claesen Wyckoff House, part of which is the oldest structure in New York City and one of the oldest in New York State, was the Commission's first designation on October 14, 1965 (Brooklyn No. 112). The west wing was built in c. 1652 and the additions during the 18th and 19th centuries. Among subsequent designations, the Ford Foundation, completed in 1967, is the youngest (Manhattan No. 238). Brooklyn Heights was the first historic district (Brooklyn H.D. 4). The Greenwich Village and Upper West Side/Central Park West Historic Districts have the largest number of buildings, each containing approximately two thousand structures, and the Hardenbergh-Rhinelander Historic District has the fewest, with seven (Manhattan H.D. 25 and 37). The landmarks law was amended in 1973 to include interiors that are customarily open and accessible to the public and scenic landmarks (mostly parks) that are located on city-owned property. The following year Central Park and the main interiors of the New York Public Library, Astor, Lenox, and Tilden Foundation were designated (Manhattan Nos. 376 and 278). Central Park is the city's largest scenic landmark, more than 840 acres in size. At present there are 9 scenic landmarks and 104 designated interiors. Among various legal decisions related to the Commission's work, the most important was made in 1978 when the United States Supreme Court upheld the constitutionality of the landmarks law in a case related to the designation of Grand Central Terminal (Manhattan No. 280). When the Landmarks Protection Bill became law in 1998, the Commission received the power to seek civil fines for violations. The Commission currently has a staff of 49 persons. In fiscal year 2002 it received 197 requests to evaluate potential landmarks and historic districts, more than 7,136 applications to work on landmark structures and 10 applications to build new buildings in historic districts. In response 12 landmarks and 4 historic districts (a total of 220 buildings) were designated, and 83 percent of the applications received were approved, including 14 new buildings (2001–02).

example of the tripartite expression of high-rise design, with its ornate arcaded base, simple shaft, and impressive pyramidal crown. Adjacent to the former Home Life building is Harding & Gooch's Postal Telegraph Building, erected for a major competitor of Western Union. In 1947 Home Life purchased the neighboring structure and connected the two buildings internally.

64 **City Hall,** City Hall Park (Joseph-François Mangin and John McComb, Jr., 1802–11), designated 1966, interior 1976. City Hall is one of the most beautiful early 19th-century public buildings in the United States. Mangin and McComb's design was the winning entry in a competition held in 1802. It is generally believed that the French-trained Mangin was responsible for the exterior, since it closely resembles 18th-century French civic struc-

tures. The exterior stonework, originally Massachusetts marble with a brownstone rear elevation, deteriorated so extensively that in 1954–56 it was replaced with Alabama limestone above a Missouri granite base. The **interior** is especially remarkable. The main entrance hall leads to a central rotunda in which a pair of spectacular cantilevered stairs curve upward to the second floor, where a series of marble Corinthian columns support a coffered dome. The lobby, stairs, and columns are original features; the dome is part of a restoration undertaken by Grosvenor Atterbury in 1912.

65 **New York County Courthouse,** also known as the Tweed Courthouse, 52 Chambers Street (John Kellum and Leopold Eidlitz, 1861–81), designated 1984. This marble building just north of City Hall is intimately associated with New York's

The stairs of the Tweed Courthouse (No. 65) were restored in 2002. Photo by Carl Forster.

The stone carvings above the windows on the Swift, Seaman & Company Building (No. 66) are unusually fine.

corrupt political boss William M. Tweed. The New York County Courthouse was the first permanent government building erected by New York City after the completion of City Hall (see above) in 1811. As conceived by John Kellum, the courthouse was a grand Italianate monument with a Corinthian portico and a long staircase facing Chambers Street. Kellum died before the building was completed, and Leopold Eidlitz then designed the south wing in a medieval-inspired style. The building contains some of the finest mid-19th-century **interiors** in New York, including Kellum's cast-iron staircases; an octagonal rotunda (largely the work of Eidlitz) with brick arcades; and Eidlitz's courtroom, which is distinguished by its encaustic tile floors, foliate columns, fireplace, and Gothic detail. Following a major restoration, completed in 2002, it became the headquarters of the New York City Department of Education.

66 **Swift, Seaman & Company Building,** 122 Chambers Street, 52 Warren Street (1857–58), designated 2000. Named for the saddlery hardware

company that occupied the building for twenty years, this handsome palazzo-style structure was built when Chambers Street was the heart of the city's commercial district. It is clad in tan-colored stone, and the arched window surrounds are extremely unusual, crowned with shells, cartouches, rosettes, and foliated scrolls.

67 **Cary Building,** 105–107 Chambers Street (King & Kellum, 1856–57), designated 1982. A masterpiece of cast-iron design, the Cary Building extends through the entire block between Chambers and Reade Streets. Its Italian Renaissance facades, with their arched windows supported by Corinthian columns, were cast in the form of rusticated stone blocks at Daniel D. Badger's Architectural Iron Works on East 14th Street. Erected by the dry goods firm of Cary, Howard & Sanger, the building reflects the mid-19th-century transformation of the area west and north of City Hall into an important commercial district. Badger pioneered in the manufacture of rolling iron shutters, and many of these are still visible on the Cary Building's windows.

68 **Broadway-Chambers Building,** 277 Broadway (Cass Gilbert, 1899–1900), designated 1992. Cass Gilbert's first New York City building epitomizes the tripartite columnar base-shaft-capital form popular on early steel-skeleton-frame skyscrapers in New York. The use of materials is especially fine here, with a classically inspired pink granite base, a shaft of red and beige brick, a capital faced in beige terra cotta highlighted with blue, green, yellow, and pink glazed detail, and a crowning green copper cornice.

69 **287 Broadway** (John B. Snook, 1871–72), designated 1989. This cast-iron commercial building in the French Second Empire style was erected as a speculative venture. To increase its allure for potential tenants, the building was crowned with an impressive mansard roof featuring lacy iron cresting and was equipped with a very early Otis passenger elevator. The iron elements were cast by Jackson, Burnet & Co., which maintained foundries on Centre Street and on East 13th Street.

70 **A. T. Stewart Store,** later the New York Sun Building, 280 Broadway (Joseph Trench & Co., 1845–46; additions: Trench & Snook, 1850–51 and 1852–53; Frederick Schmidt, 1872; Edward D. Harris, 1884; 1921), designated 1986. The A. T. Stewart Store was one of the most influential buildings ever erected in New York City, as its style, materials, use, and location helped determine the course of architecture and commerce in the city. In 1846 Alexander Turney Stewart opened New York's first department store. Located on the corner of Broadway and Reade Street, the store inaugurated the commercial development of Broadway north of City Hall. As the first Italianate commercial building in New York, it established what would become the style of choice for hundreds of stores and warehouses erected through the succeeding decades. In addition, the store was the first major commercial structure faced with Tuckahoe marble, a material that would later become common on such buildings; it was innovative also in its use of imported French plate glass for the ground-floor windows. The store expanded along Broadway, Reade Street, and Chambers Street, with three-bay modules echoing those of the original design (the final bays were built in 1884). By the early 1850s, cast iron was employed on the ground floor to support the upper walls. The building served as Stewart's retail store until 1862,

when it became a warehouse. The sixth and seventh floors are 1884 additions (the seventh-floor corners were added in 1921), built when the store was converted into offices. Offices of the *New York Sun* occupied the building between 1919 and 1952. The A. T. Stewart Store now houses municipal offices.

71 **Emigrant Industrial Savings Bank,** 51 Chambers Street (Raymond F. Almirall, 1908–12), designated 1984. The Emigrant Industrial Savings Bank was organized in 1850, under the auspices of Roman Catholic bishop John Hughes and the Irish Emigrant Society, to protect the savings of newly arrived Irish immigrants. In 1908 the bank commissioned designs for a new building that would front both Chambers and Reade Streets. This limestone-faced skyscraper in the Beaux-Arts style was the first to be laid out on an H-plan, providing light and air to almost all office spaces. The building is now owned by New York City. **Interior:** This richly decorated space has marble walls and floors, bronze grilles, original tellers' cages, and a series of stained-glass skylights with allegorical figures representing mining, manufacturing, agriculture, and other modes of employment.

72 **Hall of Records,** now Surrogate's Court–Hall of Records, 31 Chambers Street (John R. Thomas and Horgan & Slattery, 1899–1907), designated 1986, interior 1976. This boldly detailed Beaux-Arts structure was erected by New York City as a representation of the importance of civic government. Designed by Thomas, the building was completed, following his death, by a firm closely allied with New York's Tammany politicians. Built of Maine granite, the building supports a profusion of sculptural details that depict New York's history. The decoration is at its most lavish in the magnificent **interior,** particularly the foyer, with its Siena marble walls and vaulted mosaic ceiling by the artist William de Leftwich Dodge; the double-height marble lobby with a skylight and a divided stair; the encircling corridors; and the two fifth-floor courtrooms, one paneled in Santo Domingo mahogany and the other in quarter-sawn English oak.

73 **Brooklyn Bridge**, see Brooklyn, No. 17.

74 **Municipal Building,** 1 Centre Street (McKim, Mead & White, William M. Kendall, partner in charge, 1907–14), designated 1966. In 1907 New

The Municipal Building (No. 74) is crowned by Adolph Weinman's statue of Civic Fame. Photo by Carl Forster.

York City announced a competition for the design of a skyscraper office building to be erected on a site straddling Chambers Street; the building was to house administrative agencies and to incorporate a large subway station. McKim, Mead & White partner William M. Kendall's brilliant functional solution won the competition and was constructed between 1909 and 1914. The base of the limestone building is articulated by a screen of Corinthian columns flanking a central triumphal arch that bridges Chambers Street. The intricate terra-cotta vault above the street is modeled on the entrance treatment of the Palazzo Farnese in Rome. At the south end of the building is the subway entrance, an arcaded plaza covered by dramatic vaults of Guastavino tile construction. The simple office shaft rises 25 stories to a templed cupola crowned by Adolph Weinman's gold statue *Civic Fame;* Weinman also created the allegorical relief panels at the base. Since 2001 it has housed the offices of the Landmarks Preservation Commission.

75 **United States Courthouse,** 1 Foley Square (Cass Gilbert, 1933–36), designated 1975. Cass Gilbert's last building is a Classical Revival skyscraper that rises from a base of monumental Corinthian columns to a golden pyramidal crown. The building is carefully aligned with the New York County Courthouse (see below) to the north and the Municipal Building (see above) to the south, and its tower balances that of Gilbert's earlier Woolworth Building (see No. 57), located on the opposite side of City Hall Park.

76 **New York County Courthouse,** now the New York State Supreme Court, 60 Centre Street (Guy Lowell, 1913–27), designated 1966, interior 1981. In 1927 the New York County Court moved from the old "Tweed Courthouse" (see No. 65) to this spacious granite-faced building. The Boston architect Guy Lowell won a competition in 1913 with a design for a round building. Construction was delayed and the design altered to a hexagonal form; work finally began in 1919. The Roman classical style chosen was popular for courthouse architecture in the first decades of the 20th century. The monumental character of the exterior continues on the **interior,** with its central rotunda and radial corridors. In the 1930s, under the sponsorship of the federal government's artists' relief programs, Attilio Pusterla

painted a series of murals on the vestibule ceiling and on the rotunda dome; restoration work on these began in 1992.

77 **Fire Engine Company No. 7/Hook & Ladder Company No. 1,** now Hook & Ladder Company No. 1, 100 Duane Street (Trowbridge & Livingston, 1904–05), designated 1993. At the beginning of the 20th century, the fire department commissioned new firehouses from various architects, including such prestigious firms as Trowbridge & Livingston. The firm designed a bold French Renaissance building with a rusticated limestone base set below brick with heavy limestone banding. This is among the most impressive small-scale civic structures of the period.

78 **David S. Brown Store,** also known as the 8 Thomas Street Building (J. Morgan Slade, 1875–76), designated 1978. A manufacturer of laundry and toilet soaps commissioned this rare New York City example of Victorian Gothic masonry design from J. Morgan Slade, who, before his untimely death at age thirty in 1882, distinguished himself as an exceedingly accomplished architect of commercial buildings. The use of banded stone arches and other Venetian Gothic motifs reflects the influence of the English theorist John Ruskin, while the honest use of cast iron on the ground floor indicates Slade's interest in French architectural theory.

79 **319 Broadway** (D. & J. Jardine, 1869–70), designated 1989. The lone survivor of a pair of buildings known as the Thomas Twins that once occupied the two western corners of Broadway at Thomas Street, this Italianate structure has facades of iron that were cast at Daniel D. Badger's Architectural Iron Works.

80 **325–333 Broadway** (1863–64), designated 2002. When Henry Barclay erected this imposing commercial palazzo at the corner of Worth Street, it catered to retail tenants and businesses associated with the textile and dry-goods industry. Clad in marble, the simply treated elevations display stylized and abstracted neoclassical ornamentation.

81 **New York Life Insurance Company Building,** 346 Broadway (Stephen Decatur Hatch and McKim, Mead & White, 1894–99), designated

1987. The New York Life Insurance Company, one of America's oldest life insurance firms, erected its headquarters building on Broadway between Catherine Lane and Leonard Street in 1868–70. In 1894 Hatch was commissioned to extend the building eastward. Shortly thereafter he died, and the commission was taken over by McKim, Mead & White. Hatch's rear extension was built, but the company then decided to replace its earlier building. The elevations facing the narrow side streets continue Hatch's design, while McKim, Mead & White's Broadway frontage is a flamboyant palazzo-like pavilion crowned by a clock tower. Now housing municipal offices, the building retains many of New York Life's original **interior** spaces, including a marble lobby, a 13-story stair hall, a banking hall, executive offices, and the clock tower machinery room.

82 **Kitchen, Montross & Wilcox Store,** also known as 85 Leonard Street (1861), designated 1974. Commissioned by a firm of dry goods merchants, this cast-iron-fronted structure is one of the few surviving buildings in New York known to have been fabricated at the ironworks of the pioneer cast-iron founder James Bogardus. It is also one of a small group of mid-19th-century commercial buildings in the sperm-candle style, identifiable by its two-story columns resembling candles made from sperm-whale oil.

83 **359 Broadway** (Field & Correja, 1852), designated 1990. This Italianate commercial building with its unusual window enframements reflects the rapid shift from residential to commercial tenancy that occurred on Broadway south of Canal Street following the construction of the A. T. Stewart Store (see No. 70) in 1845. The stone building is of special historic importance because the upper three floors were occupied by the photographer Mathew Brady's portrait studio between 1853 and 1859. Brady, one of the most important photographers in American history, is renowned for his portraits and Civil War images.

84 **361 Broadway,** also known as the James S. White Building (W. Wheeler Smith, 1881–82), designated 1982. While most early examples of cast-iron construction appear to be attempts to simulate stone, cast-iron buildings of the late 1870s and 1880s were designed to exploit the properties of the

material itself and are often extremely flamboyant. Commissioned by James S. White, this late example of a building with cast-iron facades contains very large windows set in a framework of elaborately decorated iron columns and piers.

85 **Condict Store,** also known as 55 White Street (John Kellum & Son, 1861), designated 1988. Commissioned by John and Samuel Condict to house their saddlery business, this structure is one of New York City's most significant commercial buildings of the mid-19th century. It is also the largest surviving example of a cast-iron sperm-candle design, with thin two-story columns resembling the expensive candles made of sperm-whale oil. The facade, whose components were cast at Daniel D. Badger's Architectural Iron Works, was restored in 1988–89 as part of a residential conversion.

86 **Woods Mercantile Buildings,** 46–50 White Street (1865), designated 1979. The Woods Mercantile Buildings are handsome examples of the Italianate commercial palaces faced in Tuckahoe marble that transformed the streets adjacent to Broadway just north of City Hall into a prime business district in the 1850s and 1860s. The two buildings, designed as a single unit, have cast-iron shop fronts and are crowned by an unusual pedimented cornice emblazoned with the name and date of the buildings.

87 **Ahrens Building,** 70–76 Lafayette Street (George H. Griebel, 1894–95), designated 1992. The facades of this narrow seven-story steel-framed corner commercial building in the Romanesque Revival style are unified by three-story round-arched arcades. The building is covered with rough sandstone at the base, contrasting smooth buff brick on the superstructure, and rock-faced brown brick trim; on Lafayette Street it is embellished with three-story metal oriels. The building was erected as a speculative venture at the time when New York City was widening Lafayette Street to create a major traffic artery.

88 **Fire Engine Company No. 31,** now the Downtown Community Television Center, 87 Lafayette Street (Napoleon Le Brun & Sons, 1895), designated 1966. The firm of Napoleon Le Brun & Sons was responsible for the design of many of the city's late 19th-century firehouses. Engine Company

Fire Engine Company No. 31 (No. 88). The design of this former firehouse was inspired by the architecture of the French Renaissance. Photo by Carl Forster.

No. 31, modeled on early 16th-century Loire Valley châteaux in the style of Francis I, is the firm's most impressive civic design.

89 **94–100 Lafayette Street,** now called the Avildsen Building (Howells & Stokes, 1907–08, 1909–10), designated 2001. These two architecturally harmonious structures were built by Helen Hartley Jenkins and occupied by major hardware manufacturers for four decades. In 1952 they were joined as a single structure by Avildsen Tools & Machines, Inc. The elevations feature mainly modest neoclassical motifs executed in limestone and terra cotta. The storefronts are notable for their fine state of preservation.

90 **254–260 Canal Street** (1856–57), designated 1985. Resembling an Italian Renaissance palazzo, this building is an important early example of cast-iron architecture in New York City. There is strong evidence to suggest that this commercial palace, with its seemingly endless array of arched windows, contains iron elements cast by James Bogardus, a pioneer in the construction of cast-iron buildings, little of whose work survives.

91 **Long Distance Building of the American Telephone & Telegraph Company,** 32 Sixth Avenue (Voorhees, Gmelin & Walker, Ralph Walker, partner in charge, 1930–32), designated 1991. This massive Art Deco office building and communications center, conceived as a major enlargement and redesign of an earlier structure, was the world's largest long-distance communications center at the time of its completion. The rough-textured brick facade, with its bold sculptural massing and linear ornament, reflects a technology-inspired aesthetic in keeping with the building's function. **Interior:** The lobby has ceramic tile walls with marble trim, a terrazzo floor, and bronze doors and highlighting. Its artistic detail reinforces the building's purpose: One wall is decorated with a vast tile map of the world; the ceiling features stucco and glass mosaic allegories of long-distance communication to Africa, Asia, Australia, and Europe.

92 **2 White Street** (1808–09), designated 1966. A brick-fronted frame house with a gambrel roof and dormers, this corner building is one of the few survivors from the period when the Lower West Side

area now known as Tribeca was developing as a residential area. The house, built for Gideon Tucker, owner of the nearby Tucker & Ludlum plaster factory, has probably always had a ground-floor store.

93 **175 West Broadway** (Scott & Umbach, 1877), designated 1991. A Newark, New Jersey, architecture firm designed this exceptional late 19th-century example of a commercial building with a polychromatic brick facade. The design was inspired by European, particularly German, sources. The corbeled window arches and the corbeled brick cornice are without parallel in New York City architecture.

94 **Western Union Building,** 60 Hudson Street (Voorhees, Gmelin & Walker, Ralph Walker, partner in charge, 1928–30), designated 1991. This massive brick-clad building, which occupies an entire block, shows the influence of Dutch and German Expressionist design on American architecture. The influence is especially evident in Walker's exploitation of brick—both on the exterior, where the color lightens as the building rises in bold setbacks, and in the **interior** vestibules and lobby, with their complexly patterned orange brick walls and matching barrel-vaulted Guastavino tile ceiling. Erected as the headquarters of Western Union, the building contained the corporation's offices, equipment rooms, an auditorium, a cafeteria, shops, and classrooms for company messengers. The building now houses a variety of firms.

95 **25–41 Harrison Street,** located between Greenwich and West Streets and on a former section of Washington Street (1796–1828), designated individually 1969. Around 1800 the Lower West Side area now known as Tribeca developed into a residential neighborhood of modest brick and frame houses in the Federal style. The houses near the waterfront were gradually engulfed by the expansion of the Washington Market, and many area buildings were altered for commercial use. As part of an urban renewal project begun in the late 1960s, the nine houses in this L-shaped enclave were incorporated into the Independence Plaza housing complex; three of the houses were moved from Washington Street, including two houses designed by John McComb, Jr.—at No. 25A Harrison Street (originally 315 Washington Street, 1819), and the architect's own home, at No. 27 Harrison Street (originally 317

Western Union Building (No. 94). The former headquarters of Western Union, this building shows the influence of Dutch and German Expressionist design. Photo by Caroline Kane Levy.

Washington Street, 1796–97). All were extensively rehabilitated in the mid-1970s.

96 **Fleming Smith Warehouse,** 451–453 Washington Street (Stephen Decatur Hatch, 1891–92), designated 1978. Crowned by eccentric gables and dormers, Hatch's brick warehouse is a skillful combination of Romanesque Revival and Flemish Renaissance design. The central gable contains the date of design and the owner's initials, all wrought in metal. The building was one of the first in Tribeca to be converted for residential use.

97 **502–508 Canal Street** (1818–41), designated individually 1998. These four small brick Greek Revival– and Federal-style buildings were constructed on a block partially created from landfill during the early 19th century. Located close to the Hudson River at Greenwich Street, they were developed to serve the commercial and residential needs of their owners, including a starch and powder manufacturer and a merchant tailor. The ground story of 506 Canal Street, built in 1826, has one of the city's earliest surviving storefronts.

HISTORIC DISTRICTS

9 **SoHo–Cast Iron Historic District**, designated 1973. SoHo (from "south of Houston") is a commercial district, developed in the mid- to late 19th century to serve the wholesale dry goods trade. The district contains the world's largest collection of buildings with cast-iron fronts. Such buildings were popular between the 1850s and early 1880s because of the speed with which they could be erected and the material's strength and facility for imitating the more expensive stone traditionally used in the construction of commercial palaces. The iron parts were mass-produced at local foundries, such as Daniel D. Badger's Architectural Iron Works, and assembled at the building site. The SoHo district includes a large number of Italianate and French Second Empire cast-iron buildings from the 1850s and 1860s, including the masterful Haughwout Building (see No. 102). Some of the finest mid-19th-century cast-iron streetscapes in America can be seen on Greene Street between Canal and Grand Streets and between Broome and Spring Streets. Besides cast-iron buildings, the district also has a significant number

of the masonry structures (largely Tuckahoe marble or Dorchester stone) that the cast-iron buildings sought to emulate. After the Civil War, cast-iron buildings were erected that did not imitate stone but exhibited the technical proficiency of the foundries. Major examples of these late cast-iron designs were the work of such prominent architects as Richard Morris Hunt (Roosevelt Building, 478–483 Broadway, 1873–74), Vaux & Withers (448 Broome Street, 1871–72), Renwick & Sands (34 Howard Street, 1868), and William A. Potter (435 Broome Street, 1873). By the 1890s, cast iron was no longer favored by architects and builders, and steel-framed brick and terra-cotta loft buildings were erected in SoHo to house garment factories. The most extraordinary of these is the Little Singer Building (Ernest Flagg, 1902–04), at 561 Broadway. In the 1960s artists began moving into the district's underutilized loft spaces, leading to the growth of SoHo as a major arts center. Artists were followed by visitors attracted to the area's new cultural life and then by shoppers who came to visit SoHo's fashionable new stores. Today the area is a mix of residential, cultural, commercial, industrial, and office uses, all housed in an

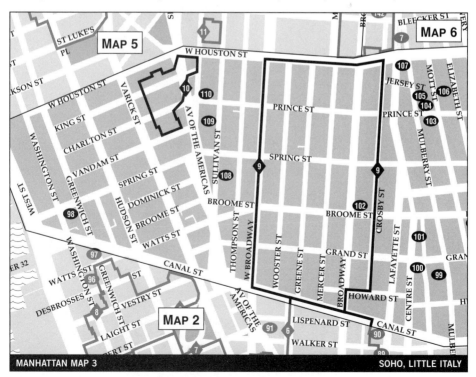

MANHATTAN

incomparable collection of commercial and industrial buildings, many of which have been beautifully restored.

⑩ Charlton-King-Vandam Historic District, designated 1966. Now located at the edge of an industrial area, this historic district is an extraordinary remnant of early 19th-century residential New York, containing the city's largest concentration of row houses in the Federal style, as well as a significant concentration of Greek Revival houses. The district was once the site of Richmond Hill, a Georgian man-

Greene Street has some of the finest cast-iron facades in the SoHo–Cast Iron District (H.D. 9). Photo by John Barrington Bayley, c. 1965.

sion that served variously as George Washington's headquarters, the official vice presidential residence, and the home of Aaron Burr. Burr had the land surveyed and mapped out the present block and street system in 1797, but he lost the property to John Jacob Astor, who was responsible for the area's development into a residential neighborhood beginning in the 1820s. Exceptional examples of Federal-style row houses line the north sides of Charlton and Vandam Streets, and King Street has fine examples of Greek Revival houses. Later additions to the district include Public School 8 (David I. Stagg, 1886), a lively Queen Anne–style building at 29 King Street, now converted into apartments.

INDIVIDUAL LANDMARKS

98 **326 Spring Street** (c. 1817), designated as the James Brown House 1969. A rare survivor from the period when the Lower West Side was a residential area, this gambrel-roofed house in the Federal style was probably erected in 1817 for the tobacconist James Brown. Original features include a facade of brick laid in Flemish bond, splayed window lintels, and a pair of dormers.

99 **149 Mulberry Street** (c. 1816), designated as the Stephen Van Rensselaer House 1969. This brick-faced, wood-frame house exemplifies the small row houses in the Federal style that were once common in Manhattan south of 14th Street. The Flemish bond brickwork, paneled stone lintels, gambrel roof, and dormer windows are characteristic of the style. The house was one of many in the area erected by Stephen Van Rensselaer; it was originally located on the northwest corner of Mulberry and Grand Streets, and was moved in 1841.

100 **Odd Fellows Hall,** 165–171 Grand Street (Trench & Snook, 1847–48; roof addition, John Buckingham, 1881–82), designated 1982. The former Odd Fellows Hall is one of the city's earliest Italianate buildings, designed only a few years after Joseph Trench had introduced the style to New York in the A. T. Stewart Store (see No. 70). The Independent Order of Odd Fellows, which was incorporated in New York in 1844, occupied the building from 1848 until the early 1880s, when the northward movement of the city's affluent residents led to

a relocation uptown. The building was subsequently converted for commercial and industrial use.

101 **New York City Police Headquarters,** now the Police Building Apartments, 240 Centre Street (Hoppin & Koen, 1905–09), designated 1978. Following the creation of Greater New York in 1898, the city's police department expanded rapidly, and a large new headquarters building was planned. In 1905 Mayor George McClellan laid the cornerstone of this monumental limestone-faced, steel-framed Edwardian Baroque structure whose tall dome is visible from the City Hall area to the south. The police department relocated in 1973, and after standing empty for over a decade, the building was converted into luxury housing.

102 **Haughwout Building,** 488–492 Broadway (John P. Gaynor, 1856–57), designated 1965. A masterpiece of early cast-iron construction, the Haughwout Building was commissioned by E. V. Haughwout for his fashionable china, silver, and glassware emporium. The iron components were manufactured at Daniel D. Badger's Architectural Iron Works and were originally painted a color referred to in 1859 as "Turkish drab." The attempt to create a beautiful building using a limited number of mass-produced parts is evident in this structure's insistent repetition of round arches and Corinthian columns, motifs adapted from the facade of the Sansovino Library in Venice. After years of neglect, the building's facades were beautifully restored and repainted their original color in 1995 under the direction of Joseph Pell Lombardi, architect.

103 **Roman Catholic Orphan Asylum,** now Saint Patrick's Convent and Girls' School, 32 Prince Street (1825–26), designated 1966. The Roman Catholic Orphan Asylum, founded in 1817, was operated by the Sisters of Charity. This large brick building with an elegant doorway is the most significant institutional building in the Federal style surviving in New York City. Originally housing both boys and girls, the asylum became a girls' institution in 1851. In 1886 the asylum was converted into a school.

104 **Saint Patrick's Old Cathedral,** Mott Street at Prince Street (Joseph-François Mangin, 1809–15; restoration, 1868), designated 1966. New York City's Roman Catholic cathedral was dedicated to the patron saint of Ireland. This original cathedral complex was built on Mott Street, in what was a rapidly developing residential neighborhood in the early 19th century. It is the oldest Roman Catholic church building in New York City. Mangin, the architect of City Hall, designed the original Saint Patrick's Cathedral in a rather fanciful Gothic-inspired style. The church was built of local stone, with facades facing Mott and Mulberry Streets. The building was extensively restored following a disastrous fire in 1866. The cathedral moved uptown to Fifth Avenue between 50th and 51st Streets in 1879 (see No. 296) and this building became known as Saint Patrick's Old Cathedral.

105 Saint Patrick's Chancery Office, later Saint Michael's Chapel, now Saint Michael's Russian Catholic Church, 266 Mulberry Street (James Renwick, Jr., with William Rodrigue, 1858–59), designated 1977. This small Gothic Revival building was designed to harmonize with the nearby cathedral. The architects were James Renwick, Jr., the designer of the new Saint Patrick's Cathedral (see No. 296), which was under construction at the time, and William Rodrigue, a relative of Archbishop John Hughes. Rodrigue, who also assisted Renwick at Saint Patrick's, had previously designed buildings for Fordham University (see Bronx No. 37).

106 Fourteenth Ward Industrial School of the Children's Aid Society (Astor Memorial Building), 256–258 Mott Street (Vaux & Radford, 1888–89), designated 1977. In the late 1880s and 1890s, the Children's Aid Society erected a series of schools to serve the city's poor, the earliest of which was this superb Victorian Gothic building with beautiful naturalistic terra-cotta ornament. The school, founded to teach skills to immigrant children, was built with funds provided by John Jacob Astor III as a memorial to his wife, a longtime supporter of the society. The building has been converted into housing.

107 Puck Building, 295–309 Lafayette Street (Albert Wagner, 1885–86 and 1892–93; Herman Wagner, 1899), designated 1983. With its seemingly endless round-arched arcades and complex brickwork, the Puck is a masterpiece of late 19th-century New York commercial architecture. The Ro-

manesque Revival building was erected to house the offices and printing plant of *Puck,* a prominent humor magazine, and the J. Ottman Lithographing Co., which printed the magazine's famous chromolithographic cartoons. The two original wings, designed by Albert Wagner, fronted only on Houston and Mulberry Streets. In the late 1890s, Lafayette Street was extended through the block, and two bays of the Puck Building's Houston Street facade and the building's entire west wall were demolished. Herman Wagner, who was related to Albert, designed the new Lafayette Street elevation to conform to the original design. The main entrance was moved from the corner of Houston and Mulberry to Lafayette Street. Both the original and later entrances are marked by statues of Shakespeare's Puck; the statue at the original entrance is by Casper Buberl, and the one on Lafayette Street is the work of Henry Baerer. The building was handsomely rehabilitated in 1983–84.

108 83 and 85 Sullivan Street (1819), designated 1973. This pair of modest houses retains original Federal-style doorways with leaded transoms (among the earliest surviving in the city), low stoops with wrought-iron railings, Flemish bond brickwork, and multipaned wooden sash windows. The houses were originally 2½ stories tall, but full third floors were added when the former single-family homes became multiple dwellings. In 1900, No. 85 housed five families.

109 116 Sullivan Street (1832; upper two floors, 1872), designated 1973. This house in the Federal style retains an extremely unusual doorway. In the manner of many local doorways, the six-paneled door is flanked by Ionic colonnettes and crowned by a fanlight. The sidelights, however, are unique survivors: each one is broken into three ovals with wooden frames carved to simulate a cloth curtain drawn through a series of rings.

110 203 Prince Street (1834), designated 1974. This handsomely restored house in the late Federal style was built on land that was once part of Aaron Burr's estate. Originally 2½ stories tall, the house received a full third floor in 1888. The reconstructed, elliptically arched entranceway above a high stoop is a fine example of Federal-style design.

Puck Building (No. 107). This Romanesque Revival building was built to house the offices of Puck, a prominent humor magazine. Photo by Carl Forster.

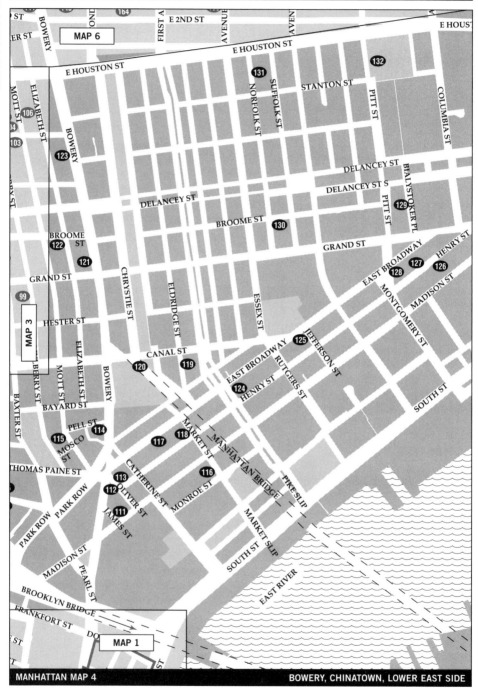

INDIVIDUAL LANDMARKS

111 **Saint James Roman Catholic Church,** 32 James Street (1835–37), designated 1966. Saint James, the second oldest Roman Catholic church building in New York, is constructed of fieldstone and has an imposing pedimented Greek Revival brownstone facade that features a pair of Doric columns. The detailing of the facade is modeled on designs published by the architect Minard Lafever, and while the building has frequently been attributed to Lafever, there is no supporting documentary evidence.

112 **Shearith Israel Graveyard,** 55–57 Saint James Place (1683–), designated 1966. This tiny graveyard is all that remains of the earliest surviving burial ground of Congregation Shearith Israel, the oldest Jewish congregation in North America. The graveyard is one of three small Manhattan cemeteries once used by the congregation. The others are on West 11th Street (see H.D. 12) and West 21st Street (see No. 15; H.D. 16).

113 **Oliver Street Baptist Church,** now Mariners' Temple (Baptist), 12 Oliver Street (attributed to Isaac Lucas, 1844–45), designated 1966. This building is one of several brownstone-fronted Greek Revival churches erected in Manhattan's newly developing residential neighborhoods in the 1830s and 1840s. The facade of the Mariners' Temple features a pair of slender Ionic columns. The little-known architect Isaac Lucas is mentioned in the 1844 church minutes, but it is not clear whether he was the architect or simply the building superintendent.

114 **Edward Mooney House,** 18 Bowery (c. 1785–89), designated 1966. Built for merchant Edward Mooney at some point between 1785 and 1789, this house in the Georgian style is thought to be the oldest surviving row house in Manhattan. At the time of construction, the Chatham Square area was developing as a fine residential neighborhood, but by the 1840s the house had become a brothel. Today the building boasts many original features above its carefully reconstructed ground story.

115 **Zion English Lutheran Church,** now the Church of the Transfiguration (R.C.), 25 Mott Street (1801; additions, Henry Engelbert, 1868), designated 1966. This former Lutheran church, one of four Georgian-Gothic landmark churches built of locally quarried Manhattan schist on the Lower East Side, became a Roman Catholic church in 1853. In 1868 the tower was added; the heavy Gothic window frames probably also date from this remodeling.

116 **William and Rosamond Clark House,** also known as the 51 Market Street House (1824–25), designated 1965. This row house in the late Federal style, apparently erected for the grocer William Clark and his wife, was built when the Lower East Side was an affluent residential neighborhood. The house retains a beautiful fanlighted entrance, as well as original ironwork and window lintels. The two upper floors were added later in the 19th century.

117 **New York Public Library, Chatham Square Branch,** 31 East Broadway (McKim, Mead & White, 1903), designated 2001. This library is situated on a busy street lined with tenements, restaurants, and shops. Built with funds from Andrew Carnegie (see No. 538), it was the first of twelve neoclassical branches designed by McKim, Mead & White. Large arched windows illuminate the reading room of the main floor, and the upper two stories are organized behind a double height Ionic arcade that dominates the limestone facade.

118 **Northern Reformed Church,** also known as the Market Street Reformed Church, later the Sea and Land Church, now the First Chinese Presbyterian Church, 61 Henry Street (1817–19), designated 1966. This is the most elegant of the four surviving Georgian-Gothic-style churches of the Lower East Side. Built of locally quarried Manhattan schist, the church still has its beautifully proportioned one- and two-story clear-glass windows. The Reformed Church became known as the Sea and Land Church in 1866 when it began ministering to local sailors.

119 **Eldridge Street Synagogue** (Congregation Khal Adath Jeshurun with Anshe Lubz), 12–16 Eldridge Street (Herter Brothers, 1886–87), designated 1980. In the late 19th century large numbers of Eastern European Jews settled on Manhattan's Lower East Side. The Eldridge Street Synagogue, the first Orthodox synagogue erected by these immigrants, is the most lavish synagogue ever built in the neighborhood. The brick and terra-cotta facade combines Moorish, Gothic, and Romanesque features in a fanciful and imposing manner. Although the sanctuary was closed in the 1950s, the building continues to be used for religious services and as a center for education, focusing on Jewish culture and immigration.

120 **Manhattan Bridge Arch and Colonnade,** Manhattan Bridge Plaza at Canal Street (Carrère & Hastings, 1910–15), designated 1975. Carrère &

Hastings's monumental gateway to the Manhattan Bridge was designed in the form of a triumphal arch flanked by curved colonnades. This "City Beautiful" project placed a grand entry at one of the key links between Manhattan and Brooklyn. Preliminary designs for the Manhattan approach were drawn in 1910, the year after the bridge opened. In 1912 Carrère & Hastings prepared final designs that included pylons carved by Carl A. Heber and a frieze by Charles Rumsey entitled *Buffalo Hunt*—a rather odd theme for a New York project. Restoration of this seriously deteriorated ensemble was completed in 2000.

Eldridge Street Synagogue (No. 119). This was the first Orthodox synagogue built by the large numbers of Eastern European Jews who settled on the Lower East Side in the late 19th century. Photo by Carl Forster.

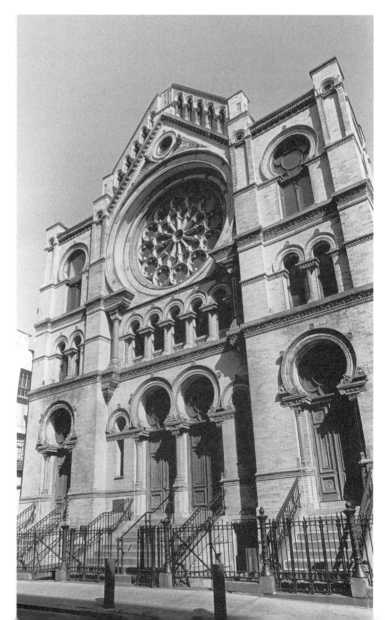

121 Bowery Savings Bank, 130 Bowery (McKim, Mead & White, Stanford White, partner in charge, 1893–95), designated 1966, interior 1994. This monumental building is the third erected at this location since the Bowery Savings Bank opened its doors in 1834. For this especially challenging L-shaped site, Stanford White designed two limestone street fronts, each in a Roman classical style with Corinthian columns supporting pediments sculpted by Frederic MacMonnies. White was the first to popularize the Roman classical style for bank design, and his choice established a trend; the Bowery became a prototype for other banks in New York and throughout the United States. The skylighted, L-shaped steel-framed **interior** creates the image of an ancient Roman temple. To the primarily poor immigrants who invested their meager incomes at this bank, entering this luxurious space must have been an awe-inspiring experience. By employing screens of monumental Corinthian columns, White created a square banking hall within a trapezoidal space. Among the major decorative features of the interior are marble mosaic floors, a yellow Siena marble teller's counter, scagliola (faux marble) columns, marble walls, coffered ceilings, and cast-iron skylights and stairs. The building is now used as a restaurant and nightclub.

122 Fire Engine Company 55, 363 Broome Street (R. H. Robertson, 1898–99), designated 1998. One of the first firehouses completed after the consolidation of Greater New York, this midblock facility combines Romanesque Revival and Beaux Arts features. With a monumental arch that serves as the apparatus bay, a company banner carved in stone, and oval windows draped with garlands, this richly ornamented structure was one of several civic improvements planned for this area at the beginning of the 20th century.

123 Young Men's Institute Building, Young Men's Christian Association (YMCA), 222 Bowery (Bradford L. Gilbert, 1884–85), designated 1998. This red brick Queen Anne–style structure, located between Spring and Prince Streets, is the only extant 19th-century YMCA branch in New York. Bradford Gilbert, one of the period's most innovative architects, chose this style for its associations to England, where the YMCA was founded in 1844, and for its progressive character. The facility catered primarily to working-class men, offering lectures, a circulating library, and a large gymnasium. After closing in 1932, the interiors were converted to residential and studio use, attracting such celebrated tenants as painter Fernand Leger and writer William Burroughs.

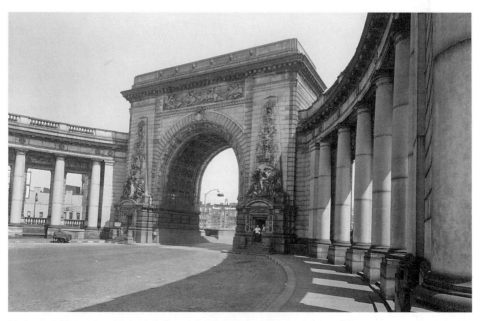

Manhattan Bridge Arch and Colonnade (No. 120). A fittingly grand gateway to one of the key links between Manhattan and Brooklyn. Photo by John Barrington Bayley, c. 1965.

MANHATTAN

124 **Pike Street Synagogue** 13–15 Pike Street (Alfred E. Badt, 1903–04), designated 1997. Designed by Alfred E. Badt for the Congregation Sons of Israel Kalwarie, this limestone-fronted building was constructed during a period when many synagogues were established on the Lower East Side. Built by immigrants from Kalwarie, Poland, it was one of the largest in the area and could accommodate 1,500 worshipers. The tripartite facade, which has an arched portico reached by twin lateral staircases, exhibits both Romanesque and classical features. The building was rehabilitated in the 1990s for multiple tenants, including a Buddhist temple.

125 **Forward Building,** 173–175 East Broadway (George A. Boehm, 1912), designated 1986. This prominent 11-story Classical Revival building, erected on the Lower East Side as the home of the *Jewish Daily Forward,* the most significant Yiddish-language newspaper published in America, symbolizes the importance of the publication to the local Eastern European Jewish community. The *Forward* was a socialist paper that fought for the Jewish masses and was closely allied with Jewish labor and social improvement organizations, notably the Amalgamated Clothing Workers Union and the Workmen's Circle (which had offices in the building). The political leanings of the *Forward* are evi-

The former Pike Street Synagogue (No. 124) was built by Polish immigrants in 1903–04. Photo by Carl Forster.

dent in the building's ornamentation, which includes a series of flaming torches (symbols of the socialist vanguard) as well as low-relief portraits of such socialist leaders as Karl Marx and Friedrich Engels on the frieze above the entrance.

126 **All Saints' Free Church (Episcopal),** later Saint Augustine's Chapel, now Saint Augustine's Episcopal Church, 290 Henry Street (1827–29; enlargement, 1849), designated 1966. This "free" church (i.e., rent was not charged for pews) is the most imposing of the four Georgian-Gothic landmark churches constructed of Manhattan schist on the Lower East Side. The design incorporates a double pediment and a projecting tower. In 1945 Trinity Church took over the operation of All Saints'. Four years later Trinity's Saint Augustine's Chapel moved into the building. Saint Augustine's became an independent parish in 1976.

127 **Henry Street Settlement,** 263 and 265 Henry Street (1827; later alterations) and 267 Henry Street (Buchman & Fox, 1900), designated 1966. In 1893 Lillian Wald, a middle-class woman of German-Jewish descent, founded the Nurses' Settlement, later renamed the Henry Street Settlement, to assist the Lower East Side populace and to help educate and Americanize the Eastern European Jewish immigrant population settling in the area. Two years later the German-Jewish philanthropist Jacob Schiff purchased 265 Henry Street for use by the organization. A single story was added to this well-preserved Federal-style row house, a survivor from a once affluent residential neighborhood; Schiff donated the building to the settlement in 1903. Three years later another German-Jewish philanthropist, Morris Loeb, purchased No. 267 from the Hebrew Technical School for Girls and gave it to the settlement. This Greek Revival house had received a Colonial Revival facade in 1900 when Buchman & Fox donated their services for the redesign of the technical school. The settlement's third building on Henry Street, No. 263, a Federal-style house with an extensively altered facade, was leased for use as classrooms and apartments in 1938 and was acquired by the settlement in 1949. Nos. 263 and 265 were restored in 1989 and 1992.

128 **281 East Broadway** (c. 1829), designated 1998. Commissioned by Issac Ludlam, a New York City surveyor, this Federal-style row house was built when the Lower East Side was one of the city's most prosperous residential districts. Among the various original features, the pedimented dormers with arched window openings are particularly notable.

129 **Willett Street Methodist Episcopal Church,** now Bialystoker Synagogue, 7–13 Bialystoker Place (1826), designated 1966. The simplest of the four early 19th-century landmark religious buildings of Manhattan schist surviving on the Lower East Side, this building has housed the Bialystoker Synagogue since 1905. The history of the building reflects the changes that occurred in this neighborhood around 1900 as tens of thousands of Eastern European Jews arrived in New York. The present congregation was founded in 1878 by Jews from Bialystok, then a part of the Russian Empire and now located in Poland.

130 **Norfolk Street Baptist Church,** now Beth Hamedrash Hagodol Synagogue, 60–64 Norfolk Street (1850), designated 1967. America's oldest congregation of Orthodox Russian Jews, established in 1852, converted this Gothic Revival church into a synagogue in 1885. Among the notable original features are the Gothic woodwork and the iron fence. The building was erected by a Baptist congre-

gation that followed its members north, finally becoming The Riverside Church (see No. 530).

131 **Anshe Chesed Synagogue,** later Anshe Slonim, 172–176 Norfolk Street (Alexander Saeltzer, 1849–50), designated 1987. Built for the city's third Jewish congregation, this is the oldest surviving building in New York City erected specifically for use as a synagogue and is the earliest synagogue on the Lower East Side. Curiously, the building was designed in a Gothic Revival style and, at the time of construction, was even compared to Cologne Cathedral. In the late 1980s, the building was converted to a visual and performing arts center.

132 **Hamilton Fish Park Play Center,** 130 Pitt Street (Carrère & Hastings, 1898–1900), designated 1982. The monumental Beaux-Arts Petit Palais in Paris was the model for this small pavilion. The play center and adjacent park were constructed as part of a movement to create parks in New York City's most densely crowded neighborhoods. Rather than a simple utilitarian structure, the building was intended as a sophisticated work that, it was hoped, would exert a positive influence on the area's poor immigrant population. The park has been redesigned several times, and the pavilion was restored in 1989–91.

Hamilton Fish Park Play Center (No. 132). In 1898 it was hoped that this sophisticated municipal building would exert a positive influence on the area's immigrant population. Photo by Carl Forster.

HISTORIC DISTRICTS

⓫ **MacDougal-Sullivan Gardens Historic District,** designated 1967. MacDougal-Sullivan Gardens, a small enclave planned around a central garden, became a prototype for related New York developments of the 1920s. In 1920 William Sloane Coffin, president of the Hearth and Home Corporation, purchased twenty-two deteriorated Greek Revival row houses, built between 1844 and 1850, and commissioned a rehabilitation from the architects Francis Y. Joannes and Maxwell Hyde. All the stoops were removed, the two street facades were given a homey Colonial Revival appearance, and,

most important, the rear yards were combined to create a private community garden. Each row house was divided into spacious, airy, and well-lit apartments affordable to middle-income people.

⓬ **Greenwich Village Historic District,** designated 1969. Greenwich Village is one of New York City's oldest and most diverse residential neighborhoods. The architecture within this district reflects the physical growth and continuing change that have occurred in Greenwich Village since the small rural community of Greenwich began to be urbanized in the 1820s. In addition, many of the buildings in the district are a reflection of the rich social and

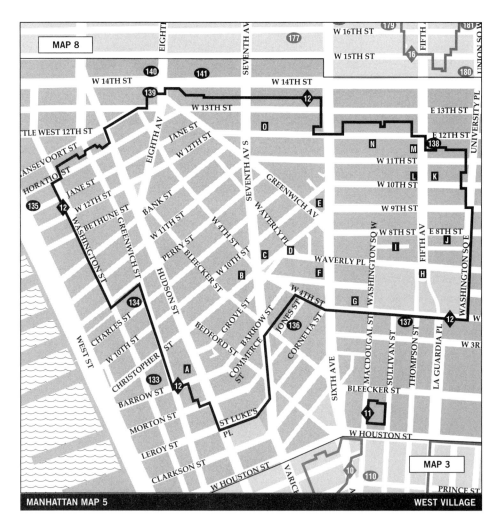

Greenwich Village Historic District (H.D. 12). Federal houses built between 1825 and 1834 on the south side of Grove Street between Bedford and Hudson Streets. Photo by Carl Forster.

cultural history of this singular neighborhood. Streets in the village of Greenwich were initially laid out in the late 18th century. By the early 19th century, the population was growing, as people moved here to escape crowding and epidemics in the more densely populated metropolis to the south. This was especially true in the 1820s, when a significant number of Federal-style row houses were erected, either of brick or of wood with brick facades. Primarily located on the streets west of Sixth Avenue, they were leased or purchased by a wide variety of middle-class households. A few were grand 3½-story houses with ornate fanlighted entrances, such as 59 Morton Street (1828), but most were more modest 2½-story structures. Excellent examples survive on Grove, Barrow, Commerce, and Hudson Streets. In the 1830s and 1840s, wealthy New Yorkers began moving to Greenwich Village as it became increasingly urbanized and lost its village character. The area between Fifth and Sixth Avenues north of Washington

Square was especially popular with these affluent households. The most prestigious houses were the Greek Revival rows with freestanding templed porticoes and elaborate iron railings on Washington Square North (1833–37). More typical Greek Revival row houses with austere entrances framed by heavy stone surrounds can be found throughout the district, most notably at 14–54 West 11th Street (1840–46). Somewhat more modest houses from this period can be found in the less affluent sections of the Village, farther west, especially on Bank and Bethune Streets, west of Seventh Avenue South. By the 1850s, as tastes changed, rows of brownstone-fronted houses were erected in Greenwich Village, although these were never as common as in neighborhoods to the north, since the area was already heavily built up. Perhaps the most significant brownstone row is the Anglo-Italianate terrace at 20–38 West 10th Street (1856–58), with low stoops and unified rusticated bases and iron balconies. Among the finest Italianate houses are those in the brick row with brownstone trim that lines the north side of Saint Luke's Place between Seventh Avenue South and Hudson Street (1851–54). In the post–Civil War period, the population of Greenwich Village changed as many middle-class families moved to newer neighborhoods uptown and poor immigrants crowded into the former single-family row houses, which were converted into multiple dwellings. In the late 19th century, large numbers of five- and six-story tenements were built, especially west of Sixth Avenue, and by the early 20th century, the Village had a significant population of Italian immigrants, as well as considerable Irish and German populations. The blocks north of Washington Square were an exception, retaining a population of middle-class native-born households. The row houses in this area were augmented by a series of early apartment buildings with elevators, spacious apartments, and servants' quarters, such as the Portsmouth and Hampshire (Ralph S. Townsend, 1882–83) at 38–50 West 9th Street, and the Ardea (J. B. Snook & Sons, 1895–1901), at 31–33 West 12th Street. In the early 20th century, the low rents and heterogeneous population of Greenwich Village began to attract artists and political and social radicals. Many buildings were converted in whole or part into artists' studios with large windows facing north, and commercial spaces began to attract coffeehouses and restaurants. The new bohemian community soon drew visitors, and

Greenwich Village became an important tourist area. The nontraditional character of the Village also began to attract a large number of gay men and lesbians, establishing Greenwich Village as a center of gay life in New York. The southern extension of Seventh Avenue and the opening of the IRT subway beneath the avenue in 1917 made the neighborhood convenient to downtown and midtown commercial districts (the Sixth Avenue subway, opened in 1930, making the neighborhood even more accessible). Property values rose, and a significant number of new apartment houses were erected, such as the Shenandoah (Emory Roth, 1928–29), at 10 Sheridan Square, and 614 Hudson Street (Emory Roth, 1929–31). Many of these buildings have small apartments planned for single people and childless couples. They attracted large numbers of young educated working women who were for the first time beginning to establish independent households and found the relatively liberal social attitudes of Village residents welcoming. In the 1950s and 1960s, Greenwich Village became one of the first city neighborhoods in America to draw residents interested in living in older urban environments and restoring the residential architecture. Greenwich Village is one of the city's most popular neighborhoods, one that maintains its reputation for welcoming a wide variety of people while it retains an extraordinary array of 19th- and 20th-century buildings.

Within the boundaries of the Greenwich Village Historic District are some of New York City's most important buildings. A selection of these is discussed individually below:

A **Saint Luke's Episcopal Church,** later Saint Luke's Episcopal Chapel, now Church of Saint Luke-in-the-Fields (Episcopal), 485 Hudson Street (attributed to Clement Clarke Moore, 1821–22). As increasing numbers of people moved north into Greenwich Village, Trinity Church donated land for construction of an Episcopal church. A modest Federal-style brick structure was erected as the centerpiece of an extraordinary urban complex that included a series of adjoining 2½-story row houses (1825–26). Church records indicate that a "plan" was drawn up by Clement Clarke Moore, a member of the congregation who would later lay out Chelsea and fund construction of Saint Peter's Episcopal Church on West 20th Street (see H.D. 15, map 7). The contract to build the church was given to John

Heath. By the late 1880s, the surrounding neighborhood was becoming home to an increasingly poor immigrant community, and the church corporation relocated to Convent Avenue and West 141st Street (see H.D. 39, map 17); in 1891 Saint Luke's, which retained some of its old congregation, became a chapel of Trinity Parish, becoming an independent congregation again only in 1976. The building burned in 1886 and again in 1981. An extensive reconstruction by Hugh Hardy of the firm Hardy Holzman Pfeiffer Associates was completed in 1985.

B **Eighth Presbyterian Church,** later Saint Matthew's Episcopal Church, now Saint John's Lutheran Church, 81 Christopher Street (1821–22; altered, Berg & Clark, 1886). This Federal-style church is one of the oldest religious buildings in Greenwich Village. Although altered in 1886, when the Romanesque Revival first story was installed, the

building retains elegant Federal-style decorative detail and a domed cupola. Eighth Presbyterian was organized in 1819 and dissolved in 1842; the building was then sold to an Episcopal congregation. In 1858, in response to the growth of the German community in the area, a Lutheran congregation purchased the structure and has maintained it ever since.

C **Stonewall Inn,** 51–53 Christopher Street. At about 1:00 A.M. on June 28, 1969, the gay bar known as the Stonewall Inn was raided by the police, setting off events that resulted in the birth of the modern gay and lesbian rights movement. Although the raid itself was not an unusual event, the fact that bar patrons fought back, forcing the police to retreat, galvanized the community. The anniversary of the riot is celebrated annually around the world with parades and other gay pride events.

D **Northern Dispensary,** 165 Waverly Place (Henry Bayard, carpenter, and John C. Tucker, mason, 1831; third-floor addition, 1855). The Northern Dispensary opened as a private medical clinic for the poor. Established in 1824, it moved into this simple triangular Federal-style building, originally only two stories tall, in 1831.

E **Jefferson Market Courthouse (Third Judicial District Courthouse),** now New York Public Library, Jefferson Market Branch, 425 Sixth Avenue (Vaux & Withers, 1874–77). The Jefferson Market Courthouse, the most prominent building in Greenwich Village, is not only a monument of American High Victorian Gothic design, but also of seminal importance in the history of the historic preservation movement. The courthouse is the masterpiece of English-born architect Frederick Clarke Withers, whose knowledge of English public architecture is evident on this building. The courthouse is faced with red brick and has black brick and yellow Ohio sandstone trim. The facades are richly ornamented with sculptural detail, including a pediment with the trial scene from *The Merchant of Venice* and a corner water fountain appropriately decorated with a wading bird, cattails, a snail, a salamander, and other water plants and animals. The building originally contained a police court, a district court, and, in the tall bell tower, a fire watch. In 1885 a survey among architects sponsored by the *American Architect and*

Jefferson Market Courthouse (Greenwich Village Historic District, entry E). A monument of American High Victorian Gothic design, the courthouse was also the focus of one of the early, pivotal preservation battles in New York City. Photo by John Barrington Bayley, c. 1965.

Building News voted the courthouse the fifth best building in the United States. The courthouse was vacated in 1958, and its future was in doubt. In 1959 a group of preservationists organized the Committee of Neighbors to Get the Clock on Jefferson Market Courthouse Started as a way of drawing attention to the building and its precarious condition. Soon this group was campaigning to have the building converted into a library, and in 1961 the New York Public Library agreed. Giorgio Cavaglieri was commissioned to design one of the earliest adaptive reuse projects in America, and the rejuvenated building reopened in 1967.

F **Saint Joseph's Church (R.C.),** 365 Sixth Avenue (John Doran, 1833–34). The parish of Saint Joseph's was established in 1829 just as Greenwich Village was becoming a populous residential district. Saint Joseph's is the second oldest Roman Catholic church building extant in New York City (after Saint Patrick's Old Cathedral—see No. 104). Built of Manhattan schist with a stuccoed front focusing on a Doric portico, this is one of the most beautifully proportioned Greek Revival church edifices in the city. The arched windows of the facade date from 1885, when architect Arthur Crooks rebuilt the fire-damaged structure.

G **Washington Square Methodist Church,** 135–139 West 4th Street (Gamaliel King, 1859–60). This Early Romanesque Revival–style marble church is a major work by Gamaliel King, an important but little-known mid-19th-century New York architect. The congregation was established on Sullivan Street in 1842, expanding into this building as the size of the congregation increased.

H **Washington Memorial Arch,** Washington Square (McKim, Mead & White, Stanford White, partner in charge, 1889–95; sculptural figures completed 1918). As part of the 1889 celebration of the centennial of George Washington's inauguration as the nation's first president, Stanford White designed a temporary wooden arch for Washington Square. It proved to be so popular that funds were raised to provide a permanent arch at the base of Fifth Avenue. The form is an adaptation of ancient Roman triumphal arches, perhaps symbolizing the triumph of republican democracy in America. The marble structure is embellished with figures of Washington

by Herman MacNeil and Alexander Stirling Calder and spandrel panels by Frederick MacMonnies. In January 1917 the arch became a symbol of bohemian Greenwich Village when John Sloan, Marcel Duchamp, and a group of friends climbed to the top and proclaimed that Greenwich Village had seceded from the Union and would thenceforth be the Free and Independent Republic of Washington Square.

I **MacDougal Alley.** Most of the buildings on MacDougal Alley are 19th-century stables erected by the owners of the large row houses on Washington Square North and West 8th Street. By 1900 the mews had become a slum, but early in the 20th century the stables were discovered by artists who converted them into studios and homes, turning the street into what was known as the "Art Alley de Luxe." Large, north-facing studio windows were added to many of the buildings. The first stable converted into a studio was No. 6, leased by sculptor Frederick Triebel in 1902. Among the artists who soon moved into the former stables were painters Guy Pène du Bois and Ernest Lawson and sculptors Henry Bush-Brown, Jo Davidson, James Fraser, Daniel Chester French, Philip Martiny, and Gertrude Vanderbilt Whitney.

J **Whitney Museum of American Art,** now New York Studio School of Drawing, Painting and Sculpture, 8–12 West 8th Street (1838; altered, Noel & Miller, 1931). In 1914 sculptor Gertrude Vanderbilt Whitney established the Whitney Studio at 8 West 8th Street, adjoining her MacDougal Alley studio. Here she planned to organize exhibits of the work of the young avant-garde American artists whose work she supported. Whitney assembled a substantial collection of new artworks, and after the Metropolitan Museum rejected her offer of a gift in 1929, she established the Whitney Museum of American Art. In 1931 Auguste L. Noel transformed the three former row houses at 8–12 West 8th Street into a museum and residence for Whitney, covering the facade with a reddish stucco and redesigning the entrance in a modern classical manner. The fledgling museum remained here until 1954. Its history as an art center continues under the auspices of the New York Studio School.

K **Lockwood de Forest House,** now New York University, The Bronfman Center for Jewish Student

Life, 7 East 10th Street (Van Campen Taylor, 1887). Lockwood de Forest was a leading decorative designer of the late 19th century and a founder, with Louis Comfort Tiffany, of the Associated Artists (see Seventh Regiment Armory, No. 455). After visiting India, de Forest established a wood workshop in Ahmadabad and incorporated Indian decorative pieces into his designs, including the library at the Andrew and Louise Carnegie House and the extraordinary teak detail on the facade of this row house, which he commissioned in 1887. The house was restored by Helpern Associates in 1994–96 after its acquisition by NYU.

L **Church of the Ascension (Episcopal),** 36–38 Fifth Avenue (Richard Upjohn, 1840–41; parish house, McKim, Mead & White, 1888–89). This symmetrically massed Gothic Revival–style brownstone church, with its central square tower, is an early work of Richard Upjohn that closely relates to his slightly earlier Trinity Church (see No.18) and slightly later Christ Church (see H.D. 5, Brooklyn map 3). In 1885–88 Stanford White was hired to redesign the interior. This early McKim, Mead & White project was one of the great collaborative efforts of the era and includes a mural and a stained-glass window by John La Farge, marble reredos by Louis Saint-Gaudens, mosaics by D. Maitland Armstrong, and a pulpit by Charles F. McKim. Following the completion of this interior project, McKim, Mead & White redesigned an earlier building to create the elegant Northern Renaissance–inspired yellow brick parish house with bottle-glass windows at 12 West 11th Street.

M **First Presbyterian Church,** 48 Fifth Avenue (Joseph C. Wells, 1844–46; chapel, McKim, Mead & White, 1893–94; church house, Edgar Tafel, 1958–60). First Presbyterian, established in 1716, built its first church on Wall Street in 1719. By 1840 Wall Street was the city's business center, and the congregation chose to move to more residential Greenwich Village. Joseph C. Wells provided the congregation with one of the finest English-inspired Gothic Revival churches in New York. The brownstone building focuses on an impressive pinnacled entrance tower. The chapel on West 11th Street was designed by McKim, Mead & White to complement Wells's original design, while the church house on West 12th Street was inspired by Prairie School design, here infused with Gothic detail.

N **New School for Social Research,** 66 West 12th Street (Joseph Urban, 1929–31). The New School was established in 1919 as a progressive center for adult education, catering especially to women. Initial courses were largely in the social sciences, but the curriculum soon expanded into the arts, psychology, and other liberal arts fields. In 1929 construction began on a new building in Greenwich Village that was as modern in its design as the school was in its educational mission. The New School is among the earliest examples of the influence of European Modernism in New York City. Viennese immigrant architect Joseph Urban was attuned to contemporary developments in Europe and designed a building of black and buff brick with ribbon windows and without applied ornament that stands in marked contrast to the earlier row houses and apartment buildings on West 12th Street. On the **interior** (designated 1997), Urban designed a magnificent egg-shaped auditorium (restored in 1992 by Prentice & Chan Olhausen) that was a model for Radio City Music Hall (see No. 294).

O **171 West 12th Street Apartments** (Emilio Levy, 1922). In the 1920s large numbers of apartment houses were erected in Greenwich Village, many with small apartments that appealed to single people and couples with no children. As social constraints were liberalized, many single women, including many lesbians, began seeking places to live on their own, and the progressive Greenwich Village community was a welcome place in which to settle. The twenty-four apartments in this building attracted many notable women, including a significant number in the circle of Eleanor Roosevelt. Among those who lived here in the years after the building's completion were Mary Dewson, one of the most important women active in the Democratic Party during the 1930s and 1940s, and her partner, radical activist Polly Porter; Communist Party leaders Grace Hutchins and Anna Rochester; and Nancy Cook and Marion Dickerman, a couple who founded the private Todhunter School and, along with Roosevelt, established the Val-Kill furniture company.

INDIVIDUAL LANDMARKS

133 **United States Appraisers' Store,** later the U.S. Federal Building, now the Archives Apartments, 641 Washington Street (Willoughby J. Ed-

MANHATTAN

The New School for Social Research (Greenwich Village Historic District, entry N) is an early example of the influence of European Modernism in New York City. Photo by Carl Forster.

brooke and others, 1892–99), designated 1966. The Department of the Treasury built this red brick Romanesque Revival building, occupying an entire square block, as a warehouse for imported goods awaiting customs appraisal. The two lowest floors were built to the designs of Supervising Architect of the Treasury Willoughby J. Edbrooke. While Edbrooke designed an additional eight stories, as did one of his successors, William M. Aiken, the upper floors, as constructed, differ from the published designs of both architects. The massive building was used as archival storage for many years and has now been converted into 479 apartments.

134 **131 Charles Street** (1834), designated 1966. This well-preserved 2½-story brick house in the Federal style provides a contrast to the later lofts and warehouses of its West Village neighborhood.

135 American Seamen's Friend Society Sailors' Home and Institute, 505–507 West Street (William A. Boring, 1907–08), designated 2000. This handsome brick building stands at the west end of Jane Street, facing the Hudson River. It was designed by William A. Boring, and construction was financed primarily by Olivia Sage, one of the era's leading philanthropists. Built at a time when New York was the busiest port in the world, it operated as a hotel, offering inexpensive lodgings to seamen and indigent sailors. Among its amenities were a chapel, a concert hall and a bowling alley, as well as a polygonal corner observatory from which a beacon shone up and down the river. Surviving crew members of the ill-fated luxury liner Titanic were brought here in April 1912 for care and recuperation. Since 1944 it has been used as a residential and transient hotel.

136 26, 28, and 30 Jones Street (1844), designated 1966. These virtually intact Greek Revival row houses typify vernacular residential design of the 1840s. Of special note are the original stoops, wrought-iron railings, modest temple-like entrances (at Nos. 26 and 28), and dentiled cornices.

137 Judson Memorial Church, Tower, and Hall, 51–55 Washington Square South (church, 1888–93; tower and hall, 1895–96—all McKim, Mead & White, Stanford White, partner in charge), designated 1966. Built as a memorial to Adoniram Judson, the first American Baptist missionary in Asia, by his son, the Reverend Dr. Edward Judson, and funded in part by John D. Rockefeller, Judson Memorial is one of Stanford White's most elegant works. White combined Italian Early Christian and Renaissance features into a rich composition that remains one of the key elements of the Washington Square skyline. The architect's choice of mottled yellow Roman brick with extensive white terra-cotta trim introduced light coloration into American church architecture. The activist congregation continues to occupy the church, but the hall and tower are now residences for New York University. Adjacent to the hall is an 1877 building designed by John G. Prague as a young men's boardinghouse.

138 Irad Hawley House, now the Salmagundi Club, 47 Fifth Avenue (1853), designated 1969. This Italianate mansion was built for Irad Hawley,

president of the Pennsylvania Coal Company, which had its yards along the Greenwich Village waterfront. The house is the last survivor of the mansions that once lined fashionable lower Fifth Avenue. The Salmagundi Club, established in 1871 for "the promotion of social intercourse among artists and the advancement of art," has occupied the house since 1917.

139 New York County National Bank, 77–79 Eighth Avenue (DeLemos & Cordes, with Rudolph L. Daus, 1906–07), designated as the Manufacturers Hanover Trust Company Building, 1988. The New York County National Bank, founded in 1855, erected this small but imposing neoclassical limestone-faced bank with Beaux-Arts motifs on a prominent intersection at the northern edge of Greenwich Village. The French influence is especially evident in the arched windows, with their visible iron framing, and in the exuberant quality of the carving.

140 New York Savings Bank, 81 Eighth Avenue (R. H. Robertson, 1896–97), designated 1988. This corner building, designed to be a visual landmark at the intersection of West 14th Street and Eighth Avenue, is an early example of Classical Revival bank design, begun only a year after the completion of McKim, Mead & White's pioneering Bowery Savings Bank (see No. 121). Faced entirely in Vermont marble, the bank has a temple front supported by a pair of Corinthian columns and is crowned by a commanding copper dome with a clerestory of twenty stained-glass windows. The **interior** of the L-shaped building consists of a grand banking hall with a shallow coffered vault supported by columns and pilasters of Siena marble. A restoration was undertaken by Robert Scarano, Jr., architect, when the building was converted into a rug and carpet emporium in 1994.

141 Andrew Norwood House, 241 West 14th Street (1845–47), designated 1978. This beautifully restored house is a survivor from a row of three transitional Greek Revival/Italianate residences erected by the stockbroker Andrew Norwood, who was an active developer in the 14th Street area. Norwood built this house, the central unit of the trio, for himself. As the first masonry buildings on the block, these houses marked the beginning of the transformation of 14th Street into a fashionable residential thoroughfare.

HISTORIC DISTRICTS

⑬ **NoHo Historic District,** designated 2000. During the 1850s, commercial activity in Manhattan eased northward, transforming the residential blocks above Houston Street into a vibrant shopping district. While the area to the south, now called SoHo, has mostly Renaissance-inspired facades executed in cast iron, the NoHo (from "north of Houston") streetscape is considerably more varied, reflecting a broad range of materials and a succession of popular architectural styles. The earliest extant structure in the district was built for James Roosevelt in 1822–23. Located at 58 Bleecker Street, the house features Flemish bond brick, brownstone lintels, and a pitched roof. By the 1840s many fine residences had been erected in the district, such as La

Grange Terrace (1832–33, see No. 152), 2–6 Bond Street (1828–29), and 3–5 Great Jones Street (1844–45). The majority of buildings are store and loft buildings or warehouses, built between 1850 and 1910. Most are located on Broadway, the district's main north-south artery. The earliest examples are 631, 633, and 635 Broadway, built on speculation in 1853–54. The design of these marble-fronted Italianate structures was influenced by the hugely successful A. T. Stewart Store (see No. 70) at 280 Broadway. There also is a significant group of cast-iron-fronted buildings: 620 Broadway (John B. Snook, 1858), 436–440 Lafayette Street (Edward H. Kendall, 1870–71), and 1–5 Bond Street (Stephen Decatur Hatch, 1879–80). Among the most impressive retail stores built after the Civil War is 668–674 Broadway, designed by George E. Harney for the

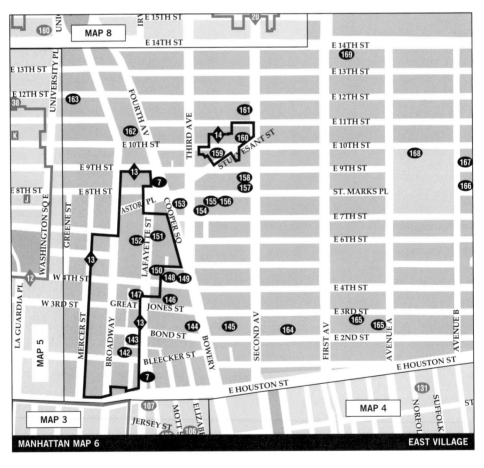

men's clothiers Brooks Brothers in 1873–74. This exuberant corner building is decorated with variegated brick and sandstone, iron columns, and elaborate tie plates. Other exceptional buildings from this period include 10–20 Astor Place (Griffith Thomas, 1875–76), 746–750 Broadway (Orlando Potter, 1881–83) and the Manhattan Savings Institution (Stephen Dectaur Hatch, 1889–91) at 644–646 Broadway. During the last decades of the 19th century, a group of nationally prominent architects were active in the district. H. J. Schwartzmann, architect-in-chief of the 1876 Centennial Exposition in Philadelphia, designed the Mercantile Exchange at 628–630 Broadway (1882–83), which features unusual floral details, and George B. Post was responsible for the Schermerhorn Building (1890–91), an early steel-frame skyscraper, at 696–701 Broadway. Several important buildings were designed by architects who played major roles in the World's Columbian Exposition of 1893 in Chicago, including the Cable Building (McKim, Mead & White, 1892–94) at 611–621 Broadway, the Bayard-Condict Building (Louis Sullivan, 1897–99, see No. 142), and a full-block annex to the Wanamaker's store (D. H. Burnham, 1903–07) at 756–770 Broadway. In the decades that followed, the area entered a period of slow decline. This trend began to reverse in the 1950s, and the turnaround accelerated in the late 1970s, when loft conversions attracted a new generation of commercial, residential, and institutional tenants.

14 **Saint Mark's Historic District,** designated 1969. The land within this district was once part of Peter Stuyvesant's "bouwerie," or farm. The transformation of the area into an urban neighborhood began in the late 18th century when Petrus Stuyvesant, the great-grandson of the Dutch governor, began to subdivide the land into building lots. Stuyvesant Street, running due east-west (at an angle to the later grid), dates from this era, as do the Nicholas and Elizabeth Stuyvesant Fish House (1803–04; see No. 159), the Nicholas William Stuyvesant House (1795) at 44 Stuyvesant Street, and Saint Mark's-in-the-Bowery Church (see No. 160). Major development in the district began in 1839 with the construction of 102 East 10th Street and continued through the 1860s with the construction of Greek Revival, Italianate, and Anglo-Italianate row houses. The Fish House had a large garden that was not developed until 1859–61, when "the Triangle" was erected. This magnificent unified complex of Anglo-Italianate brownstone and brick houses faces onto Stuyvesant and East 10th Streets.

INDIVIDUAL LANDMARKS

■ WEST OF SECOND AVENUE

142 **Bayard-Condict Building,** 65–69 Bleecker Street (Louis Sullivan; Lyndon P. Smith, associate architect, 1897–99), designated 1975. New York City's only work by Louis Sullivan, the Bayard-Condict is a superb illustration of Sullivan's ideas on skyscraper design. The structure of this 12-story steel-frame loft building, clad entirely in white terra cotta, is clearly manifested in the six emphatic vertical bays of the facade. The building is divided horizontally into three sections, demonstrating Sullivan's conviction that a skyscraper should have an ornate base to attract people's attention, a shaft of identical stories stacked atop one another, and a decorated crown to cap the building's upward thrust. The design is enhanced by Sullivan's distinctive organic ornament. In 2003 the original storefronts were recreated.

143 **Robbins & Appleton Building,** 1–5 Bond Street (Stephen Decatur Hatch, 1879–80), designated 1979. The Robbins & Appleton Building is an impressive French Second Empire cast-iron commercial structure erected as a factory for a firm that manufactured watch cases. Three of the floors were leased to D. Appleton & Co., a prominent publishing firm of the era. The facade, with its rows of large windows and its massive mansard roof, has been restored and repainted in imitation of stone.

144 **Bond Street Savings Bank,** now the Bouwerie Lane Theater, 330 Bowery (Henry Engelbert, 1873–74), designated 1967. The Atlantic Savings Bank commissioned this Italianate cast-iron building in 1873; by the time the bank was completed, it was known as the Bond Street Savings Bank. This institution soon failed, and in 1879 the property was conveyed to the German Exchange Bank, which catered to the area's large German immigrant population. The former bank has housed a theater since 1963.

145 **New York Marble Cemetery,** interior of the block bounded by East 2nd and 3rd Streets, Second Avenue, and the Bowery (1830–), designated 1969. Entered through an alley off Second Avenue, Manhattan's first nonsectarian cemetery was founded in 1830 as a commercial venture in a then-fashionable section of the city. The cemetery consists of 156 underground vaults of Tuckahoe marble. There are no monuments, only plaques set into the north and south walls bearing the names of the original vault owners.

146 **Fire Engine Company No. 33,** 44 Great Jones Street (Flagg & Chambers, 1898–99), designated 1968. This Beaux-Arts firehouse is one of the grandest small-scale civic buildings in New York City. The design is dominated by a monumental arch capped by a flamboyant cartouche. The metal infilling of the arch and the metal brackets of the cornice are evidence of the influence that contemporaneous French design had on Ernest Flagg, one of the most sophisticated French-trained architects active in New York.

147 **Schermerhorn Building,** also known as the 376–380 Lafayette Street Building (Henry J. Hard-

enbergh, 1888–89), designated 1966. With its varied materials and colors and its use of wide, segmentally arched openings, this corner building is among New York's most monumental commercial structures of the 1880s. Although the solidity of the masonry walls is mitigated by wide window openings, enormous squat stone columns resting on granite bases accentuate the weight of the building's structure. William C. Schermerhorn replaced the old family mansion and rented the new building to a manufacturer of boys' clothing.

148 **Old Merchant's House,** also known as the Seabury Tredwell House, 29 East 4th Street (1831–32), designated 1965, interior 1981. The Old Merchant's House was built on speculation by Joseph Brewster as part of a row of six identical dwellings. Brewster lived here for a few years, then sold the house to the prosperous hardware merchant Seabury Tredwell in 1836. Gertrude, Tredwell's eighth child, was born in a second-floor bedroom in 1840 and lived in the house until her death in 1933, maintaining the house "as Papa wanted it." At Gertrude's death, a relative saved the house and its contents,

Old Merchant's House, also known as the Seabury Tredwell House (No. 148). This house museum, with its landmark-designated interior, shows the life of an affluent 19th-century family. Photo by Carl Forster.

converting the building into a museum that illustrates the life of an affluent 19th-century family. The 3½-story row house is in a transitional late Federal–Greek Revival style. The exterior is basically Federal in design, distinguished by its Flemish bond brickwork, marble entrance enframement with a Gibbs surround, sloping roof punctuated by dormers, and delicate railings (restored). The **interior,** on the other hand, contains stylish Greek forms, notably the Ionic column screen that separates the front and rear parlors on the main floor. In 1971 a major restoration of the house was undertaken by the architect Joseph Roberto and the designer Carolyn Roberto.

149 **Samuel Tredwell Skidmore House,** 37 East 4th Street (1845), designated 1970. This 3½-story Greek Revival row house with a freestanding Ionic portico is one of the few surviving houses from the period in the mid-19th century when the East Village was an affluent residential neighborhood. The house was built for the businessman Samuel Tredwell Skidmore, a cousin of Seabury Tredwell, whose house still stands to the west at 29 East 4th Street (see above).

150 **De Vinne Press Building,** 393–399 Lafayette Street (Babb, Cook & Willard, 1885–86; addition, 1890–92), designated 1966. Theodore De Vinne, who was in the forefront of the revival of printing as an art form, was responsible for the printing of many major magazines, including *The Century* and *Scribner's Monthly.* De Vinne's Romanesque Revival printing house is a masterpiece of 19th-century commercial architecture with a sophisticated fenestration pattern and subtle terra-cotta detail. The focus of the front elevation is a trio of three-story arches with deeply recessed window frames that accent the massive quality of the walls.

De Vinne Press Building (No. 150). Note the sophisticated fenestration pattern on this 19th-century commercial building. Photo by Carl Forster.

151 Astor Library, now the Joseph Papp Public Theater, 425 Lafayette Street (south wing, Alexander Saeltzer, 1849–53; center section, Griffith Thomas, 1856–69; north wing, Thomas Stent, 1879–81), designated 1965. New York's first public library was built with a bequest from John Jacob Astor. The building, which appears to be a single unified structure, was actually erected in three campaigns, each with a different architect of record. The German-born Alexander Saeltzer established the building's form with his use of the German round-arched, or *Rundbogenstil,* style, with its roots in Northern Italian Romanesque design. The building served for many years as the headquarters of the Hebrew Immigrant Aid Society (HIAS) but was vacant and endangered in 1965 when the theatrical producer Joseph Papp persuaded the city to acquire it. In 1966 architect Giorgio Cavaglieri converted the building for use by one of America's most innovative theatrical institutions. In recent years all the windows have been beautifully restored by Buck Cane Architects.

152 La Grange Terrace, also known as Colonnade Row, 428, 430, 432, and 434 Lafayette Street (attributed to Seth Geer, 1832–33), designated 1965. These four houses survive from a row of nine Greek Revival marble-fronted residences that, at the time of their completion, were among the grandest dwellings in New York and were occupied by members of New York's leading families. Erected, and possibly designed, by the developer Seth Geer and named for the Marquis de Lafayette's estate in France, the row is unified by the use of a Corinthian colonnade that was once crowned by a continuous band of anthemia (now visible only at No. 434). The buildings began to deteriorate in the post–Civil War era as the wealthy moved out of this neighborhood, and the houses were subdivided into apartments and commercial spaces. The row now contains apartments, restaurants, and theaters.

153 Cooper Union, Cooper Square (Frederick A. Peterson, 1853–59; later rooftop additions), designated 1965. Dedicated to "the advancement of science and art," Cooper Union was established as a school offering free education to working-class men and women. The Italianate building, faced in brownstone, was among the first structures to employ rolled iron beams (fabricated at Peter Cooper's Tren-

La Grange Terrace, also known as Colonnade Row (No. 152). For a brief period one of the city's toniest addresses, only four of these grand dwellings survive. Photo by Carl Forster.

ton, New Jersey, foundry) and was also among the earliest buildings designed to accommodate an elevator. The original structure rose only five stories, with income-producing stores on the first floor. Several rooftop additions have led to significant structural alterations, including the replacement in 1886 of the original rectangular second-floor windows with segmental arched openings (Leopold Eidlitz, architect). In 1975–76 the cast-iron storefronts were restored (new pieces were cast in aluminum by the school's art students) and the street level was converted into a library; these changes were part of an extensive renovation designed by John Hejduk, who served as dean of Cooper Union's architecture school.

154 **Metropolitan Savings Bank,** now the First Ukrainian Evangelical Pentecostal Church, 9 East 7th Street (Carl Pfeiffer, 1867), designated 1969. Built to serve the largely German inhabitants of this East Village neighborhood, the Metropolitan Savings Bank is a significant example of French Second Empire design. Pfeiffer handled the Second Empire idiom in a sophisticated manner, creating a dynamically massed structure on a relatively small site. In 1937 the marble building was purchased by the First Ukrainian Assembly of God, and it has since served as a church.

155 **German-American Shooting Society Clubhouse,** 12 St. Mark's Place (William C. Frohne, 1889–89), designated 2001. Prior to the 20th century, St. Mark's Place was the heart of Kleindeutschland, or Little Germany. Many organizations and societies were established in the area to support the immigrant community, including shooting clubs, which offered facilities for target practice. This yellow brick clubhouse served as the headquarters of twenty-four companies. A rare example of the German Renaissance style in New York, the building features fanciful ornament, a steep mansard roof, and tall ornate dormers. Particularly noteworthy is the arched panel at the center of the fourth story, depicting a target and crossed rifles above an eagle with outstretched wings.

156 **20 Saint Mark's Place,** also known as the Daniel Leroy House (1832), designated 1969. In the 1830s the south side of Saint Mark's Place between Second and Third Avenues was developed with an elegant row of 3½-story brick houses erected on speculation by Thomas E. Davis. The sole intact survivor is No. 20, whose exceptional marble entrance surround is ornamented with vermiculated blocks. The original residents appear to have been the South Street merchant Daniel Leroy and his wife, Elizabeth Fish.

German-American Shooting Society Clubhouse (No. 155). This German Renaissance style building recalls the era when the East Village was called Kleindeutschland. Photo by Carl Forster.

157 **New York Free Circulating Library, Ottendorfer Branch,** now the New York Public Library, Ottendorfer Branch, 135 Second Avenue (William Schickel, 1883–84), designated 1977, interior 1981. The German-American philanthropists Oswald Ottendorfer, publisher of the *Staats-Zeitung,* and his wife, Anna, built this library and the adjacent German Dispensary (see below) as part of their efforts to improve the minds and bodies of their fellow German immigrants. The library is an ornate red brick Queen Anne– and Renaissance-inspired building with extensive terra-cotta detail that incorporates such symbols of wisdom and knowledge as globes, owls, books, and torches. Even before it was completed, the Ottendorfers donated their library to the New York Free Circulating Library, a privately funded library system (see No. 419). The Ottendorfer is now the oldest operating branch of the New York Public Library system. Its **interior** retains its original character, with reading rooms on the first

and second floors and cast-iron book stacks at the rear of the first floor and on the glass-floored mezzanine.

158 **Deutsches (German) Dispensary,** now Stuyvesant Polyclinic, 137 Second Avenue (William Schickel, 1883–84), designated 1976. The German Dispensary and the neighboring Ottendorfer Library (see above) were commissioned by Anna and Oswald Ottendorfer, philanthropists concerned with the welfare of New York's German immigrant community. This exuberant Italian Renaissance–inspired structure, designed by the German-born architect William Schickel, is among the first buildings in New York to display extensive ornamental terra cotta, including busts of important figures in the history of medicine.

159 **Nicholas and Elizabeth Stuyvesant Fish House,** also known as the Stuyvesant-Fish House,

New York Free Circulating Library (No. 157) and Stuyvesant Polyclinic (No. 158). These two buildings were built by philanthropists Oswald and Anna Ottendorfer to help their fellow German immigrants. Photo by Carl Forster.

21 Stuyvesant Street (1803–04), designated 1965. The Fish House was built by Petrus Stuyvesant, great-grandson of the last director general of New Amsterdam, on land owned by the Stuyvesant family since the 17th century. The brick dwelling in the Federal style was a wedding gift to Stuyvesant's daughter Elizabeth and her husband, Nicholas Fish, a veteran of Valley Forge.

160 Saint Mark's-in-the-Bowery Church (Episcopal), East 10th Street at Second Avenue (1799; tower, Town & Thompson, 1826–28; portico, 1854), designated 1966. The second oldest church building in Manhattan, Saint Mark's is a survivor from the period when the East Village was sparsely populated. The land on which the church is built, the former site of Dutch governor Peter Stuyvesant's private chapel (Stuyvesant is buried in the churchyard), was sold to the Episcopal Church for one dollar by Stuyvesant's great-grandson. The original fieldstone church was a simple pedimented structure with beautifully proportioned window openings. In 1828, by which time the area around the church was developing into the city's most affluent residential neighborhood, a stylish Greek Revival tower was constructed, turning the church into one of the most prominent buildings in the vicinity. An Italianate cast-iron portico was added in 1854. As the community changed over the years, the church building deteriorated significantly; at the same time the Saint Mark's congregation developed into one of the most politically and socially committed in the city. A restoration project was begun in 1975 that included training local residents in construction; this project, which continued even after a fire severely damaged the church in 1978, was completed in 1983.

161 Louis N. Jaffe Art Theater (Yiddish Art Theater/Yiddish Folks Theater), now Village East City Cinemas, 189 Second Avenue (Harrison G. Wiseman, 1925–26), designated 1993. In the 1920s Second Avenue below 14th Street was known as the Yiddish Rialto. Erected as a home for the Yiddish Art Theater by Jewish civic leader Louis Jaffe, this is the most prominent of the theaters that once housed Yiddish productions. The design, with its large central arch, gold-hued cast-stone facing, and symbolic Judaic ornament, resembles the form of contemporary synagogues designed in what was known as the

"Semitic" style, an original combination of Moorish, Byzantine, and Middle Eastern motifs. Although the Yiddish Art Theater, a company inspired by the European "art theater" movement, only performed in this building for four seasons, the theater remained a Yiddish stage, generally known as the Yiddish Folks Theater. With the Yiddish theater in decline, the building was converted into a movie house in 1946. It again became a legitimate stage in 1953, hosting the famous Phoenix Theater repertory company, which produced classic and modern plays with such great actors as Hume Cronyn, Jessica Tandy, Eli Wallach, Farley Granger, Lillian Gish, and Eva LeGallienne. Later the theater premiered *Oh! Calcutta!* and *Grease.* In 1990–91 the **interior** was converted into a multiplex cinema, preserving much of the exotic polychromatic ornament of the lobby, proscenium, and auditorium walls and ceiling.

162 Grace Church (Episcopal) Complex, 800 and 804 Broadway and 92, 94–96, and 98 Fourth Avenue (church, James Renwick, Jr., 1843–46; with additions, James Renwick, Jr., Edward T. Potter, Heins & La Farge, and William W. Renwick; rectory, James Renwick, Jr., 1846–47; Grace House, James Renwick, Jr., 1880–81; Grace Church Houses, now Grace Church School: Memorial House, James Renwick, Jr., 1881–83; Clergy House, Heins & La Farge, 1902–03; Neighborhood House, Renwick, Aspinwall & Tucker, 1906–07), designated 1966. Grace Church is one of the most significant early examples of Gothic Revival architecture in America. Designed in a French Gothic mode, the marble church and its picturesque rectory were among the first works of James Renwick, Jr. The church is strategically sited at a point where Broadway curves, so that the vista up Broadway from the Battery terminates with the church tower. This location underscores the Episcopal parish's standing as one of the most prestigious religious organizations in New York City. Over the years the church has had many additions and alterations, all of them in keeping with Renwick's original scheme. Among these are Renwick's Grace House (1880–81), which connects the church and rectory; his 1883 replacement of the original wood spire with the present marble spire; Edward T. Potter's Chantry (1879; alterations by William W. Renwick, 1910); and a chancel extension (Heins & La Farge, 1903). As the nature and needs of the congregation changed in response to population changes in the surrounding area, new buildings were added to the complex, including a series of structures on Fourth Avenue that display great stylistic coherence. In 1881 James Renwick designed Grace Memorial House in a Gothic style that echoes his earlier church design. This building is thought to have housed New York's first day-care center. Twenty-one years later the building was expanded to the south with the addition of the Clergy House, an exact copy of the original building. The complex was further expanded in 1907 with the more austere Neighborhood House. An addition to the Grace Church School was built behind the facades of the Memorial House, the Clergy House, and part of the Neighborhood House in 1974–75.

163 **Police Athletic League Building,** originally Grammar School 47, 34½ East 12th Street (Thomas R. Jackson, 1855), designated 1998. Constructed for the Board of Education in 1855, this freestanding Italianate structure was one of the earliest public schools in New York City built exclusively for girls. Designed by the prolific architect Thomas R. Jackson, it is crowned by a bracketed cornice with triangular pediments above the end pavilions. The school was reorganized as a high school for girls (later known as the Wadleigh School, see No. 547) in 1897, and as Girl's Technical High School in 1902. The building was acquired by the Police Department in 1958.

■ EAST OF SECOND AVENUE

164 **New York City Marble Cemetery,** 52–74 East 2nd Street (1831–), designated 1969. Opened one year after the nearby New York Marble Cemetery (see No. 145), this cemetery was the second nonsectarian burial ground in the city. Among the distinguished citizens buried beneath the stone markers and monuments are members of the Fish, Kip, Lenox, and Roosevelt families.

165 **First Houses,** 29–41 Avenue A and 112–138 East 3rd Street (Frederick L. Ackerman, 1935–36), designated 1974. First Houses was the nation's earliest public-sponsored low-income housing project and the first effort of the city's newly established Housing Authority. The L-shaped complex was planned as a renovation of older tenements; every

third building was to be removed, creating a series of courtyards. As work proceeded, however, the remaining buildings had to be substantially reconstructed. The open space to the rear of the buildings was landscaped with trees, benches, fanciful sculpture, and playgrounds.

166 **Children's Aid Society, Tompkins Square Lodging House for Boys and Industrial School,** also known as the Eleventh Ward Lodging House, 296 East 8th Street (Vaux & Radford, 1886), designated 2000. Between 1879 and 1892, Calvert Vaux and George Kent Radford completed approximately twelve facilities for the Children's Aid Society. Each was a gift from a private individual, and this facility was donated by Mrs. Robert L. Stuart, the wife of a sugar refiner. To distinguish the building from the surrounding tenements, the architects fashioned a picturesque brick design featuring an elaborate roof punctuated by dormers, gables, and a corner tower. Most tenants were homeless newsboys and bootblacks, aged seven to seventeen. It became a school in 1900 and was converted to apartments in 1978.

167 **Charlie Parker Residence,** 151 Avenue B (c. 1849), designated 1999. The world-famous alto saxophonist Charlie "Bird" Parker occupied the ground story of this row house from 1950 to 1954. Parker moved to New York in the late 1930s and soon established himself as one of jazz's most gifted performers. Parker leased the apartment with his common-law wife, Chan Richardson, at the height of his career, having achieved considerable success as the cofounder of bebop, the modern jazz style that he invented with trumpeter Dizzy Gillispie. Two children were born to the couple during their residency here. Restored in the 1990s, the Gothic Revival facade displays many original details, including a pointed-arch entranceway and a projecting box cornice embellished with trefoil relief.

168 **New York Public Library, Tompkins Square Branch,** 331 East 10th Street (McKim, Mead & White, 1904), designated 1999. Located between Avenues A and B on the north side of Tompkins Square, this three-story limestone structure was designed by the architect Charles Follen McKim, who was responsible for many important libraries in New York, including twelve branches financed by Andrew Carnegie. Above the second story windows, a shield incorporates the seal of the City of New York, and rosettes commemorate Aldus Manutius and Cristophe Plaintin Press, major figures in the history of printing.

⓯ Grace Chapel (Episcopal) and Hospital, now Immaculate Conception Church (R.C.) and Clergy House, 406–412 East 14th Street (Barney & Chapman, 1894–96), designated 1966. Barney & Chapman designed two distinguished and distinc-tive Episcopal church complexes in the French Gothic style—Grace Chapel and the Church of the Holy Trinity (see No. 506). This chapel of brick and terra cotta was built by Grace Church (see No. 162) as a free church that would minister to all, regardless of income—that is, no pew rents were charged. Adjoining the church is an austere complementary structure erected as a hospital. In 1943 the chapel was converted into a Roman Catholic church, and the hospital became a clergy house.

The legendary jazz musician Charlie Parker lived in this Gothic Revival house (No. 167) from 1950 to 1954. Photo by Carl Forster.

HISTORIC DISTRICT

⑮ Chelsea Historic District and Extension, designated 1970 and 1981. In 1750 Captain Thomas Clarke purchased a large plot of land along the Hudson River and laid out a country estate that he called Chelsea. A portion of the property was deeded to Clarke's grandson Clement Clarke Moore in 1813. Moore, a wealthy, well-educated scholar, poet, and country gentleman, is remembered today as the author of "A Visit from Saint Nicholas." As the city moved northward, Moore realized that his land would soon be ripe for development. With the advice and assistance of James N. Wells, Moore had the area divided into building lots with restrictions placed on the design and quality of new housing. Between 1825 and 1860, almost the entire area was built up. The district is especially rich in Greek Revival row houses, notably Cushman Row (1839–40), at 408–418 West 20th Street between Ninth and Tenth Avenues, and also contains New York City's largest concentration of Anglo-Italianate row houses, identifiable by their low stoops and sunken basements. Moore donated land on West 20th Street for Saint Peter's Episcopal Church (1836–38), an early example of the Gothic Revival in America, and also gave the land on which the General Theological Seminary was constructed. The oldest surviving building on the Episcopal seminary's block is a small Gothic Revival stone structure of 1836; most of the campus was the work of Charles C. Haight, who prepared a master plan in 1883 and designed a series of Collegiate Gothic buildings.

INDIVIDUAL LANDMARKS

⑰⓪ Chelsea Apartments, now the Chelsea Hotel, 222 West 23rd Street (Hubert, Pirsson & Co., 1883–85), designated 1966. The famous Chelsea Hotel was built as one of the city's earliest cooperative apartment houses. The facade of the picturesque Queen Anne building, executed in a variety of materials, is enhanced by tiers of remarkable iron balconies ornamented with flowers. Since its conversion into a hotel in 1905, the Chelsea has attracted many

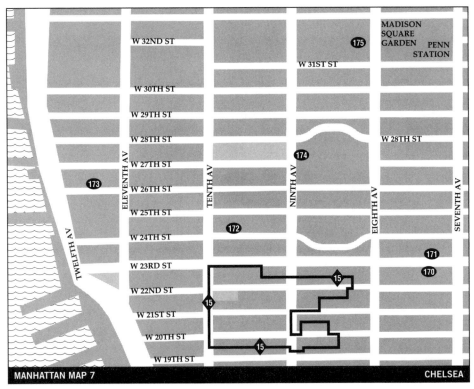

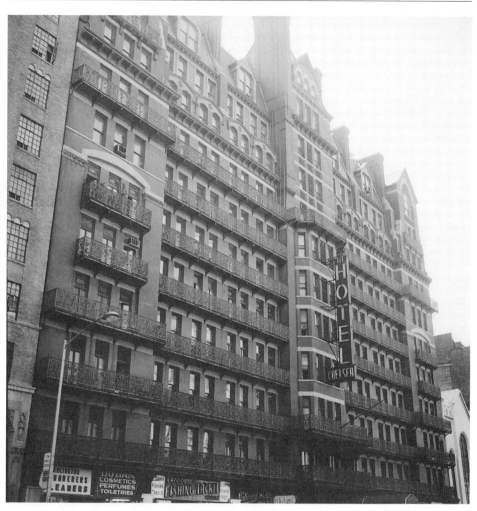

The Chelsea Hotel (No. 170) attracts many famous artists and musicians. Its picturesque Queen Anne–style facade is enhanced by tiers of iron balconies. Photo by Peter Choy.

famous writers, artists, and musicians, including Brendan Behan, Thomas Wolfe, Dylan Thomas, Mark Twain, Tennessee Williams, Virgil Thomson, and Sid Vicious; it was also the location for Andy Warhol's movie *Chelsea Girls*.

171 New York Public Library, Muhlenberg Branch, 209–211 West 23rd Street (Carrère & Hastings, 1906), designated 2001. Faced in limestone, this neoclassical library was designed by Carrère & Hastings, architects of the main building of the New York Public Library. Built to serve the Chelsea community, it was probably named for William Augustus

Muhlenberg, first rector of the Church of the Holy Communion on West 20th Street. This library was the eleventh branch built in Manhattan with funds donated by Andrew Carnegie.

172 437–459 West 24th Street (1849–50), designated individually 1970. This long row of twelve paired houses was erected by the builder Philo V. Beebe to provide housing for the merchants and professionals who moved into the Chelsea neighborhood in the 1840s. Most of these transitional Greek Revival/Italianate dwellings have deep landscaped yards and retain their original stoops, iron railings, and other details.

65

173 **Starrett-Lehigh Building,** 601–625 West 26th Street (Cory & Cory; Yasuo Matsui, associate; consulting engineers, Purdy & Henderson, 1930–31), designated 1986. The striking Starrett-Lehigh Building is an enormous freight terminal and warehouse, occupying an entire block. It was built as a joint venture of the Starrett Investing Corporation and the Lehigh Valley Railroad (trains could pull right into the ground story of the building). The building—with its setback massing, polygonal corners, and horizontal bands of steel ribbon windows alternating with brick spandrels and concrete floorplates—was in the forefront of modern design when it was erected in 1930–31. This was one of only a handful of American designs included in the Museum of Modern Art's pioneering "International Style" exhibition of 1932.

174 **Church of the Holy Apostles (Episcopal),** 300 Ninth Avenue (Minard Lafever, 1845–48; additions, Minard Lafever, 1853–54; transepts, Richard Upjohn & Son, 1858), designated 1966. Lafever's only surviving building in Manhattan is a rare New York example of an Italianate church. The brick building, which has a prominent spire, has been enlarged several times. In 1853–54 it was extended 25 feet with the construction of a new chancel, and in 1858 transepts were constructed to the designs of Charles Babcock of the firm Richard Upjohn & Son. The building contains several stained-glass windows designed by William Jay Bolton that survived a devastating fire in 1990. Following the fire, the socially active congregation raised money for its continuing efforts to feed the hungry while at the same time restoring this exceptional church building.

175 **United States General Post Office,** now the James A. Farley Building, Eighth Avenue at West 31st Street (McKim, Mead & White, William M. Kendall, partner in charge, 1908–13), designated 1966. The McKim, Mead & White firm designed this enormous granite structure as a companion to Pennsylvania Station, which stood across the street until 1963. Along Eighth Avenue, a monumental Corinthian collonade stretches two full city blocks. Plans call for the building to be converted into a major transit facility, named for the late New York senator, Daniel Patrick Moynihan.

Starrett-Lehigh Building (No. 173). This huge freight terminal and warehouse was one of the few American designs included in the Museum of Modern Art's "International Style" exhibition of 1932. Photo by Carl Forster.

■ WEST OF UNION SQUARE AND PARK AVENUE SOUTH

HISTORIC DISTRICTS

⑯ Ladies' Mile Historic District, designated 1989. The Ladies' Mile Historic District developed largely in the decades following the Civil War, when commerce intruded on the residential neighborhoods between Union and Madison Squares. In the late 1860s, businesses such as Arnold Constable (881–887 Broadway; Griffith Thomas, 1868–76) and Lord & Taylor (see No. 186) erected imposing Italianate and French Second Empire marble or cast-iron department stores along Broadway. They were soon joined by Gorham Silver Manufacturing Company (see No. 185), W. & J. Sloane (880–886 Broadway; W. Wheeler Smith, 1881–82), and other prestigious emporiums. Sixth Avenue also became a center for department stores, with B. Altman & Co. opening on the southwest corner of West 19th Street in 1877 (D. & J. Jardine, architect; additions, 1880–1909). Altman's

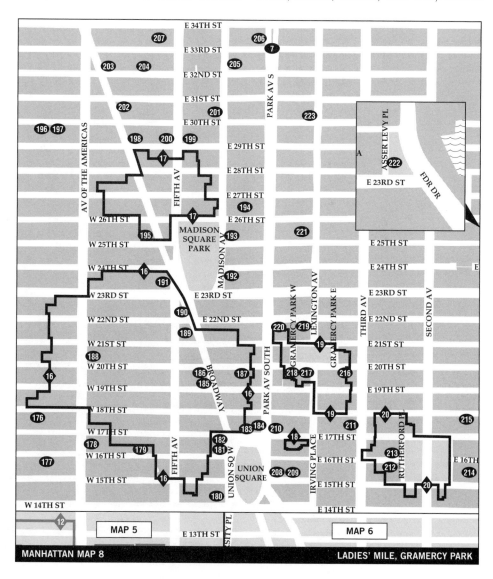

was followed by a succession of other stores, culminating in the 1895–97 construction of the monumental Siegel-Cooper Department Store (DeLemos & Cordes, architect) between West 18th and West 19th Streets. Fifth Avenue attracted smaller shops, publishing houses (see Scribner's, No. 189), the offices of charitable institutions such as the Methodist Book Concern (Edward Hale Kendall, 1888–90) at No. 148–152 and the Presbyterian Building (Rowe & Baker, 1894–95) at No. 154–158, and skyscrapers (see Flatiron Building, No. 190). With the exception of 23rd Street, with its large department stores (notably Stern Brothers, 32–46 West 23rd Street; Henry Fernbach, 1878, with later additions), the side streets in the district were redeveloped around 1900 with loft buildings in which many of the goods sold in the nearby stores were manufactured. The finest of these is the Viennese Secession–influenced Spero Building (Robert D. Kohn, 1907–08) at 19–27 West 21st Street. A wave of restoration and rehabilitation began in the 1980s as the area was rediscovered by architects, photographers, publishing houses, advertising firms, and other businesses. These businesses have in turn attracted restaurants, boutiques, and other fashionable shops to Broadway, Fifth Avenue, and the adjacent side streets, while many of the former department stores on Sixth Avenue have been restored for national merchandising chains.

⬧17 Madison Square North Historic District, designated 2001. A pair of intersecting north-south streets, Broadway and Fifth Avenue, define the character of this large historic district. Following the opening of Madison Square in 1847, the blocks adjoining the park attracted residential development, particularly four- and five-story row houses faced in brick or brownstone. Approximately 25 percent of the district's buildings were planned as single-family residences. Along the south side of West 28th Street stands a row of five contiguous structures, built between 1855 and 1862. Despite commercial alterations, this block is unique for maintaining its resi-

Ladies' Mile Historic District (H.D. 16). The large store windows on the second floor of many of these buildings allowed riders of the elevated railway to peer into the stores on Sixth Avenue. Photo by Caroline Kane Levy.

dential scale. After the Civil War, the district's character was transformed by commercial development, chiefly hotels, theaters, clubs, and restaurants. Among various hotels to survive from this period are 39–41 West 27th Street (Renwick, Aspinwall & Company, 1890), the Breslin (1903–5) at the southeast corner of Broadway and 29th Street, and the Prince George (Howard Greenley, 1904–5, 1912–13), the last and largest hotel built in the district. Madison Square emerged as an important mercantile center

The Madison Square North Historic District (H.D. 17) contains a great variety of commercial buildings, including 256 Fifth Avenue. Photo by Carl Forster.

after 1880. The first phase of development consisted of small commercial buildings, most notably the real-estate office of the Astor family at 21 West 26th Street (Thomas Stent, 1883), and 256 Fifth Avenue (Alfred Zucker and John Edelman, 1893), a Moorish Revival structure that was initially leased to the portrait photographer Napoleon Sarony. In subsequent decades, larger office and loft buildings rose throughout the district. Early examples include the classically inspired Baudouine and Revillon Buildings (both 1896) at 1181 Broadway and 13–15 West 28th Street. The Townsend Building (Cyrus L.W. Eidlitz, 1896) at Broadway and 25th Street, the St. James Building (Bruce Price, 1896–98) at 1133 Broadway, and the Brunswick Building (Francis H. Kimball, 1906–07) at 225 Fifth Avenue attracted a remarkable concentration of architectural firms as tenants, including Carrère & Hastings, C. P. H. Gilbert, and John Russell Pope. After 1900 most developers catered to wholesale merchants who sought large floors interrupted by a minimum of columns. Among the most architecturally distinguished loft buildings were the neoclassical Neptune Building (Maynicke & Franke, 1909–10) at 23–25 East 26th Street and the neo-Gothic Croisic Building (Frederick C. Browne, 1905–7) at Fifth Avenue and 26th Street, both overlooking Madison Square, and 256–261 Fifth Avenue, an Art Deco gem with remarkable polychrome terra cotta designed by Eli Jacques Kahn in 1928–29. Few buildings have been constructed in the historic district since the Depression era, and most of the structures continue to serve their original, or a related, purpose.

INDIVIDUAL LANDMARKS

176 **126, 128, 130–132, 136, and 140 West 18th Street Stables** (1864–65), designated individually 1990. These five landmark buildings are rare survivors of a row of thirteen private carriage houses designed in a utilitarian round-arched style. Erected on a street devoted exclusively to stables, they served the large residences built north of 14th Street in the mid-19th century.

177 **New York House and School of Industry,** now the Young Adults Institute, 120 West 16th Street (Sidney V. Stratton, 1878), designated 1990. Founded in 1850, the New York House and School of Industry was organized by members of several of New York's wealthiest families to assist destitute women by providing them with employment in the form of needlework, ranging from mundane sewing to the production of fancy embroidery. The charity's 1878 headquarters is thought to be the earliest building in the Queen Anne style in the city. The stone, terra-cotta, and slate trim, the paneled oriel with multipaned windows, and the free use of classical motifs are characteristic of highly sophisticated Queen Anne design. The building has been restored by Anderson Associates, architects.

178 574 Sixth Avenue (Simeon B. Eisendrath, 1903–04), designated 1990. Erected as a retail store for the Knickerbocker Jewelry Company, this building has a simple, rationally massed facade crowned by an exuberant cornice that was designed to attract the attention of riders on the Sixth Avenue Elevated, which ran in front of the building.

179 5, 7, 9, 17, 19, 21, and 23 West 16th Street (c. 1845–46), designated individually 1990. In the 1840s the streets adjacent to Fifth Avenue just north of 14th Street were developed with row houses. Most of these structures were demolished as commerce invaded the area in the late 19th century, but West 16th Street retains a significant number of Greek Revival houses. The most impressive are the four survivors of a row of nine wide houses—Nos. 5, 7, 9 and 17—each of which has a full-height curving bay on its front facade, an extremely rare feature in New York. In 1930 the family-planning pioneer Margaret Sanger moved her Birth Control Clinical Research Bureau into No. 17. Nos. 19 and 21 are simpler houses displaying fine ironwork, while No. 23 has a magnificent cast-iron balcony and stoop railing. All the houses have wide stone entrance enframements with battered sides and eared corners; this is a classic Greek form copied from the window surrounds on Greek temples.

180 Lincoln Building, 1–3 Union Square West (R. H. Robertson, 1889–90), designated 1988. The Lincoln Building is representative of the early skyscraper form as it evolved in New York, where architects chose to adapt already-popular styles to this new building type. Robertson designed the Lincoln

126, 128, 130–32, 136, and 140 West 18th Street Stables (No. 176). A reminder of New York's equestrian past. Photo by Caroline Kane Levy.

Building in the same Romanesque Revival style that he used for churches, houses, and other structures. The building, faced in limestone, granite, red brick, and terra cotta, marks an important transitional phase in skyscraper engineering; it was constructed with a metal framing in combination with traditional masonry bearing walls.

181 Bank of the Metropolis, 31 Union Square West (Bruce Price, 1902–03), designated 1988. Price was an important early skyscraper designer with a particular interest in adapting the tripartite form of the column to tall buildings. This neo-Renaissance limestone-faced example is clearly massed in Price's preferred base-shaft-capital manner. The Bank of the Metropolis, founded in 1871 to serve the needs of businesses in the Union Square area, maintained its offices on the square until 1918, when it was absorbed by the Bank of Manhattan.

182 Decker Building, now the Union Building, 33 Union Square West (John Edelmann in the employ of Alfred Zucker, 1892–93), designated 1988. A rare example of a Moorish-inspired skyscraper, the headquarters of the Decker Piano Company was designed by John Edelmann, mentor and friend of Louis Sullivan. Many features of the Decker Building, most notably the naturalistic ornament, reflect Sullivan's influence. Between 1968 and 1974 Andy Warhol's Factory occupied the sixth floor. The base was handsomely restored in 1995.

183 Century Building, now Barnes & Noble Bookstore, 33 East 17th Street (William Schickel, 1880–81), designated 1986. The red brick Century Building is a rare New York example of a Queen Anne–style commercial structure. Erected to house the prestigious Century Publishing Company, publisher of *The Century* and *St. Nicholas* magazines, the building is characteristic of the finest Queen Anne design in its free use of classical motifs in stone and terra cotta and its employment of the style's trademark sunflowers. After standing vacant for many years, the building was converted into a bookstore, and the facade received an award-winning restoration.

184 Everett Building, 200 Park Avenue South (Goldwin Starrett & Van Vleck, 1908), designated 1988. Located on the north side of Union Square, the Everett Building exemplifies an important develop-

ment in the design of commercial high-rise buildings—the construction of functional, fireproof structures with large windows, open floor space, and simple classical detail. This emphasis on functionalism reflects the influence of Chicago skyscraper designs; in fact, the architect, Goldwin Starrett, had worked for four years in the Chicago office of Daniel Burnham.

185 Gorham Manufacturing Company Building, 889–891 Broadway (Edward Hale Kendall, 1883–84; alteration, John H. Duncan, 1912), designated 1984. This commercial building in the Queen Anne style was erected for the Gorham Manufacturing Company, a leading American silver firm, for its retail outlet in the exclusive Ladies' Mile shopping district. The Gorham is an early example of a mixed-use building: only the lower two floors were occupied by the store; the upper floors were rented as bachelor apartments. By 1893, however, the building was entirely in commercial use. The architect John H. Duncan is responsible for a remodeling of the building in 1912 that entailed the removal of a corner tower and the addition of roof dormers. The building now contains shops at street level and apartments above.

186 Lord & Taylor Store, 901 Broadway (James H. Giles, 1869–70), designated 1977. Two English immigrants, Samuel Lord and George Taylor, founded the dry goods firm Lord & Taylor around 1830. The business joined the northward migration of Manhattan's commercial establishments when it opened this impressive French Second Empire store in the fashionable Ladies' Mile shopping district. James H. Giles's original cast-iron building was considerably larger than the present structure; much of the Broadway frontage was rebuilt after Lord & Taylor moved in 1914 to its present home on Fifth Avenue at 39th Street. The building is noteworthy for its bold three-dimensional massing, its large windows, and the chamfered corner topped with a mansard roof that was designed to attract the attention of shoppers traveling south on Broadway from uptown residential neighborhoods. The facade has been restored and given a new ground story by Kutnicki Bernstein Architect.

187 Theodore Roosevelt Birthplace, now the Theodore Roosevelt Birthplace National Historic Site, 28 East 20th Street (Theodate Pope Riddle,

1923), designated 1966. At his death in 1919, Theodore Roosevelt was revered as a great American hero. Three years earlier his boyhood home, a modest Gothic Revival row house on East 20th Street (much altered after the Roosevelt family moved uptown in 1872), had been demolished. The Woman's Roosevelt Memorial Association, founded with the intention of honoring Roosevelt's memory, purchased the birthplace site, along with the adjacent home (also significantly altered) of Theodore's uncle, Robert Roosevelt. The association proceeded to demolish the uncle's house and to commission Theodate Pope Riddle, one of the first female architects in America, to reconstruct Theodore Roosevelt's childhood home as it had existed in 1865, when a mansard roof had been added and the interiors redesigned. A modest museum wing was built on the adjoining site. In 1963 the house was donated to the National Park Service.

188 **Church of the Holy Communion (Episcopal) Complex,** Sixth Avenue at West 20th Street (church, 1844–46; rectory and parish house, c. 1850; Sisters' House, 1854—all Richard Upjohn), designated 1966. Although a small building, the former Church of the Holy Communion had one of the most influential designs of the 19th century. Holy Communion was the first asymmetrical Gothic Revival church edifice in the United States and was the prototype for hundreds of similar buildings erected all across the country. Upjohn designed the building to resemble a small medieval English parish church; the rectory and other additions complement the church in style and massing. The church's founder, the Reverend William Muhlenberg, a leader of the evangelical Catholic movement within the Episcopal Church, was closely involved with the design; it was apparently he who suggested the use of transepts and other features that were more common in Roman Catholic churches of the era. As part of his work at Holy Communion, Muhlenberg organized Saint Luke's Hospital, established a library that became the Muhlenberg Branch of the New York Public Library (see No.171), and founded the first boys' choir and the first Episcopal sisterhood in America. The small three-story building on Sixth Avenue was the Sisters' House. The parish later consolidated with Calvary Church and Saint George's Church (see H.D. 16 and 20, map 8), and its complex of buildings has been converted to secular use.

189 **Scribner Building,** now the United Synagogue of America, 153–157 Fifth Avenue (Ernest Flagg, 1893–94), designated 1976. The publishing firm Charles Scribner's Sons commissioned this building for use as a bookstore and corporate headquarters. The limestone-fronted building, Flagg's first commercial work, indicates the architect's sophisticated understanding of contemporary French design, especially evident in the use of heavy load-bearing corner piers that flank a more open central area with large windows, attenuated iron colonnettes, and a wide shop front. The Scribner company was founded in 1846 by Charles Scribner and flourished, under various names, until Scribner's death in 1871. By the late 1870s, Scribner's sons had taken over the firm, which grew into one of America's most prestigious publishing houses, introducing works by Henry James, Edith Wharton, F. Scott Fitzgerald, and Ernest Hemingway, among others. The Fifth Avenue building, designed by Charles Scribner II's brother-in-law, was the first built specifically for the company. In 1913 the company moved into a new store farther north on Fifth Avenue (see No. 291).

190 **Flatiron Building,** Broadway and Fifth Avenue at 23rd Street (D. H. Burnham & Co., 1901–03), designated 1966. The Chicago architect Daniel Burnham designed this triangular steel-framed skyscraper on what was, at the beginning of the 20th century, among the most prominent sites in New York City—Madison Square at the junction of Fifth Avenue and Broadway—anchoring the north end of the prestigious Ladies' Mile shopping district. Built as offices for the Fuller Construction Company (see No. 316), the skyscraper was dubbed the Flatiron because its shape resembles that of a clothing iron. Many early 20th-century painters and photographers were inspired by the building's singular form, and it became a world-famous symbol of the romantic New York skyline. The slender 22-story building is clad in traditional Italian Renaissance ornament, most of it white terra cotta; the light coloration was again revealed in 1991 when the building was cleaned and restored (Hurley & Farinella, architect). The small metal and glass extension (known as the cowcatcher) at the apex of the building was designed by the Burnham firm in 1902. To celebrate the building's centennial, the sculptural group on the roof was recreated.

Flatiron Building (No. 190)
Daniel Burnham's memorable
design for this prominent site.
Landmarks Preservation
Commission collection.

191 **Sidewalk Clock,** 200 Fifth Avenue at West 23rd Street (Hecla Iron Works, 1909), designated 1981. Clocks were once an important part of the street fabric of American cities. Large cast-iron sidewalk clocks, many of which served as advertisements for jewelers and other businesses, proliferated in the early 20th century. In Manhattan four such clocks are landmarks (see Nos. 289, 428, and 505). There are, in addition, two landmark clocks in Queens (see Nos. 6 and 43) and one in Brooklyn (see No. 10). This clock, as the words on its faces announce, was installed by the Fifth Avenue Building (now the Toy Center), which opened in 1909. It is the most ornate sidewalk clock in New York City. A fluted Ionic column supports the clock, which is framed by wreaths of oak leaves and crowned by a cartouche.

192 **Metropolitan Life Insurance Company Tower,** 1 Madison Avenue (Napoleon Le Brun & Sons, Pierre Le Brun, architect in charge, 1907–09), designated 1989. The 54-story tower that rises along the east side of Madison Square was planned by the Metropolitan Life Insurance Company as the world's tallest building and was intended as a corporate symbol. Designed by Pierre Le Brun, the tower evokes the form of the famous campanile in the Piazza San Marco in Venice. Despite the fact that much of the tower's ornament was removed in a renovation of 1960–64, the tower's form is intact, as are the most prominent features of the design, the ornate four-faced clock and the crowning cupola and lantern.

193 **Appellate Division Courthouse,** New York State Supreme Court, 27 Madison Avenue (James Brown Lord, 1896–99), designated 1966, interior 1981. This small Beaux-Arts limestone courthouse is especially notable for the manner in which art is incorporated into the design to create a structure that is unified architecturally and symbolically. The three-dimensional exterior, with its projecting Corinthian porticoes, supports an extensive display of sculpture by sixteen artists on themes relating to the law. Of special note are Daniel Chester French's *Justice,* at the peak of the pediment; Frederick Ruckstuhl's *Wisdom* and *Force,* flanking the entrance stair; and statues representing important figures in the history of justice standing along the roofline. **Interior:** The magnificent main hall, courtroom, and anteroom are richly decorated with furniture designed specifically

for the courthouse by Herter Brothers and with an elaborate series of allegorical murals painted by ten American artists, including Edwin Blashfield, Kenyon Cox, and H. Siddons Mowbray.

194 **New York Life Insurance Company Building,** 51 Madison Avenue (Cass Gilbert, 1926–28), designated 2000. The last of three important Manhattan skyscrapers designed by Cass Gilbert, this 40-story office building was constructed to serve as the headquarters of the New York Life Insurance Company. Built on the original site of Madison Square Garden, which it acquired through foreclosure after 1917, the building fills an entire city block. While the setback massing conforms to the 1916 zoning law, the intricate limestone ornament was inspired by Gothic, Renaissance, and contemporary French sources. Renovated in 1994, the octagonal crown is now clad with gold-toned ceramic tiles.

195 **Trinity Chapel (Episcopal) Complex,** now the Serbian Orthodox Cathedral of Saint Sava and Parish House, 15 West 25th Street (chapel, Richard Upjohn, 1850–55; clergy house, R. & R. M. Upjohn,

An entrance to the New York Life Insurance Company Building (No. 194) facing Madison Avenue. Photo by Carl Forster.

1866; parish school, Jacob Wrey Mould, 1860), designated 1968. This symmetrically massed, Early English Gothic–inspired building was erected to serve the congregants of Trinity Church (see No. 18) who in the mid-19th century were moving to the newly developing neighborhoods around Madison Square. To the east of the church and the adjoining clergy house is the parish school (now the parish house), a small polychromatic building that is an early and notable example of the Victorian Gothic style in the United States as well as Mould's only surviving building in New York City. In 1943 the complex was acquired by the Serbian Orthodox Church.

196 **23rd Police Precinct Station House,** 134–138 West 30th Street (R. Thomas Short, 1907–08), designated 1998. Built to serve the Tenderloin district, an area that was once considered the most crime-ridden in the city, this fortresslike police station features a rusticated granite base arranged to simulate rounded towers and a bold crenellated roof parapet. Short, who designed many notable apartment buildings with the firm Harde & Short, was responsible for the building's imposing and somewhat theatrical character.

197 **130 West 30th Street** (Cass Gilbert, 1927–28), designated 2001. Stylized lions, hunting scenes, and winged guardian figures embellish this midblock 18-story loft building in the fur district. Designed by Cass Gilbert, who is chiefly known for office buildings and civic structures, these unusual terra-cotta reliefs were inspired by ancient Assyrian sources. A rare example of this style in New York, its decorative features were fabricated by the Atlantic Terra Cotta Company.

198 **Gilsey House,** 1200 Broadway (Stephen Decatur Hatch, 1869–71), designated 1979. The exuberant French Second Empire cast-iron building that

Gilsey House (No. 198). An exuberant French Second Empire cast-iron building.
Photo by Carl Forster.

dominates the intersection of Broadway and West 29th Street was a premier 19th-century New York hostelry. With its projecting frontispieces and extraordinary mansard roof, the baroque structure was erected when this section of Broadway was being transformed into New York's entertainment district. In 1979 the building was converted into housing. In 1992 the facades were restored and repainted in a cream color by Building Conservation Associates.

199 **Church of the Transfiguration (Episcopal),** also known as the Little Church Around the Corner, 1 East 29th Street (church and rectory, 1849–50; church addition, 1852; lych-gate, Frederick Clarke Withers, 1896; lady chapel, 1906; mortuary chapel, 1908), designated 1967. The Church of the Transfiguration consists of a series of Gothic Revival structures built around a quiet garden. The original one-story church and adjoining rectory were designed by an unidentified architect in 1849, and

the guildhall, transepts, and tower were added a few years later. Frederick Clarke Withers's English-inspired lych-gate was described by a contemporary critic as "the one touch necessary to make the surroundings of the church . . . the most picturesque and charming of any in New York." The church acquired its sobriquet in 1870, when the minister of a fashionable church nearby, declining to conduct a funeral service for an actor, referred the mourners to "the little church around the corner." The church has welcomed actors ever since.

200 **Marble Collegiate Church,** 272 Fifth Avenue (Samuel A. Warner, 1851–54), designated 1967. Like West End Collegiate (see No. 395) on the Upper West Side, Marble Collegiate traces its history back to the city's first church, a Reformed congregation established by Dutch colonists in 1628. This Early Romanesque Revival building, with its Gothic trim and Wren-like steeple, is clad entirely

Founded in 1903, the Colony Club (No. 201) was designed by Stanford White.
Photo by John Barrington Bayley, 1964.

in the Tuckahoe marble from which the church derives its name. The church has had a number of famous preachers, most prominent among them the Reverend Norman Vincent Peale.

201 **Colony Club,** now the American Academy of Dramatic Arts, 120 Madison Avenue (McKim, Mead & White, Stanford White, partner in charge, 1904–08), designated 1966. Founded in 1903, the Colony Club was the first private women's club in New York City to erect its own clubhouse. Stanford White's building was modeled on 18th-century houses in Annapolis, Maryland (he even escorted building committee members on a trip to view the original houses), with header-bond brickwork laid in a diaper pattern. By 1914 the club had outgrown this building, and a new clubhouse was erected on Park Avenue (see H.D. 33, map 14). Since 1963 the building has housed the American Academy of Dramatic Arts, the oldest professional acting school in the English-speaking world.

202 **Grand Hotel,** 1232–1238 Broadway (Henry Engelbert, 1868), designated 1979. The Grand Hotel is a handsome marble-fronted building erected at a time when Broadway between Madison and Herald Squares was being transformed into a glittering entertainment district. French Second Empire in style, the hotel is distinguished by its pavilion massing, its chamfered corner, and its imposing mansard roof with large pedimented dormers and ocular windows.

203 **Hotel Martinique,** 1260 Broadway (Henry J. Hardenbergh, 1897–98, 1901–03, 1909–11), designated 1998. Constructed in three phases, the French Renaissance–style Hotel Martinique was built and named for its owner, the developer William R. H. Martin. Hardenbergh—who specialized in luxury hotels, including the original Waldorf and Astoria hotels, as well as the Plaza—embellished the Martinique's visible facades with picturesque features, including a boldly scaled mansard roof with towers and dormer windows. During the 1970s and 1980s the hotel served as an emergency shelter and became one of the city's most notorious welfare hotels. The building was renovated in the late 1990s.

204 **Aberdeen Hotel,** 17 West 32nd Street (Harry B. Mulliken, 1902–04), designated 2001. Located between the Fifth Avenue shopping district

and Herald Square, the Aberdeen was one of several hotels built in the area during the first decade of the 20th century. Designed in the Beaux Arts style, the brick and limestone facade is draped with three-dimensional ornament, from the rusticated base with its elaborate sculpted entranceway to the broken pediment and crown that draws attention to the upper stories. During the 1920s the Aberdeen was one of the first hotels in New York to admit women travelers unaccompanied by men.

205 **Grolier Club,** 29 East 32nd Street (Charles W. Romeyn, 1889), designated 1970. Founded in 1884 for "the literary study and promotion of the arts pertaining to the production of books," the Grolier Club occupied this building from 1890 until 1917, when it moved to larger quarters on East 60th Street. The highly original late Romanesque Revival design was executed in Roman brick and stone.

206 **Della Robbia Bar (The Crypt),** now a restaurant **(interior),** 4 Park Avenue (Warren & Wetmore with R. Guastavino Company and Rookwood Pottery Company, 1910–13), designated 1994. The Della Robbia Bar, also known as the Crypt, of the former Vanderbilt Hotel, is an outstanding example of a ceramic interior and one of the few such early 20th-century spaces that survive. Entered from 33rd Street, the vaulted space is constructed from structural, textured, ivory-colored Guastavino tiles (similar to those used at the Oyster Bar at Grand Central Terminal—see No. 280) combined with colorful ceramic ornament, embellished with flowers, faces, and other motifs, produced by the Rookwood Pottery Company of Cincinnati, one of the country's leading art pottery manufacturers.

207 **Empire State Building,** 350 Fifth Avenue (Shreve, Lamb & Harmon, 1929–31), designated 1981. Among the best-known symbols of New York City, the Empire State Building was designed to be the world's tallest building and is a product of the frenzy of skyscraper construction that produced the great Art Deco towers of the late 1920s and early 1930s. The building was conceived by General Motors vice president John Raskob and was promoted by former New York governor Al Smith, who served as president of the Empire State Corporation. Unfortunately, the Depression left much of the office space vacant; the building was saved from bankruptcy by

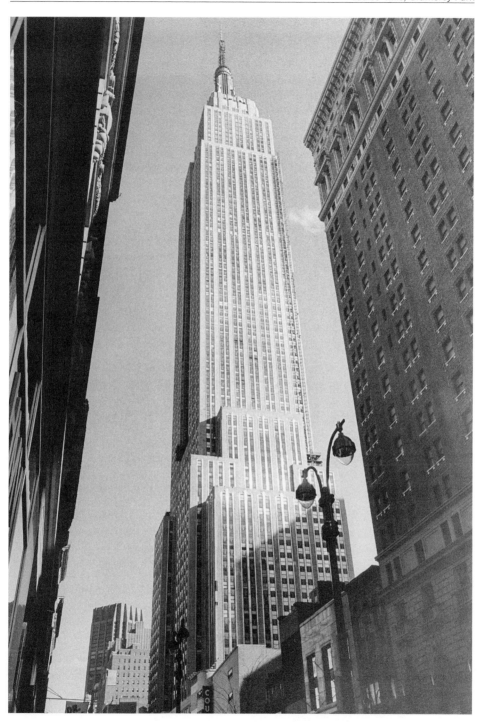

Empire State Building (No. 207). This prominent symbol of New York City was saved from bankruptcy during the Depression by the popularity of its observation deck. Photo by Carl Forster.

the popularity of its observation deck. The brick-clad edifice with a stone base was massed in accordance with zoning laws while accommodating the constraints of elevator placement, a restricted budget, and an effort to have no office space more than 28 feet from a window. **Interior:** The lobby is laid out in a functional manner with all corridors leading to the elevators. The walls are covered with two varieties of German marble highlighted by aluminum detailing. Major ornamental features include aluminum bridges, bronze medallions depicting the crafts and industries involved with the building's construction, and a marble panel with an aluminum relief of the building superimposed on a map of New York, the Empire State.

■ UNION SQUARE AND EAST OF PARK AVENUE SOUTH

HISTORIC DISTRICTS

18 **East 17th Street/Irving Place Historic District,** designated 1998. The majority of structures in this small historic district were built following the opening of Union Square in 1839. During subsequent decades, it became one of the city's most fashionable residential enclaves, attracting the families of successful merchants, bankers, and politicians. The earliest houses, designed in the Greek Revival and Italianate styles, were built between the late 1830s

TALLEST

Until 1892 the tallest structure in New York was Trinity Church (see Manhattan No. 18), with its steeple reaching a height of 284 feet. In the decade that followed, the term *skyscraper* gained popularity, and a succession of designated landmarks would compete to claim the swiftly fleeting title of the world's tallest building. This development coincided with a period of technological innovation, including the invention of the safety elevator and the introduction of skeletal steel construction. The Renaissance-inspired Park Row Building (Manhattan No. 58), completed in 1899 opposite City Hall Park, held the distinction of world's tallest building for nine years. While, contrary to popular belief, the Flatiron Building was never the world's loftiest, a block away the Metropolitan Life Insurance Company Tower held the title for three short years, 1909–12 (Manhattan Nos. 190 and 192). Twice the height of the Venice campanile on which it was modeled, it stands 700 feet tall. The last unregulated skyscraper in New York was the Equitable Building, completed in 1915 (Manhattan No. 23). Construction of this massive 38-story building provoked considerable controversy, and in 1916 the first zoning law in the United States was passed, restricting the height and bulk of future buildings. The impact of this legislation was most strongly felt in the 1920s and 1930s, a period when "setback" skyscrapers defined the Manhattan skyline.

The 60-story neo-Gothic Woolworth Building, completed in 1913, was the world's loftiest until 1929, when it was briefly surpassed by the Manhattan Company Building and the Chrysler Building, and finally the 102-story Empire State Building (see Manhattan Nos. 57, 37, 326, 207), completed in 1931. Crowned by a winged spire that was conceived as a mooring mast for zeppelins, this iconic tower held the title for an impressive forty-two years. Also worth note from this era are the Downtown Athletic Club, a rare example of a skyscraper clubhouse, and the twin-towered Waldorf-Astoria (Manhattan Nos. 9 and 335), once the city's tallest hotel. Beyond Midtown Manhattan two isolated pinnacles deserve special attention—the slender domed Williamsburgh Savings Bank, the tallest building in Brooklyn (and for sixty years Long Island), and The Riverside Church on the Upper West Side, with a neo-Gothic spire housing 30 floors of offices and the world's largest carillon (Brooklyn No. 44 and Manhattan No. 530).

and 1850s. Following the Civil War, Union Square became the heart of the city's art and entertainment district. These changes altered the character of the block, and many of the houses were leased to tenants with ties to commerce in the immediate area. At the east end of the block stands 49 Irving Place, the district's most architecturally distinctive and culturally significant structure. Built in 1843–44 and expanded in 1853–54, the facade incorporates a well-preserved cast-iron porch and entranceway. Claims that it was once home to author Washington Irving are false, but the house did have many prominent tenants, including the interior decorator Elsie de Wolfe and theatrical agent Elizabeth Marbury, who rented the house for almost twenty years, and the photographer Clarence White, who lived here and ran a photography school on the premises during 1917–20. Multiple dwellings began to appear on the block in the late 1880s, first as converted row houses, and later as six-story apartment buildings, including the Fanwood Apartments (1890–91), an early work by George F. Pelham at 112–114 East 17th Street, and the Irving (1901–02), at 118 East 17th Street. Compatible in scale and detailing, these later Renaissance Revival buildings attracted mostly working- and middle-class residents.

19 **Gramercy Park Historic District and Extension,** designated 1966 and 1988. The special character of Gramercy Park is largely the result of a plan established by the developer Samuel B. Ruggles, who purchased a large tract of land in 1831 with the intention of creating a prime residential neighborhood around a small private park open only to the owners of adjacent lots. To attract builders, Ruggles not only planned the park and enclosed it with a tall iron fence (still extant), but also laid out Irving Place and Lexington Avenue. It was not, however, until the 1840s that fine row houses, many still standing on the west and south sides of the park, were erected and sold to prominent citizens. Somewhat smaller row houses were built on the blocks to the south of the park; several fine examples from the 1850s can be found on East 18th Street. In conjunction with this residential development, impressive buildings such as Calvary (Episcopal) Church (Park Avenue South at East 21st Street; James Renwick, Jr., 1846) and the Friends Meeting House (see No. 216) were constructed, helping to establish Gramercy Park as a neighborhood of great prestige. Later in the century, as the area's preeminence

waned, several early apartment houses were built; the Queen Anne–style Gramercy (34 Gramercy Park East; George DaCunha, 1883) and the neo-Gothic 36 Gramercy Park East (James Reily Gordon, 1908–10) are prime examples. Clubs were also attracted to the neighborhood—both the Players (see No. 218) and the National Arts Club (see No. 217) are housed in converted residences. By the early 20th century, the Gramercy Park area was home to an affluent, artistic group of people living in older buildings, in new duplex cooperatives (e.g., 24 Gramercy Park South; Herbert Lucas, 1908), and in renovated row houses. On several blocks the old-fashioned row houses were rediscovered and redesigned with stucco facades embellished with simple artistic details. This is especially evident on East 19th Street between Irving Place and Third Avenue, known as the Block Beautiful, where, beginning in 1909, the architect Frederick H. Sterner renovated many houses.

20 **Stuyvesant Square Historic District,** designated 1975. Stuyvesant Square was laid out in 1846 on land donated to the city by Peter Gerard Stuyvesant. The square is divided by Second Avenue, and each of its two parts is surrounded by an original cast-iron fence. Stuyvesant Square provides a fine setting for two of New York's most distinguished landmarks, the Friends Meeting House and Seminary (see No. 212) and Saint George's Church (Episcopal) (see No. 213). The earliest Greek Revival houses in the district were erected in 1842–43 at 214–216 East 18th Street, when residential development reached north of 14th Street. Most of the district's houses, however, were built in the 1850s, when late Greek Revival, Italianate, and Anglo-Italianate rows were constructed. One of the latest single-family dwellings in the district is the Sidney Webster House (1883) at 245 East 17th Street, the only surviving residence in New York City designed by the architect Richard Morris Hunt.

INDIVIDUAL LANDMARKS

208 **Union Square Savings Bank,** 20 Union Square East (Henry Bacon, 1905–07), designated 1996. The bold academic classicism of this white granite bank building with its Corinthian temple front reveals the design aesthetic of Henry Bacon, an architect best known for the monumental Lincoln Memorial in Washington, D.C. The Institution for the Savings of Merchants' Clerks, established in 1848, was renamed the Union Square Savings Bank in 1904. The bank remained an independent institution until 1968, when it merged with another bank. The building is now used as a theater.

209 Century Association Building, now Century Center for the Performing Arts, 109–111 East 15th Street (Gambrill & Richardson, 1869), designated 1993. Not only is this the oldest surviving clubhouse building in Manhattan, but it appears to be an early work of Henry Hobson Richardson, who would later become one of America's most influential architects. Charles Gambrill began planning the clubhouse in 1866, before Richardson was a member of the club or Gambrill's partner, but by the time the building was erected, the firm Gambrill & Richardson had been formed and Richardson had become a Centurion. Although it is not clear what the relative contribution of each partner was to the design, the massing and the employment of a mansard roof and stylized neo-Grec detail resemble features on other early buildings by Richardson and may reflect his French training. The Century Association moved to 43rd Street (see No. 282) in 1891. In 1996–97 the building was rehabilitated and converted into a theater.

210 Germania Life Insurance Company Building, now the W Hotel, 201 Park Avenue South (50 Union Square East) (D'Oench & Yost, 1910–11), designated 1988. Prominently located on a corner site overlooking Union Square, the headquarters of the Germania Life Insurance Company (renamed Guardian Life in 1918 in response to anti-German sentiment during World War I) is a 20-story tower with a tripartite massing. The building is crowned by an enormous mansard roof atop which stands an early example of electric signage.

211 Scheffel Hall, 190 Third Avenue (Weber & Drosser, 1894–95), designated 1997. This small ornate building recalls the period when Manhattan's Lower East Side was known as Kleindeutchland or Little Germany. Designed by Henry Adam Weber and Hubert Drosser, the white terra-cotta facade was closely modeled on the Fredrichsbau, an early 17th-century building at Heidelberg Castle. Built as a beer hall and restaurant, it was named for the German poet

Joseph Victor von Scheffel, author of *Gaudeamus*, a collection of student songs. After 1928 it was used by the German-American Athletic Club, and beginning in the 1970s, Fat Tuesday's, a popular jazz club.

212 Friends Meeting House and Seminary, 15 Rutherford Place and 226 East 16th Street (attributed to Charles T. Bunting, 1861), designated 1969. This austere brick meetinghouse and the adjoining seminary, with its finely proportioned massing and original multipaned windows, were erected by a group of Quakers known as the Hicksites, who were more traditional in their mode of worship than the Orthodox Quakers (see No. 216). Having been divided since the mid-19th century, the two groups reconciled in 1958, retaining this building as their meetinghouse.

213 Saint George's Church (Episcopal), Rutherford Place at East 16th Street (Blesch & Eidlitz, 1846–56), designated 1967. This massive round-arched stone building dominating Stuyvesant Square is one of the first and most significant examples of Early Romanesque Revival church architecture in America. The exterior, probably the work of the Bavarian-born architect Otto Blesch, reflects the influence that the German round-arched style known as *Rundbogenstil* had on American design in the 1840s. The interiors were the work of Leopold Eidlitz, who also restored the church after it was damaged by fire in 1865. The design was ideally suited to the requirements of its rector, Stephen Higginson Tyng, an ardent leader of the evangelical wing of the Episcopal Church and one of the greatest preachers of his time. The original stone spires were removed in 1889; the church's facade was restored in the 1980s. The church is only one part of a larger complex (included in the Stuyvesant Square Historic District) composed of Saint George's Chapel (M. L. & H. G. Emery, 1911–12), a neo-Romanesque building located to the north of the church; the rectory, set to the rear of the church, designed in the early 1850s by Eidlitz; and the romantic, asymmetrically massed Saint George Memorial House (now apartments), a gift from J. P. Morgan that was designed by Leopold Eidlitz's son, Cyrus L. W. Eidlitz, in 1886.

214 Stuyvesant High School, 345 East 15th Street (C. B. J. Snyder, 1905–07), designated 1997. Following the consolidation of Greater New York in

1898, many new high schools were built, including Stuyvesant, which was designed in the Beaux Arts style with Secessionist detail by C. B. J Snyder. The curriculum originally focused on manual training. Science became a specialty in the 1920s, and the school gained a reputation as one of the city's most prestigious. Girls were first admitted in 1969. Alumni include three Nobel Prize winners. Stuyvesant relocated to Battery Park City in 1992, and the building was converted for use by several programs run by the Department of Education.

215 326, 328, and 330 East 18th Street (1853), designated 1973. These three Italianate brick row houses form a pleasant enclave in the middle of the blockfront of East 18th Street between First and Second Avenues. The houses have deep front yards, a rarity in Manhattan, and superb cast-iron verandas.

216 Friends Meeting House, now Brotherhood Synagogue, 144 East 20th Street (King & Kellum, 1857–59), designated 1965. A doctrinal split in the Quaker community led to the construction of two Manhattan meetinghouses in the mid-19th century (see No. 212). New York's Orthodox Quaker community, the more worldly of the city's two Quaker congregations, commissioned the prominent firm King & Kellum to design a meetinghouse for this site on Gramercy Park. The chaste but beautifully detailed Italianate building was constructed of extremely fine yellow sandstone from Ohio. The meetinghouse was carefully restored (James Stewart Polshek, architect) in the 1970s as part of its conversion into a synagogue.

217 Samuel Tilden House, now the National Arts Club, 15 Gramercy Park South (Vaux & Radford, 1881–84), designated 1966. Calvert Vaux's masterful Victorian Gothic facade resulted from a remodeling of two earlier row houses. This work was undertaken for Samuel J. Tilden, a lawyer who resigned as governor of New York to run for the presidency in 1876, losing in the electoral college to Rutherford B. Hayes. Reflecting the influence of John Ruskin's architectural theories, the house's polychromatic facade is enlivened with sculptural ornament depicting various plants, animals, and birds native to the New York area as well as with busts of notable writers and thinkers, chosen to reflect

Tilden's literary interests. At his death, Tilden's private library, and a considerable fortune, helped to establish the New York Public Library (see No. 278). In 1906 the National Arts Club, an organization dedicated to supporting the arts, purchased the building.

218 The Players, 16 Gramercy Park South (1845; redesign, McKim, Mead & White, Stanford White, partner in charge, 1888–89), designated 1966. This single-family Gothic Revival–style brownstone house has been occupied as a club by the Players since 1888. Original Gothic drip lintels on the upper floors survive from the original row house facade. Edwin Booth, who established the Players as a club for men in the theatrical profession, commissioned his friend Stanford White to redesign the building. White removed the stoop and added the elegant Italian Renaissance–inspired two-tiered porch with its magnificent ironwork, as well as the stained-glass windows and the cornice that incorporates theatrical masks.

219 Russell Sage Foundation Building and Annex, 122–120 East 22nd Street (Grosvenor Atterbury, with John A. Tompkins II, 1912–13 and 1922–23, annex 1930–31), designated 2000. Oliva Sage founded the Russell Sage Foundation with a $10 million bequest in 1907. Grosvenor Atterbury based his design of the headquarters on 16th-century Florentine models, cladding the facades with rock-faced sandstone. In subsequent decades, the foundation became a leading reform social service organization and a pioneer in "scientific philanthropy." During the mid-1920s, a series of granite shields and sculptural panels were installed between the second-story windows. Modeled by sculptor Rene Chambellan, these reliefs illustrate the foundation's various activities and concerns. The penthouse and annex were added to serve related organizations, most notably the Office of the Regional Plan and the New School for Social Research. Sold to the Catholic Charities of the Archdiocese of New York in 1949, the building was converted to apartments in the mid-1970s.

220 Church Missions House, now the Protestant Welfare Agencies Building, 281 Park Avenue South (Robert W. Gibson and Edward J. N. Stent, 1892–94), designated 1979. Beginning in the late 19th century,

The Players (No. 218) was established as a club for men in the theatrical profession. Photo by Peter Choy.

the area immediately south of East 23rd Street became a center for the offices of charitable organizations. The Church Missions House, a steel-frame structure whose facade was modeled on a medieval Flemish guildhall, was the headquarters for the missionary activities of the Episcopal Church. The building was restored in the early 1990s by Kapell & Kastow; it continues to house social service organizations.

221 **Sixty-ninth Regiment Armory,** 68 Lexington Avenue (Hunt & Hunt, 1904–06), designated 1983. The 69th Regiment Armory was the first New York City armory built after the Seventh Regiment Armory (see No. 455) that was not designed in the form of a medieval fortress. Hunt & Hunt rejected the medieval form in favor of a French Beaux-Arts mode with a severe military aspect. The armory is famous as the home of "the Fighting 69th," New York's only official Irish regiment, and as the site of the legendary 1913 Armory Show, which introduced modern art to the American public.

222 **Public Baths,** Asser Levy Place at East 23rd Street (Brunner & Aiken, 1904–06), designated

1974. In the late 19th century, progressive social reformers lobbied for the creation of public baths that would help alleviate sanitary problems in New York City's slum neighborhoods, where few residents had access to a bath or a shower. Appropriately, the design precedent for the Asser Levy Place baths was the public baths of ancient Rome, as evidenced by the paired columns and semicircular thermal windows. Now a swimming pool and recreation center, the building was restored by the Parks Department in 1989–90.

223 **New York School of Applied Design for Women,** later Pratt–New York Phoenix School of Design, now Touro College, Lexington Avenue Campus, 160 Lexington Avenue (Harvey Wiley Cor-

bett, 1908–09), designated 1977. In the late 19th century, women began to enter the art world in increasing numbers and became especially active in the decorative arts. The New York School of Applied Design for Women was established in 1892 to offer "women instruction which may enable them to earn a livelihood . . . in the application of ornamental design to manufacture and the arts." The school, which specialized in such fields as book illustration, textile and wallpaper design, and interior decoration, was unusual in that its programs were geared specifically to the education of poor women. The architect of the school's facility, Harvey Wiley Corbett, was also an instructor there. He designed an idiosyncratic version of a classical temple, complete with casts from the Parthenon frieze.

Public Baths (No. 222). Designed according to Roman prototypes, this building was constructed to address appalling sanitary conditions in New York City's slums. Landmarks Preservation Commission collection.

INDIVIDUAL LANDMARKS

■ WEST OF SEVENTH AVENUE

224 **New Amsterdam Theater,** 214 West 42nd Street (Herts & Tallant, 1902–03), designated 1979. As home to the Ziegfeld Follies, as well as Eva Le Gallienne's Civic Repertory Theater and George White's "Scandals," this legendary theater has presented scores of great actors in memorable produc-

tions. The theater has a narrow Beaux-Arts-inspired entrance facade on West 42nd Street with a vertical sign dating from 1937, when the theater was used as a movie house. The **interior** is adorned with splendid Art Nouveau decoration. The lobby, foyers, reception room, staircases, smoking room, and auditorium contain ornate terra-cotta panels evoking theatrical themes; murals by George Peixotto, Robert Blum, and others; faience stairway balustrades; art tiles designed by Henry Mercer; and ornate plaster, stone, and wood carving. The theater closed in

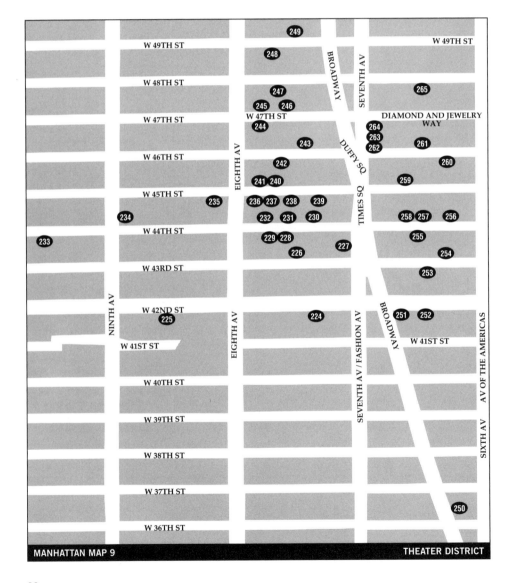

New Amsterdam Theater (No. 224). This legendary theater has splendid Art Nouveau decoration throughout the interior. Photo courtesy of Whitney Cox.

1985. In 1995–97 the Walt Disney Company undertook a major restoration under the direction of Hardy Holzman Pfeiffer, architect, that rejuvenated the extraordinary interior.

225 **McGraw-Hill Building,** 330 West 42nd Street (Raymond Hood, Godley & Fouilhoux, 1930–31), designated 1979. The 35-story McGraw-Hill Building is a major work of the great skyscraper architect Raymond Hood. The massing, with horizontal setbacks that allow the building to be read as a modern slab, and the simple detailing illustrate the transition between the decorative Art Deco style and the more austere slab forms of International Style design. With the McGraw-Hill Building, Hood also introduced to New York the idea of horizontal ribbon windows, a feature that would become common on modern skyscrapers. Color was an important element of the design. Almost the entire building is faced in blue-green terra cotta; the metal windows were originally apple green with a band of vermilion across the top; the entranceway is clad in alternating bands of blue and green metal; and the building is crowned by a sign with the corporate name spelled out in 11-foot-tall letters originally painted white with an orange stripe. The building was erected west of Eighth Avenue in an area zoned for industrial use because it housed not

THE PRINTED WORD

In the vicinity of City Hall are several landmarks associated with daily newspapers: the *New York Times*, the *New York Evening Post*, and the *New York Sun*, which occupied the former A. T. Stewart Store for more than three decades (Manhattan Nos. 62, 55, and 70). Following the introduction of the telephone and the subway, many newspapers moved north, erecting prominent skyscrapers in Midtown. Notable examples include the French-inspired New York Times Building and the Modernist Daily News Building (Manhattan Nos. 226 and 327). On the Lower East Side is the Forward Building, an 11-story neoclassical building that was home to the most significant Yiddish-language newspaper in America (Manhattan No. 125). Rockefeller Center has several structures associated with the news media, most notably the Associated Press Building at 45 Rockefeller Plaza, whose entrance is crowned with a stainless-steel relief called *News* by Isamu Noguchi (Manhattan No. 294).

Several buildings constructed by popular magazines have been designated. One of the oldest is the offices of the Century Publishing Company, built in the Queen Anne style in 1881 and now occupied by a Barnes & Noble bookstore, followed by the Romanesque Revival–style Puck offices and printing plant, which began construction in 1885, and the massive De Vinne Press Building of 1890–92, where such leading magazines as the *Century*, *St. Nicholas*, and *Scribner's Monthly* were published (Manhattan Nos. 183, 107, and 150). Most companies founded in the 20th century were located in Midtown, including Hearst Magazines, the publisher of *Cosmopolitan*, *Good Housekeeping*, and *House Beautiful*. The company has had several locations in Manhattan, most notably an Art Deco structure at 951–969 Eighth Avenue (Manhattan No. 368). Also of interest is the lively lobby of the Time & Life Building, housing such magazines as *Time*, *Fortune*, *Life*, and *Sports Illustrated* (Manhattan No. 346).

Book publishing companies have also erected a number of prominent buildings in Manhattan. These include a cast-iron commercial structure occupied by D. Appleton & Co. at 1–5 Bond Street, an early skyscraper built by the American Tract Society, a publisher of religious literature, and two French-inspired works by the architect Ernest Flagg for Charles Scribner's Sons at 153–157 Fifth Avenue and 597 Fifth Avenue (Manhattan Nos. 143, 60, 189, and 291). The distinguished ground-floor interior of the latter building, which originally served as the company's flagship store, is also designated. On West 42nd Street is Raymond Hood's McGraw-Hill Building. Built as a printing plant and offices, the blue-green elevations incorporate elements associated with both the Art Deco and International Styles (Manhattan No. 225). More recently Scholastic, a leading publisher of children's books, constructed a new building at 577 Broadway in the SoHo–Cast Iron District (Manhattan H.D. 9).

Among the various clubhouses designated by the Commission, two are specifically related to literature and publishing: the Century Association, founded in 1846, and the Grolier Club, established in 1884 to study and promote the "arts pertaining to the production of books" (Manhattan Nos. 209, 282, and 205). Other literary landmarks include the Algonquin Hotel, a center of literary and theatrical activity during the 1920s and 1930s, and the Chelsea Hotel, home to such noted authors as Thomas Wolfe, Dylan Thomas, and Arthur Miller (Manhattan Nos. 284 and 170). The Poe Cottage, where Edgar Allen Poe wrote *Annabel Lee* and *The Bells* in the late 1840s, and the Langston Hughes House have also been designated (Bronx No. 31 and Manhattan No. 569).

only McGraw-Hill's corporate offices but also its printing plant. McGraw-Hill moved to Rockefeller Center in 1970, and the building remains in use as offices.

226 New York Times Building, originally the Times Annex, 217–247 West 43rd Street (Buchman & Fox, 1912–13; Ludlow & Peabody, 1922–24; Albert Kahn, Inc., 1930–32), designated 2001. Founded on Nassau Street in 1851, this world-famous newspaper moved to 42nd Street in 1905, constructing a skyscraper headquarters at the crossing of Broadway and Seventh Avenue. In 1912 the first section of the Times Annex was built on 43rd Street. Designed by Buchman & Fox to resemble the nearby tower, it featured identical materials and neo-Gothic details. The Annex soon became the newspaper's headquarters, accommodating editorial and executive departments, as well as all printing operations. The second stage of construction added five additional bays, as well as a seven-story tower in the French Renaissance style. This châteauesque feature gave the expanded Annex new prominence, making it visible from all corners of the entertainment district. In subsequent years, a west wing was added; in 1942 it was renamed the New York Times Building. Printing operations were discontinued in 1997.

227 Paramount Building, 1501 Broadway (Rapp & Rapp, 1926–27), designated 1988. The theater architects Rapp & Rapp designed this dramatically massed skyscraper (at its completion, the tallest in the Times Square area) as offices for Paramount Pictures, as a home for the Paramount Theater (demolished), and as an advertisement for the Paramount Corporation. The motion picture company's trademark, a mountain encircled by five-pointed stars, is echoed in the mountainlike massing of the building and its surmounting four-faced clock, on which the hours are marked by five-pointed stars. The clock is crowned by a glass globe that, when illuminated, is visible for miles and is a focal point of the Times Square area. The clocks and globe were restored in 1997; the marquee in 2001.

228 Little Theater, now the Helen Hayes Theater, 238 West 44th Street (Ingalls & Hoffman, 1912; interior remodeling, Herbert J. Krapp, 1917–20), designated 1982, interior 1987. The construction of the Little Theater marked a new direction in Broadway theater design. The theater was commissioned by the producer Winthrop Ames to house the type of drama known as intimate theater. The small size (the theater seated only 299 people) and the use of the primarily domestic Colonial Revival style on both the exterior and **interior** contribute to the feeling of intimacy. The balcony was added in 1917 in an effort to make the theater more profitable.

229 Erlanger Theater, now the Saint James Theater, 246–256 West 44th Street (Warren & Wetmore, 1926–27), designated 1987. The restrained Beaux-Arts facade of this theater is the work of an important New York architecture firm. Commissioned by the producer Abraham Erlanger, the theater was renamed the Saint James by new owners following Erlanger's death in 1930. The **interior,** which contains a large auditorium, is unusual in its reliance on spatial organization rather than on ornament for effect. The Saint James has housed such great American musicals as *Oklahoma!, The King and I,* and *Hello, Dolly!*

230 Shubert Theater, 221–233 West 44th Street (Henry B. Herts, 1912–13), designated 1987. This is the flagship playhouse of the Shubert Organization, a major force in the construction of theaters and the production of plays in New York and elsewhere in the United States since the early 20th century. Built as a memorial to Sam Shubert, the oldest of the three Shubert brothers, the building also served as the headquarters of the Shubert theatrical empire. The theater was designed in a lavish manner with Venetian Renaissance sgraffito decoration on the exterior and, on the **interior,** elaborate plasterwork and murals by J. Mortimer Lichtenauer. The Shubert has been home to many hit productions, among them the record-breaking *A Chorus Line.* In 1996 architect Francesa Russo of Campagna & Russo restored the original color scheme and murals and recreated the central ceiling mural.

231 Broadhurst Theater, 235–243 West 44th Street (Herbert J. Krapp, 1917–18), designated 1987. One of many Broadway theaters built by the Shuberts, the Broadhurst opened under the personal management of the playwright George Broadhurst. Built as a companion to the Plymouth Theater (see

Theaters along West 44th Street, between Broadway and Eighth Avenue.
Photo by Carl Forster.

No. 238), the building has a handsome neoclassical facade of patterned brick and terra cotta. The plan of the Adamesque **interior** is characteristic of the many theaters designed by Krapp: the space is wider than it is deep and has a single curving balcony. Among the celebrated actors to have appeared in plays at the Broadhurst are Eva Le Gallienne, Lionel and Ethel Barrymore, Leslie Howard, Barbara Stanwyck, Humphrey Bogart, Karl Malden, Rosalind Russell, Joel Grey, Katharine Hepburn, George C. Scott, and Dustin Hoffman.

232 **Majestic Theater,** 245–257 West 44th Street (Herbert J. Krapp, 1926–27), designated 1987. The Majestic, a large musical house (seating 1,800), was built by Irwin Chanin as one of a trio of theaters; the others were the Royale (see No. 237) and the Theater Masque (see No. 236). The eclectic exterior is in a style that Chanin and his architect referred to as "modern Spanish." The **interior** is decorated in a neoclassical manner and is laid out in the so-called stadium plan that Chanin and Krapp first introduced at their Forty-sixth Street Theater (see No. 242). Among the hit musicals that have played the Majestic are *Carousel, South Pacific, The Music Man, Camelot, The Wiz,* and *The Phantom of the Opera.*

233 **Actors Studio,** originally the Seventh Associate Presbyterian Church, 432 West 44th Street (c. 1858), designated 1991. The Actors Studio, founded in 1947, is best known for its association with Lee Strasberg, who became director of the studio in 1949. Strasberg was the leading American advocate of the Method acting technique pioneered by Konstantin Stanislavsky at the Moscow Art Theater. In 1955 the Actors Studio purchased this late Greek Revival church structure and converted it for use as a drama school. In 1995 the building was restored by Davis, Brody & Associates, architect.

234 **Film Center Building (interior),** 630 Ninth Avenue (Ely Jacques Kahn, 1928–29), designated 1982. The ground-floor vestibule, lobby, and hall-way of the Film Center, composing one of the most beautiful Art Deco interiors in New York, were de-signed by Kahn in his idiosyncratic manner. Much of the interior reflects a pre-Columbian influence. Of special interest are the geometrically patterned ter-razzo floors, the ziggurat shape of the plaster ceil-ings, the superb metalwork, and—the lobby's most striking feature—the polychromatic mosaic on the wall between the elevator banks.

235 **Martin Beck Theater,** now the Al Hirschfeld Theater, 302–314 West 45th Street (C. Albert Lans-burgh, 1923–24), designated 1987. Among the most spectacular theaters in the Broadway theater district, this Moorish-inspired structure was built by the producer Martin Beck, who operated the theater until his death in 1940. The **interiors** reflect Beck's desire to build the most lavish legitimate theater in the Broadway area. The fantastical Moorish-Byzan-tine-style spaces were designed by Lansburgh in col-laboration with the painter Albert Herter. Since the 1960s the Martin Beck Theater has been a popular venue for musicals and has housed such hits as *Bye Bye Birdie, Man of La Mancha,* and *Into the Woods.* As a tribute to the famed illustrator, the theater was renamed in 2002.

236 **Theater Masque,** now the Golden Theater, 252–256 West 45th Street (Herbert J. Krapp, 1926–27), designated 1987. Built by Irwin Chanin in conjunction with the Majestic (see No. 232) and the Royale (see No. 237), the Theater Masque, which was renamed for the producer John Golden in 1937, is a small house planned for intimate dramas. Both the exterior and the **interior** of the theater were designed in the "modern Spanish" style used by Krapp for several of his Chanin commissions. *Tobacco Road*

The Al Hirshfeld Theater (No. 235) is a Moorish-inspired building with lavish interior details. Photo by Justin Van Soest.

premiered at the Masque in 1933 and was followed by many other successful productions, including, in recent years, *The Gin Game, Crimes of the Heart, 'Night Mother,* and *Glengarry Glen Ross.*

237 **Royale Theater,** 242–250 West 45th Street (Herbert J. Krapp, 1926–27), designated 1987. The Royale and its neighbors the Theater Masque (see No. 236) and the Majestic (see No. 232) were built as a trio by Irwin Chanin; all were designed in the "modern Spanish" style that he favored. The **interior** continues the Spanish-inspired detail and is particularly notable for the groin-vaulted ceiling of the auditorium, which features a large mural by Willy Pogany entitled *Lovers of Spain.* One of the most popular theaters on Broadway, the Royale has been home to *Diamond Lil* (starring Mae West), *The Magnificent Yankee,* Moss Hart's *Light Up the Sky,* Julie Andrews's American debut in *The Boy Friend,* Thornton Wilder's *The Matchmaker,* Laurence Olivier in *The Entertainer,* Tennessee Williams's *Night of the Iguana,* and *The Subject Was Roses.*

238 **Plymouth Theater,** 234–240 West 45th Street (Herbert J. Krapp, 1917–18), designated 1987. The Plymouth, planned by the Shuberts as a companion to the Broadhurst (see No. 231), has always been one of Broadway's most successful theaters. It has housed *Abe Lincoln in Illinois, Private Lives, Dial 'M' for Murder, The Caine Mutiny Court Martial, The Odd Couple, Plaza Suite,* and *Equus.* The Plymouth and the Broadhurst were the first designs of the prolific theater architect Herbert J. Krapp, and they reflect his interest in the use of patterned brickwork on the exterior and Adamesque design for the **interior.**

239 **Booth Theater,** 222–232 West 45th Street (Henry B. Herts, 1912–13), designated 1987. The Italian Renaissance–inspired Booth and the neighboring Shubert Theater (see No. 230) were designed as a pair by the prominent theater architect Henry B. Herts. The **interior** of the Booth was planned as an intimate setting for drama. The theater has been enormously successful, housing such important American plays as *You Can't Take It with You; The Time of Your Life; Come Back, Little Sheba; That Championship Season; For Colored Girls; Sunday in the Park with George;* and *Having Our Say.*

240 **Music Box Theater,** 239–247 West 45th Street (C. Howard Crane & E. George Kiehler, 1920), designated 1987. Producer Sam Harris built this theater to house Irving Berlin's *Music Box Revues.* The revues ran for five years, after which time the theater housed many successful plays and musicals, including George S. Kaufman and George and Ira Gershwin's *Of Thee I Sing,* Kaufman and Edna Ferber's *Dinner at Eight* and *Stage Door,* Moss Hart and Irving Berlin's *As Thousands Cheer,* and several hits by Kaufman and Hart, including *The Man Who Came to Dinner.* The elegant English-inspired neoclassical exterior is articulated by a porch supported by four attenuated columns; the Adamesque **interior** features delicate plasterwork and murals.

241 **Imperial Theater (interior),** 249 West 45th Street (Herbert J. Krapp, 1923), designated 1987. Built by the Shuberts, the Imperial has long been one of the most successful Broadway theaters. Planned as a showcase for musicals and revues, the theater has premiered such hits as *Rose-Marie; Oh, Kay!; Annie Get Your Gun; Gypsy; Oliver!; Fiddler on the Roof; Cabaret; Dreamgirls;* and *Les Miserables.* The Imperial has an elegant Adamesque interior with fine plasterwork.

242 **Forty-sixth Street Theater,** now the Richard Rodgers Theater, 226–236 West 46th Street (Herbert J. Krapp, 1924), designated 1987. The first Broadway theater built by the Chanin Organization, the Forty-sixth Street is an elaborate Renaissance-inspired work that features several innovations in theater design, notably a single entrance and, on the interior, stadium-type seating with a steeply raked orchestra and a single balcony (Irwin Chanin thought such seating would democratize theatergoing). Many hit musicals have played the Forty-sixth Street, including *Good News, Finian's Rainbow, Guys and Dolls, Damn Yankees,* and *1776.*

243 **Globe Theater,** now the Lunt-Fontanne Theater, 203–217 West 46th Street (Carrère & Hastings, 1909–10), designated 1987. Built as the headquarters of the influential Broadway producer Charles Dillingham, the Beaux-Arts Globe is the only surviving theater designed by Carrère & Hastings. After serving as a movie house for many years, the Globe was returned to legitimate theater use in 1958; at the same time, however, its interior was gutted and its name was changed. Dillingham had been able to attract many major stars to play the Globe, including Sarah Bernhardt, Lynn Fontanne, Fred and Adele Astaire, and Fanny Brice. In more recent years the theater has been favored for musicals, chief among them *The Sound of Music* and *Beauty and the Beast.*

244 **Mansfield Theater,** now the Brooks Atkinson Theater, 256–262 West 47th Street (Herbert J. Krapp, 1925–26), designated 1987. Named originally for the 19th-century American actor Richard Mansfield, and renamed in 1960 for the theater critic Brooks Atkinson, this theater is one of six erected in the 1920s by the Chanin Organization. The theater was designed in the "modern Spanish" style favored by Irwin Chanin. The exceptional **interior** reflects the expertise of Chanin, Krapp, and Roman Meltzer, the former architect to Czar Nicholas II who supervised the ornamental scheme, which includes fine plasterwork and murals. The theater has housed a number of successful dramas and comedies, including *Green Pastures, Come Blow Your Horn, Talley's Folly,* and *Noises Off.*

245 **Biltmore Theater (interior),** now Manhattan Theater Club, 261–265 West 47th Street (Herbert J. Krapp, 1925–26), designated 1987. One of six Broadway theaters built by Irwin Chanin (see No. 325), the Biltmore has a handsome Adamesque interior laid out in an unusual horseshoe-shaped plan. The theater, home to such productions as *No Exit* and *Hair,* was rehabilitated in 2003.

246 **Barrymore Theater,** 243–251 West 47th Street (Herbert J. Krapp, 1928), designated 1987. Built by the Shuberts to honor their star performer, Ethel Barrymore, this theater is among Krapp's most interesting designs—its facade takes the form of a giant classical Roman window with a terra-cotta grid. The **interior** is unusual for its mock-Elizabethan decoration. Ethel Barrymore appeared in the first production at the theater as well as in three other plays performed there between 1929 and 1931. Among the theater's many successful productions were *Gay Divorce* (with Fred Astaire), *The Women, Key Largo, A Streetcar Named Desire,* and *Raisin in the Sun.*

247 **Longacre Theater,** 220–228 West 48th Street (Henry B. Herts, 1912–13), designated 1987. The Longacre was designed in the French neoclassical style for the Broadway producer and baseball magnate Harry Frazee (who owned the Boston Red Sox). The **interior,** with its simple French-inspired decor (now somewhat altered), incorporated many innovations in design, planning, and ventilation. Although the theater has had a checkered history, it has housed a number of long-running hits, notably *Ain't Misbehavin'* and *Children of a Lesser God.*

248 **Forrest Theater (interior),** later the Coronet Theater, now the Eugene O'Neill Theater, 230–238 West 49th Street (Herbert J. Krapp, 1925–26), designated 1987. Built by the Shuberts, the Forrest was named for the celebrated American actor Edwin Forrest (see Fonthill, Bronx No. 55) and renamed in honor of the great American playwright Eugene O'Neill in 1953. The auditorium is an elegant example of the Adamesque design favored by Krapp. The most famous production staged in this theater was *Tobacco Road,* which moved to the Forrest in 1934, several months after opening at the Theater Masque (see No. 236), and which ran for 3,182 performances, then a Broadway record. In 1994 a restoration of the interior was undertaken by Francesa Russo of Campagna & Russo, architect.

249 **Ambassador Theater (interior),** 215–223 West 49th Street (Herbert J. Krapp, 1919–21), designated 1985. Krapp made lavish use of paint and plaster in the Adamesque style to create the illusion of opulence on the interior of this theater. The Ambassador is one of numerous Broadway houses commissioned by the Shuberts in the 1920s; it has since housed more than 120 different productions, including in recent years *Bring In 'Da Noise, Bring In 'Da Funk.*

■ EAST OF SEVENTH AVENUE

250 **Greenwich Savings Bank,** 1352–1362 Broadway (York & Sawyer, 1922–24), designated 1992. This "temple of thrift" is a sophisticated rendition of academic classicism by the noted bank architects York & Sawyer. The firm manipulated such features as a high rusticated base and Corinthian colonnades on each of the three street fronts to create a monumental architectural statement. The irregular shape of the site is masterfully handled on the **interior** where a majestic elliptical banking hall is set within a trapezoid. Limestone, sandstone, and varicolored marbles create an impressive classical space that retains many of its original bronze furnishings. After several years of vacancy, the interior is now used for special events.

251 **Knickerbocker Hotel,** 1462–1470 Broadway (Marvin & Davis, with Bruce Price, 1901–06; annex at 143 West 41st Street, Trowbridge & Livingston, 1906), designated 1988. In the first decade of the 20th century, several grand hotels were erected in the Times Square area; the only survivor is the Knickerbocker. Financed by John Jacob Astor IV, this Beaux-Arts red brick building with terra-cotta detail and a prominent mansard roof was among the city's most lavish hostelries and was a popular dining and dancing spot in New York's new theater district. The hotel closed during the Depression, and the building was converted for office use.

252 **Bush Tower,** 130–132 West 42nd Street and 133–137 West 41st Street (Helmle & Corbett, 1916–18, 1921), designated 1988. The setback massing of Bush Tower, built by the Bush Terminal Company as an international merchandise market, became a prototype for the skyscrapers erected in New York City in the following decade. According to Corbett, the setbacks were a purely aesthetic solution, planned prior to the passage of the 1916 zoning law. The narrow neo-Gothic midblock building is unusual for its decorated brick side elevations.

253 **Henry Miller's Theater,** 124–130 West 43rd Street (Allen, Ingalls & Hoffman, 1917–18), designated 1987. This theater was designed to the specifications of the actor/producer/director Henry W. Miller and was the venue of Miller's own productions until his death in 1926. The building was converted to a movie house in 1969 and later to a dance club. It is presently used as a theater.

254 **Town Hall,** 113–123 West 43rd Street (McKim, Mead & White, Teunis J. van der Bent, partner in charge, 1919–21), designated 1987. Town Hall was built by the League for Political Education as a meeting hall for the city. It was planned to accommodate lectures, concerts, and movies and to serve as a clubhouse for members of the league. As soon as it opened, Town Hall became a popular venue for speaking engagements; guest speakers included many of the most eminent figures of the 20th century, among them Theodore Roosevelt, Henry James, Booker T. Washington, Margaret Sanger, Winston Churchill, and Woodrow Wilson. The **interior** includes a simple lobby and a Colonial Revival–style auditorium that is celebrated for its acoustics.

255 **Lambs Club,** now the Manhattan Church of the Nazarene, 128 West 44th Street (McKim, Mead & White, Stanford White, partner in charge, 1903–05; addition, George A. Freeman, 1915), designated 1974. Founded in 1874, the Lambs was a club for actors and theater enthusiasts. In 1903 the commission for the Lambs' new clubhouse went to the firm McKim, Mead & White—all three principals were members. Stanford White was responsible for the Colonial Revival design ornamented with lambs' and rams' heads. The size of the building was doubled in 1915 when an addition to the west, a virtual copy of White's original, was constructed.

256 **Belasco's Stuyvesant Theater,** now the Belasco Theater, 111–121 West 44th Street (George Keister, 1906–07), designated 1987. The actor, director, and manager David Belasco, one of the most important figures in the history of the American stage, conceived this theater as a "living room" in which actors and audience would come in close contact. The use of the homey Colonial Revival style for the exterior heightens the domestic theme. The **interior** is especially noteworthy for its Tiffany glass lamps, column capitals, and ceiling panels and for the eighteen murals by the Ashcan school artist Everett Shinn.

257 **Hotel Gerard,** now the Gerard Apartments, 123 West 44th Street (George Keister, 1893–94), designated 1982. The Gerard exhibits an unusual combination of Romanesque, Gothic, and Northern European Renaissance forms. This apartment hotel was in the vanguard of the movement that was to transform the low-rise residential area north of Times Square into a district of theaters, hotels, and related facilities.

258 **Hudson Theater,** 139–141 West 44th Street (J. B. McElfatrick & Son and Israels & Harder,

The Lyceum Theater (No. 259) has the most imposing facade in the Broadway theater district. Photo by Carl Forster.

1902–04), designated 1987. The Hudson, one of the oldest theaters in Midtown, was built by the producer Henry B. Harris as a showcase for his stars. The theater has a restrained Beaux-Arts facade and an exuberant **interior** with elegant plasterwork and stained glass. It was restored in 1990 and is now part of the adjacent hotel.

259 Lyceum Theater, 149–157 West 45th Street (Herts & Tallant, 1902–03), designated 1974, interior 1987. The Beaux-Arts facade of the Lyceum is the most imposing in the Broadway theater district. Built for the early 20th-century theater impresario Daniel Frohman, the playhouse was designed by New York's most talented theater architects. Although it is a two-balcony house, the **interior** is relatively small and was planned for intimate plays. Lush plaster detail embellishes walls and ceilings and is adorned with the initial *L*. The theater is further enhanced by mar-

ble paneling and lobby murals by James Wall Finn. The Lyceum has housed many of Broadway's most famous comedies and dramas, including a run of classic plays produced in the late 1960s by the APA-Phoenix Theater. The list of great stars who have performed at the Lyceum is unparalleled and includes William Gillette, Ethel Barrymore, Billie Burke, Walter Huston, Bette Davis, Miriam Hopkins, Cornel Wilde, Joseph Cotton, Maurice Evans, John Garfield, Montgomery Clift, Ruth Gordon, Melvyn Douglas, Alan Bates, Lauren Bacall, Angela Lansbury, Billy Dee Williams, Helen Hayes, Rosemary Harris, Brian Bedford, and Nancy Marchand.

260 Public School 67, later the High School of the Performing Arts, now the Jacqueline Kennedy Onassis High School for International Careers, 120 West 46th Street (C. B. J. Snyder, 1893–94), designated 1982. P.S. 67 is the first school known to have been designed by C. B. J. Snyder, who as superintendent of school buildings for New York City's Board of Education for thirty years was responsible for the design of many of the city's finest school buildings. This Romanesque Revival structure enjoyed fame as the home of the High School of the Performing Arts from the founding of the school in 1948 until 1985, when it moved to a new facility. The school's curriculum emphasizes studies in music, drama, and dance, and its graduates include Eliot Feld, Arthur Mitchell, Rita Moreno, Liza Minnelli, Al Pacino, Ben Vereen, and Edward Villella. After a fire, the building was restored in 1991–93.

261 Church of Saint Mary-the-Virgin (Episcopal) Complex, 133–145 West 46th Street (Napoleon Le Brun & Sons, Pierre Le Brun, architect in charge, 1894–95), designated 1989. This religious complex consists of a French Gothic–inspired limestone-clad church, its flanking brick-faced clergy house and mission house, and a brick-clad rectory and lady chapel that face onto West 47th Street. The church was built for a congregation in the forefront of the American Anglo-Catholic movement, and the buildings were planned to further Anglo-Catholic worship. J. Massey Rhind's extensive sculptural decoration complements Pierre Le Brun's design. Saint Mary's is thought to be the first church built with a steel frame.

262 I. Miller Building, 1522–1554 Broadway (Louis H. Freeland, 1926), designated 1999. Four marble statues, representing leading actresses of the 1920s, decorate the former Times Square branch of the I. Miller shoe chain. Located at the corner of 46th Street, this three-story structure was remodeled in 1926 by Louis H. Freeland as a tribute to the theatrical profession. Promoted as the "Show Folks Shoe Shop," the store invited the public to nominate the actresses who would decorate the niches. Alexander Stirling Calder executed the portraits, depicting Ethel Barrymore as Ophelia, Marilyn Miller as Sunny, Rosa Ponselle as Norma, and Mary Pickford as Little Lord Fauntelroy.

263 Embassy Theater (interior), now the Times Square Vistors Center, 1556–1560 Broadway (Thomas W. Lamb, with Rambusch Studio, 1925), designated 1987. The former Embassy Theater,

planned as an experiment to determine whether an elegant, intimate movie house would attract an exclusive high-society audience, has an ornate French-inspired interior designed by architect Thomas W. Lamb and the decorating firm of Rambusch Studio that features elaborate plasterwork and murals by Arthur Crisp. As part of the effort to create a salon-like atmosphere, a woman (the heiress Gloria Gould) was appointed manager of the theater. The exclusivity lasted only a few years; in 1929 the Embassy became the first newsreel theater in the country.

264 Palace Theater (interior), 1564–1566 Broadway (Kirchhoff & Rose, 1912–13), designated 1987. The legendary Palace Theater, built as a vaudeville house, has hosted a greater number of stars and a greater variety of entertainment than any other Broadway theater. Although built by Martin Beck, it was operated primarily by Beck's rival E. F. Albee of the Keith-Albee Circuit, which produced vaudeville nationwide. The first production at the Palace was a flop, but the appearance of Sarah Bernhardt in May 1913 marked the beginning of an era of unprecedented success. The Palace featured such great vaudeville stars as Bob Hope, Ed Wynn, Sophie Tucker, George Jessel, Will Rogers, Jimmy Durante, the Marx Brothers, W. C. Fields, Harry Houdini, and Eddie Cantor. Succumbing to changes in the entertainment industry, the Palace became a movie house in 1932, but since the opening of *Sweet Charity* in 1966 it has become a theater for musicals. The theater was refurbished in 1990–91 (Fox & Fowle, architect) and reopened, appropriately, with *The Will Rogers Follies.*

265 Cort Theater, 138–146 West 48th Street (Thomas W. Lamb, 1912–13), designated 1987. Among the oldest and most beautiful Broadway theaters, the Cort is an adaptation of the Petit Trianon (1762) at Versailles. The theater was designed for the producer John Cort by one of America's most prominent theater architects. The elegant **interior** is decorated with French neoclassical detail and a mural depicting a dance in the gardens of Versailles. The theater has housed a large number of dramas, including many revivals. Among the long-running shows that have played the Cort are *The Diary of Anne Frank, Sunrise at Campobello, The Magic Show, Sarafina,* and *The Heiress.*

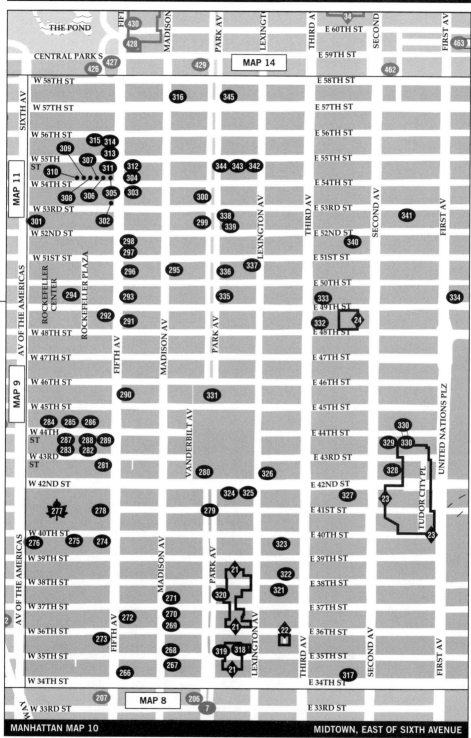

■ WEST OF PARK AVENUE

INDIVIDUAL LANDMARKS

266 **B. Altman & Co. Department Store,** now B. Altman Advanced Learning Super Block (New York Public Library, Science, Industry and Business Library; Oxford University Press; and City University of New York, Graduate School and University Center), 355–371 Fifth Avenue and 188–198 Madison Avenue (Trowbridge & Livingston, 1905–13), designated 1985. The imposing B. Altman & Co. store was among the first of the great department stores on Fifth Avenue. Designed to complement the nearby mansions, the store was a major catalyst for the transformation of Fifth Avenue into a boulevard lined with magnificent stores. Although the building appears to be a single unified Italian Renaissance–inspired structure, it was erected in several stages, with the first Fifth Avenue wing opening in 1906. B. Altman went out of business in 1989. The exterior of the vacant building was restored by Hardy Holzman Pfeiffer, architects, and the interior has been reconfigured for three separate organizations, largely by Gwathmey Siegal & Associates, architect.

267 **Thomas and Fanny Clarke House,** now the Collectors Club, 22 East 35th Street (McKim, Mead & White, Stanford White, partner in charge, 1901–02), designated 1979. For his friend the art collector and dealer Thomas Benedict Clarke, Stanford White designed one of his most delightful town houses. The street facade combines what is basically a Colonial Revival brick front with an unusual medieval-inspired multipaned bowed window reminiscent of those favored by the British architect Richard Norman Shaw in the 1870s. In 1937 the house was purchased by the Collectors Club, a leading organization devoted to philately.

268 **Church of the Incarnation (Episcopal) and Rectory,** 205 and 209 Madison Avenue (church, Emlen T. Littell, 1864; restoration and additions, D. & J. Jardine, 1882; rectory, Edward P. Casey, 1905–06), designated 1979. The Church of the Incarnation was erected at the time Murray Hill was being developed as a prestigious residential neighborhood. Built of brownstone with light-colored sandstone trim, the Gothic Revival structure's most prominent feature is its tall broached spire. D. & J. Jardine restored and enlarged the building following a fire in 1882. The church contains some of the finest ecclesiastical artwork in America, including stained-glass windows designed by William Morris, Edward Burne-Jones, Louis Comfort Tiffany, and John La Farge; sculpture by the American masters Daniel Chester French and Augustus Saint-Gaudens; and a monument designed by Henry Hobson Richardson. A rectory built adjacent to the church in 1868–69 was largely rebuilt and given a new facade in a neo-Jacobean style in 1905–06 and is currently used as a parish house.

269 **Pierpont Morgan Library and Annex,** 29–33 East 36th Street (McKim, Mead & White, Charles F. McKim, partner in charge, 1902–07; annex, Benjamin Wistar Morris, 1927–28), designated 1966, interior 1982. When J. P. Morgan commissioned a library to house his collection of books and manuscripts, Charles F. McKim responded with an architectural masterpiece. McKim based his design on the attic story of the Nymphaeum of 1555, built in Rome for Pope Julius III. The facade of Tennessee marble laid up without mortar centers on an entrance in the form of a Palladian arch. To either side are lions carved by Edward Clark Potter and roundels and panels by Andrew O'Connor and Adolph Weinman. The refined simplicity of the exterior belies the richness of the **interior.** The original library has three public rooms, each magnificently decorated. The colorful marble entrance hall is crowned by a domed ceiling adorned with murals and plasterwork by H. Siddons Mowbray, a leading muralist of the period, who derived his inspiration from the work of Raphael. The East Library is dominated by triple tiers of bookcases and is ornamented with lunettes by Mowbray. The West Library, which was Morgan's study, has been called "one of the great achievements of American interior decoration." In 2002 the Landmarks Preservation Commission approved expansion plans for the library complex, designed by architect Renzo Piano.

270 **Phelps Stokes–J. P. Morgan, Jr. House,** 231 Madison Avenue (1852–53; enlarged, R. H. Robertson, 1888), designated 2002. This freestanding mansion was one of three brownstone Italianate houses built for the Phelps family on the east side of Madison Avenue between 36th and 37th Streets.

J. Pierpont Morgan acquired the greatly expanded structure in 1904, and it served as the home of his son J. P. Morgan, Jr., until 1944, when it was converted to the headquarters of the Lutheran Church in America. The building was acquired by the Pierpont Morgan Library in 1988.

271 **Joseph Raphael De Lamar House,** now the Consulate General of the Republic of Poland, 233 Madison Avenue (C. P. H. Gilbert, 1902–05), designated 1975. This Beaux-Arts mansion, the largest in Murray Hill and one of the grandest in all of New York, was designed for a Dutch-born entrepreneur who made his fortune in the California Gold Rush. The subtly asymmetrical house, with an entrance that is flanked by marble columns and crowned by a pair of putti, is surmounted by an exceptionally imposing mansard.

272 **Tiffany & Co. Building,** 397–409 Fifth Avenue (McKim, Mead & White, Stanford White, partner in charge, 1903–06), designated 1988. Upon the completion of this Italian Renaissance–inspired white marble palace, Tiffany & Co. became one of the first large stores to move north of 34th Street on Fifth Avenue. Stanford White's sophisticated design, closely modeled on the 16th-century Palazzo Grimani in Venice, adapted Michele Sanmicheli's residential design to the needs of a prestigious jewelry emporium. The facade was restored in 2003.

273 **Gorham Building,** 390 Fifth Avenue (McKim, Mead & White, Stanford White, partner in charge, 1904–06), designated 1998. Intended as a showcase for the Gordham Manufacturing Company, this elegant corner building is decorated with bronze balconies and friezes crafted by its staff. Stanford White, architect of the nearby Tiffany & Co. Building (see above), based his design on early Florentine Renaissance models, crowning the elevations with a prominent copper cornice.

274 **Knox Building,** now part of the Republic National Bank Building, 452 Fifth Avenue (John H. Duncan, 1901–02), designated 1980. With its limestone and white brick facades, the Knox Building is a fine example of Beaux-Arts commercial architecture. Erected for a prominent hat company at a time when business development was sweeping north along Fifth Avenue, the building is conspicuously

sited on the corner immediately south of the New York Public Library's plaza.

275 **American Radiator Building,** now the Bryant Park Hotel, 40 West 40th Street (Raymond Hood, 1923–24), designated 1974. Raymond Hood's first New York City skyscraper is highlighted by conservative Gothic-inspired detail but was, at the time of its construction, quite daring in its dramatic exploitation of the setback massing required by the 1916 zoning law. The building's most unusual feature is its black brick, chosen by Hood in an attempt to devise a unified facade (the facades of most earlier skyscrapers were light-colored masonry punctuated by dark window openings). The gold crown was originally brightly lit at night to simulate the glow of a hot radiator. The restored building was converted to a hotel in 2001.

276 **Bryant Park Studios,** 80 West 40th Street (Charles A. Rich, 1900–01), designated 1988. The Bryant Park Studios, like a handful of other buildings erected in New York City around 1900, was designed as combined living and studio spaces for artists. The large windows with unobstructed north light (Bryant Park is across the street) illuminate the double-height studios. The building was commissioned by successful portrait painter Abraham Anderson, who kept a studio here. Among the building's other residents were the artists Edward Steichen and Fernand Leger. The studios continue to be used by design firms, although residential occupancy has ended.

277 **Bryant Park Scenic Landmark,** Sixth Avenue at West 42nd Street (east end, Carrère & Hastings, 1898–1911; main park, Lusby Simpson, 1933–34; redesign, Hanna/Olin, landscape architect, and Lynden B. Miller, garden designer, 1988–91), designated 1974. Bryant Park was built on the site of two of New York's most famous 19th-century structures, the Crystal Palace and the Croton Reservoir. Established in 1884, the park was not actually laid out until the 20th century. The terraces and kiosks at the east end were designed by Carrère & Hastings as part of the New York Public Library (see below) commission and include the sculptor Herbert Adams's Bryant Memorial. The main park, planned in the tradition of formal French gardens, was laid out as a Depression-era public works project. The park was restored and sections of it were redesigned in 1988–91, creating one of the most successful oases in New York City. Of special interest, at the west end of the park, is the Josephine Shaw Lowell Fountain (Charles Platt, 1912), the first major monument in New York dedicated to a woman; Lowell was a pioneering social reformer.

278 **New York Public Library, Astor, Lenox and Tilden Foundations,** 476 Fifth Avenue (Carrère & Hastings, 1898–1911), designated 1967, interior 1974. The main building for the New York Public Library, the design for which was won in competition by Carrère & Hastings, is perhaps the greatest masterpiece of Beaux-Arts architecture in the United States. The library, a private foundation

housed in a city-owned building, was established in 1895 when the Astor Library (see No. 151), the Lenox Library, and the Tilden Trust (see No. 217) consolidated their holdings. The majestic building, constructed of Dorset marble from Vermont, is enormous in scale, yet its broad front stairs and projecting central pavilion are not overpowering. They draw the public into one of the world's leading research institutions. The exterior is embellished with sculpture by Edward Clark Potter (the lions), Frederick MacMonnies (the fountains), Paul Wayland Bartlett (figures above the entrances), and George Gray Barnard (the end pediments). The **interiors,** notably the main lobby (Astor Hall), the staircases, and the central hall, are distinguished by the outstanding quality of their design, materials, and con-

The Bryant Park Studios (No. 276) was designed as combined living and studio spaces for artists. Photo by Carl Forster.

struction. A major restoration of both the exterior and interior was begun in the 1980s.

279 **Park Avenue Viaduct,** also known as the Pershing Square Viaduct, Park Avenue from East 40th Street to Grand Central Terminal (Warren & Wetmore, design, 1912; construction, 1917–19), designated 1980. Grand Central Terminal (see below) was designed with complex systems for the efficient circulation of trains, surface traffic, and pedestrians. The Park Avenue Viaduct was conceived in 1903 by the architecture firm Reed & Stem as an expeditious way of moving traffic along Park Avenue and around the massive terminal. As designed by Warren & Wetmore in 1912, the viaduct consists of three low, broad arches—all originally open—composed of steel girders cantilevered from granite piers; ornate iron railings run along the roadway above the arches.

280 **Grand Central Terminal,** East 42nd Street at Park Avenue (Reed & Stem and Warren & Wetmore; William Wilgus, engineer, 1903–13), designated 1967, interior 1980. One of the world's great railway terminals, often referred to as the gateway to the nation, Grand Central is an outstanding Beaux-Arts design. The engineer William Wilgus and the architects Reed & Stem were responsible for the terminal's innovative plan, with its extensive tunnels, ramp system, and upper and lower concourses. The monumental facades and the sumptuous interior spaces were the work of Whitney Warren. Grand

New York Public Library, Astor, Lenox, and Tilden Foundations (No. 278). Arguably the greatest masterpiece of Beaux-Arts design in the United States. Photo by John Barrington Bayley, c. 1965.

Central was designed on an axis with Park Avenue; Jules-Felix Coutan's clock and *Transportation* statue at the apex of the building terminate the avenue's northward vista. The **interiors** are laid out in a formal, axial Beaux-Arts manner with a grand waiting room and an even grander concourse, famous for its windowed east and west elevations—through which shafts of light penetrate the space—and its high vaulted ceiling appropriately decorated with constellations highlighted by electric stars. Ramps lead down to the more modest lower concourse, planned for suburban trains, and to the famous Oyster Bar, whose vaulted ceiling is covered in Guastavino tiles. The landmark designation of Grand Central Terminal sustained a series of legal challenges that culminated in a 1978 United States Supreme Court decision affirming the validity of New York City's landmarks law. Under the auspices of the Metropolitan Transportation Authority, the terminal was restored by Beyer Blinder Belle, architect, in 1994–98.

281 Manufacturers Trust Company Building, 510 Fifth Avenue (Skidmore, Owings & Merrill, Gordon Bunshaft, partner in charge, 1953–54), designated 1997. During the 1950s Gordon Bunshaft distinguished himself as one of the most gifted interpreters of European Modernism. This elegant structure ranks among his most influential works and was the first bank in the United States designed in the International Style. Located at the southwest corner of 43rd Street, the large plate-glass windows are framed by aluminum mullions that rise five stories to provide unobstructed views of the interiors, particularly the second-story banking hall and street-level vault. The novelty of the design proved to be an asset, and the building was a critical and commercial success.

282 Century Association Clubhouse, 7 West 43rd Street (McKim, Mead & White, 1889–91), designated 1967. McKim, Mead & White's design for the Century Association, a club organized in 1847

Grand Central Terminal (No. 280). Once considered the "gateway to the nation," the Beaux-Arts Grand Central Terminal also played a seminal role in the history of the American historic preservation movement. Photo by John Barrington Bayley, c. 1965.

"to promote the advancement of art and literature," established the Italian Renaissance palazzo mode as the favored style for the many private clubhouses built in American cities in the late 19th and early 20th centuries. In New York City this influence is evident in such later buildings as the Metropolitan Club (see No. 430) and the University Club (see No. 305). The facade of the Century, combining light-colored stone, Roman brick, and terra cotta, is highlighted by magnificent ironwork. The club moved here from its previous home on East 15th Street (see No. 209). The building was restored in 1992 by Jan Hird Pokorny, architect.

283 **Fire Engine Company No. 65,** 33 West 43rd Street (Hoppin & Koen, 1897–98), designated 1990. Erected at a time when 43rd Street between Fifth and Sixth Avenues was being developed as the location of some of the city's most prestigious clubs and hotels, this four-story Italian Renaissance–inspired firehouse was designed to resemble the nearby Century Association Clubhouse (see above).

284 **Algonquin Hotel,** 59–61 West 44th Street (Goldwin Starrett, 1902), designated 1987. The Algonquin Hotel is famous for playing host to literary and theatrical visitors, most prominently the legendary Round Table, a group of critics, writers, and humorists including Robert Benchley, Heywood Broun, George S. Kaufman, Ring Lardner, Dorothy Parker, and Alexander Woollcott, who convened on the premises almost daily in the 1920s.

285 **New York Yacht Club,** 37 West 44th Street (Warren & Wetmore, 1899–1900), designated 1979. This clubhouse in the Beaux-Arts style was the first building by the architects Warren & Wetmore, best known for their later work at Grand Central Terminal (see No. 280). It is one of the most lighthearted buildings of the era. As befits the home of the nation's most prestigious yacht club, the building presents a limestone facade designed on a nautical theme. The most prominent feature is the trio of windows carved to resemble the sterns of baroque galleons. Elsewhere on the ornate street front, restored in the early 1990s, are seashells, dolphins, dripping seaweed, and other marine ornament.

286 **Harvard Club of New York City,** 27 West 44th Street (McKim, Mead & White, Charles F.

McKim, partner in charge, 1893–94; rear addition on West 45th Street, 1900–05; west additions, 1913–16), designated 1967. Appropriately, the Harvard Club was designed in a colonial-inspired style reminiscent of the early buildings on the university's Cambridge, Massachusetts, campus. Charles F. McKim, who had unsuccessfully studied engineering at Harvard and later designed several buildings and memorial gates on the Harvard campus, was responsible for the original building of dark red "Harvard brick" with limestone trim. The same style and materials were used by McKim, Mead & White for the early 20th-century additions. Davis Brody Bond designed the west wing, completed in 2003.

287 **Association of the Bar of the City of New York,** 42 West 44th Street (Cyrus L. W. Eidlitz, 1895–96), designated 1966. This imposing limestone building, with street facades on both 43rd and 44th Streets, illustrates Eidlitz's individualistic approach to the handling of classical architectural forms. Eidlitz designed the building for the Association of the Bar, New York's leading legal organization, which was founded in 1870 "for the purpose of maintaining the honor and dignity of the profession of the law, of cultivating social relations among its members, and increasing its usefulness in promoting the due administration of justice."

288 **General Society of Mechanics and Tradesmen,** 20 West 44th Street (Lamb & Rich, 1890; additions, Ralph S. Townsend, 1903–05), designated 1988. This Renaisance Revival building was constructed in two separate campaigns that created a single unified design. The original building was erected by the Berkeley School, a private boys' school that emphasized military drill exercise. In 1899 the property was acquired by the General Society of Mechanics and Tradesmen, an organization founded in 1785 to foster education in the mechanical trades. In 1903 Andrew Carnegie, who was a member of the society, provided a gift of $250,000 to renovate the building. The original top story was replaced with three stories, and the building's magnificent wrought-iron fire escapes were installed.

289 **Sidewalk Clock** (see No. 191), 522 Fifth Avenue at West 44th Street (Seth Thomas Company, 1907), designated 1981. Installed on Fifth Avenue at 43rd Street by the American Trust Company, this clock was moved to its present location, a block farther north, in the 1930s. The clock has an unusually ornate base and is crowned by a cast-iron pineapple.

290 Fred F. French Building, 551 Fifth Avenue (H. Douglas Ives and Sloan & Robertson, 1926–27), designated 1986. The prominent Fred F. French real-estate firm erected this skyscraper with massed setbacks for its corporate headquarters and for rental income. The use of detail inspired by ancient Mesopotamian art is an indication of the exotic historicism that was prevalent during the 1920s. The exotic influence is especially evident at the base, where the bronze entrances and storefronts are embellished with mythological figures and Near Eastern ornament, and at the crown, with its vivid polychromatic terra-cotta decoration. **Interior:** The ornamental motifs in the magnificent lobby pick up exterior design elements. The lobby has a vaulted ceiling, bronze doors, and other elaborate Near Eastern features.

291 Scribner Building, 597 Fifth Avenue (Ernest Flagg, 1912–13), designated 1982, interior 1989. Almost two decades after moving into its building at 153–157 Fifth Avenue, between 21st and 22nd Streets (see No. 189), Charles Scribner's Sons followed Manhattan's fashionable retailers to Midtown. Ernest Flagg, Charles Scribner II's brother-in-law, was again commissioned to design a store and office building for the firm. Flagg elaborated on his earlier design, which had become an identifiable image of the Scribner firm, and created a 10-story French-inspired limestone-fronted building with a facade that reflects the nature of the steel skeleton frame. As befitted a prestigious bookstore, the vaulted **interior** was designed to resemble a small library. Appropriately the plaster ceiling contains cartouches embellished with the initials *CS,* as well as open books and lamps of learning. The restored ground floor was converted to a clothing store in 1996.

292 Goelet Building, now Swiss Center Building, 608 Fifth Avenue (Victor L. S. Hafner and Edward Hall Faile, 1930–32), designated 1992. The Goelet family, one of New York's major landowners and developers, erected a large mansion on the corner of Fifth Avenue and West 49th Street in 1880. Robert Goelet replaced the house with this Art Deco

building, which consists of a two-story commercial base articulated by large glass display windows and eight office floors clad in green and white marble. The central decorative element on the second story of the Fifth Avenue front is the Goelet crest—a swan set above intertwined *Gs.* Swans are also evident on the ceiling of the **interior** vestibule. The vestibule and lobby are among the finest Art Deco spaces in New York, with their complex floor plan, varicolored marbles, aluminum and aluminum-leaf highlights, nickel silver doors, and stylized ornamentation. The lower floors were restored in 1997 in the spirit of the original design by the firm Garrison & Siegel, architect.

293 Saks Fifth Avenue, 611 Fifth Avenue (Starrett & Van Vleck, 1922–24), designated 1984. The department store specialists Starrett & Van Vleck designed this luxurious emporium in 1922 in a Renaissance-inspired style appropriate to the exclusive commercial character of Fifth Avenue. Saks's relocation from Herald Square to Fifth Avenue at East 50th Street marks the final chapter in the northward migration of Manhattan's large retail stores, a development that began early in the 20th century.

294 Rockefeller Center (Associated Architects; other architects as noted): **RCA Building and Lobby,** now the General Electric Building, 30 Rockefeller Plaza (1932–33); **RCA Building West,** now the General Electric Building, 1250 Sixth Avenue (1932–33); **RKO Building,** now the Amax Building, 1270 Sixth Avenue (1931–32); **Radio City Music Hall,** 1260 Sixth Avenue (1931–32); **British Empire Building,** now the British Building, 620 Fifth Avenue (1932–33); **La Maison Français,** 610 Fifth Avenue (1933); **Palazzo d'Italia,** 626 Fifth Avenue (1933–34); **International Building and Lobby,** 630 Fifth Avenue (1933–34); **International Building North,** 636 Fifth Avenue (1933–34); the former **Time-Life Building,** now 1 Rockefeller Plaza (1936–37); **Associated Press Building,** 50 Rockefeller Plaza (1938); the former **Eastern Airlines Building,** now 10 Rockefeller Plaza (1939); **U.S. Rubber Company Building,** now the Simon & Schuster Building, 1230 Sixth Avenue (1939; extension, Harrison & Abramovitz, 1954–55); **Esso Building,** now the Warner Communications Building, 75 Rockefeller Plaza (Carson & Lundin, 1946–47); **Manufacturers Hanover Trust Build-**

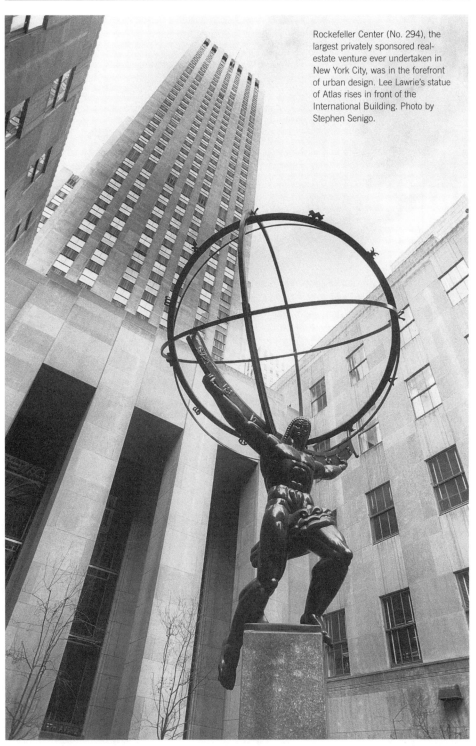

Rockefeller Center (No. 294), the largest privately sponsored real-estate venture ever undertaken in New York City, was in the forefront of urban design. Lee Lawrie's statue of Atlas rises in front of the International Building. Photo by Stephen Senigo.

ing, now 600 Fifth Avenue (Carson & Lundin, 1950–52); **Promenade,** also known as Channel Gardens; **Sunken Plaza; Rockefeller Plaza;** and **Rooftop Gardens,** all designated 1985. Rockefeller Center, one of America's most significant architectural and urban design projects, has been copied many times, but it has never been equaled. The center, which incorporates office buildings, stores, theaters, and open space, unites a sophisticated business sense with good design in the largest privately sponsored real-estate venture ever undertaken in New York City. The genesis of Rockefeller Center was the desire of John D. Rockefeller, Jr., to help the Metropolitan Opera build a new home. Rockefeller agreed to lease a large plot of land—bounded by 48th and 51st Streets, Fifth and Sixth Avenues—on which the new opera house would be built and where he would erect a series of profitable office buildings. Unfortunately, the stock market crash of 1929 forced the Met to abandon the project. Despite the Depression and the withdrawal of the opera company, Rockefeller and his advisers continued to plan a large commercial complex. The layout and the design of the original buildings were handled by the Associated Architects, a group directed by Raymond Hood that included the architects Reinhard & Hofmeister, advisers to Rockefeller since the inception of the project, and Corbett, Harrison & MacMurray, specialists in skyscraper design. The plan consisted of a monumental central building—the RCA Building—surrounded by smaller office towers, low-rise buildings on Fifth Avenue that were to be leased to foreign tenants, and strategically placed open spaces such as the promenade (popularly known as the Channel Gardens because it runs between the British and French buildings) and the sunken plaza that would draw people into the underground shops. The limestone-faced buildings combine simple modern massing with a traditional artistic scheme. All the artworks in Rockefeller Center have humanistic themes—for example, progress through science, and technology and peace through international understanding. Among the most famous pieces are Paul Manship's *Prometheus* and Lee Lawrie's *Atlas.* Several of the buildings have significant **interiors.** The ground floor of the RCA Building is most famous for its lobby murals by José Maria Sert (in part replacing murals by Diego Rivera) and Frank Brangwyn. The International Building's lobby is a dramatic four-story space embellished with

rich materials and metallic sculptures by Michio Ihara installed in 1978. The success of the initial project led Rockefeller to plan additional buildings on sites adjacent to the original complex.

The major entertainment facility at Rockefeller Center is Radio City Music Hall. Opened in 1932, this 6,200-seat theater—the world's largest at the time of its construction—was planned by the impresario Samuel Rothafel (better known as Roxy) for live entertainment, but it soon became a movie theater in which the feature films were preceded by stage shows starring the precision dancers known as the Roxyettes (later the Rockettes). On the **interior** (designated 1978), the huge auditorium was planned to be as intimate as possible. It consists of a great arched proscenium in the form of a rising sun and a large orchestra with three shallow balconies. The decoration of the theater was undertaken by Donald Deskey, who created a modern, well-integrated scheme for the carpets, wall coverings, and furnishings. Like other Rockefeller Center buildings, the theater contains several major artworks, including Ezra Winter's monumental foyer mural, *Fountain of Youth,* and a series of murals in the men's and women's lounges.

295 **Villard Houses,** later the Helmsley Palace Hotel, now the New York Palace Hotel and the Urban Center, 451–457 Madison Avenue and 24 East 51st Street (McKim, Mead & White, Joseph M. Wells, designer, 1882–85), designated 1968. Commissioned by the railroad entrepreneur Henry Villard, this masterpiece of late 19th-century urban design involved the skillful combination of six brownstone houses into a single monumental U-shaped unit set around an open court. The complex is not only one of the most beautiful in New York but was also among the first major projects in the United States to adapt specific European architectural precedents. In this case, the architect Joseph M. Wells of the McKim, Mead & White office took as a model the Palazzo della Cancelleria in Rome. The massing, arcades, window enframements, and rosette details of the Roman palace were used in the New York project, but in a novel manner, to accord with the New York site and with the demands of a late 19th-century residential commission. In the early 1970s, demolition of the complex was threatened, but in 1975–80 the houses were incorporated into the Palace Hotel and the north wing was re-

DECO DESTINATIONS

The Chrysler Building and Empire State Building are world-famous landmarks (Manhattan Nos. 326 and 207). These splendid Art Deco towers have become icons of the skyline, celebrated for their height, vertical massing, and sumptuous decoration. While the style takes its name from the 1925 Exposition International des Art Decoratifs held in Paris, a great range of decorative sources were absorbed by American designers, from the work of Austria's Wiener Werkstätte and the German Expressionists to Mayan and other Native American forms. Among the architects to adopt this style, Ralph Walker and Raymond Hood are particularly well represented in Manhattan. Walker's finest work is concentrated below Canal Street, where he built several important structures for the communications industry, as well as the former Irving Trust Building, which has a smooth limestone skin arranged to simulate drapery folds or a fluted column (Manhattan Nos. 50, 91, 94, and 19). In Midtown are a number of outstanding buildings by Hood, including the gold-tipped American Radiator Building, the Daily News Building (and interior), and the McGraw-Hill Building (Manhattan Nos. 275, 327, 225). Hood also collaborated on the design and planning of Rockefeller Center (Manhattan No. 294). The 1920s was a period of great prosperity, and three leading real-estate developers built handsome skyscrapers to serve as their headquarters: Fred F. French, the Fuller Construction Company, and Irwin Chanin (Manhattan Nos. 290, 316, 325). Chanin's office was responsible for a number of theaters and two of the most memorable twin-towered apartment houses bordering Central Park West, the Century and the Majestic (Manhattan Nos. 372 and 377). Other notable examples on the Upper West Side include the Eldorado Apartments, the Master Building and the Midtown Theater, which has a facade of polychrome terra cotta (Manhattan Nos. 400, 423, 418)

Worth visiting in the Bronx is the Dollar Savings Bank and its impressive interior, the Park Plaza Apartments, and the Paul J. Rainey Memorial Gates at the Bronx Zoo, sculpted by Paul Manship (Bronx Nos. 29, 18, 35). Queens offers a small and unusually varied selection of Art Deco buildings, including the Marine Air Terminal at LaGuardia Airport with its circular rotunda and mural by James Brooks, as well as a several examples clustered in downtown Jamaica, including a polychromatic furniture store, a set-back office building, and a streamlined nightclub (Queens Nos. 10, 45, 42, and 41).

served as office and gallery space for organizations involved in architectural and design issues.

296 **Saint Patrick's Cathedral (R.C.) Complex,** Fifth Avenue between East 50th and 51st Streets (cathedral, rectory, and cardinal's residence, James Renwick, Jr., 1853–88; lady chapel, Charles T. Mathews, 1901–06), designated 1966. In 1852, when New York's Roman Catholic archdiocese purchased the site for a new cathedral, the area near Fifth Avenue and 50th Street was relatively uninhabited, but by the time Saint Patrick's was inaugurated in 1879 (the spires were not completed until

1888), the area had become one of the city's finest residential districts. James Renwick, Jr.'s design was influenced by continental Gothic buildings, in particular Cologne Cathedral. Although the marble building was not constructed exactly to Renwick's specifications (several major structural changes were made), his Fifth Avenue facade, with its three entrances and twin spires, is among the most impressive 19th-century ecclesiastical works in America. Early in the 20th century, Renwick's east front was removed and reconstructed at Our Lady of Lourdes Church (see No. 537) and the present lady chapel was built.

MANHATTAN

297 **647 Fifth Avenue,** also known as the George W. Vanderbilt House, now Versace (Hunt & Hunt, 1902–05; addition, Charles L. Fraser, 1917), designated 1977. This town house in the Louis XV style and its neighbor the Morton and Nellie Plant House (see below) are reminders of the residential character of Fifth Avenue early in the 20th century. The house, one of a pair known as the Marble Twins, was commissioned by George W. Vanderbilt and sold to his brother William K. Vanderbilt before it was completed. It is the last survivor of a group of Vanderbilt residences built on this section of Fifth Avenue. The house was designed by the sons of Richard Morris Hunt, the architect of George Vanderbilt's famous Biltmore estate in North Carolina. Robert Goelet and his wife, Elsie, were the only residents prior to the 1917 sale of the house to the art dealers Gimpel & Wildenstein. Versace sponsored an extensive restoration of the facade in 1995–96.

298 **Morton and Nellie Plant House** and **Edward and Frances Holbrook House,** now Cartier, Inc., 651–653 Fifth Avenue and 2–4 East 52nd Street (Robert W. Gibson, 1903–05 and C. P. H. Gilbert, 1904–05), designated 1970. Banker, yachtsman, and baseball club owner Morton Plant built this elegant Italian Renaissance–inspired house, which is the finest surviving mansion on Fifth Avenue south of 59th Street. The Plant house and the adjacent Holbrook house at 4 East 52nd Street were successfully converted into a shop for the Cartier jewelry company by William Welles Bosworth around 1917.

299 **Racquet and Tennis Club,** 370 Park Avenue (McKim, Mead & White, William S. Richardson, partner in charge, 1916–19), designated 1979. The Racquet and Tennis Club is one of the few survivors from the period when Park Avenue north of Grand Central Terminal was lined with luxurious masonry apartment houses and institutional buildings. In keeping with the prestige of the site chosen for its new home, the club engaged the services of McKim, Mead & White, even though by 1916 the firm's two leading designers, McKim and White, were no longer alive. A younger partner, William S. Richardson, was responsible for this project, designed in the form of an Italian Renaissance palazzo, the style that the firm had established for clubhouses almost thirty years earlier with its Century Associa-

tion (see No. 282). The most interesting features of the subdued front elevation are the recessed loggia and the frieze in the form of a tennis net with crossed rackets.

300 **Lever House,** 390 Park Avenue (Skidmore, Owings & Merrill, Gordon Bunshaft, partner in charge, 1950–52), designated 1982. The construction of the 24-story glass and stainless steel Lever House heralded the beginning of a new wave in American skyscraper design and a turning point in the history of modern architecture. Lever House established the suitability of the International Style for office building design and signaled the transformation of the style from one associated with an idealistic European social movement into one symbolizing corporate America. Lever House also signaled the beginning of the transformation of Park Avenue south of 59th Street from a street of masonry apartments and institutions into an avenue of glass towers. Lever House was the first skyscraper in the form of a vertical slab erected in New York City after the passage of the 1916 zoning resolution; the setbacks required by the 1916 law were not necessary if a building occupied only 25 percent of its lot. Bunshaft's design is especially dramatic because the slab is set perpendicular to Park Avenue and appears to float above the street and above the one-story base and open plaza. In 2003 SOM completed replacement of the deteriorated signature curtain wall, accompanied by the installation of sculpture and seating designed by Isamu Noguchi.

301 **CBS Building,** 51 West 52nd Street (Eero Saarinen & Associates, 1961–64, completed by Kevin Roche and John Dinkeloo), designated 1997. The CBS Building is one of New York's most important skyscrapers. In a departure from the metal and glass curtain walls that dominated Park and Sixth Avenues after the Second World War, Saarinen's stated goal was to create "the simplest skyscraper in New York." The powerfully sculptural elevations consist of angled dark gray granite piers that alternate with single panes of matching tinted glass.

Lever House (No. 300), a turning point in the history of 20th-century architecture, was restored in 2000–03. Photo by Florian Holzherr. Courtesy Skidmore, Owings & Merrill.

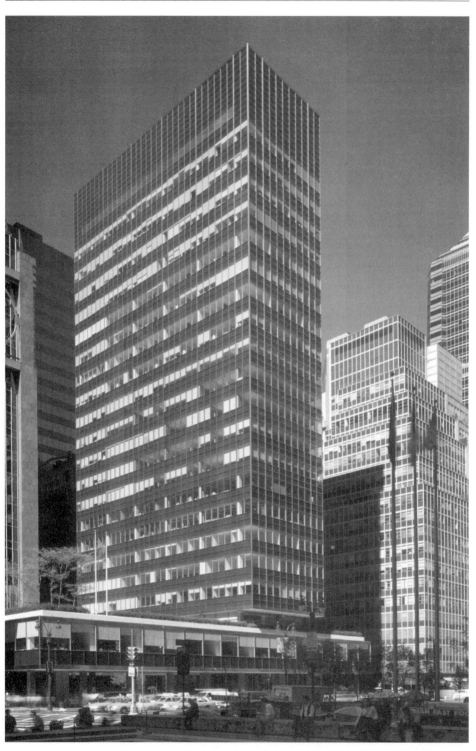

Completed in 1964, the building has been widely praised and was cited by the Architectural League and the Municipal Art Society for excellence.

302 **Saint Thomas Church (Episcopal) and Parish House,** Fifth Avenue at West 53rd Street (Cram, Goodhue & Ferguson, 1906–13), designated 1966. Saint Thomas, a major design by Cram, Goodhue & Ferguson, is a limestone-faced building that makes dramatic use of its corner site. Replacing a church that burned in 1905, the neo-Gothic design, with an asymmetrically placed tower, combines features from English and French medieval architecture. The initial plan for the church was devised by Ralph Adams Cram, but it appears to have been Bertram Goodhue who developed the idea into the magnificent building that was erected in 1911–13. Beyer Blinder Belle were the architects for a facade restoration completed in 1997.

303 **William H. and Ada S. Moore House,** 4 East 54th Street (McKim, Mead & White, 1898–1900), designated 1967. This marble-fronted house was commissioned by W. E. D. Stokes, builder of the Ansonia Hotel (see No. 390), but four months before its completion, Stokes sold the house to Ada S. Moore. Moore and her husband, the Chicago lawyer and corporate titan William H. Moore, a founder of U.S. Steel and other large corporations, moved into one of McKim, Mead & White's most beautiful Italian Renaissance–inspired town houses. After Ada Moore's death in 1955, the house had a succession of philanthropic and commercial tenants.

304 **Aeolian Building,** 689–691 Fifth Avenue (Warren & Wetmore, 1925–27), designated 2002. During the first quarter of the 20th century, the Aeolian Company was a leading manufacturer of roll-operated musical instruments, including organs and pianos. This building was built to serve as its headquarters, and the French Renaissance–inspired design was awarded a gold medal by the Fifth Avenue Association. Since 1930 the flagship Elizabeth Arden Red Door Salon has occupied the ground story.

305 **University Club,** 1 West 54th Street (McKim, Mead & White, Charles F. McKim, partner in charge, 1896–1900), designated 1967. Charles F. McKim designed the University Club in the spirit of Italian High Renaissance palazzi. The nine-story structure is divided into three horizontal sections, each defined by the tall arched windows that light the clubhouse's major rooms (lounge, library, and dining room); subsidiary floors are subtly placed between them. The building is faced with pink Milford granite and ornamented with the seals of various universities, executed in marble by Daniel Chester French, and a large club seal by Kenyon Cox.

306 **Moses Allen and Alice Dunning Starr House,** now Petrola House, also known as 5 West 54th Street (R. H. Robertson, 1897–99), designated 1981. The neurologist Moses Allen Starr commissioned this meticulously detailed town house at a time when many wealthy New Yorkers were building houses in the area; it is one of five adjacent town houses erected in the late 1890s that are designated landmarks. The subtle Renaissance-inspired building has a limestone base; its upper floors are clad in Roman brick trimmed with limestone.

307 **Philip and Carrie Lehman House,** also known as 7 West 54th Street (John H. Duncan, 1899–1900), designated 1981. Philip Lehman, son of a founder of the banking firm Lehman Brothers and himself a partner in the firm, commissioned this limestone-fronted Beaux-Arts town house, one of five adjacent landmark residences on the north side of West 54th Street. After Philip's death in 1947, the house was occupied by his son Robert, who amassed an extraordinary art collection; this collection was later given to the Metropolitan Museum of Art, where it is now installed along with interiors removed from the house.

308 **James J. and Josephine Goodwin Residence,** now U.S. Trust Company, also known as 9–11 West 54th Street (McKim, Mead & White, Charles F. McKim and William Mead, partners in charge, 1896–98), designated 1981. The wealthy businessman James Junius Goodwin, a cousin and business partner of J. P. Morgan's, was responsible for commissioning one of McKim, Mead & White's finest Colonial Revival residences. Modeled on Charles Bulfinch's Third Harrison Gray Otis House (1806) in Boston, this elegant brick structure was planned as a double house; the Goodwins resided in the larger unit at No. 11. The building underwent an award-winning restoration and conversion into a bank in 1980–81.

309 **13 and 15 West 54th Street** (Henry J. Hardenbergh, 1896–97), designated 1981. This pair of houses was built as a speculative venture. Hardenbergh's love of Northern European architecture, evident at his famous Dakota Apartments (see No. 378), is also seen in these residences with their banded window enframements and tapered pilasters. In 1906 No. 13 was purchased by John D. Rockefeller; it was the home of his son, John D. Rockefeller, Jr., until about 1918. Later, Governor Nelson Rockefeller of New York used the house as an office; he died here in 1979. Nelson Rockefeller purchased No. 15 in 1955, and for many years it housed the Museum of Primitive Art (now the Michael Rockefeller Collection at the Metropolitan Museum of Art).

310 **Rockefeller Apartments,** 17 West 54th Street and 24 West 55th Street (Harrison & Fouilhoux, 1935–37), designated 1984. In their simplicity, their use of industrial materials, their smooth wall surfaces, and especially their fenestration, these two brick apartment houses exemplify early International Style design in the United States. The windows consist of bands of metal sash, often grouped in curving bays, that provide 15 percent more light than required by city building codes. Commissioned by Nelson Rockefeller, these buildings represent the first of many collaborations between Rockefeller and Wallace K. Harrison. In 1997 the cooperative organization undertook a major restoration, most notably of the extraordinary windows, under the supervision of William Leggio Architects.

311 **Gotham Hotel,** now the Peninsula Hotel, 696–700 Fifth Avenue (Hiss & Weekes, 1902–05), designated 1989. The Italian Renaissance–inspired Gotham Hotel is among the handsomest surviving early 20th-century luxury hotels in New York City. The 20-story limestone building was designed to harmonize with the adjoining University Club (see No. 305) and to complement the St. Regis Hotel (see below), begun one year earlier on a site across Fifth Avenue.

312 **St. Regis Hotel,** 699–703 Fifth Avenue and 2 East 55th Street (Trowbridge & Livingston, 1901–04; extension, Sloan & Robertson, 1927), designated 1988. Planned by Colonel John Jacob Astor as New York's finest luxury hotel, the St. Regis is

among the most elegant Beaux-Arts buildings in the city. As befits its location on New York's most prestigious avenue, the hotel "established a new standard of excellence . . . superior to that of any hotel in this country, and probably over any hotel in the world," commented one critic on the occasion of the hotel's opening. The 1927 addition complements the original design. The hotel reopened, following an extensive refurbishing, in 1991.

313 **712 Fifth Avenue Building,** later the Rizzoli Building, now part of the Henri Bendel Store, 712 Fifth Avenue (Albert S. Gottlieb, 1907–08), designated 1985. When the Fifth Avenue Presbyterian Church commissioned this commercial building for a site adjacent to the church, Fifth Avenue was primarily residential. Thus the building was designed in accordance with 18th-century French prototypes as a five-story limestone-fronted structure that would blend with the nearby houses and maintain the elegant character of the street. The first tenant was the fashionable decorating establishment of L. Alavoine & Co. From 1964 to 1985, the Rizzoli bookstore and publishing company occupied the premises.

314 **Coty Building,** now part of the Henri Bendel Store, 714 Fifth Avenue (Woodruff Leeming, 1907–08; glass front, René Lalique, 1910), designated 1985. The former Coty Building, originally a row house erected in 1871, received a new commercial front in 1907–08. The building was leased in 1910 by the French perfumer François Coty, who commissioned what is now the only extant architectural glasswork in New York City designed by the great French glassmaker René Lalique. Lalique's composition of intertwining vines initially rose from the second through the fifth floors (the narrow second-floor level has been lost) and was designed to fit within the preexisting commercial frame. The facade, including the glass, was restored in 1989–90 by Beyer Blinder Belle, architect.

315 **Harry B. and Evelina Hollins Residence,** later the Calumet Club, now the Consulate General of Argentina, 12–14 West 56th Street (McKim, Mead & White, 1899–1901; alteration, J. E. R. Carpenter, 1924), designated 1984. The banker and broker Harry B. Hollins commissioned this handsome Colonial Revival brick house in 1899, at a time when many town houses were being built in north

Midtown. Commerce soon overwhelmed the neighborhood, and in 1914 the house was converted into the Calumet Club. Ten years later the club removed the original central entrance and constructed the porch and wing to the east. Since 1947 the house has been occupied by the Argentine consulate.

316 **Fuller Building,** 41 East 57th Street (Walker & Gillette, 1928–29), designated 1986. Erected as the headquarters of the Fuller Construction Company, this prominently sited corner building was planned to house retail stores and art galleries on the first six floors and offices above. The design, with its modernist interpretation of classical architectural forms, reflects the conservative aspects of the Art Deco style. The building has a black Swedish granite base; the upper floors are clad in a light-colored limestone. A pair of figures by the noted sculptor Elie Nadelman crowns the imposing three-story entrance. The styl-

ized modern classicism of the exterior continues on the **interior,** where the vestibules and lobby are richly decorated with marble walls, mosaic floors, and bronze detail. Of special note are the round mosaic floor panels representing the company's three successive headquarters buildings—the Tacoma Building in Chicago, the Flatiron Building (see No. 190) and the Fuller Building—and the bronze elevator doors depicting scenes of building construction.

■ **EAST OF PARK AVENUE**

HISTORIC DISTRICTS

21 **Murray Hill Historic District,** designated 2002. Most of the buildings in this tree-lined neighborhood are mid-19th-century row houses. The historic district takes its name from the 18th-century

Originally a stable, this handsome building on East 38th Street in the Murray Hill Historic District (H.D. 21) was altered to become the architectural offices of the celebrated firm Delano & Aldrich. Photo by Carl Forster.

country estate of Robert Murray. With the opening of Lexington Avenue and Fourth (now Park) Avenue by the 1840s, the blocks were partitioned and sold to developers. The earliest residences, at 102–112, 105–111, and 123–127 East 35th Street, were built in 1853–54. These brownstone-fronted buildings have low stoops with Italianate details. In 1859 the Church of the New Jerusalem began construction at 114–124 East 35th Street. Designed to complement the neighboring residences, it features a high base and tall pedimented windows. Construction during the mid-1860s, as the last remaining lots were developed, included a group of five French Second Empire–style houses at 115–123 East 38th Street, and a pair of Renaissance Revival brownstones at 107 and 109 East 36th Street. Well-known residents during the late 19th century included Admiral David G. Farragut, Dr. Charles Parkhurst, and Mary Lincoln Isham, granddaughter of Abraham and Mary Todd Lincoln. Several large mansions were constructed after 1900, most notably the Lanier House at 123–125 East 35th Street (see No. 318), designed in the Beaux-Arts style by Hoppin & Koen. In 1916 the celebrated architects Delano & Aldrich converted a stable at 126 East 38th Street into their studio, producing an exquisitely detailed neoclassical facade with circular windows across the third floor. The Town House Apartments, at 108 East 38th Street, was one of the last structures built in the district, completed in 1930. Designed by Bowden & Russell (with Emery Roth), this Art Deco building features a 25-story set-back tower, scalloped brick spandrels, and polychrome terra-cotta ornament.

22 **Sniffen Court Historic District,** designated 1966. New York City's second smallest historic district consists of ten round-arched stables erected in 1863–64 on a small court set perpendicular to East 36th Street between Lexington and Third Avenues. Although the source of the court's name is obscure, it is believed that it recalls John Sniffen, a local builder. In the 1920s the modest two-story brick buildings were converted into stylish residences. One stable became the home and studio of the sculptor Malvina Hoffman, several of whose works adorn the wall at the far end of the alley.

23 **Tudor City Historic District,** designated 1988. Fred F. French, one of New York's most active developers following World War I, began buying di-

lapidated row houses and tenements on the far east end of 42nd Street in 1925. In December of that year he announced that construction would begin on "the largest housing project ever undertaken in mid-Manhattan." French and his architectural staff, headed by H. Douglas Ives, designed a complex of apartment houses and apartment hotels with Tudor detail. The choice of a Tudor style and "olde English" names such as The Cloister, Essex House, and Windsor Tower, the location of the development on a bluff set apart from its surroundings, the absence of through streets, and the presence of two small private parks lent a suburban character to the complex. This ambience was appropriate since Tudor City sought to attract middle-class tenants who might have moved to the suburbs had they not been sufficiently impressed by the community's amenities and its convenient proximity to the nearby Midtown commercial district.

24 **Turtle Bay Gardens Historic District,** designated 1966. As part of a movement to reclaim the deteriorated brownstone row houses of the east Midtown area, Charlotte Martin purchased twenty run-down houses on East 48th and 49th Streets in 1919–20. She commissioned Edward C. Dean and William Lawrence Bottomley to renovate the houses into single-family units and apartments, to redesign the facades, and to combine the rear yards into an Italian Renaissance–inspired garden, although as an amateur architect Martin is thought to have had significant input into the designs. Iron turtles were placed on the fence posts, and Martin dubbed the development Turtle Bay Gardens. Ever since, the beautiful enclave has attracted people in the arts, including the architect Edward Dean, Katharine Hepburn, Mary Martin, Tyrone Power, Stephen Sondheim, Leopold Stokowski, and E. B. White.

INDIVIDUAL LANDMARKS

317 **Civic Club,** now Estonian House, 243 East 34th Street (Thomas A. Gray, 1898–99), designated 1978. The Civic Club was founded by Frederick Goddard, a wealthy New Yorker involved in turn-of-the-century social reform efforts who sought specifically to improve the lives of people residing between 23rd and 42nd Streets east of Fourth (now Park) Avenue. Goddard not only founded the Civic Club but also erected its Beaux-Arts clubhouse. The building remained in the Goddard family until 1946, when it was sold to the Estonian Educational Society, an organization that sponsors activities for Estonian-Americans.

318 **James F. D. and Harriet Lanier House,** 123 East 35th Street (Hoppin & Koen, 1901–03), designated 1979. At the beginning of the 20th century, many of the old residences in Murray Hill were replaced by imposing new town houses. The banker James Franklin Doughty Lanier and his wife demolished two modest houses of 1854 and erected this richly detailed Beaux-Arts dwelling designed by architects who had studied at the École des Beaux-Arts and worked in the offices of McKim, Mead & White.

319 **James Hampden Robb and Cornelia Van Rensselaer Robb House,** 23 Park Avenue (McKim, Mead & White, Stanford White, partner in charge, 1888–92) designated 1998. Stanford White designed this freestanding town house for James Hampden Robb, a retired businessman and civic leader. Five stories tall, the street facades display a wealth of Renaissance-inspired detail, rendered in iron spot brick, brownstone, and terra cotta. The house was acquired by the Advertising Club in 1923 and converted to apartments in 1977.

320 **Adelaide L. T. Douglas House,** now the Guatemalan Permanent Mission to the United Nations and Guatemalan Consul General, 57 Park Avenue (Horace Trumbauer, 1909–11), designated 1979. New York socialite Adelaide L. Townsend Douglas commissioned this house from the fashionable Philadelphia architect Horace Trumbauer a year after her divorce from William Douglas, the initial developer of Douglaston, Queens. Trumbauer designed the house in the Louis XVI style that he favored for urban residences. The facade contains especially interesting sculpted friezes.

The Robb House (No. 319) is considered to be one of Stanford White's finest urban residences. Photo by Carl Forster.

321 **152 East 38th Street** (1858; redesign, Robertson Ward, 1934–35), designated 1967. This house is an example of the extensive redesign that many of New York's older houses underwent in the 1920s and 1930s. Set far back from the lot line, the house appears originally to have been an outbuilding on an estate belonging to a member of President Martin Van Buren's family. In 1934 the developer Russell A. Pettengill commissioned Robertson Ward to convert the building and its neighbor into a residence and office for his own use. The old facade was stuccoed, and a low wall with thin colonnettes and other Regency-inspired detail was constructed near the front of the lot. In 1944 the house was sold to the publisher Cass Canfield.

322 **George S. Bowdoin Stable,** 149 East 38th Street (Ralph S. Townsend, 1902), designated 1997. This Dutch Renaissance Revival stable building is one of Manhattan's most ornate. Built for William R. H. Martin, a businessman and real-estate developer, the brick and stone facade rises to a stepped gable decorated with the bust of a bulldog. To convey the building's function, a pair of sculpted horse heads also project from the lower cornice. Acquired by Bowdoin in 1907, it was converted to a garage in 1918 and later to a single-family residence.

323 **Jonathan W. Allen Stable,** 148 East 40th Street (Charles E. Hadden, builder, 1871), designated 1997. This charming Second Empire–style brick structure was built for Jonathan W. Allen, a broker who lived on East 42nd Street. Two stories tall, the ground floor accommodated both horses and carriages, while the second story provided living quarters for the groom. It was converted to commercial use by the mid-1940s.

324 **Bowery Savings Bank Building,** 110 East 42nd Street (York & Sawyer, William Louis Ayres, partner in charge, 1921–23 and 1931–33), designated 1996. In 1920 the Bowery Savings Bank decided to move its headquarters from its historic location on the Bowery (see No. 121) to a site on East 42nd Street in the rapidly developing Midtown office district. The prominent architecture firm York & Sawyer was responsible for the Italian Romanesque–inspired building with its enormous arched entrance and monumentally scaled **interior.** The vast basilica-like banking hall (65 feet high, 80 feet wide, and 197 feet 6 inches long), with its plaster ceiling designed in imitation of wood beams, is richly decorated with a variety of marbles, sandstones, and limestone, bronze screens and tellers' cages, and an intricate marble Cosmati floor. The elevator lobby is especially notable for its blue mosaic ceiling with gold stars. In 1931–33 a six-story addition, dubbed the chapel, with fine interior detail, was erected to the east of the original building. The banking hall is now used for special events.

325 **Chanin Building,** 122 East 42nd Street (Irwin S. Chanin, with Sloan & Robertson, 1927–29), designated 1978. This Art Deco structure, designed in part by its builder, Irwin S. Chanin, is one of the most significant New York skyscrapers of the 1920s, as it is one of the earliest with a solid base, setback massing, and a buttressed crown inspired by the form of Eliel Saarinen's influential entry in the 1922 Chicago Tribune Building competition. The base is ornamented with decoration by Rene

George S. Bowdoin Stable (No. 322). A stepped Flemish gable distinguishes the facade of this well-preserved stable building in Murray Hill. Photo by Carl Forster.

Chambellan, including a terra-cotta frieze with stylized curvilinear and angular naturalistic forms set in a complex pattern that is the quintessence of Art Deco design. Below this frieze is a bronze band illustrating the theory of evolution—beginning with primitive marine life and extending as far as birds.

326 **Chrysler Building,** 405 Lexington Avenue (William Van Alen, 1928–30), designated 1978. The Chrysler's stunning Art Deco design is the embodiment of the romantic New York skyscraper. The 77-story edifice, distinguished by its abundant automotive imagery (for example, silver hood ornaments

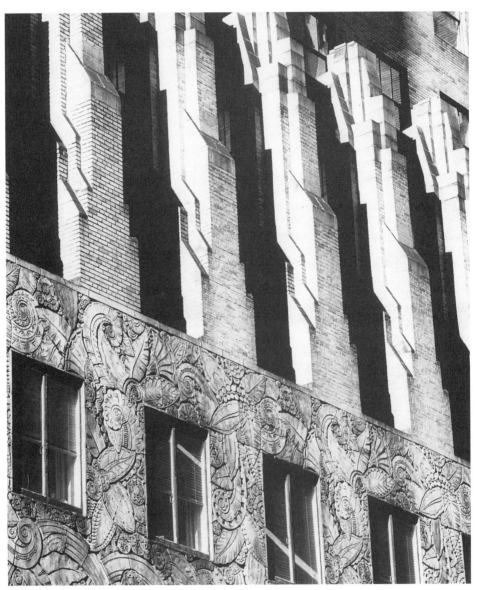

▲ Chanin Building (No. 325). A major Art Deco skyscraper. Detail of the decorated terra-cotta frieze by Rene Chambellan. Photo by Stephen Senigo.

▶ Chrysler Building (No. 326). A romantic Art Deco symbol of New York City. Photo by Carl Forster.

embellish the setbacks and stylized racing cars appear at the thirty-first floor) and a striking crown, was a personal symbol of Walter P. Chrysler and an advertisement for his corporation, as well as a speculative investment in office space. The black Belgian granite entrance arches lead into the spectacular **interior.** The lobby contains red Moroccan marble walls and yellow Siena marble floors; a ceiling mural by Edward Trumbull, which, according to a contemporary source, depicts "the vision, human energy, and engineering ability which made possible the structure"; steel, aluminum, and onyx ornament; and elevator cabs richly detailed in exotic woods that are among the most glorious ever created.

327 Daily News Building, 220 East 42nd Street (Raymond M. Hood, 1929–30), designated 1981, interior 1998. Joseph Patterson, founder of the *Daily News,* commissioned this building as the home and symbol of America's first tabloid and the country's largest newspaper. As designed by Hood, the building combines Art Deco and modernist forms in a striking manner. The flat roof and freestanding slab-like massing are significant modern innovations, but Hood's use of striped brickwork and an entrance adorned with a large relief panel of light rays shining on a diverse urban populace are characteristic decorative forms of Art Deco design. The *Daily News* remained a major tenant until 1995. **Interior:** At the center of this darkly lit interior is a giant globe set beneath a domed ceiling of faceted black glass. Conceived as a dramatic entranceway and as a permanent science exhibit devoted to planet Earth, the lobby was expanded by Harrison & Abramowitz in 1957–60. While many of the original Modernistic features were retained, some decorative elements were reconfigured and updated.

328 Ford Foundation Building, 321 East 42nd Street and 320 East 43rd Street (Eero Saarinen Associates, later Kevin Roche John Dinkeloo Associates, 1963–67), designated 1997. Built in 1963–67 to serve as the headquarters of the nation's largest private foundation, the Ford Foundation is one of the most widely admired examples of modern architecture in New York. Twelve stories tall, the granite and Cor-ten steel facades were designed by Kevin Roche to complement the neighboring Tudor City complex. **Interior:** Conceived as a grand civic gesture and to enhance staff working conditions, the

terraced atrium was originally landscaped by Dan Kiley, who collaborated frequently with Eero Saarinen. Visible from both the street and offices, the lushly planted garden is one of the city's most memorable public spaces.

329 Beaux-Arts Institute of Design, 304 East 44th Street (Frederic C. Hirons, of the firm Dennison & Hirons, 1928), designated 1988. The Society of Beaux-Arts Architects, dedicated to furthering the architectural ideas promulgated at the École des Beaux-Arts in Paris, held a competition for the design of a new school in 1927. The winning entry combines traditional Beaux-Arts ideas of symmetry, solidity, monumentality, and the use of symbolic artwork (by Rene Chambellan) with ornament reflecting the contemporary Art Deco design aesthetic. The building was rehabilitated in 1989–92.

330 Beaux-Arts Apartments, 307 and 310 East 44th Street (Kenneth M. Murchison and Raymond M. Hood, of the firm Raymond Hood, Godley & Fouilhoux, 1929–30), designated 1989. This pair of apartment houses was among the first in New York City to reflect the trend toward modernism, as evidenced in the horizontal massing, the use of steel casement windows, and the lack of applied ornament. The buildings contain studio and one-bedroom apartments planned for artists and others who wished to live in the artistic community that grew up around the nearby Beaux-Arts Institute of Design (see above).

331 New York Central Building, now the Helmsley Building, 230 Park Avenue (Warren & Wetmore, 1927–29), designated 1987. The New York Central Building, set astride Park Avenue just north of Grand Central Terminal (see No. 280), was the linchpin of the Terminal City complex of hotels and office buildings sponsored by the New York Central Railroad. Designed by the same architects responsible for the exterior of the railroad terminal, this tower once dominated Park Avenue and the surrounding Midtown business district with its distinctive design and monumental pyramidal roof capped by an ornate cupola. **Interior:** The impressive lobby, planned as a corridor connecting 45th and 46th Streets, echoes the magnificence of the exterior. The building's design and ornamentation celebrate the prowess of the New York Central Railroad, which

Critic Ada Louise Huxtable called the headquarters of the Ford Foundation (No. 328) a "civic gesture of beauty and excellence." Photo by Carl Forster.

had its headquarters on the premises. A sense of imperial grandeur is created by the marble walls and bronze detail, which includes extensive use of the railroad's initials. The Chinese red elevator doors open into cabs with red walls, wood moldings, gilt domes, and painted cloudscapes.

332 William Lescaze House and Office, 211 East 48th Street (William Lescaze, 1933–34), designated 1976. The pioneer modern architect William Lescaze designed this house for his family and incorporated an office into the basement level. The building, actually a redesign of an old row house, is generally considered to be the first truly "modern" house in New York. It has a complex, rationally designed street front with precisely balanced solids and voids. The stuccoed facade is pierced by casement ribbon windows and expanses of glass block; this is the first use of glass block in New York City.

333 Amster Yard, now Instituto Cervantes, 211–215 East 49th Street (1869–70; renovation, Harold Sterner, 1945), designated 1966. James Amster commissioned Sterner to convert this group of 1860s structures into shops, offices, and apartments grouped around a landscaped courtyard.

334 Panhellenic Tower, now the Beekman Tower Hotel, 3 Mitchell Place (John Mead Howells, 1927–28, annex 1928–20), designated 1998. An outstanding Art Deco skyscraper, the Panhellenic Tower was built to provide affordable housing for women entering the job market. Designed by John Mead Howells, a frequent collaborator with Raymond Hood, the 28-story structure is distinguished by its orange-tan brick and bold vertical striping. The lower floors incorporate handsome sculptural reliefs by Rene Chambellan.

335 Waldorf-Astoria Hotel, 301 Park Avenue (Schultze & Weaver, Lloyd Morgan, partner in charge, 1929–31), designated 1993. The famous Waldorf-Astoria Hotel on Park Avenue is the modern reincarnation of the legendary pair of hotels erected by the Astor family (John Jacob Astor immigrated from Waldorff, Germany) in the 1890s on the present-day site of the Empire State Building. The Park Avenue building combines a transient hotel with a pair of vertically massed residential skyscraper towers each surmounted by a crowning beacon. The

hotel has a gray limestone base with matching gray brick above and is ornamented at street level with Art Deco–style storefronts, lamps, entries, and screens, a soaring winged statue, and other features in nickel silver, a silver-colored alloy of nickel, zinc, and copper that was extremely popular in the late 1920s and early 1930s.

336 Saint Bartholomew's Church (Episcopal) and Community House, Park Avenue at East 50th Street (Bertram Goodhue, 1914–19; community house, Mayers, Murray & Phillip, 1926–28), designated 1967. Superbly sited in a terraced garden amid the corporate towers of Park Avenue, the Byzantine-inspired Saint Bartholomew's is an outstanding example of the work of Goodhue. The church is constructed of fine materials—salmon-colored brick highlighted with bands of limestone—and is ornamented with carvings, many of them representative of the life of Saint Bartholomew. The famous triple-arched entrance portal (1900–03), designed by Stanford White of the firm McKim, Mead & White for the congregation's previous home on Madison Avenue, was a memorial to Cornelius Vanderbilt II; Goodhue was required to incorporate this element into his design. The entrance, with its bronze doors and carved panels, the work of Daniel Chester French and Andrew O'Connor (central bay), Herbert Adams (north), and Philip Martiny (south), was modeled on the portal to the Provençal Romanesque church Saint Gilles-du-Gard near Arles, France. The community house, designed by Goodhue's successor firm after his death, is completely in harmony with the church.

337 General Electric Building, 570 Lexington Avenue (Cross & Cross, 1929–31), designated 1985. The Radio Victor Corporation of America (RCA) was a subsidiary of General Electric when it commissioned this Art Deco building as its headquarters. But when, in 1931, as part of an effort to gain corporate independence, the firm moved to Rockefeller Center, it deeded this building to General Electric. The octagonal brick tower, rising from a base with rounded corner, is one of the most expressive skyscrapers of its era. Especially noteworthy features are the complex brickwork and terra cotta in colors chosen to blend with the neighboring Saint Bartholomew's Church (see above) and the use of details symbolic of the building's tenant: the corner clock whose projecting arms grasp electric bolts; the spectral figures with boltlike bodies above the shop fronts; and the stylized figures at the building's crown, each with a halo of electric rays. In 1995, after the building was donated to Columbia University, an extensive restoration was completed by Ernest de Castro of the WCA Design Group.

338 **Seagram Building,** 375 Park Avenue (Ludwig Mies van der Rohe, with Philip Johnson and Kahn & Jacobs, 1955–58), designated 1989. The only building in New York designed by the modern master Mies van der Rohe, the Seagram Building is considered to be the greatest of the International

Style skyscrapers erected in the postwar era, when this style became a symbol of corporate America. Seagram's president, Samuel Bronfman, and his daughter, the architect Phyllis Lambert, selected Mies and gave him a virtually unlimited budget for the project. The juxtaposition of the extruded bronze frame with the rectangular bronze spandrel panels and transparent glass surfaces of the curtain wall creates the tight geometry and the contrast between solid and void that typify the finest International Style design. The tower rises behind a plaza with a pair of fountains. **Interior:** The fine materials and careful detailing of the exterior are evident in the lobby, designed by Philip Johnson, with its

Seagram Building (No. 338). The only building in New York designed by the master architect Mies van der Rohe, the Seagram Building is considered the greatest International Style skyscraper. Photo by Carl Forster.

travertine walls and floor, bronze mullions, and elevator cabs with stainless steel and bronze mesh panels. The broad stairs at the rear lead to the Four Seasons Restaurant (see below).

339 Four Seasons Restaurant (interior), 99 East 52nd Street (Philip Johnson, 1958–59), designated 1989. An integral part of Mies van der Rohe's Seagram Building (see above), the Four Seasons Restaurant has one of the most elegant International Style interiors in the United States. Planned as a first-class restaurant, the beautifully proportioned interior spaces display travertine, bronze, aluminum, wood, rawhide, and other materials, all of which have been installed with expert craftsmanship that accentuates their natural beauty. For this design Johnson collaborated with an interior designer, a lighting consultant, horticulturists, artists, and furniture and industrial designers to create a unified series of environments, including the long narrow lobby, the Grill Room, and the Pool Room.

340 Rockefeller Guest House, 242 East 52nd Street (Philip Johnson, in association with Landis Gore and Frederick C. Genz, 1949–50), designated 2000. Built without traditional ornament, the Rockefeller Guest House is one of the earliest buildings in New York to reflect the influence of the celebrated architect Mies van der Rohe. Just two stories tall, this brick, steel, and glass pavilion was commissioned by Blanchette Rockefeller, an important patron of the Museum of Modern Art, to display her art collection and entertain guests. Donated to the museum in 1955 and sold later, the house attracted many tenants associated with modern art, including the building's architect, who lived here from 1971 to 1979.

341 312 and 314 East 54th Street (attributed to Robert & James Cunningham, builders, 1866), designated 1968 and 2000. Once common but now exceptionally rare, this pair of matching frame row houses near Second Avenue has modest Italianate and Second Empire style details. Both buildings continue to be used as private residences.

342 Central Synagogue (Congregation Ahavath Chesed), 652 Lexington Avenue (Henry Fernbach, 1871–72), designated 1966. Central Synagogue is the oldest building in New York State in continuous use by a single Jewish congregation. The congrega-

tion was founded in 1846 on the Lower East Side by Jews from Bohemia. Following the city's population northward, the congregation purchased a corner site on Lexington Avenue at East 55th Street and commissioned the design of a new sanctuary from the Prussian-born Jewish architect Henry Fernbach. The masterful Moorish-inspired form reflects the heritage of Jews in Moorish Spain and was a response to the 19th-century debate on the appropriate style for synagogues. The earliest Moorish-inspired synagogues were in Germany, but beginning with the 1866 design for America's oldest Reformed congregation, Congregation B'nai Jeshurun in Cincinnati, Moorish temples were erected throughout the United States. The brownstone-faced Central Synagogue, with its banded arches and onion domes, is a masterpiece of the style. restoration. Following a major renovation, the synogogue was gutted by fire in 1998. Hardy Holzman Pfeiffer planned the current restoration.

343 Mary Hale Cunningham House, 124 East 55th Street (1880–81; new facade, Harrie T. Lindeberg, of Albro & Lindeberg, 1909), designated 2001. The electrification of the New York Central Railroad and the covering of the tracks made the blocks adjoining Park Avenue increasingly attractive to development. In 1907 Mary Hale Cunningham acquired a modest apartment building at the middle of the block and converted it to a private residence. The architects Albro & Lindeberg supervised the remodeling, fashioning a neo-Tudor facade with a monumental keyed enframement extending over the second and third stories. Since the 1930s this well-preserved town house has been leased to a succession of commercial tenants.

344 William and Helen Ziegler, Jr. House, 116–118 East 55th Street (William L. Bottomley, 1926–27), designated 2001. This unusually wide neo-Georgian residence was built for William and Helen Ziegler, Jr. The three-bay front is beautifully detailed, featuring Flemish bond brickwork with burnt leaders, paneled wood shutters, and a steeply pitched slate roof. Following Ziegler's death in 1958, the house was converted to offices.

345 Ritz Tower, 465 Park Avenue (Emery Roth, with Thomas Hastings, 1925–27), designated 2002. Located at the northeast corner of Park Avenue and 57th Street, the Ritz Tower was once the tallest residential building in New York. Thomas Hastings, the surviving member of the prominent architectural firm Carrère & Hastings, helped enrich the tan brick elevations, contributing a rusticated limestone base and the terra-cotta ornament that distinguishes the five setbacks. Financed by journalist Arthur Brisbane, the project was a great success and attracted such tenants as William Randolph Hearst, Greta Garbo, and Le Pavilion, one of America's most influential French restaurants.

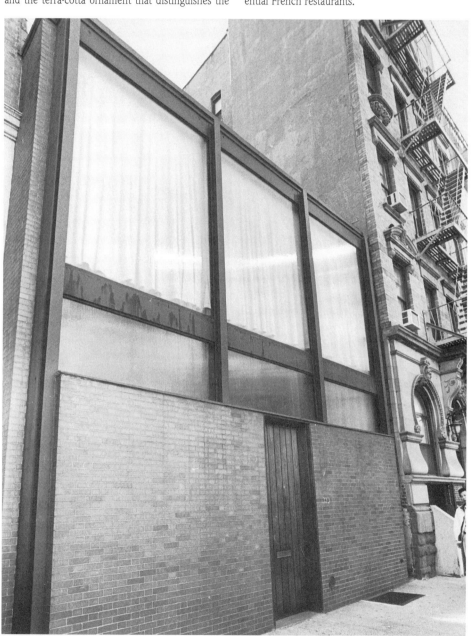

Completed in 1950, the Rockefeller Guest House (No. 340) is one of Philip Johnson's earliest works in New York. Photo by Carl Forster.

INDIVIDUAL LANDMARKS

346 **Time & Life Building (interior),** 1261–1267 Sixth Avenue (Harrison & Abramowitz & Harris, 1956–60), designated 2002. A joint venture of Rockefeller Center and Time Inc., this office building has one of the most distinctive public interiors in New York. Entered from 50th and 51st Streets, the lobby reveals a lively and eclectic decorative scheme, juxtaposing a gridded wall of stainless steel to serpentine terrazzo paving, as well as abstract works of art, including mural-size pieces by Fritz Glarner and Josef Albers.

347 **Winter Garden Theater (interior),** 1634–1646 Broadway (W. Albert Swasey, 1910–11; remodeling, Herbert J. Krapp, 1922–23), designated 1988. Built around 1885 as the American Horse Exchange, a stable and auction mart, this building was converted into a theater in 1910–11 for the Shuberts. The present seating arrangement and decor date largely from the remodeling of 1922–23. The enormous theater contains some of Krapp's finest Adamesque ornament. In its early years the Winter Garden attracted lavish revues; it premiered with *La Belle Paree,* which introduced Al Jolson. The revamped theater has attracted both revues, such as

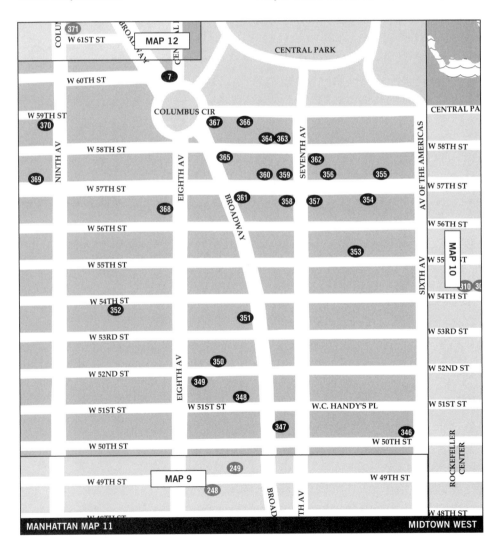

the *Ziegfeld Follies* of 1934, which starred Fanny Brice, and a series of musicals, including *Wonderful Town, West Side Story, Funny Girl, Mame, Pacific Overtures,* and *Cats,* the longest-running play in Broadway history.

348 Hollywood Theater, later the Mark Hellinger Theater, now Times Square Church, 217–239 West 51st Street (Thomas W. Lamb, 1929), designated 1988, interior 1987. The Hollywood, originally entered from Broadway (entry demolished), is the sole survivor of the great Broadway movie palaces. The exterior, with its combination of modernist elements (a massing derived from Frank Lloyd Wright's Unity Temple and a series of figures inspired by those on Eliel Saarinen's Helsinki Railroad Station), hides a lavish Baroque-inspired **interior** with rich gilded plaster surfaces, large mirrors, murals of nymphs and clouds, and ornate chandeliers. Run as a movie theater for only five years, the theater was converted into a legitimate house and renamed for a noted columnist and producer. The building was sold to the Times Square Church in 1991.

349 Alvin Theater, now the Neil Simon Theater, 244–254 West 52nd Street (Herbert J. Krapp, 1926–27), designated 1985. Built to house the musical comedies of the producers Alex Aarons and Vinton Freedley (whose names were merged in the theater's original name), the Alvin is one of the prolific theater architect Herbert J. Krapp's most impressive Adamesque designs. **Interior:** The lobbies and auditorium continue the use of the Adamesque detail seen on the exterior. The theater has housed an extraordinary number of hit productions since its debut with George and Ira Gershwin's *Funny Face,* including the Gershwins' *Girl Crazy* and *Porgy and Bess,* Ethel Merman in *Anything Goes,* Henry Fonda in *Mister Roberts,* Judy Holliday in *Bells Are Ringing,* and James Earl Jones in *The Great White Hope.*

350 Guild Theater, later the ANTA Theater, now the Virginia Theater, 243–259 West 52nd Street (Crane & Franzheim, 1924–25), designated 1985. The Theater Guild, an organization founded by members of the theater community for the express purpose of presenting high-quality plays, commissioned this building as a theater and a theatrical resource center. The facade design was inspired by 15th-century Tuscan villas. The guild produced a series of clas-

sical and modern plays (premiering Eugene O'Neill's *Mourning Becomes Electra* and *Ah, Wilderness!*) with all-star casts before it was forced to give up the theater in 1943. From 1950 to 1981, the American National Theater and Academy (ANTA) owned the theater; among its productions was the American premiere of *A Man for All Seasons.*

351 Hammerstein's Theater (interior), now the Ed Sullivan Theater, 1697–1699 Broadway (Herbert J. Krapp, 1927), designated 1988. The neo-Gothic style chosen for the vestibule, lobbies, and auditorium of the former Hammerstein's Theater is unique on Broadway. The theater was built by Arthur Hammerstein (see Queens No. 31) as a memorial to his father, Oscar Hammerstein I, and no expense was spared in making the interiors as imposing as possible. Unfortunately, the theater was never successful as a legitimate playhouse. It served for many years as a dance hall and then became a radio theater. In 1945 it was converted for use by television and housed *The Ed Sullivan Show,* the longest-running program in television history. Since 1993 it has been the location for *The Late Show with David Letterman,* following an extensive renovation and partial restoration of the theater.

352 Eleventh District Municipal Court/Seventh District Magistrates' Court, now the Midtown Community Court, 314 West 54th Street (John H. Duncan, 1894–96), designated 1989. This courthouse is an example of the imposing small-scale civic buildings erected throughout New York City in the late 19th century. For the limestone and brick structure, Duncan employed Renaissance forms ornamented with terra-cotta detail incorporating symbols of justice. After serving several other uses, the building was converted back into a courthouse in 1995.

353 Mecca Temple, now the City Center 55th Street Theater, 131 West 55th Street (H. P. Knowles, 1922–24), designated 1983. Famed since 1943 as the home of several of New York's major performing arts organizations, the City Center Theater was originally a temple for the Ancient Order of Nobles of the Mystic Shrine, better known as the Shriners. A Moorish-inspired design, the building is faced in sandstone blocks and is crowned by a huge tiled dome. The facade is enlivened by entrances featuring brightly colored terra cotta and glazed tile in an

Islamic design. The temple consists of a huge auditorium above a basement banquet room (now the Manhattan Theater Club) and a 12-story wing to the rear that originally housed lodge and club rooms (now offices). Mecca Temple was never a financial success, and in 1942 New York City foreclosed on the property. Mayor Fiorello La Guardia conceived of the idea of converting the hall into a cultural center that offered tickets at affordable prices. The City Center of Music and Drama was officially organized in 1943. City Center's constituents have included the New York City Ballet, the New York City Opera, the Joffrey Ballet, and the Alvin Ailey Dance Theater.

354 **130** and **140 West 57th Street Studio Buildings** (Pollard & Steinam, 1907–08), designated 1999. These buildings were constructed when 57th Street was the city's main cultural district. Pollard & Steinam, who specialized in apartment houses and studio buildings, gave the neo-Renaissance elevations projecting double-height bay windows to provide the north light prized by artists. The building at No. 130 attracted many notable residents, including William Dean Howells and Childe Hassam.

355 **Steinway Hall,** 109–113 West 57th Street (Warren & Wetmore, 1924–25), designated 2001. Founded in 1853, the world-famous Steinway Piano Company built this 16-story building in 1924–25. Inspired by ancient Greek sources, the limestone facade has a music-themed sculptural group at the base by Leo Lentelli and a 4-story tower ornamented with Ionic colonnades and urns. In addition to serving as the firm's headquarters, with showrooms, offices, and a recital hall, the building offered leased space to cultural organizations active in the immediate area. Sold to the Manhattan Life Insurance Company in 1958, it was reacquired by Steinway & Sons in 1999.

356 **Louis H. Chalif Normal School of Dancing,** 163–165 West 57th Street (G. A. & H. Boehm, 1916), designated 1999. Russian ballet master Louis H. Chalif built this school when many of the city's most important cultural institutions were located on West 57th Street. Five stories tall, the tan-gray brick and polychrome terra-cotta facade is decorated with motifs borrowed from Italian Renaissance and Mannerist sources, including masks, skulls, urns, and lyres. The

Chalif School relocated in 1933, and in subsequent years the building was owned by music publisher Carl Fisher and Columbia Artists Management.

357 **Carnegie Hall,** West 57th Street at Seventh Avenue (William B. Tuthill, 1889–91; office wing, William B. Tuthill, 1892–95; studio wing, Henry J. Hardenbergh, 1896–97), designated 1967. Carnegie Hall, one of America's greatest concert halls, was built by steel magnate Andrew Carnegie as part of his efforts toward "the improvement of mankind." Known originally as the Music Hall, the Carnegie Hall auditorium opened in 1891 with the American conducting debut of Tchaikovsky and since then has hosted many of the world's leading musicians. The building, faced in Roman brick and terra cotta and designed in an Italian Renaissance–inspired style, was originally crowned by a mansard roof; this roof was replaced by a full top floor early in the 1890s. The hall has two major additions: Tuthill's office tower on West 56th Street and Hardenbergh's studio tower on West 57th Street. Carnegie Hall was saved from demolition in 1960 when it was purchased by the city; it was refurbished in 1981–90 by James Stewart Polshek & Partners. An office tower, designed by Cesar Pelli & Associates and containing improved backstage facilities, was erected immediately to the east of the studio tower in 1986–90.

358 **Rodin Studios,** 200 West 57th Street (Cass Gilbert, 1916–17), designated 1988. Named for one of the most innovative artists living at the time, the Rodin was the latest of the series of buildings erected in Manhattan in the first years of the 20th century to provide combined studio and residential space for artists. The building contained double-height studios, most of them facing north onto West 57th Street, and duplex living units at the rear. The building has a reinforced concrete frame that is faced in polychromatic rough brick with extensive iron and terra-cotta trim in a French Gothic style that complements the American Fine Arts Society (see No. 360) across the street. Cass Gilbert had previously used this style on his Woolworth Building (see No. 57). The Rodin Studios now houses offices, and the duplex units have been subdivided.

359 **Osborne Apartments,** 205 West 57th Street (James E. Ware, 1883–85, enlargement of top story, 1889; addition to west, Alfred S. G. Taylor, 1906), designated 1991. The Osborne, an early luxury apartment building, is located in the area that by the mid-1880s was rapidly becoming the city's first center of apartment-house construction. Ware's robust Italian Renaissance–inspired building with medieval detail is clad in heavy, rock-faced blocks of red sandstone and features elegant carved ornamental panels. The building's plan—the Osborne contains duplex apartment units—is reflected in its elevations. There are twelve floors in the front and fourteen at the rear.

360 **American Fine Arts Society,** now the Art Students League, 215 West 57th Street (Henry J.

Hardenbergh, 1891–92), designated 1968. With its design adapted from a hunting lodge erected by Francis I in the forest of Fontainebleau in the early 16th century, this building is one of several New York City landmarks that reflect Hardenbergh's interest in Northern European architecture. The American Fine Arts Society was incorporated in 1889 by the New York Architectural League, the Society of American Artists, and the Art Students League to raise funds for a building that would contain offices, galleries, and studios for the three organizations. Each originally had space in the building; it is now used solely by the Art Students League.

Carnegie Hall (No. 357). One of America's greatest concert halls, Carnegie Hall was built by steel magnate Andrew Carnegie as part of his efforts toward "the improvement of mankind." Photo by Carl Forster.

ARTISTS' NEW YORK

New York has long been a magnet for visual artists. Their impact on the city's character is indisputable, where they worked and lived, and in the cultural institutions where their production is displayed. As the number of artists working here grew, so did the number of organizations to support and educate them, such as the Cooper Union, the New York School of Applied Design for Women, and the Art Students League (Manhattan Nos. 153, 223, and 360). After the opening of the League's impressive home on West 57th Street in 1892, many structures were built in Midtown that catered to artists, including two studio buildings named for artists—the Rodin and the Gainsborough (Manhattan Nos. 358 and 366). The latter building has especially beautiful tilework and is decorated with a bust of the painter and a relief depicting *A Festival Procession of the Arts*. These live-work spaces became increasingly popular after 1900, and a cluster of these cooperative buildings, frequently occupied by nonartists, stands along a single block—the 67th Street Cooperative Studio Building (1901–3) at 23–27 West 67th Street, the Central Park Studios (1904–5) at 11–15 West 67th Street, the Atelier Building (1904–5) at 29–33 West 67th Street, and the Hotel des Artistes (1915–18) at 1 West 67th Street (Manhattan H.D. 25) Another studio building of architectural distinction is the Bryant Park Studios of 1901, where Edward Steichen and Fernand Leger worked (Manhattan No. 276). Buildings used by artists as clubs have also been designated: the Irad Hawley House at 47 Fifth Avenue, home to the Salmagundi Club since 1917; the Samuel Tilden House, purchased in 1906 by the National Arts Club; and two structures built by the Century Association, 109–111 East 15th Street and 7 West 43rd Street (Manhattan Nos. 138, 217, 209, and 282).

In Greenwich Village, structures that exemplify the district's bohemian past include the Washington Memorial Arch, the Church of the Ascension, the Lockwood de Forest House, and the original home of the Whitney Museum of American Art on West 8th Street (Manhattan H.D. 12; H, L, K, J). Now the Studio School, the rear of the latter building faces McDougal Alley, a street of stables that was converted to mainly sculptor's studios after 1900 (Manhattan H.D. 12, I). Gertrude Vanderbilt Whitney, the museum's founder, had her workshop here, as did Daniel Chester French. The Commission also designated the 69th Regiment Armory, where the famed Armory Show of 1913 was held, and several structures associated with American photographers, such as Matthew Brady, who worked on the upper floors of 359 Broadway; Clarence H. White, who lived and ran a photography school at 122 East 17th Street; and Alice Austen, who for many years lived in a picturesque house overlooking the Narrows on Staten Island (Manhattan Nos. 221, 83, H.D. 18, and Staten Island No. 26).

Manhattan's Upper East Side has a great concentration of art-related landmarks. While some of these buildings were purpose-built, such as the Metropolitan Museum of Art and the Solomon R. Guggenheim Museum, others were originally private residences, most notably the Frick Collection, the Cooper-Hewitt Museum, the National Academy of Design at 1083 Fifth Avenue, and the Neue Galerie at 1048 Fifth Avenue (Manhattan Nos. 471, 472, 446, 477, H.D. 35 and 36). Following the Whitney Museum's move to 945 Madison Avenue in 1966, the blocks adjoining it attracted many art galleries, and in 1970 Alexander Calder was commissioned to create a black-and-white terrazzo sidewalk in front of Nos. 1014–1018 Madison Avenue (Manhattan H.D. 35). Recently restored, it is a unique work in the sculptor's oeuvre.

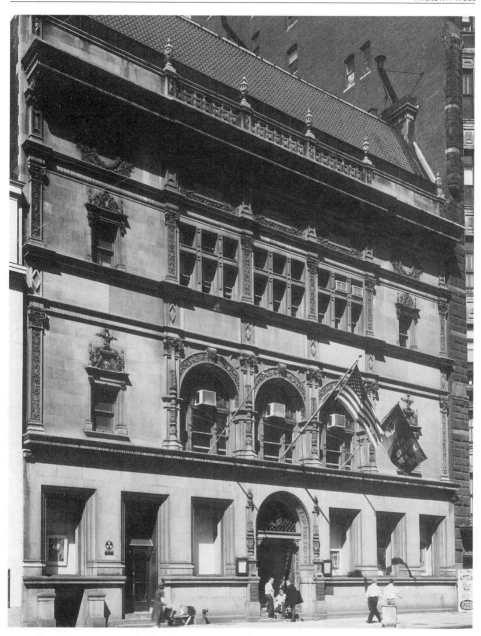

The American Fine Arts Society (No. 360) reflects architect Henry Hardenbergh's interest in Northern European architecture. Photo by John Barrington Bayley, c. 1965.

361 **A. T. Demarest & Company and Peerless Motor Car Company Buildings,** 224–228 West 57th Street (Francis H. Kimball, 1909), designated 2000. For more than six decades, these adjoining buildings have been associated with the automobile industry. Located on Broadway, in what was once the heart of Manhattan's automobile row, the architecturally harmonious structures were designed and built separately in 1909. Clad almost entirely in glazed terra cotta, they feature complementary neo-

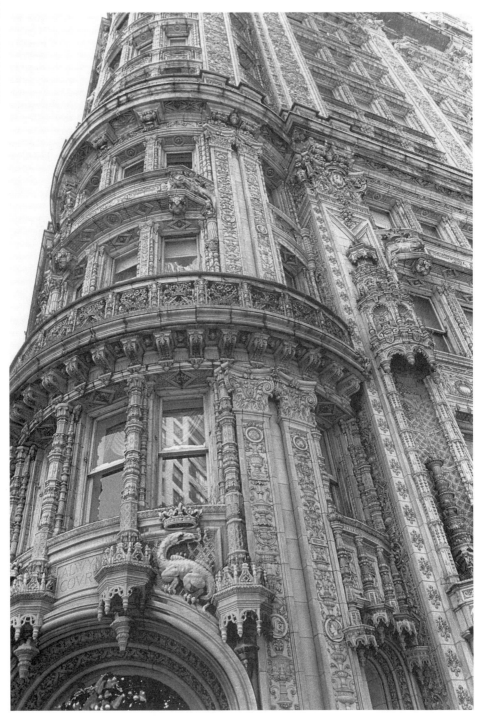

Alwyn Court Apartments (No. 362). A profusion of terra-cotta ornament decorates this early apartment house. Detail of corner bay. Photo by Carl Forster.

Gothic and Romanesque Revival details. The buildings were acquired by the General Motors Corporation in 1918 and used as offices until they were sold to the Hearst Corporation in 1977.

362 **Alwyn Court Apartments,** 182 West 58th Street (Harde & Short, 1907–09), designated 1966. Almost every inch of this apartment house is covered with terra-cotta ornament in the Francis I style. Located just south of Central Park, in an area that attracted a significant number of Manhattan's early apartment houses, Alwyn Court originally boasted expansive 14-room apartments (subdivided during the Depression), each with five baths. The facade was cleaned and restored in 1980–81.

363 **Helen Miller Gould Carriage House,** now the Unity Center of Practical Christianity, 213 West 58th Street (York & Sawyer, 1902–03), designated 1989. Although planned for a utilitarian function, this structure is a sophisticated example of early French Renaissance–inspired design, resembling a town house on the Place Vendôme in Paris. Built for the eldest daughter of the "robber baron" Jay Gould, the carriage house is an early work of York & Sawyer, an architecture firm best known for its banks.

364 **Fire Engine Company No. 23,** 215 West 58th Street (Alexander H. Stevens, 1905–06), designated 1968. Fire Engine Company No. 23 is a straightforward Beaux-Arts limestone and brick building that served as a model for other early 20th-century firehouses. The building is one of the first to have been designed by the fire department's superintendent of buildings rather than by an outside architect.

365 **United States Rubber Company Building,** 1790 Broadway (Carrère & Hastings, 1911–12), des-

This elegant office building (No. 365) is a rare skyscraper by the architects Carrère & Hastings. Photo by Carl Forster.

ignated 2000. Among the various automobile-related structures built along this section of Broadway in the early 20th century, this corner office building is notable for its height and Beaux Arts design. Carrère & Hastings designed few skyscrapers, and the powerful elevations display a strong vertical emphasis, with continuous stone piers to direct views toward a projecting copper cornice. The lowest floors were remodeled in 1959.

366 **Gainsborough Studios,** 222 Central Park South (Charles W. Buckham, 1907–08), designated 1988. The Gainsborough was planned as combined living and studio space for artists. The double-height windows facing Central Park provide north light to the studios; duplex apartments are located at the rear. The facade (restored in 1988) acknowledges the building's artist residents with its bust of Thomas Gainsborough, a frieze by Isidore Konti entitled *A Festival Procession of the Arts,* and an art tile mural produced at Henry Mercer's Moravian Tile Works.

367 **240 Central Park South Apartments** (Mayer & Whittlesey, 1939–40), designated 2002. The modern character of this distinguished apartment house is expressed through the absence of traditional ornament, the use of industrial materials, and a particularly innovative plan. Covering only half of an irregularly shaped lot, the complex consists of two buildings, a courtyard, and a series of rounded shop fronts along Broadway. Clad in orange brick, the apartments have steel casement windows and cantilevered balconies facing Central Park. One of the largest luxury apartment buildings of its day, it has an entrance court decorated with "The Quiet City," a mosaic by Amédée Ozenfant.

368 **Hearst Magazine Building,** 951–969 Eighth Avenue (Joseph Urban and George B. Post & Sons, 1927–28), designated 1988. Built as the headquarters of William Randolph Hearst's publishing empire, this building was designed by the Viennese-born and -educated architect Joseph Urban, a lead-

Gainsborough Studios (No. 366). The building's original artist residents are acknowledged in the bust of Thomas Gainsborough rising above the frieze A Festival Procession of the Arts. Photo by Carl Forster.

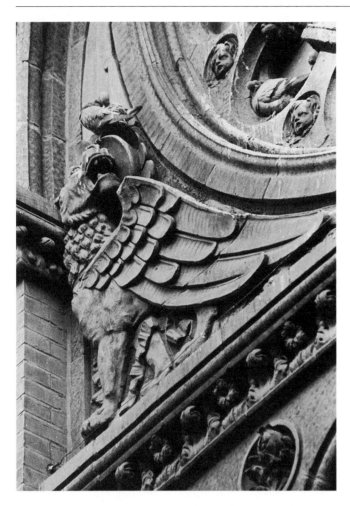

Winged lions, excecuted in terra cotta, frame the rose window of the Catholic Apostolic Church (No. 369). Photo by Carl Forster.

ing theater designer of the 20th century. The six-story building, faced in cast limestone, was planned as the base of a skyscraper. It combines Art Deco ornament, Viennese Secessionist forms, and baroque theatricality that exemplify Urban's architectural vision. Of special note are the paired sculptural figures representing comedy and tragedy, art and music, sport and industry, and printing and science.

369 Catholic Apostolic Church, now Church for All Nations, 417–419 West 57th Street (Francis H. Kimball, 1885–86), designated 2001. The Catholic Apostolic Church was one of Kimball's first independent commissions in New York. Designed in a style that contemporaries described as "scholarly Gothic," it was one of the earliest buildings in Manhattan to make extensive use of architectural terra

cotta. A large rose window, set into a pointed-arch surround, dominates the brick facade, flanked by reliefs of angels, winged lions, and evangelical beasts.

370 Roosevelt Hospital, William J. Syms Operating Theater, 400 West 59th Street (W. Wheeler Smith, 1890–92), designated 1989. W. Wheeler Smith worked in conjunction with the prominent surgeon Charles McBurney to create the most advanced operating theater in the world for Roosevelt Hospital. McBurney examined modern operating facilities throughout Europe and America before he accepted a final design. Although the building's interior has been altered, its distinctive exterior form (a rectangle with a semiconical roof) and utilitarian appearance continue to express its original function.

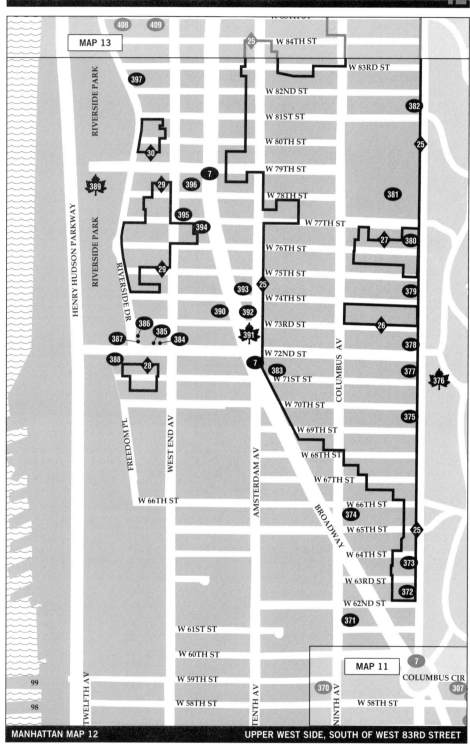

■ EAST OF COLUMBUS AVENUE

HISTORIC DISTRICTS

②⑤ Upper West Side/Central Park West Historic District, designated 1990. Extending westward from the western edge of Central Park, this large district evokes the distinctive qualities of the Upper West Side, from its powerful iconography of twin towers along Central Park West, to its active commerce along Columbus Avenue, to its residential side streets. The district is defined by a large concentration of architecturally distinctive buildings erected on the Upper West Side during the fifty years in which substantial development occurred in the neighborhood. The inauguration of the Ninth Avenue elevated railway in 1879 along what is now

Upper West Side/Central Park West Historic District streetscape (H.D. 25). The north side of West 78th Street between Amsterdam and Columbus Avenues. Photo by Caroline Kane Levy.

Columbus Avenue opened the vast unoccupied regions of the Upper West Side to speculative development, and hundreds of neo-Grec, Romanesque Revival, Queen Anne, and neo-Renaissance row houses were built on the side streets between Central Park West and Amsterdam Avenue, while tenements for the working class and French flats for middle-class households were constructed on or near Amsterdam and Columbus Avenues. A few grand apartment houses, such as the Dakota (see No. 378), were built in this early period, but most apartment-house construction in the district dates to the early years of the 20th century, when the neighborhood's great Beaux-Arts apartment buildings were erected, including the Prasada (Charles Romeyn, 1904–07), the Langham (Clinton & Russell, 1904–07), the Kenilworth (Townsend, Steinle & Haskell, 1906–08), and the Saint Urban (Robert T. Lyons, 1904–05). Beginning in 1902, West 67th Street was transformed into a unique enclave of apartment houses, most designed in a neo-Gothic mode with double-height studio spaces for artists. In the 1920s many large apartment houses and apartment hotels were built along Central Park West and other streets in the district, but most construction ceased with the advent of the Great Depression in 1929. During the entire span of development, important institutional buildings were also erected, including museums, churches, and synagogues, several of which are individual landmarks (see below).

②⑥ Central Park West–West 73rd–74th Streets Historic District, designated 1977. Now entirely subsumed within the Upper West Side/Central Park West Historic District (see above), this square block contains some of the finest residential design on the Upper West Side. The earliest buildings in the district are eighteen row houses on West 73rd Street, which survive from a row of twenty-eight designed by Henry J. Hardenbergh in 1882–85 for Edward S. Clark, president of the Singer [Sewing Machine] Manufacturing Co., in a style compatible with the nearby Dakota Apartments (see No. 378). Clark's grandson Frederick Ambrose Clark developed much of West 74th Street in 1902–04 with a long neo-Georgian row designed by Percy Griffin. The Clarks sold the Central Park West frontage in 1902, and Clinton & Russell's elegant Langham Apartments in the Beaux-Arts style was erected in 1904–07.

27 **Central Park West–76th Street Historic District,** designated 1973. This small historic district is now located entirely within the Upper West Side/Central Park West Historic District (H.D. 25). Row houses began to appear on West 76th Street in 1887; by 1900, forty-four of them had been built within the district. Central Park West retains examples of the three types of buildings erected on that avenue beginning in the 1890s: the Kenilworth (Townsend, Steinle & Haskell, 1906–08), a Beaux-Arts-style apartment house designed for upper-middle-class families; the neo-Gothic Church of the Divine Paternity (now Fourth Universalist Society; William A. Potter, 1897–98); and the New-York Historical Society (see No. 380), one of two major museums located along the park. The district also includes Harde & Short's Studio Building (1907–09) at 44 West 77th Street, an apartment house that contains two-story artists' studios with attached duplex residential units.

INDIVIDUAL LANDMARKS

371 **Kent Automatic Parking Garage,** later the Sofia Brothers Warehouse, now the Sofia Apartments, 33–43 West 61st Street (Jardine, Hill & Murdock, 1929–30), designated 1983. This flamboyant brick and polychrome terra-cotta Art Deco building was erected as a parking garage that employed a patented automatic parking system: an electrical "parking machine" engaged each car by its rear axle and towed it from an elevator to a parking spot. Unfortunately, the novel system failed. The building served as a more conventional garage until 1941, when it became the Sofia Brothers Warehouse. In 1983–84 the warehouse was converted into luxury apartments.

372 **Century Apartments,** 25 Central Park West (Irwin S. Chanin, 1931), designated 1985. The twin-towered Century, a sophisticated example of residential Art Deco design in New York, is a major element of Central Park West's distinctive skyline. Much of the Century's aesthetic interest lies in the successful manipulation of such features as brickwork, windows, bays, and balconies and the spare use of ornament to highlight entrances, setbacks, towers, and other elements.

373 **New York Society for Ethical Culture,** 2 West 64th Street (Robert D. Kohn, 1909–10), designated 1974. The Ethical Culture meetinghouse is among a small group of exceptional buildings designed by Robert D. Kohn in the Secessionist mode, a reform style that developed in Vienna. The austere geometry and abstract classicism of Viennese design are evident in this structure and in Kohn's New York Evening Post Building (see No. 55). For both buildings Kohn's wife, Estelle Rumbold Kohn, provided sculptural decoration.

374 **First Battery Armory,** later the 102nd Medical Battalion Armory, now television studios, 56 West 66th Street (Horgan & Slattery, 1900–03), designated 1989. The First Battery, founded in 1867, was a largely German-American volunteer unit of the National Guard. The unit was one of several in New York City that built medieval-inspired armories around 1900. This relatively small building has a lively facade, with turrets, crenellations, and other castlelike features, some functional and others merely decorative.

375 **Shearith Israel Synagogue** (the Spanish and Portuguese Synagogue), 99 Central Park West (Brunner & Tryon, 1896–97), designated 1974. As the Jewish population in the United States expanded, especially in the second half of the 19th century, debate arose over the appropriate style for synagogues. In the post–Civil War years, Moorish-inspired designs were popular. Late in the century, after archaeologists discovered the ruins of the Second Temple in Jerusalem, built during the Roman occupation of Palestine, this classical monument became the model for new synagogues. Congregation Shearith Israel is believed to have been the first to adopt this style when it erected its new home on Central Park West, and it influenced the design of hundreds of other synagogues nationwide. Shearith Israel, founded in 1654 by Sephardic Jews who arrived in New York from a Dutch colony in Brazil, is the oldest Jewish congregation in North America. This synagogue is the fourth erected by the congregation since it built its initial home in 1730.

376 **Central Park Scenic Landmark,** Fifth Avenue to Central Park West, 59th Street to 110th Street (Frederick Law Olmsted and Calvert Vaux, designed 1858), designated 1974. One of the great man-made monuments of the 19th century, Central Park was the first large-scale public park in the United States, and its success influenced park design all across the country. The design embodies 19th-century attitudes toward nature and the ideals of a democratic society. The park was planned as a naturalistic landscape in which urban dwellers of all backgrounds could mingle and find respite from the pressures of life. Olmsted and Vaux transformed what was in part a rugged, swampy area with scattered settlements (including Seneca Village, a small community of African-Americans and Irish immigrants) into a bucolic setting of meadows, lakes, and forests punctuated with modest buildings designed by Vaux. Four separate road and path systems wend through the park: pedestrian walkways, carriage drives, bridle paths, and transverse roads that carry crosstown traffic. These systems pass over and under one another by way of stone and cast-iron bridges of exceptional beauty. Among the major features of the park are the 33-acre Sheep Meadow; the 1,200-foot-long Mall, with its rows of American elms; Bethesda Terrace, with Jacob Wrey Mould's intricate carved representations of plants and birds native to New York in each season and a fountain by Vaux crowned by Emma Stebbins's sculpture *Angel of the Waters of Bethesda;* the heavily forested 30-acre Ramble; the formal Conservatory Garden; and such beautiful bodies of water as the Lake and Harlem Meer. Major restoration projects undertaken by the Parks Department and the Central Park Conservancy since the 1970s have returned much of Central Park to its original glory.

377 **Majestic Apartments,** 115 Central Park West (Irwin S. Chanin, 1930–31), designated 1988. The Majestic is one of the four great twin-towered

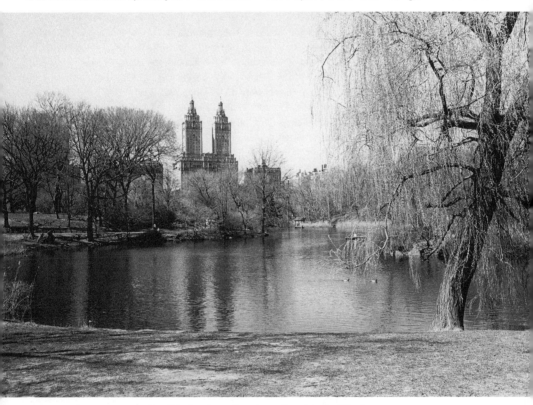

Central Park Scenic Landmark (No. 376). The first large-scale public park in the United States, Central Park influenced park design across the country. Also shown are the San Remo Apartments (No. 379). Photo by Carl Forster.

apartment buildings that define the Central Park West skyline. This Art Deco building is the earlier of Irwin Chanin's two Central Park West apartment houses and is somewhat simpler than the nearby Century (see No. 372). The towers are a response to a 1929 building regulation that limited the height of an apartment building's street wall but permitted tall towers on large plots.

378 Dakota Apartments, 1 West 72nd Street (Henry J. Hardenbergh, 1880–84), designated 1979. One of New York's best-known buildings, the Dakota was erected at a time when the Upper West Side was sparsely populated. The building was commissioned by Edward S. Clark, president of the Singer [Sewing Machine] Manufacturing Company and an active West Side developer. Hardenbergh's in-

NEW TO NEW YORK

Arguably the most important decisions made by the Commission concern proposed new buildings within historic districts and proposed additions to designated buildings. A variety of shifting ideological positions shape these decisions, including whether new construction should fit seamlessly into the historic streetscape so as to be indistinguishable from its neighbors or be recognizably new, a reflection of its time and culture. In undertaking these difficult reviews, the Commission must balance such criteria as the physical character of the designated property, the quality of the proposed design, and, if it is located in an historic district, the immediate context.

The Watchtower Bible & Tract Society's dormitory and library was one of the earliest new constructions within an historic district approved by the Commission. It is located at 119 Columbia Heights, a residential block in the Brooklyn Heights Historic District (Brooklyn H.D. 4). Completed in 1970, Ulrich Franzen's sensitive yet contemporary design respects the scale of the adjoining neo-Grec row houses without direct imitation. These nearby residences have also won the Commission's approval: 222 Columbia Heights (Alfredo De Vido, 1982), 54 Willow Street (Alfredo De Vido, 1987), and 6 Grace Court Alley (Joseph Stella, 1994). In the Greenwich Village Historic District (Manhattan H.D. 12), two buildings have followed a similarly contextual strategy. The first of these, designed by Hugh Hardy, replaced a Greek Revival row house that was severely damaged when a bomb ripped large holes through the street facade in 1970. Completed in 1979, the brick facade includes a double-height-angled window that recalls this tragic event while respecting the block's historic character. In 1986 the six-story Washington Court apartments were built on Sixth Avenue, between Waverly and Washington Place. Designed by James Stewart Polshek & Partners, the brick, limestone, and terra-cotta elevations complement the adjoining row houses. In an entirely different context, the Commission approved 353 Central Park West (Yorgancioglu Architects, 1992), a brick apartment house with cascading setbacks at the northwest corner of 95th Street in the Upper West Side/Central Park West Historic District (Manhattan H.D. 25).

In districts that have a less residential character, a broader range of solutions have been employed. In 1971 the Commission approved the relocation of a designated landmark from the Washington Market to the corner of Fulton Street and Beekman Place in the South Street Seaport Historic District (Manhattan H.D. 3). Following disassembly, the cast-iron building elements were stolen, and the new building (Beyer Blinder Belle, 1983) has arcaded metal facades that recall the earlier structure. Other new buildings in the district include the canopied Fulton Market Building (Benjamin Thompson & Associates, 1983) at 11 Fulton Street and the Seamen's Church Institute (1989-91) at 241 Water Street, an inventive collage of modern and traditional forms by the Polshek Partnership.

A significant group of buildings have been erected in SoHo (Manhattan H.D. 9) since designation in 1973, including 130 Prince Street (Lee Manners & Associates, 1988), Bar 89 at

terest in Northern European architecture is evident in the building's somewhat Germanic design, with its picturesque gables rising above Central Park. In plan, the Dakota has a central courtyard with an entrance in each corner. A cleaning and restoration of the facade in the 1990s revealed the cream-colored shade of the brick and the beautifully carved stone detailing.

379 San Remo Apartments, 145–146 Central Park West (Emery Roth, 1929–30), designated 1987. Soaring over Central Park, the San Remo is one of the most significant components of the Central Park West skyline. The building was designed by Emery Roth at the pinnacle of his career as a designer of apartment houses. The San Remo and the nearby Beresford (see No. 382) are examples of

89 Mercer Street (Ogawa/Depardon, 1995), and the neotraditional Scholastic Building at 557 Broadway. Designed by Aldo Rossi (with Gensler Associates) in 1997, the Scholastic Building's white, red, and terra-cotta colored facades feature a grid of monumental columns that harmonize with the adjoining loft buildings on Broadway and Mercer Street. Another interesting project was designed by Joseph Pell Lombardi. Completed in 2003, 101 Greene Street is an exact copy of its cast-iron neighbor. In the Ladies' Mile Historic District (Manhattan H.D. 16), the Caroline, a mixed-use project designed by Rick Cook & Associates, was completed in 2003. This building consists of two distinct masses, one aligned with the retail streetscape of Sixth Avenue and the other with a group of early-20th-century high-rises on West 23rd Street.

The Commission works closely with cultural institutions that seek to expand. In the case of the Jewish Museum, a 1962 entry pavilion was replaced by a larger and more sympathetic masonry wing. Designed by Kevin Roche and executed by masons trained at the workshop of St. John the Divine, the scale and stonework precisely match those of the adjoining Felix and Frieda S. Warburg mansion (Manhattan No. 482). Across Central Park, at the American Museum of Natural History (Manhattan No. 381), an entirely different strategy was pursued by the Polshek Partnership, one using modern materials and forms. Completed in 2000, the much acclaimed Rose Center for Earth and Space consists of a shimmering cube of transparent structural glass that encloses the planetarium and galleries on West 81st Street, as well as the adjacent Arthur Ross Terrace. The Polshek Partnership was also responsible for the Brooklyn Museum of Art's new entrance pavilion and plaza (Brooklyn No. 75). At present the Pierpont Morgan Library is undergoing a major expansion designed by Renzo Piano. Threaded neatly between two designated properties (Manhattan Nos. 269 and 270), the project includes a new public entrance on Madison Avenue and an enclosed courtyard, as well as a reading room, auditorium, and galleries.

Several major skyscrapers have been built with the Commission's approval. The first of these, the former Helmsley Palace, is located at the rear of the Villard Houses (Manhattan No. 295). Completed in 1980, the hotel's dark metal and tinted glass facade was designed to function as a "quiet background" to this famous brownstone ensemble. Other examples include Carnegie Hall Tower (Cesar Pelli & Associates, 1986–90) linked to Carnegie Hall and clad with complementary brickwork; and 712 Fifth Avenue (Kohn, Pedersen & Fox, with Beyer Blinder Belle, 1989–91), a marble and limestone office building set 50 feet behind two landmark structures, including the Coty Building, which preserves and highlights a grid of etched glass by René Lalique (Manhattan Nos. 313, 314, and 357). The Hearst Headquarters, designed by Foster & Partners, is currently under construction. A 42-story glass and metal tower was approved as an addition to the 6-story Hearst Magazine Building (Manhattan No. 368), an Art Deco structure that was originally conceived as the base for an office building that was never realized.

Roth's sophisticated adaptation of Italian Renaissance forms to high-rise residential design.

380 **New-York Historical Society,** 170 Central Park West (York & Sawyer, 1903–08; wings, Walker & Gillette, 1937–38), designated 1966. This museum and research facility, designed in a severe Classical Revival style, was built to house a rich repository of artwork and historical material relating primarily to the history of New York City and New York State and collected since the organization of the society in 1804. The granite-faced central pavilion with its Ionic colonnade is complemented by end wings added several decades after the main building was erected.

381 **American Museum of Natural History,** Central Park West at West 77th Street (Vaux & Mould, 1874–77; south and part of west elevation, Cady, Berg & See, 1888–1908; east wing, Trowbridge & Livingston, 1912–34; Theodore Roosevelt Memorial Hall, John Russell Pope, 1931–34; library, Kevin Roche John Dinkeloo Associates, 1990–92), designated 1967, interior 1975. Five years after the museum's incorporation in 1869, construction began on a spacious site known as Manhattan Square with Vaux & Mould's High Victorian Gothic building, now barely visible in a court at the west side of the site. In 1888 Cady, Berg & See prepared a master plan for the institution that envisioned a monumental Romanesque Revival complex to be constructed of pink granite; only the south front and a portion of the west front (undertaken by the architect Charles Volz) were completed. In 1912 Trowbridge & Livingston began planning a series of Classical Revival pavilions; only the east wing was erected. John Russell Pope's Theodore Roosevelt Memorial Hall, now the museum's main entrance, is in the form of a massive triumphal arch. The acclaimed Rose Center for Earth and Space (Polshek Partnhsip), as well as the Arthur Ross Terrace and a new entrance on Columbus Avenue, were completed in 2000. The **interior** of Memorial Hall is among New York's great monumental spaces, with a barrel-vaulted ceiling, giant Corinthian columns, and rich marble walls and floors, all reminiscent of the grandeur of ancient Rome. The room, reopened in 1991 following a restoration by the Roche firm, contains a series of murals by William A. Mackay that depict events in Roosevelt's life.

382 **Beresford Apartments,** 211 Central Park West (Emery Roth, 1928–29), designated 1987. The Italian Renaissance–inspired Beresford, with its three prominent octagonal towers, is one of the masterpieces of the famed apartment-house designer Emery Roth. The building is among the most prominent elements of Central Park West's distinctive skyline.

■ **WEST OF COLUMBUS AVENUE**

HISTORIC DISTRICTS

28 **West 71st Street Historic District,** designated 1989. This small, nearly block-long district on a quiet cul-de-sac ends in a wall that separated the street from the railroad tracks to the west. The district consists of thirty-three row houses, erected in six groups over only a three-year period (1893 to 1896), a single town house of 1903–04, and an apartment building erected in 1924. The block's cohesive quality results from the consistent use of Renaissance-inspired detail on all the masonry row houses.

29 **West End–Collegiate Historic District,** designated 1984. Named for the nearby West End Collegiate Church (see No. 395), this historic district consists primarily of row houses that developers built on speculation in the last fifteen years of the 19th century. Many of the city's most talented architects specializing in row-house design—including C. P. H. Gilbert, Lamb & Rich, and Clarence True—were active in the district, creating blockfronts with an eclectic blend of Italian, French, and Flemish Renaissance stylistic forms, among others. Lamb & Rich's 1891 blockfront in the Francis I style on the west side of West End Avenue between West 76th and West 77th Streets is among the most beautiful on the Upper West Side. In the first decades of the 20th century, several apartment houses were built in the district, reflecting the decline in row-house construction as land values rose and as the apartment house became an increasingly acceptable residential alternative for affluent New Yorkers. Jazz great Miles Davis lived at 312 West 77th Street for many years.

30 **Riverside Drive–West 80th–81st Street Historic District,** designated 1985. This small historic district illustrates, in microcosm, the early residential development of the West End section of New York's Upper West Side. Development began on West 81st Street in 1892, with the construction of a row of five transitional Romanesque Revival/neo-Renaissance row houses designed by Charles Israels (Nos. 308–314). Two years later Israels designed an additional row on West 80th Street (Nos. 307–317). Another wave of row-house construction occurred in 1897–99, when the architect/developer Clarence True built the houses on and adjacent to Riverside Drive. These large brick and stone row houses are characteristic of True's Northern European–inspired designs. Contemporaneous with the row houses are three modest French flats erected on West 80th Street for middle-class families. In 1926 one of True's houses was demolished and replaced by a 16-story neoclassical apartment building designed by Maurice Deutsch.

INDIVIDUAL LANDMARKS

383 **Dorilton Apartments,** 171 West 71st Street (Janes & Leo, 1900–02), designated 1974. Perhaps the most flamboyant apartment house in New York, the Dorilton is an enormous Beaux-Arts pile with striking French-inspired sculptural decoration and an iron gate reminiscent of those that guard French palaces. The Dorilton was erected to cater to the prosperous upper-middle-class families who were moving into apartment houses on the Upper West Side in increasing numbers in the early years of the 20th century.

384 **309 West 72nd Street House,** also known as the William E. Diller House (Gilbert A. Schellenger, 1899–1901), designated 1991. William E. Diller, a physician and an active builder of single-family houses, erected this impressive Renaissance Revival town house as a speculative venture (he never lived here). Built on a site with restrictive covenants that required high-quality construction, the house complements the neighboring residences commissioned by the Kleeberg, Prentiss, and Sutphen families (see below).

385 **John and Mary Sutphen House,** 311 West 72nd Street (C. P. H. Gilbert, 1901–02), designated 1991. The Sutphen House and the neighboring Kleeberg and Prentiss Houses (see below) are all French-

inspired limestone-fronted dwellings built on oddly shaped lots in accordance with restrictive covenants that required the construction of high-quality residences. These restrictions were inaugurated by John Sutphen's father, who once owned the entire Riverside Drive frontage between West 72nd and West 73rd Streets.

386 **Frederick and Lydia Prentiss House,** 1 Riverside Drive (C. P. H. Gilbert, 1899–1901), designated 1991. One of a group of extraordinary town houses at the southernmost end of Riverside Drive designed by the prolific architect C. P. H. Gilbert, this limestone-fronted Beaux-Arts structure is set on a curved lot and has two visible facades, one of which fronts a triangular court shared with the neighboring Sutphen House (see above).

387 **Philip and Maria Kleeberg House,** 3 Riverside Drive (C. P. H. Gilbert, 1896–98), designated 1991. The Kleebergs' elegant town house, designed in the French Renaissance style, is one of four landmark residences located at the gateway to Riverside Drive. Gilbert's design for this limestone-fronted house takes full advantage of its wide curving lot, incorporating a recessed bay above the entrance, a large projecting bay, and a fourth-story loggia.

388 **Chatsworth Apartments and Annex,** 340 and 344 West 72nd Street (John E. Scharsmith, 1902–04 and 1905–06), designated 1984. Prominently sited at the southern end of Riverside Park and Drive, the Beaux-Arts Chatsworth and its annex were built to house the affluent families moving into Upper West Side apartment houses in the early 20th century. The Chatsworth originally offered such amenities as a conservatory, a sun parlor, a café, a billiards room, a barber shop, a beauty salon, and electric bus service along West 72nd Street to and from Central Park.

389 **Riverside Park and Riverside Drive Scenic Landmark,** West 72nd Street to St. Clair Place (Frederick Law Olmsted, design, 1873–75; initial construction, 1875–80; additions, Clifton Lloyd, 1934–37), designated 1980. Riverside Park was initially established in 1865 as a way of increasing real-estate values on the Upper West Side. Riverside Drive was laid out as a separate entity in 1870. Three years later the city's Parks Department asked Olmsted, one of the landscape architects of Central Park (see No. 376) and Prospect Park (see Brooklyn No. 79), to draw up a formal plan for the park and drive. It was Olmsted's idea to treat the two as a single design that would take advantage of the natural beauty of the site. The curving drive was landscaped with trees, walkways, and viewing sites, and the hillside leading down toward the New York Central's railroad tracks and the Hudson River was planted. The wide, straight walkway within the park (located on top of the railroad tracks) and the paths and playgrounds alongside the river were not part of Olmsted's design but were laid out by Clifton Lloyd at the time of the construction of the Henry Hudson Parkway, during Robert Moses's tenure as Parks Commissioner. Since the late 19th century, Riverside Drive has acquired some of New York's finest monuments. The most prominent of these are Grant's Tomb (see No. 531) and the Soldiers' and Sailors' Monument (see No. 416). On a more modest scale are such important works of public sculpture as Anna Hyatt Huntington's *Joan of Arc* (base by John V. Van Pelt) at West 93rd Street, Karl Bitter's *Franz Sigel* (base by William Welles Bosworth) at West 106th Street, and the Firemen's Memorial by Attilio Piccirilli (sculptor) and H. Van Buren Magonigle (architect) at West 100th Street.

390 **Ansonia Hotel,** 2101–2119 Broadway (Paul E. M. DuBoy, 1899–1904), designated 1972. The largest and most exuberant of the multiple dwellings in the Beaux-Arts style erected on the Upper West Side, the Ansonia was built as an apartment hotel by W. E. D. Stokes, a major developer in the area. Stokes advocated all-masonry fireproof construction, including soundproof partitions between floors and apartments, a feature that has attracted many distinguished musicians, singers, and conductors.

391 **Verdi Square Scenic Landmark,** Broadway and Amsterdam Avenue at West 72nd Street, designated 1975. This small triangular park is dominated by a statue of Giuseppe Verdi, commissioned by New York's Italian community from the Sicilian sculptor Pasquale Civiletti and unveiled in 1906.

The granite pedestal is encircled by figures representing characters from four of Verdi's operas. The statuary was restored in 1996–97.

392 **Central Savings Bank,** now the Apple Bank for Savings, 2100–2108 Broadway (York & Sawyer, 1926–28), designated 1990. York & Sawyer, the leading architect of banks in New York City in the 1920s, was responsible for several banks in the Italian Renaissance palazzo style. The freestanding Central Savings Bank is the grandest of these, with its massive rusticated limestone facades and magnificent exterior ironwork crafted by Samuel Yellin of Philadelphia. Like York & Sawyer's earlier Brooklyn Trust Company Building (see Brooklyn No. 20), this building is modeled after the work of the 16th-century Veronese architect Michele Sanmicheli. The **interior** banking hall is among the grandest and most ornate in New York City, with its huge gilded and coffered barrel-vaulted ceiling, marble floor laid in a geometric pattern, rusticated sandstone walls, and marble teller's counter capped by intricate iron screens created by master ironworker Yellin.

393 **Beacon Theater (interior),** 2124 Broadway (Walter W. Ahlschlager, 1927–28), designated 1979. The lavishly appointed lobbies, stairways, and auditorium of the Beacon, with their eclectic Greek, Roman, Renaissance, and rococo detail, are characteristic of the great movie palaces built in the 1920s. The Beacon, one of the last surviving movie palaces in New York City, is now used primarily for concerts.

394 **Belleclaire Hotel,** 2171–2179 Broadway (Emery Roth of the firm Stein, Cohen & Roth, 1901–03), designated 1987. The earliest known design by Roth, the Belleclaire is one of the fine apartment hotels erected on the Upper West Side at the start of the 20th century. The design is unusual in its use of ornamental motifs inspired by contemporary Secessionist architecture in Central Europe in combination with more traditional French Beaux-Arts motifs. The facades contain fine carved detail and complex window sash.

Ansonia Hotel (No. 390). The soundproof construction of this grand apartment hotel has made it popular with musicians, singers, and conductors. Photo by Caroline Kane Levy.

395 **West End Collegiate Church and Collegiate School,** West End Avenue at West 77th Street (Robert W. Gibson, 1892–93), designated 1967. The West End Collegiate Church traces its roots back to the organization of the first church in New Amsterdam in 1628. Appropriately, when the church was built on the Upper West Side, a style evocative of Dutch Renaissance architecture was chosen. The massing and the use of stepped gables, strapwork ornament, and finials are reminiscent of the design of the early 17th-century Butcher's Market in Haarlem, the Netherlands. The school building, erected to house the oldest private secondary school in America, founded in 1638, was built as a part of the church complex; the Collegiate School is now an independent institution.

396 **Apthorp Apartments,** 2201–2219 Broadway (Clinton & Russell, 1906–08), designated 1969. The Astor estate commissioned this monumental apartment house, which covers an entire square block of the Upper West Side. Clinton & Russell's adaptation of an Italian Renaissance palazzo includes a large, landscaped central courtyard separated from the street by handsome iron gates.

397 **103, 104, 105, and 107–109 Riverside Drive and 332 West 83rd Street** (Clarence True, 1898–99), designated 1991. The architect/developer Clarence True erected these five houses as part of a row of six (No. 102 has been demolished), using his signature Elizabethan Revival mode of design, which combined English and French Renaissance forms; the idiosyncratic style is unique to True's residential work on the Upper West Side. The facades of Nos. 103 and 104 were redesigned by Clinton & Russell and rebuilt in 1910–11 in a manner that recalled the original, after a lawsuit brought by a neighboring property owner forced the removal of the original stoops and bow fronts, which encroached on the public way. The facades of Nos. 105 and 107–109 were redesigned by Bosworth & Holden and Tracy, Swartwout & Litchfield, respectively, and rebuilt in the same years. Because No. 332 was around the corner on West 83rd Street, its facade did not have to be rebuilt.

West End Collegiate Church and Collegiate School (No. 395). The design of the school building is evocative of Dutch Renaissance architecture. Photo by Carl Forster.

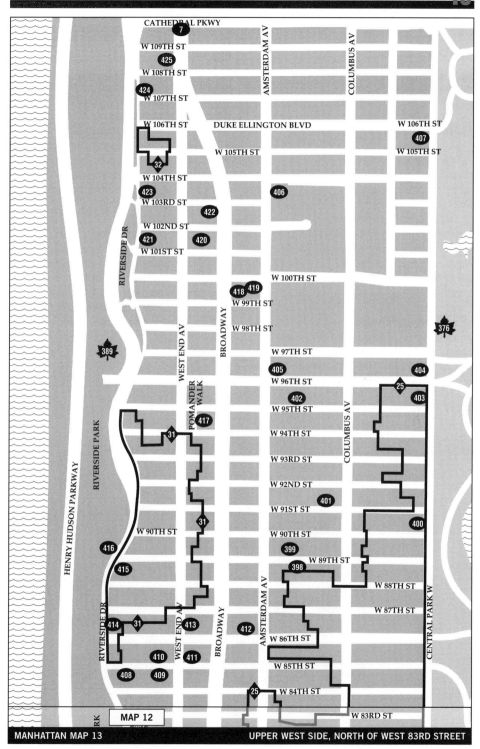

MANHATTAN

■ EAST OF AMSTERDAM AVENUE

HISTORIC DISTRICT

Upper West Side/Central Park West Historic District. See Map 12.

INDIVIDUAL LANDMARKS

398 **Public School 166,** 132 West 89th Street (C. B. J. Synder, 1897–99), designated 2000. One of the oldest extant public schools on the Upper West Side, this building served as the prototype for five schools in Manhattan and the Bronx. C. B. J. Snyder, superintendent of school buildings during 1891–1923, frequently employed the Collegiate Gothic style in his designs due to its long-standing association with higher education. Richard Rogers, Jonas Salk, and J. D. Salinger were students here.

399 **Claremont Stables,** now the Claremont Riding Academy, 175 West 89th Street (Frank A. Rooke, 1892), designated 1990. Designed in the Romanesque Revival style, the Claremont is the oldest functioning commercial stable in Manhattan.

The building was erected as a livery stable for the rental of horses and carriages.

400 **Eldorado Apartments,** 300 Central Park West (Margon & Holder, with Emery Roth, 1929–31), designated 1985. The Art Deco Eldorado is the northernmost of the four great twin-towered apartment buildings that line Central Park West. It is believed that Margon & Holder designed the Art Deco detailing but that Emery Roth, one of the leading apartment-house designers of the period, was responsible for the plan and the massing, which closely resemble Roth's contemporary work on the San Remo Apartments (see No. 379).

401 **Trinity School** (including the former Saint Agnes Parish House), 121–147 West 91st Street (school, Charles C. Haight, 1893–94; parish house, William A. Potter, 1888–92), designated 1989. Trinity School, established in 1709, followed New York's population north and settled on the Upper West Side in 1894. Haight designed an English Collegiate Gothic structure not unlike his contemporary work at Yale University. The building incorporates large windows that maximize natural light and air circulation. Adjacent to the school is the Ro-

Trinity School (No. 401). The large windows were designed to maximize natural light and air circulation. Photo by Carl Forster.

manesque Revival granite-and-red-sandstone parish house originally built for use by Trinity Church's Saint Agnes Chapel. When the church was demolished in 1944, the parish house was converted into classrooms.

402 **Charles A. Vissani House,** 143 West 95th Street (James W. Cole, 1889), designated 1991. Appropriately, this Gothic Revival town house was commissioned by the Very Reverend Charles A. Vissani, the first Commissary General of the Holy Land for the United States. It housed not only Vissani but also a group of Franciscan priests who worked with him in his mission to develop interest in the preservation of the holy places in Jerusalem and Palestine. The building is now divided into apartments.

403 **354 and 355 Central Park West** (Gilbert A. Schellenger, 1892–93), designated 1987. These two survivors from a row of five neo-Renaissance dwellings are rare examples of row houses built on Central Park West.

404 **First Church of Christ, Scientist,** 1 West 96th Street (Carrère & Hastings, 1899–1903), designated 1974. New York City's oldest Christian Science congregation erected this magnificent church, which is built entirely of Concord granite. The building was designed by Carrère & Hastings shortly after the firm won the competition for the New York Public Library (see No. 278). The church displays a rare combination of English Baroque massing (not unlike the churches of Nicholas Hawksmoor) and French Beaux-Arts detail.

405 **East River Savings Bank,** 743 Amsterdam Avenue (Walker & Gillette, 1926–27, enlarged 1931–32), designated 1998. Constructed in two phases, this neoclassical structure was built as the first branch of the East River Savings Bank. A giant Ionic colonnade supports a massive entablature, giving the building a monumental street presence. The 1931–32 addition doubled the number of bays facing Amsterdam Avenue while maintaining the original materials and classical vocabulary.

406 **Association Residence for Respectable Aged Indigent Females,** now a branch of Hostelling International–USA, 891 Amsterdam Avenue (Richard Morris Hunt, 1881–83; addition, Charles A. Rich, 1907–08), designated 1983. The Association for the Relief of Respectable Aged Indi-

Association Residence for Respectable Aged Indigent Females (No. 406). One of Richard Morris Hunt's few surviving buildings in New York City has been converted into a hostel. Photo by Carl Forster.

gent Females, one of New York City's first charitable institutions, was chartered in 1814 to aid those who were left poor widows by the Revolutionary War and the War of 1812. As the number of needy clients increased, a large new home was needed; in 1881 the Amsterdam Avenue blockfront between West 103rd and 104th Streets was purchased. This building is among the few extant structures in New York City designed by Richard Morris Hunt; it is also a rare example of 19th-century institutional architecture that has been successfully adapted to a new use. The design of the Gothic-inspired brick-and-stone building clearly reflects Hunt's knowledge of contemporary French architecture. The conversion to New York's first youth hostel was completed in 1990.

407 **New York Cancer Hospital,** later the Towers Nursing Home, 455 Central Park West and 32 West 106th Street (Charles C. Haight, 1884–86, and additions, 1889–90), designated 1976. Founded in 1884, the former New York Cancer Hospital was the first institution in the United States (and the second in the world, after the London Cancer Hospital) dedicated to the study and treatment of cancer. Haight's design was inspired by Le Lude, one of the great Renaissance châteaus of the Loire Valley. The five massive round towers were planned to provide a maximum amount of light and air to the wards and to facilitate nursing supervision from the center of each ward; it was also thought that the shape prevented air stagnation and the accumulation of dirt and germs in corners.

■ WEST OF AMSTERDAM AVENUE

HISTORIC DISTRICTS

61 **Riverside Drive–West End Historic District,** designated 1989. The West End section, the portion of the Upper West Side located west of Broadway, developed somewhat later than the area near Central Park, which was served by the elevated trains running along Columbus Avenue. Although the earliest buildings in the district are the row houses at 267–271 West 88th Street (Nelson M. Whipple, 1884), development did not begin in earnest until three years later. Between 1887 and 1897, row houses were built on speculation along the length of West End Avenue and adjacent side

streets. Notable examples include the neo-Renaissance rows with gold or beige brick and terra-cotta detail designed by Thom & Wilson, C. P. H. Gilbert, and Ralph Townsend in 1893–95 on West 88th and West 89th Streets, and several groups designed between 1890 and 1901 by Clarence True on West End Avenue at West 90th and West 92nd Streets and on West 88th through West 92nd Streets between West End Avenue and Riverside Drive, mostly in his favorite Elizabethan Revival style. The two blockfronts of row houses on West End Avenue between 90th and 91st Streets illustrate the low scale and architectural quality of this avenue prior to its reconstruction as a street of apartment buildings. Most of the multiple dwellings that replaced the West End Avenue row houses in the early decades of the 20th century were the work of specialists in apartment-house design and planning. Among the finest apartment houses are Schwartz & Gross's Chautauqua (1911–12) at No. 574, with its Sullivanesque ornament; George & Edward Blum's Evanston (1910) at No. 610, with its unusual terra-cotta and iron detail; Neville & Bagge's neo-Renaissance building at No. 590 (1915), with its beautiful ocher-colored terra-cotta ornament; and Emery Roth's No. 580 (1926–27), ornamented with the bold High Renaissance features that this architect favored on his large buildings of the 1920s. In the early 20th century, Riverside Drive also became a prime location for elegant apartment houses, such as the Clarendon (Charles Birge, 1906–07) at No. 137–139. Many of the apartment houses erected on Riverside Drive during its peak period of development in the 1920s follow the curve of the drive: No. 160 (Gaetan Ajello, 1922) has a convex front, while the facade of the block-long building at No. 171–177, between West 89th and West 90th Streets (J. E. R. Carpenter, 1925–26), is concave. The extraordinary Normandy is located on Riverside Drive between West 86th and West 87th Streets (see No. 414). There are two important religious structures in the district. The Gothic Revival Fourth Presbyterian Church (now Annunciation Greek Orthodox Church) on West End Avenue and West 91st Street (Heins & La Farge, 1893–94) served the area's first residents, who were predominantly Protestant. Congregation B'nai Jeshuran (Schneider & Herts, 1917–18) on West 88th Street was built for the increasing number of Jewish residents in the neighborhood; its impressive facade with austere granite walls and a great arched entrance was a prototype for the "Semitic" synagogue designs that became popular in the 1920s.

32 Riverside Drive–West 105th Street Historic District, designated 1978. This small district built on the gentle slope leading to Riverside Drive consists of residences erected in 1899–1902. The cohesive quality of the district's row houses and town houses is the result of five factors: the brief construction span; the use of English basements with entries at or near the sidewalk level; the use of similar materials, mainly limestone, to create a unified streetscape; the exuberant Beaux-Arts detail chosen by all four architecture firms active in the district (Janes & Leo, Mowbray & Uffinger, Hoppin & Koen, and Robert D. Kohn); and the covenants that required buildings of "suitable character and such as are a benefit to the neighborhood."

INDIVIDUAL LANDMARKS

408 Red House, 350 West 85th Street (Harde & Short, 1903–04), designated 1982. With its combination of French Gothic and Renaissance elements, the Red House recalls early 16th-century residences in the style of Francis I. This red brick and white terra-cotta building is the first of the four major French Gothic–inspired apartment houses designed by Harde & Short (see Nos. 302, 434, and H.D. 27, map 12) and is a reflection of the changing character of the Upper West Side in the early years of the 20th century, when apartment houses began to supplant row houses as the dominant type of residence.

409 316, 318, 320, 322, 324, and 326 West 85th Street (Clarence True, 1892), designated 1991. This row of six brick houses trimmed with Maynard red sandstone is among the most unusual designed by Clarence True. The houses were commissioned by Charles Judson, with whom True shared a business address. The well-preserved row is of note for the Spanish tile used on the rectangular oriels and projecting false roofs and for its brickwork laid in a rusticated manner to echo the rusticated stonework on the entrance level.

410 329, 331, 333, 335, and 337 West 85th Street (Ralph S. Townsend, 1890–91), designated

1991. Townsend's row of five Queen Anne/Romanesque Revival brick-and-brownstone houses was erected in the decade when much of the Upper West Side west of Broadway was emerging as a desirable residential neighborhood.

411 John B. and Isabella Leech House, 520 West End Avenue (Clarence True, 1892), designated 1988. The Leech residence is an unusual work by the prolific West Side architect/developer Clarence True. The corner house combines Romanesque, Gothic, and Elizabethan forms and is enlivened by superb carved detail. Built for a wealthy cotton broker, the house is a rare example of an individually designed single-family town house on West End Avenue.

412 Belnord Apartments, 201–225 West 86th Street (Hiss & Weekes, 1908–09), designated 1966. Built at a time when apartment houses were becoming the most popular type of residence on the Upper West Side, the Belnord, designed in the Italian Renaissance style, is an enormous building, encompassing an entire city block. The three main entrance arches on West 86th Street, with their sgraffito decoration, lead to a large landscaped courtyard.

413 Saint Paul's Methodist Episcopal Church and Parish House, now the Church of Saint Paul and Saint Andrew (United Methodist), 540 West End Avenue (R. H. Robertson, 1895–97), designated 1981. The design of Saint Paul's Methodist Episcopal Church and the parish house adjoining the church on West 86th Street reflects a major shift from the picturesque Romanesque Revival to a style dominated by Classical and Renaissance-inspired forms. With its bold octagonal campanile, tiled buttresses, and singular terra-cotta detail, Saint Paul's exemplifies the eclecticism of the 1890s in its successful combination of elements from many sources, including Early Christian, early Italian Renaissance, Spanish Renaissance, and German Romanesque architecture.

414 Normandy Apartments, 140 Riverside Drive (Emery Roth & Sons, 1938–39), designated 1985. The Normandy is a masterpiece of the apartment-house specialist Emery Roth. Overlooking the Hudson River, this twin-towered building is the last of Roth's major prewar apartment houses. The building combines the Italian Renaissance forms that Roth had perfected at the Beresford (see No. 382) and the San Remo (see No. 379) on Central Park West with new Moderne features such as streamlined corners and concave entrances featuring mosaic detail.

415 **Isaac L. and Julia B. Rice House,** now the Yeshiva Ketana of Manhattan, 346 West 89th Street at Riverside Drive (Herts & Tallant, 1901–03), designated 1980. The Rice mansion is one of only two freestanding houses that survive on Riverside Drive. The noted theater architects Herts & Tallant designed this mansion for the lawyer, writer, and chess expert Isaac Rice and his wife, Julia, a physician who, although she never practiced, was involved in medical issues and was responsible for the creation of quiet zones around New York City hospitals. Villa Julia, as the Rices called their home, combines Georgian and Beaux-Arts forms in a highly individualistic manner. In 1908 C. P. H. Gilbert undertook alterations (most barely visible) for the second owner, Solomon Schinasi, a partner in the tobacco firm Schinasi Brothers (see No. 424).

416 **Soldiers' and Sailors' Monument,** Riverside Drive at West 89th Street (Stoughton & Stoughton, with Paul E. M. DuBoy, 1897–1902), designated 1976. The Soldiers' and Sailors' Memorial Arch (see Brooklyn No. 78) and this monument on Riverside Drive are physical manifestations of the nostalgia for the Civil War era that swept across the United States in the late 19th century as the horrors of the war faded into history. Although a Civil War monument was proposed as early as 1869, it was not until 1897 that enough interest was generated to hold a design competition. The monument was originally intended for Grand Army Plaza, near the entrance to Central Park; the design that won the competition needed to be reworked when the site was changed to Riverside Drive. Construction of the marble monument and its related terraces began in 1900. The cylindrical building is an enlarged version of the Hellenistic Monument of Lysicrates in Athens.

417 **Pomander Walk,** 3–22 Pomander Walk, 261–267 West 94th Street, and 260–274 West 95th Street (King & Campbell, 1921), designated 1989. One of the most surprising residential enclaves in New York City, Pomander Walk consists of sixteen two-story neo-Tudor houses facing onto a private

walk and eleven additional houses on West 94th and West 95th Streets. This picturesque complex was built by the restaurateur and developer Thomas Healy in an attempt to re-create the village atmosphere evoked in Lewis Parker's popular play *Pomander Walk.*

418 **Midtown Theater,** now the Metro Theater, 2624–2626 Broadway (Boak & Paris, 1932–33), designated 1989. In the 1920s and 1930s, Broadway on the Upper West Side was lined with neigh-

Pomander Walk (No. 417). An attempt by developer Thomas Healy to re-create a village atmosphere in a dense urban setting. Photo by Carl Forster.

borhood movie theaters. The Art Deco Midtown has one of the finest theater facades in New York. The street front is clad entirely in colored terra cotta, primarily beige and black. The focus of the design is a medallion with a bas-relief of figures and masks representing comedy and tragedy. The marquee, with its horizontal chrome banding, is largely original.

419 **New York Free Circulating Library, Bloomingdale Branch,** now the Ukrainian Academy of Arts and Sciences, 206 West 100th Street

(James Brown Lord, 1898), designated 1989. The Bloomingdale Branch library was commissioned by the New York Free Circulating Library, an organization established in 1878 by wealthy New Yorkers to provide for the "moral and intellectual elevation of the masses." To serve the increasingly populous Upper West Side, the library erected this fireproof steel-frame building designed in the French classical style. The library became a branch of the New York Public Library in 1901; in 1961 the building was sold to a private organization for use as a research facility devoted to the study of Ukrainian culture.

420 **854, 856, and 858 West End Avenue and 254 West 102nd Street** (Schneider & Herter, 1892–93), designated 1990. These four Queen Anne/Romanesque Revival brownstone houses are the sole surviving examples of a type of site planning commonly employed on West End Avenue corners in the 1890s, when this street was being developed with speculative row houses for upper-middle-class buyers. Each of these groups featured residences along the avenue, a prominent corner house, and an additional house facing the side street.

421 **William and Clara Baumgarten House,** 294 Riverside Drive (Schickel & Ditmars, 1900–01), designated 1991. This Beaux-Arts town house near West 102nd Street is one of the few luxury residences of its type to survive on Riverside Drive. The limestone structure was commissioned by William Baumgarten, who served as head of the famous interior design firm Herter Brothers and later established his own decorating company.

422 **Marseilles Hotel,** 2689–2693 Broadway (Harry Allan Jacobs, 1902–05), designated 1990. The Marseilles is among the most prominent of the grand apartment hotels erected on the Upper West Side. The Beaux-Arts building—with its limestone base, brick facing, terra-cotta trim, and mansard roof—was built in anticipation of the opening of an IRT subway station at West 103rd Street.

423 **Master Building,** 310–312 Riverside Drive (Harvey Wiley Corbett of the firm Helmle, Corbett & Harrison, with Sugarman & Berger, associated architects, 1928–29), designated 1989. This innovative mixed-use structure is a significant work by Corbett, an influential designer of skyscrapers. The building was planned as a 29-story apartment hotel that would incorporate the Nicholas Roerich Museum—including galleries, a library, and an auditorium—on its ground floor. The building is among the finest Art Deco high-rise structures in New York City. Among its notable features are the patterned brickwork that varies from dark to light as the building rises, the dramatic setbacks and irregular massing of the upper floors, the ornamental crown, and the innovative use of corner windows.

424 **Morris and Laurette Schinasi House,** 351 Riverside Drive (William B. Tuthill, 1907–09), designated 1974. This flamboyant marble residence, one of only two freestanding mansions surviving on Riverside Drive, was built by a wealthy cigarette manufacturer and partner in the tobacco firm Schinasi Brothers. The early 16th-century French Renaissance style popular for the châteaux along the Loire was adapted here to an urban setting overlooking the Hudson.

425 **Manhasset Apartments,** 301 West 108th Street and 300 West 109th Street (Joseph Wolf, 1899–1901; enlarged, Janes & Leo, 1901–05), designated 1996. The Beaux-Arts-style Manhasset is one of the most imposing apartment houses erected on the Upper West Side at the time when this neighborhood was the center of apartment-house construction in New York. The lower eight stories were erected in 1899–1901, but when the developer defaulted, the new owner commissioned Janes & Leo to add three stories, including the monumental mansard roof. Janes & Leo also designed the grand entrance pavilions. Construction was finally completed in 1905, and apartments in the two wings were rented to affluent families.

The Master Building (No. 423) by architect Harvey Wiley Corbett is one of New York City's finest Art Deco high-rise buildings. Photo by Carl Forster.

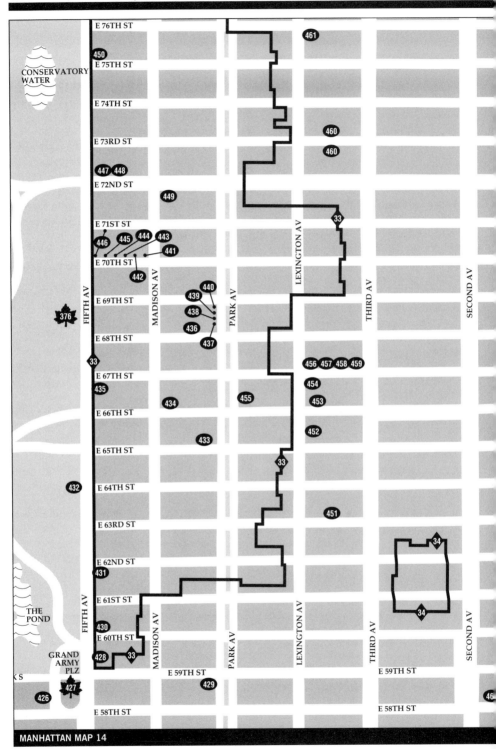

MAP **14**

MANHATTAN

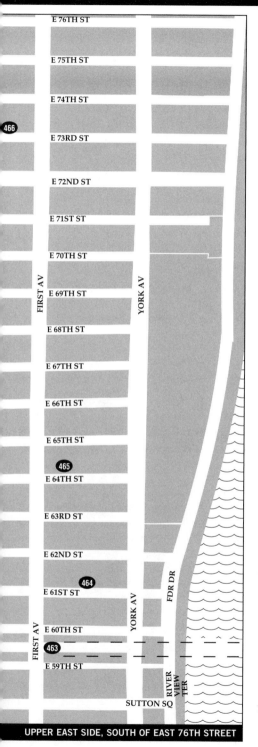

E 76TH ST
E 75TH ST
E 74TH ST
E 73RD ST
E 72ND ST
E 71ST ST
E 70TH ST
E 69TH ST
E 68TH ST
E 67TH ST
E 66TH ST
E 65TH ST
E 64TH ST
E 63RD ST
E 62ND ST
E 61ST ST
E 60TH ST
E 59TH ST

FIRST AV
YORK AV
FDR DR
YORK AV
FIRST AV
RIVER VIEW TER
SUTTON SQ

466
465
464
463

UPPER EAST SIDE, SOUTH OF EAST 76TH STREET

■ WEST OF PARK AVENUE

HISTORIC DISTRICT

33 **Upper East Side Historic District,** designated 1981. This district is composed largely of the mansions, town houses, apartment houses, private carriage houses and garages, and institutional buildings erected by or for New York City's wealthiest citizens in the first decades of the 20th century. The earliest wave of development in the district occurred in the 1870s when brownstone and brick row houses were constructed by speculative builders for sale to middle-class households; this movement was spurred by the opening of the Third Avenue elevated railway in 1878. A number of these houses are still extant (largely on Madison Avenue), but most were demolished or redesigned in the late 19th and early 20th centuries when a more affluent population transformed the streets north of 59th Street into the city's premier residential neighborhood. It was in these years that many members of America's financial and social elite commissioned substantial town houses from some of the nation's finest architects. The district contains major residential works by McKim, Mead & White; Carrère & Hastings; Warren & Wetmore; Ernest Flagg; Mott B. Schmidt; Delano & Aldrich; and other leading architects.

There are so many superb houses in the district that not all can be noted. The district contains major town houses in the Beaux-Arts style, such as the Ernesto and Edith Fabbri House (Haydel & Shepard, 1898–1900) at 11 East 62nd Street, the Marshall Orme and Caroline Astor Wilson House (now New India House, Warren & Wetmore, 1900–03) at 3 East 64th Street, and the William and Maria Schieffelin House (now the Lotos Club, Richard Howland Hunt, 1898–1900) at 5 East 66th Street. Important buildings in other styles include the Venetian Renaissance–inspired Joseph and Kate Pulitzer House (McKim, Mead & White, Stanford White, partner in charge, 1900–03) at 11 East 73rd Street; the Roman Renaissance–inspired William and Gladys Ziegler, Jr., House (now New York Academy of Sciences, Sterner & Wolfe, 1919–20) at 2 East 63rd Street; the Jacobean Thomas and Florence Lamont House (now Visiting Nurse Service of New York, Walker & Gillette, 1920–21) at 107 East 70th Street; the Colo-

Upper East Side Historic District streetscape (H.D. 33), 11 East 62nd Street. One of the many Beaux-Arts town houses that characterize this district. Photo: Landmarks Preservation Commission collection.

nial Revival–style Park Avenue Houses (see below); and two early Modern works by architect William Lescaze—the Raymond and Mildred Kramer House (1934–35) at 32 East 74th Street and the Edward A. and Dorothy Norman House (1940–41) at 124 East 70th Street. In addition, the neighborhood's residents constructed fine new institutions: churches, such as the neo-Gothic Park Avenue Baptist (now Central Presbyterian, Henry C. Pelton and Allen & Collens, 1920–22) on Park Avenue and East 64th Street and Saint James Episcopal (Ralph Adams Cram, 1923–24) on Madison Avenue and East 71st Street; synagogues, such as the impressive Temple Emanu-El (Robert D. Kohn, Charles Butler, and Clarence S. Stein, associated architects with Mayers, Murray & Phillip, consultants, 1927–29) on Fifth Avenue and East 65th Street; and private clubs, such as the Metropolitan (see No. 430), the Knickerbocker (see No. 431), the Colonial Revival–style Colony (Delano & Aldrich, 1914–16) on Park Avenue and East 62nd Street, and the English Georgian–style Links (Cross & Cross, 1916–17) at 36 East 62nd Street. Some of the wealthiest families also built or purchased private carriage houses (or, after the invention of the automobile, private garages), most of them located on the blocks east of Park Avenue, with the largest and finest concentration on East 69th Street between Third and Lexington Avenues.

By the second decade of the 20th century, as the maintenance of private homes became increasingly expensive and inconvenient, luxurious apartment houses were erected in increasing numbers on Fifth and Park Avenues and other streets in the district. Some of these brick and limestone buildings were designed by the architects who were also responsible for town houses, such as Walter B. Chambers (563 Park Avenue, 1909–10) and York & Sawyer (660 Park Avenue, 1926–27), but most were the work of architects such as J. E. R. Carpenter, George & Edward Blum, and Rosario Candela, who specialized in luxury apartment house design and planning. At the same time the apartment houses were being constructed, Madison Avenue, which had originally been a residential street, was transformed into a fashionable commercial thoroughfare. The lower floors of old row houses were converted into elegant shops, and the upper stories became apartments or offices. Although most buildings in the district predate World War II, noteworthy mid-20th-century

structures include Paul Rudolph's 101 East 63rd Street (1966–68), Philip Johnson's Asia House (now Russell Sage Foundation and Robert Sterling Clarke Foundation, 1958–60) at 112 East 64th Street, and Marcel Breuer & Associates' Whitney Museum of American Art (1964–66) on Madison Avenue and 75th Street.

INDIVIDUAL LANDMARKS

426 **Plaza Hotel,** 768 Fifth Avenue and 2 Central Park South (Henry J. Hardenbergh, 1905–07; addition, Warren & Wetmore, 1921), designated 1969. The Plaza's status as one of the world's great luxury hotels has been maintained since it opened in 1907. Located on a prominent site—overlooking Central Park (see No. 376), Grand Army Plaza (see below), and Fifth Avenue—this elegant building was designed in a free adaptation of French Renaissance architecture, taking full advantage of the vistas provided by the surrounding open space. Warren & Wetmore's 58th Street addition is a simplified version of Hardenbergh's original design.

427 **Grand Army Plaza Scenic Landmark,** Fifth Avenue at 59th Street (Carrère & Hastings, 1913–16), designated 1974. A modest plaza was laid out on this site as part of the design of Central Park (see No. 376). Although Richard Morris Hunt had proposed a formal plaza for the site as early as 1863, it was the sculptor Karl Bitter's 1898 proposal for a Parisian-inspired plaza that was eventually acted upon. In 1912 Joseph Pulitzer bequeathed $50,000 for the erection of a fountain, and a competition was held for the design. In 1913 the project was awarded to Thomas Hastings, who closely followed Bitter's plan. Hastings laid out one of the most urbane public spaces in the city: a formal, axial, elliptical space divided in half by 59th Street. The plaza is the setting for Hastings's Pulitzer Fountain, which is crowned by Bitter's bronze statue of Pomona, goddess of abundance. North of 59th Street is Augustus Saint-Gaudens's masterful General Sherman Monument, set on a base by Charles McKim. This statue, which had been unveiled in 1903, was moved to align with the new fountain. The fountain was restored and the Sherman statue regilded in 1988–90.

428 **Sidewalk Clock,** 783 Fifth Avenue at East 59th Street (E. Howard Clock Company, 1927), designated 1981. Located in front of the Sherry-Netherland Hotel, this clock was probably installed around the time the hotel opened in 1927 (see No. 191).

429 **Pepsi-Cola Building,** 500 Park Avenue (Skidmore, Owings & Merrill, Gordon Bunshaft, partner in charge; Natalie de Blois, senior designer, 1958–60), designated 1995. The Pepsi-Cola Company expanded rapidly in the 1950s under the direction of Alfred N. Steele (who was married to Joan Crawford). The construction of an International Style headquarters on fashionable Park Avenue was part of Steele's efforts to promote the company. Design was directed by noted SOM partner Gordon Bunshaft, who had previously designed Lever House (see No. 300) only a few blocks to the south. The senior designer, responsible for major work on this project, was Natalie de Blois, among the first women ac-

tively involved with corporate architecture. The small building, one of the most elegant of its era, is clad in what appears to be a weightless screen of gray-green glass and aluminum.

430 **Metropolitan Club,** 1–11 East 60th Street (McKim, Mead & White, Stanford White, partner in charge, 1891–94; addition, Ogden Codman, 1912), designated 1979. The 19th-century architecture critic Montgomery Schuyler described the Metropolitan Club as "the largest, most imposing, and most luxurious of the clubhouses of New York." This building, designed in the Italian Renaissance style, is a masterpiece of late 19th-century American architecture and a major example of the design skills of Stanford White. The Metropolitan Club was founded in 1891 by a group of prominent New Yorkers disgruntled by the rejection of several of their friends from membership in the Union Club. The marble exterior of the new club was specifically planned to be as unostenta-

Pepsi-Cola Building (No. 429). An elegant example of corporate identity through architecture. Photo by Carl Forster.

tious as possible, with rich detail limited to the interior. Since the club wished to have a lounge overlooking Central Park, the entrance is on the side, through elaborate iron gates and a court demarcated by a two-story wing with a shallow niche. The east side of the court is flanked by an earlier row house (11 East 60th Street) redesigned for the club in 1912.

431 **Knickerbocker Club,** 2 East 62nd Street (Delano & Aldrich, 1913–15), designated 1979. The exclusive Knickerbocker Club, founded in 1871 in reaction to the relaxation of admissions standards at other private men's clubs, commissioned this clubhouse in 1913. The architects Delano & Aldrich specialized in the design of refined adaptations of 18th- and early 19th-century American and English architecture, as can be seen in this elegant brick building and in several nearby landmark houses. A restoration of the structure was completed in 1991.

432 **The Arsenal,** now the Administration Building of the New York City Department of Parks and Recreation, Central Park at East 64th Street (Martin E. Thompson, 1847–51), designated 1967. Built "to house and protect the arms of the state," the Arsenal was designed as a mock-medieval castle, complete with octagonal towers. After only a few years of use as an arsenal, the structure was converted into a police station; it later served as the first home of the American Museum of Natural History. In 1934 the building became the headquarters of New York City's Parks Department.

433 **Sara Delano Roosevelt and Franklin and Eleanor Roosevelt Houses,** now the Sara Delano Roosevelt Memorial House, 47–49 East 65th Street (Charles A. Platt, 1907–08), designated 1973. This double town house of unified English Georgian–inspired design has a single central entrance. Access to the individual units was gained through doors in the vestibule; Sara Roosevelt lived to the left, and her son and daughter-in-law lived to the right. It was in his fourth-floor bedroom in this house that Franklin Roosevelt convalesced from polio in 1921–22. After Sara's death in 1941, the building was purchased for use by nearby Hunter College.

434 **45 East 66th Street Apartments** (Harde & Short, 1906–08), designated 1977. The firm Harde & Short was responsible for several of New York's

most flamboyant apartment buildings in the early years of the 20th century, including the Red House (see No. 408), Alwyn Court (see No. 362), and this impressive structure on the corner of East 66th Street and Madison Avenue. The building is faced in red brick with black mortar and has a profusion of French Gothic–inspired terra-cotta detail. As is characteristic of the architects' work, the street facades have large multipaned windows. The facades were magnificently restored in 1987–88.

45 East 66th Street Apartments (No. 434). One of several flamboyant apartment buildings built by the architecture firm Harde & Short. Photo by Caroline Kane Levy.

159

435 R. Livingston and Eleanor T. Beeckman House, now the Permanent Mission of Serbia and Montenegro to the United Nations, 854 Fifth Avenue (Warren & Wetmore, 1903–05), designated 1969. This elegant limestone dwelling, one of the few mansions still standing on Fifth Avenue, is in the style of the urban town houses erected in France during the reign of Louis XV. It was built for Robert Livingston Beeckman, a member of a prominent New York family, and was purchased by the Yugoslav government in 1946.

436 J. William and Margaretta C. Clark House, later Automation House, now Richard L. Feigen & Co., 49 East 68th Street (Trowbridge & Livingston, 1913–14), designated 1970. The socially well-connected architecture firm Trowbridge & Livingston designed this Colonial Revival house for the family of J. William Clark, heir to the Clark sewing thread fortune. Restored in 1991 by Buttrick, White & Burtis, the town house has elegant Federal-inspired detail, including a pair of arched openings on the ground floor and a variety of window lintels on the upper floors.

437 Percy and Maud H. Pyne House, now the Americas Society, 680 Park Avenue (McKim, Mead & White, Charles F. McKim, partner in charge, 1906–12), designated as Center for Inter-American Relations, 1970. Charles F. McKim designed this house for the financier and philanthropist Percy Pyne and his wife in 1906, but construction did not begin until 1910, when the railroad tracks along Park Avenue were finally covered. One of the earliest town houses on Park Avenue, it set an 18th-century design precedent that was followed by the three succeeding houses on this block, erected between 1916 and 1926. In 1965 demolition began on this house and its two neighbors, the Filley and Sloane houses (see below). In response to a public outcry, the Marquesa de Cuevas, granddaughter of John D. Rockefeller, purchased the houses and donated them to various organizations.

438 Oliver D. and Mary Pyne Filley House, now the Spanish Institute, 684 Park Avenue (McKim, Mead & White, 1925–26), designated 1970. The last of the four landmark town houses to be built on this block, this house was erected for the

680, 684, 686, and 690 Park Avenue (Nos. 437–440) are among the early mansions constructed on Park Avenue after the railroad tracks were covered. Photo by John Barrington Bayley, 1964.

daughter and son-in-law of Percy and Maud Pyne—for whom McKim, Mead & White had designed the adjacent house (see above) sixteen years earlier—on the site of the Pynes' garden.

439 **William and Frances Crocker Sloane House,** now the Italian Cultural Institute, 686 Park Avenue (Delano & Aldrich, 1916–19), designated 1970. Delano & Aldrich excelled at the design of Colonial Revival buildings, and this house, designed for the president of the prominent W. & J. Sloane furniture store, is a characteristic example. It is one of four stylistically related landmark houses on this block and one of three saved from demolition in 1965 (see No. 437).

440 **Henry P. and Kate T. Davison House,** now the Consulate General of Italy, 690 Park Avenue (Walker & Gillette, 1916–17), designated 1970. Henry P. Davison, one of the founders of Bankers Trust, commissioned this English Georgian–style brick house, the second of four related landmark buildings that create the unique blockfront of Park Avenue between East 68th and 69th Streets. The construction of these houses reflects the development of Park Avenue as a prestigious residential neighborhood following the covering of the avenue's railroad tracks around 1910. The building served as a residence until 1952, when it was converted into the Italian consulate.

441 **Gustav and Virginia Pagenstecher House,** also known as the 21 East 70th Street House, now Hirschl & Adler Galleries (William J. Rogers, 1918–19), designated 1974. The last of the five landmark town houses to be erected on the north side of East 70th Street, the Pagenstecher House is a limestone structure designed in an austere French neoclassical style. At the second floor a pair of tall round-arched windows is set in deep reveals.

442 **Dave Hennen and Alice Morris House,** now Knoedler & Company (Thornton Chard, 1909–10), designated as 19 East 70th Street, 1974. This especially austere early Italian Renaissance–inspired limestone town house, built on land previously owned by the wealthy landholder and philanthropist James Lenox, was erected for a client who would later become the U.S. ambassador to Belgium. The building now houses the Knoedler Gallery, which celebrated its 150th anniversary in 1996.

443 **Alvin W. and Angeline Krech House,** also known as the 17 East 70th Street House (Arthur C. Jackson, 1909–11), designated 1974. The Krech family's French neoclassical limestone town house lends a dignified character to the north side of East 70th Street. Alvin Krech was, according to his obituary, "one of the prominent figures in American finance and industry," serving as chairman of the Equitable Trust Company and as a railroad administrator.

444 **John Chandler and Corinne deBébian Moore House,** also known as the 15 East 70th Street House (Charles I. Berg, 1909–10), designated 1974. This house in the French neoclassical style is one of five adjacent landmarks erected on land that had been owned by James Lenox and the Lenox estate until 1907, when plots were sold to individuals who erected new town houses.

445 **11 East 70th Street** (John H. Duncan, 1909–10), designated 1974. Of the five landmark town houses on this block, No. 11 was the only one built on speculation. The builder Cornelius Luyster, Jr., commissioned the dwelling from the well-known architect John H. Duncan, who designed a subdued residence in the French neoclassical style.

446 **Henry Clay and Adelaide Childs Frick House,** now the Frick Collection and Frick Art Reference Library, 1 East 70th Street and 10 East 71st Street (Carrère & Hastings, 1913–14; entrance pavilion and library, John Russell Pope, 1931–35; garden addition, Harry Van Dyke, John Barrington Bayley, and G. Frederick Poehler, 1977; garden, Russell Page), designated 1974. The palatial residence of the steel magnate Henry Clay Frick, built on the entire Fifth Avenue blockfront formerly occupied by the Lenox Library, was planned by Thomas Hastings as both a residence and a gallery for the display of Frick's great art collection. Modeled on 18th-century French sources, the house is placed on a terrace set back from Fifth Avenue and surrounded by a retaining wall, thus heightening the structure's formal monumentality. Following the death of Adelaide Frick in 1931, the house was enlarged and converted into a museum, which opened to the public in 1935. This conversion and the construction of the adjoining reference library on East 71st Street were undertaken by John Russell Pope several years before he designed the National Gallery in Washington.

447 Oliver Gould and Mary Brewster Jennings House, 7 East 72nd Street (Flagg & Chambers, 1898–99), designated 1977. The Jennings House and the neighboring Sloane House (see below) are two of the finest Beaux-Arts residences in New York City; they lend a note of Parisian elegance to Manhattan's Upper East Side. Appropriately, both houses were designed by French-trained architects, and both are now owned by a French school. Built for a wealthy businessman and his family, the limestone-fronted Jennings House displays a rich surface texture, with vermiculated blocks on the ground floor and rusticated stonework above. The house is crowned by a particularly bold convex mansard with exuberant copper detail.

448 Henry T. and Jessie Sloane House, 9 East 72nd Street (Carrère & Hastings, 1894–96), designated 1977. Henry T. Sloane, son of the founder of the W. & J. Sloane furniture store, commissioned this luxuriant Beaux-Arts house from the French-trained architects Carrère & Hastings. Sloane and his wife lived here for only a short time before their scandalous divorce in 1898. After being briefly occupied by Joseph Pulitzer, the house was purchased by James Stillman, president of National City Bank.

449 Gertrude Rhinelander Waldo House, now the Polo/Ralph Lauren Store, 867 Madison Avenue (Kimball & Thompson, 1895–98), designated 1976. Designed in the style of the early French Renaissance châteaux of the Loire Valley, this enormous limestone mansion was built by an eccentric society matron who never lived in the house. Rather, she resided across the street, and the house remained empty until 1920, when it was converted for commercial use. Ralph Lauren instituted a major rehabilitation of the property in 1984.

450 Edward S. and Mary Stillman Harkness House, now the Commonwealth Fund, 1 East 75th Street (Hale & Rogers, 1907–08), designated 1967. Built by the son of one of the six original partners in the Standard Oil Company, the Harkness House is an Italian Renaissance–inspired mansion faced entirely with marble. Following the death of Mary Harkness in 1950, the house became the headquarters of the Commonwealth Fund, a philanthropic foundation that Edward Harkness's mother had founded in 1918. The building is surrounded by a spectacular cast- and wrought-iron fence that has been restored.

■ **PARK AVENUE TO THIRD AVENUE**

451 Cyril and Barbara Rutherford Hatch House, 153 East 63rd Street (Frederick J. Sterner, 1917–19), designated 1977. Shortly after their marriage, the New York socialites Barbara Rutherford (daughter of Mrs. William K. Vanderbilt) and Cyril Hatch commissioned this handsome Mediterranean-inspired town house. Following the Hatches' divorce in 1920, the spacious house, which has an interior courtyard, was occupied by Charles Dillingham, owner of the Globe Theater (see No. 243) and one of the country's most prominent theatrical producers, and then by Charles L. Lawrance, a pioneer in aeronautical engineering. Subsequent owners have included Louise Hovick, better known as the burlesque queen Gypsy Rose Lee, artist Jasper Johns, and filmmaker Spike Lee.

452 Church of Saint Vincent Ferrer (R.C.) Complex, 869 Lexington Avenue and 141–151 East 65th Street (church, Bertram Goodhue, 1914–18; priory, William Schickel, 1880–81; Holy Name Society Building, Wilfred E. Anthony, 1930; school, Elliot L. Chisling-Ferrenz & Taylor, 1948), designated 1967. Shortly after completing Saint Thomas Church (see No. 302), Bertram Goodhue received the commission for this Roman Catholic church erected by the Dominican order. Goodhue's design uses academic Gothic forms in a free manner. The austere exterior is faced in Plymouth granite with white limestone carvings by Lee Lawrie that appear to grow organically from the massive stonework. Immediately south of the church is the older priory, a Victorian Gothic design that is one of the few surviving examples of the ecclesiastical work of the architect William Schickel. In the 20th century, the church complex expanded along East 65th Street with the construction of the neo-Gothic Holy Name Society Building and Saint Vincent Ferrer School.

453 131–135 East 66th Street (Charles A. Platt and Simonson, Pollard & Steinam, 1905–06), designated 1967. This distinguished limestone-fronted building reflects the popular adaptation of the Italian Renaissance palazzo form to the New York apartment house. The cooperative was the first apartment house designed by the prestigious architect Charles A. Platt, who worked here in association with a firm that specialized in the design of buildings with double-height artists' studios and duplex living quarters. Platt himself moved into the building upon its completion.

Gertrude Rhinelander Waldo House (No. 449). This enormous mansion was built in the style of early French Renaissance châteaux found in the Loire Valley. Photo: Landmarks Preservation Commission collection.

454 **130–134 East 67th Street** (Rossiter & Wright, 1907), designated 1980. This building, on the corner of Lexington Avenue and East 67th Street, was designed as a pendant to the adjacent apartment house at 131–135 East 66th Street (see above). Like its neighbor, the East 67th Street structure is a cooperative building, faced in limestone and designed in the Italian Renaissance style, and it also has double-height studios.

455 **Seventh Regiment Armory,** 643 Park Avenue (Charles W. Clinton, 1877–79), designated 1967, interior 1994. The socially prominent Seventh Regiment was formed in 1806 and in 1824 became the first regiment to adopt the term *National Guard.* In 1874 the city leased this Park Avenue site to the regiment, which raised the money to build a monumental new armory. Clinton, a Seventh Regiment veteran, designed the armory with a 187-by-290-foot drill shed and an administration building in the form of a medieval fortress. The building became a prototype for the later medieval-inspired armories that appeared in large numbers in New York (see Brooklyn Nos. 52, 86, and Bronx No. 32) and throughout the country. The wealth and importance of the Seventh Regiment are evident in the decoration of the armory's **interiors,** notably the individual regiment rooms used by officers and for formal public occasions on the first floor and the second-floor company rooms. The finest rooms are the exotic Veterans' Room and the Library, extraordinary surviving Aesthetic Movement interiors executed by the Associated Artists (Louis Comfort Tiffany, Stanford White, and others). Other rooms were decorated by such leading American designers as Herter Brothers, Alexander Roux & Co., Pottier & Stymus, Sydney V. Stratton, and Kimball & Cabus. The drill room, measuring 200 by 300 feet and 100 feet high, where the regiment practiced, is one of the largest unobstructed spaces in New York and the oldest balloon shed, or barrel-vaulted roof supported on visible arch trusses, in America.

456 **Mount Sinai Dispensary,** also known as the 149–151 East 67th Street Building, now the Kennedy Child Study Center (Buchman & Deisler and Brunner & Tryon, 1889–90), designated 1980. Mount Sinai Hospital, the oldest Jewish hospital in New York City, first opened a dispensary for the treatment of outpatients in 1875. As the demand for services grew, this Italian Renaissance–inspired struc-

ture, faced in brick, stone, and terra cotta, was erected to house both an enlarged dispensary and the hospital's nursing school. The design is the combined work of two prominent Jewish architecture firms.

457 **19th Police Precinct Station House,** originally 25th Police Precinct, 153–155 East 67th Street (Nathaniel D. Bush, 1886–87), designated 1999.

Nathaniel D. Bush designed at least twenty structures for the New York Police Department between 1862 and 1895. This midblock structure is typical of his work, combining elements of the *Rundbogenstil,* Renaissance Revival, and neo-Grec styles. After the Civil War the neighborhood was rapidly expanding, and this was the second of four institutional buildings completed on the block. Rehabilitated in 1992, it is one of only two structures designed by the architect that remain in police use.

458 **Fire Engine Company 39 and Ladder Company 16 Station House,** 157–159 East 67th Street (N. Lebrun & Son, 1884–86), designated 1998. This six-story firehouse was originally built to serve as the headquarters of the New York City Fire Department. Inspired by Romanesque architecture and the work of H. H. Richardson, the brick and granite facade has round-arched windows with balconies and an elaborately carved entrance portico. Restored by the Stein Partnership in 1992, the upper floors are now used by the adjoining police precinct.

459 **Park East Synagogue** (Congregation Zichron Ephraim), 163 East 67th Street (Schneider & Herter, 1889–90), designated 1980. Park East is a late manifestation of the use of Moorish forms in synagogue design (see Central Synagogue, No. 342). The congregation was organized in 1888 by Rabbi Bernard Drachman, who believed in the importance of adapting Orthodox practices and traditions to American customs. This conviction was a direct response to the increasing popularity of Reform Judaism, especially among the German Jews settling in substantial numbers on the Upper East Side in the late 19th century. This synagogue's architectural style was seen as a link between 19th-century Judaism and the flowering of Jewish culture in Moorish Spain.

Seventh Regiment Armory (No. 455). The medieval style was copied by many other armories in New York and around the country. Photo by Carl Forster.

Fire Engine Company 39 (No. 458) provides a superb centerpiece to one of Manhattan's best-preserved rows of 19th century public architecture. Photo by Carl Forster.

460 **161–179 and 166–182 East 73rd Street** (Nos. 161 and 163, Thomas Rae, 1896–97; Nos. 165 and 167, George L. Amoroux, 1903–04; No. 171, 1860; No. 173, Hobart H. Walker, 1893; No. 175, 1860; No. 177–179, Charles F. Hoppe, 1906; No. 166, Richard M. Hunt, 1883–84; No. 168, Charles W. Romeyn, 1899; No. 170, Frank Wennemer, 1890–91; No. 172–174, Frank Wennemer, 1889; No. 178, John H. Friend, 1902; No. 180, William Schickel & Co., 1890–91; No. 182, Andrew Spense Mayer, 1890), designated 1980; No. 166, 1981. Beginning in the final decades of the 19th century, as the blocks of the Upper East Side between Fifth and Park Avenues were being transformed into streets of mansions and town houses erected for New York's wealthiest citizens, many of

the streets to the east were redeveloped with carriage houses. These carriage houses were erected in locations that were convenient to the large houses but sufficiently far away that the smells and noise of the stables did not mar the quality of life on the residential streets. In the years immediately preceding these developments, East 73rd Street between Lexington and Third Avenues was lined with modest row houses erected around 1860; two of these buildings, Nos. 171 and 175, have survived. In 1883 Richard Morris Hunt designed the first private carriage house on the street, a Romanesque Revival building at No. 166, built for Henry G. Marquand, for whom Hunt also designed a lavish mansion on Madison Avenue. The ten carriage houses that followed were erected either by individuals for their own use or by speculative builders who sold the structures to nearby residents. The most distinguished of these is No. 168, a neo-Flemish building complete with stepped gable and strapwork ornament designed for banker William Baylis. Since only the very wealthy could afford to maintain a private carriage house, most people who owned horses boarded them in commercial stables such as the five-story Romanesque Revival building at No. 182. In the early years of the 20th century, the majority of the carriage houses and stables were converted for automotive use. In this same period, commercial garages, such as the handsome building in the Beaux-Arts style at No. 177–179, began to appear in the neighborhood. By the 1920s, as the maintenance of a private garage became prohibitively expensive, most of the carriage houses were converted into private residences. At the same time, the two surviving row houses were rehabilitated, each by a prominent New York architect for his own residence—Erastus D. Litchfield at No. 171 and Francis L. Pell at No. 175.

461 **Saint Jean Baptiste Roman Catholic Church,** 1067–1071 Lexington Avenue (Nicholas Sirracino, 1910–13), designated 1969. Saint Jean Baptiste, built to serve a largely French-Canadian Roman Catholic congregation, is an impressive example of Italian Mannerist–inspired design. Of special note on this limestone-faced church are the Corinthian portico, paired towers, and dome. Construction was funded by streetcar magnate Thomas Fortune Ryan, who, it is said, sought to replace a smaller building in which he had once been forced to stand during mass. The church was restored in 1995–96.

■ EAST OF THIRD AVENUE

HISTORIC DISTRICT

34 Treadwell Farm Historic District, designated 1967. Once part of the farm of Adam Treadwell, the older brother of Seabury Tredwell [sic], whose house (see Old Merchant's House, No. 148) is now a museum, this district was transformed by speculative builders into a neighborhood of modest row houses in 1868–76. Later in the 19th century, the neighborhood deteriorated, but it was rediscovered after World War I by affluent New Yorkers searching for housing convenient to the new Midtown commercial area. Between 1919 and 1922, almost every house in the district was altered; many of the facades were simplified by the removal of stoops and other projecting features. In 1930 Martin Hedmark designed the Swedish Baptist Church (now Trinity Baptist) at 250 East 61st Street in an unusual Scandinavian Modern style; the church features exceptional brickwork and ironwork.

INDIVIDUAL LANDMARKS

462 311 and 313 East 58th Street (1856–57), designated 1967, 1970. These two vernacular houses with Italianate details are reminders of the simple dwellings that once dotted Midtown. Both houses are below sidewalk level as a result of the construction of a new approach to the Queensboro Bridge in 1930.

463 Queensboro Bridge (see Queens No. 4). Beneath the Manhattan side of the bridge, near First Avenue, are a series of cavernous spaces clad with Guastavino tiles. Originally built to serve as a farmer's market, these spaces have been restored by Hardy Holzman Pfeiffer to function as a supermarket and restaurant.

464 Abigail Adams Smith Museum, 421 East 61st Street (1799), designated 1967. In 1795 Colonel William S. Smith and his wife, Abigail, the daughter of John and Abigail Adams, established the estate of Mount Vernon along the East River. In 1798, before all the estate buildings were complete,

the Smiths were forced to sell their property to William T. Robinson; it was Robinson who constructed the combined coach house and stable that is now the Abigail Adams Smith Museum. The building's conversion into a hotel in 1826 entailed substantial alterations to the interior and the construction of a veranda. The Colonial Dames of America purchased the property in 1924 and converted the hotel into a museum that has been open to the public since 1939.

465 City and Suburban Homes Company, First Avenue Estate (in part), 1168–1200 First Avenue, 401–423 East 64th Street, and 402–416 East 65th Street (James E. Ware, James E. Ware & Sons, and Philip H. Ohm, 1898–1915), designated 1990. The First Avenue Estate is the oldest extant project built by the City and Suburban Homes Company, a limited-dividend corporation dedicated to the construction of decent affordable housing for the working poor. The company was founded and supported by some of New York's most prominent citizens, who when investing in City and Suburban shares agreed to limit their return to 5 percent. City and Suburban's development projects were experimental housing; thus the various buildings have different plans and room arrangements. This complex was begun before the Avenue A Estate (see No. 503), but it was completed later. The light-colored brick buildings were designed by James E. Ware, an architect active in the design of housing for the working poor, and by City and Suburban's own architect, Philip H. Ohm. Since their completion, the model tenements have housed large numbers of working people in quality apartments of a sort not easily found in New York City by those with limited income.

466 Bohemian National Hall (Národní Budova), 321 East 73rd Street (William C. Frohne, 1895, 1897), designated 1994. In the late 19th century, Yorkville became a center for Czech and Slovak immigrants, and this social hall was erected to serve the community's needs. The ornate Renaissance-inspired building was planned as a general meeting hall for all Czech and Slovak organizations and included a restaurant, a bar, club rooms, bowling alleys, a shooting gallery, a ballroom/theater, and classrooms where children of immigrants were taught Czech language, history, and culture.

UPPER EAST SIDE, EAST 76TH STREET TO EAST 94TH STREET

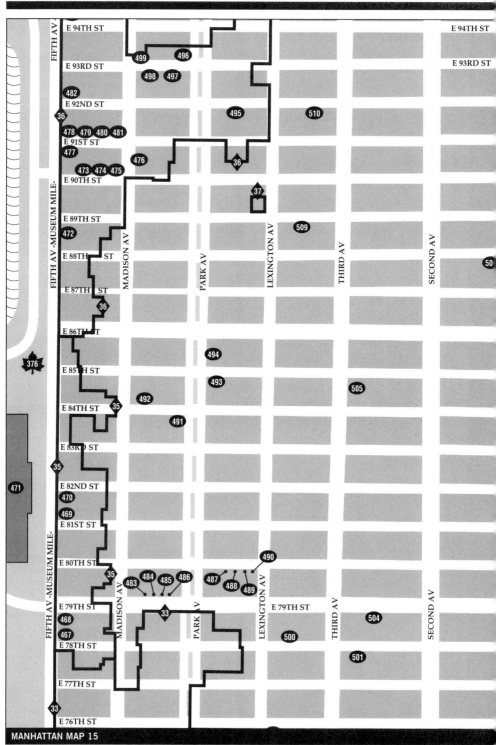

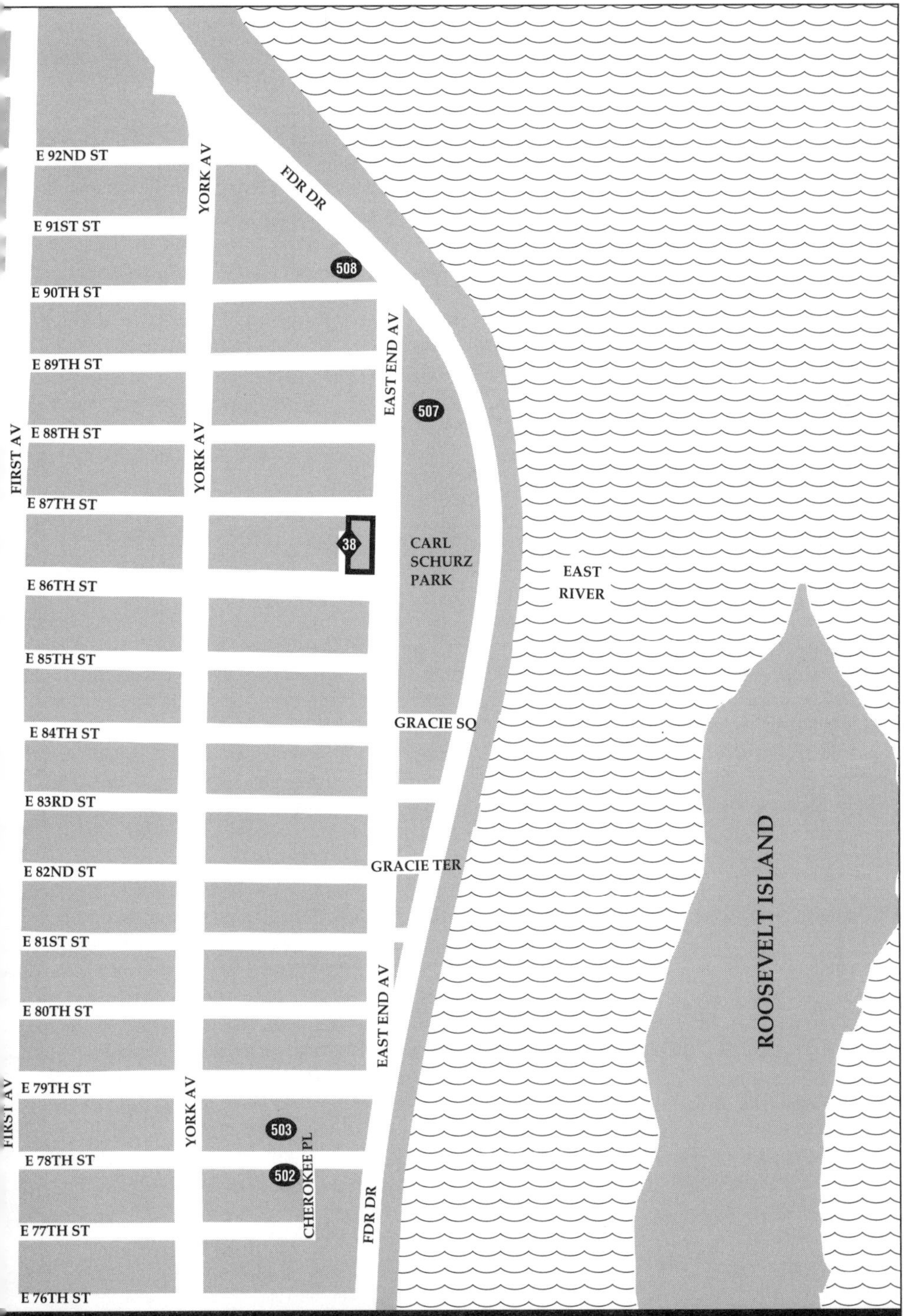

MAP **15**

MANHATTAN

E 92ND ST

E 91ST ST

508

E 90TH ST

E 89TH ST

E 88TH ST

E 87TH ST

38

CARL
SCHURZ
PARK

EAST
RIVER

E 86TH ST

E 85TH ST

E 84TH ST

GRACIE SQ

E 83RD ST

E 82ND ST

GRACIE TER

E 81ST ST

E 80TH ST

ROOSEVELT ISLAND

E 79TH ST

503

E 78TH ST

502

E 77TH ST

E 76TH ST

YORK AV

FDR DR

EAST END AV

507

FIRST AV

YORK AV

EAST END AV

FIRST AV

YORK AV

CHEROKEE PL

FDR DR

UPPER EAST SIDE, EAST 76TH STREET TO EAST 94TH STREET

■ WEST OF MADISON AVENUE

HISTORIC DISTRICTS

㉟ Metropolitan Museum Historic District, designated 1977. Located across Fifth Avenue from Central Park and the Metropolitan Museum of Art, this district traces the three main stages of residential development on the Upper East Side. Many modest row houses were built on speculation on the district's side streets in the 1870s and 1880s, especially after the Third Avenue Elevated began operation in 1878. Examples of these early houses are still evident in the district, notably at 22 and 26 East 78th Street, two Italianate houses (Silas M. Styles, 1871), and 4 East 78th Street, a Queen Anne–style house (Edward Kilpatrick, 1887–89). The area was then transformed into one of New York's most exclusive residential neighborhoods beginning in the 1890s, when the city's financial and social elite constructed mansions and town houses. Especially fine examples of these houses can be seen on the block bounded by East 78th and 79th Streets and Fifth and Madison Avenues, where the town houses designed by Warren & Wetmore; C. P. H. Gilbert; Ogden Codman; McKim, Mead & White; Horace Trumbauer; and other leading architects remain remarkably intact. In the second decade of the 20th century, such luxury apartment houses as 998 Fifth Avenue (see No. 469) began to replace the mansions. This development continued into the 1920s, when most of the restrained limestone and brick buildings on Fifth Avenue were erected and when the more progressive Art Deco apartment house, designed by Howells & Hood for *Daily News* publisher Joseph M. Patterson, was built in 1927–28 at 3 East 84th Street. The apartment building at 1001 Fifth Avenue, with an early postmodern facade, was designed by Philip Johnson and constructed in 1978–80.

㊱ Carnegie Hill Historic District, designated 1974, expanded 1993. The history of building construction in Carnegie Hill (generally the area between East 86th and East 96th Streets and Fifth and Lexington Avenues) is quite complex, with overlapping phases of residential development. By the mid-19th century, this area had scattered houses, including a number of wooden dwellings, such as 120 and 122 East 92nd Street (see No. 495). With the opening of the elevated rail lines on Third Avenue (1878) and Second Avenue (1880), speculative development of row houses for middle-class residents in the neo-Grec, Romanesque Revival, and Queen Anne styles began on the side streets and along Madison Avenue. There is a hierarchy to these houses, with the largest on the blocks between Fifth and Madison Avenues, close to Central Park, such as Cleverdon & Putzel's row of four-story houses at 5–25 East 94th Street (1892–94) and Thomas Graham's similar row at 6–14 East 92nd Street (1890–92); narrower, three-story houses between Madison and Park Avenues, including James E. Ware's row at 1285–1293 Madison Avenue (1889–90); and the smallest houses to the east of Park Avenue. The most notable ensemble is on East 95th Street between Park and Lexington Avenues, where four obscure architects—Frank Wennemer, Louis Entzer, Jr., Flemer & Koehler, and C. Abbott French & Co.—created one of the city's loveliest streets between 1887 and 1892. A second phase of development was inaugurated by Andrew Carnegie when he purchased the Fifth Avenue blockfront between East 90th and East 91st Streets in 1898 for the construction of a large mansion (see No. 477). In the first decades of the 20th century, other wealthy families moved to the area, building large houses or redesigning the older row houses. Many of the mansions are individual landmarks (see below), but others are not, including the English neoclassical William and Elsie Woodward House at 9 East 86th Street (formerly the Town Club, Delano & Aldrich, 1916–18); Henry and Annie Phipps' Italian Renaissance town house (now the Liederkranz Society, Grosvenor Atterbury, 1902–04) at 6 East 87th Street; Ogden Codman's French neoclassical house for Archer and Helen Huntington (now the National Academy of Design, 1913–15) at 1083 Fifth Avenue; and the four austere Colonial Revival town houses designed by Delano & Aldrich (1919–22) for R. Fulton Cutting's four children at 15 East 88th Street and 12–16 East 89th Street (now Saint David's School). At the same time that the mansions were being built, apartment houses planned for other wealthy families were beginning to rise in the area. Among the earliest were George & Edward Blum's white brick and terra-cotta Capitol at 12 East 87th Street (1910–11) and 1067 Fifth Avenue (1914–17), only the second luxury apartment house on Fifth Avenue, designed by C. P. H. Gilbert in an adaptation of the Francis I style that he favored for town-house designs. Major apartment-house construction occurred on Fifth and Park Avenues in the 1920s, including seven Fifth Avenue buildings by the noted designer of luxury apartments J. E. R. Carpenter. As wealthy families moved to Carnegie Hill, several society churches and schools also relocated to the area, notably the Church of the Heavenly Rest (Episcopal), which erected Mayers, Murray & Phillip's neo-Gothic church with facade sculpture by Lee Lawrie in 1927–29 on the corner of Fifth Avenue and East 90th Street; Brick Presbyterian, which commissioned a Colonial Revival church for a site on Park Avenue between East 91st and East 92nd Streets from York & Sawyer in 1937; the Spence School, which moved into a restrained Colonial Revival building (John Russell Pope, 1929) at 20 East 91st Street; and the Colonial Revival Nightingale-Bamford School (Delano & Aldrich, 1929), at 20–24 East 92nd Street. In the second decade of the 20th century, Madison Avenue lost some of its residential character, as the lower stories of row houses were converted into fashionable stores. After World War II some of the mansions were demolished and replaced by undistinguished apartment buildings, and many of the row houses and mansions were converted for school, museum, and other institutional uses. At this time the neighborhood also became home to the Guggenheim Museum (see No. 472), one of the great buildings of the mid-20th century. Carnegie Hill now contains a lively mix of residential, commercial, and institutional buildings.

INDIVIDUAL LANDMARKS

467 **James B. and Nanaline Duke House,** now the New York University Institute of Fine Arts, 1 East 78th Street (Horace Trumbauer, 1909–12), designated 1970. This enormous freestanding house, modeled on the 18th-century Château Labottière in Bordeaux, is one of the most magnificent mansions in New York. Duke was born a poor boy in North Carolina and eventually rose to become a figure of unrivaled power in the American tobacco industry. Nanaline Duke and her daughter Doris gave the mansion to New York University in 1957, and it has been successfully adapted for use as the university's graduate school of art history.

468 **Payne and Helen Hay Whitney House,** now the Office of Cultural Services, Embassy of France, 972 Fifth Avenue (McKim, Mead & White,

Stanford White, partner in charge, 1902–09), designated 1970. Financier Oliver H. Payne commissioned this house as a wedding gift for his nephew Payne Whitney and Whitney's bride, Helen Hay. The bowfront marble mansion is one of Stanford White's most successful Italian High Renaissance–inspired designs. The Republic of France acquired the building in 1952.

469 **998 Fifth Avenue** (McKim, Mead & White, William S. Richardson, partner in charge, 1910–12), designated 1970. This magnificent Italian Renaissance–inspired building, with street elevations clad entirely in limestone with yellow marble trim and a

998 Fifth Avenue (No. 469). This early apartment house designed by McKim, Mead & White became the model for hundreds of other buildings later erected on the East Side. Photo by Carl Forster.

spectacular copper cornice, was the first luxury apartment house erected on Fifth Avenue north of 59th Street. The expansive simplex and duplex units appealed to an elite clientele, and the building was rapidly rented. In its form and detail, the building became the model for New York City apartment houses, with hundreds later erected on Fifth, Park, and other avenues.

470 **1009 Fifth Avenue,** also known as the Benjamin N. and Sarah Duke House (Welch, Smith & Provot, 1899–1901), designated 1974. Soon after its completion, this Beaux-Arts town house, erected on speculation, was sold to Benjamin N. Duke, a director of the American Tobacco Company. In 1907 Benjamin's brother James purchased the house, where he lived until the completion of his own nearby mansion (see No. 467) in 1912. Until recently the house was occupied by other members of the Duke family. A superb restoration was completed in 1985.

471 **Metropolitan Museum of Art,** Fifth Avenue at East 82nd Street (major wings by Calvert Vaux and Jacob Wrey Mould, 1870–80; Thomas Weston with Arthur L. Tuckerman, associate, 1883–88; Arthur L. Tuckerman, 1890–94; Richard Morris Hunt, 1894–95; Richard Howland Hunt and George B. Post, 1895–1902; McKim, Mead & White, 1904–26; Kevin Roche John Dinkeloo Associates, 1967–90), designated 1967, interior 1977. In their original design for Central Park (see No. 376), Frederick Law Olmsted and Calvert Vaux sited the Metropolitan Museum of Art on a plot west of Fifth Avenue at 82nd Street. The original museum building, a High Victorian Gothic structure designed by Vaux and Jacob Wrey Mould (and now partially visible as the inner wall of the Lehman Wing), was built set back from Fifth Avenue, although Vaux planned for a larger museum facing the avenue. As the Metropolitan expanded its collections, a series of wings was added. The early wings, such as Weston and Tuckerman's south wing (now visible in the Petrie

Sculpture Court), were built in the park; the focus changed, however, with the design of Richard Morris Hunt's Beaux-Arts central pavilion (completed by Richard Howland Hunt following his father's death in 1895) on Fifth Avenue. On the **interior** the vestibule, Great Hall, and stairway, designed by Richard Morris Hunt and constructed under the supervision of his son, with George B. Post as consulting architect, provide a fitting introduction to the expanded museum. Beginning in 1904 the Metropolitan undertook additions on Fifth Avenue designed by Charles F. McKim of the firm McKim, Mead & White that represent a simplified version of Hunt's design. Kevin Roche John Dinkeloo Associates was commissioned to prepare a master plan for the museum in 1967; the last of the firm's modern stone-and-glass wings was completed in 1990. Its American Wing, built at the northwest corner of the complex, incorporates the facade of the former Bank of New York (Martin E. Thompson, 1823–25), which was saved from destruction and moved to the museum in 1924.

472 **Solomon R. Guggenheim Museum,** 1071 Fifth Avenue (Frank Lloyd Wright, 1956–59), designated 1990. Established by Solomon R. Guggenheim as a repository of nonobjective (i.e., abstract) art, the Guggenheim Museum is housed in one of the most acclaimed buildings of the 20th century. The museum is the major New York City work of the American master Frank Lloyd Wright and is often considered to be the crowning achievement of his later career. The building's organic form, a reversed spiral, was intended as a reflection of the natural shapes to be found across the street in Central Park. The **interior,** with its vast open space and spiraling cantilevered ramp punctuated by exhibition alcoves, is among Wright's most spectacular. In the basement is a circular auditorium also designed by the architect. In 1989–92 an addition by Charles Gwathmey of Gwathmey Siegel & Associates was constructed, and Wright's building was restored.

Solomon R. Guggenheim Museum (No. 472). Many consider the Guggenheim Museum to be the crowning achievement of architect Frank Lloyd Wright's later career. Photo by Caroline Kane Levy.

PRESERVING THE MODERNS

Modern architecture was introduced in New York City during the 1930s, in such buildings as the New School for Social Research (Manhattan H.D. 12, N) and in three town houses designed by William Lescaze. The earliest, located in Turtle Bay, was built as the Swiss-born architect's home and studio (Manhattan No. 332). Subsequent examples, the Raymond C. and Mildred Kramer House at 32 East 74th Street (1935), and the Edward and Dorothy Norman House at 124 East 70th Street (1940), are located within the Upper East Side Historic District (Manhattan H.D. 33). Designed to contrast with their older brick, brownstone, and limestone neighbors, these houses have unornamented white brick and stucco facades that incorporate steel frame windows, glass blocks, and lally or pipe columns. Modern aesthetics also influenced the design and planning of the Rockefeller Apartments and 240 Central Park West (Manhattan Nos. 310 and 367).

Interest in European Modernism, which came to be known as the International Style, increased dramatically after the Second World War. The uninterrupted green glass and aluminum curtain walls of the United Nations Secretariat, erected in 1947–52, were greeted by the architectural community as a sign of progress. In the decades that followed, Park Avenue was transformed from a street of mostly masonry apartment buildings to one of gleaming glass skyscrapers. Lever House, completed in 1952, led the group, followed by the bronze-faced Seagram Building and jewel-like Pepsi Cola Building (Manhattan Nos. 300, 338, and 429). Notable for their modern materials and formal elegance, these widely praised structures redefined the image of corporate America. Other noteworthy designations from this era include the Rockefeller Guest House, Manufacturer's Trust Company Building, the lobby of the Time & Life Building, and Asia House at 112 East 64th Street (Manhattan Nos. 340, 281, 346, and H.D. 33). Some of the most remarkable landmarks from the mid-20th century are also great feats of engineering. Most were executed in reinforced concrete and have a strong sculptural character. While the Solomon R. Guggenheim Museum, CBS Building, and Trans World Airlines Flight Center at Kennedy International Airport are classic examples (Manhattan Nos. 472 and 301, Queens No. 50), the Municipal Asphalt Building, Begrisch Hall on the campus of Bronx Community College, and the Civic Center Synagogue at 49 White Street in the Tribeca North Historic District also deserve attention (Manhattan No. 508, Bronx No. 26, and Manhattan H.D. 8). The Ford Foundation Building, completed in 1967, is the youngest designated landmark (Manhattan No. 328). Clad in granite and Cor-ten steel, the building contains one of the city's most beautiful and unique interiors—a terraced garden.

473 **Grafton W. and Anne Minot House,** also known as the 11 East 90th Street House (A. Wallace McCrea, 1929), designated 1974. The present austere facade of this house was inspired by 18th-century French designs. It replaces the original Beaux-Arts front designed by Barney & Chapman and built in 1902–03 for William and Louise McAlpin. A. Wallace McCrea specialized in this type of townhouse modernization. The building is now part of the Cooper-Hewitt Museum complex (see No. 477).

474 **Emily Trevor House,** also known as the 15 East 90th Street House (Mott B. Schmidt, 1927–28), designated 1974. This red brick house, with its carefully detailed limestone portico and trim, is an essay in English 18th-century design. It was built for the sister of John B. Trevor, whose house is located on East 91st Street (see No. 481).

475 **17 East 90th Street** (F. Burrall Hoffman, Jr., 1917–19), designated 1974. This handsome Colonial Revival brick house with an unusual street-level arcade was commissioned by Robert and Charlotte Fowler, who apparently never lived here, since the property was sold in 1919.

476 **1261 Madison Avenue** (Buchman & Fox, 1900–01), designated 1974. This elegant Beaux-Arts apartment house has a characteristic limestone facade with a mansard roof, iron balconies, and three-dimensional carved detail. Its construction in 1900 reflected a change in the character of the area now known as Carnegie Hill, as imposing new apartment houses intended for affluent residents joined the neighborhood's earlier tenements and row houses.

477 **Andrew and Louise Carnegie House,** now the Cooper-Hewitt National Design Museum, Smithsonian Institution, 2 East 91st Street (Babb, Cook & Willard, 1899–1903), designated 1974. After Andrew Carnegie purchased this large plot on a relatively undeveloped section of Fifth Avenue, he evicted a few squatters and demolished a riding academy and several tenements so that he could build what he envisioned as "the most modest, plainest and most roomy house in New York." The 64-room house synthesized "modest and plain" Georgian-inspired brickwork with Beaux-Arts ornament and incorporated the most advanced mechanical and structural systems of the day. Carnegie chose the site because it permitted him to lay out a large garden; the original landscape plan, probably by Schermerhorn & Foulks, is largely extant. In 1972 the mansion became the property of the Smithsonian Institution, which commissioned architect Hugh Hardy to convert the building into a museum of design. The Carnegie site also includes the Colonial Revival **George L. McAlpin House** at 9 East 90th Street (George Keister, 1902–03), which became the home of Carnegie's daughter in 1920. The two houses were connected in 1996–97 and other changes made (including the skillful addition of a ramp for handicapped access to the front entrance) by James Stewart Polshek & Partners, architects.

478 **Otto and Addie Kahn House,** now the Convent of the Sacred Heart, 1 East 91st Street (J. Armstrong Stenhouse, with C. P. H. Gilbert, 1913–18), designated 1974. British architect J. Armstrong Stenhouse worked with C. P. H. Gilbert to create this magnificent limestone mansion, modeled on the 15th-century Palazzo della Cancelleria in Rome. The client, the banker Otto Kahn, was one of New York's most generous patrons of the arts; he twice aided in saving the Metropolitan Opera, backed many American theatrical organizations, and sponsored the American tours of such European institutions as Stanislavsky's Moscow Art Theater and Diaghilev's Ballet Russe. Since 1934 the house has served as the Convent of the Sacred Heart's prestigious school for girls. The facade was cleaned and restored in 1994.

479 **James A. and Florence Sloane Burden House,** now the Convent of the Sacred Heart, 7 East 91st Street (Warren & Wetmore, 1902–05), designated 1974. William Sloane and his wife, Emily Vanderbilt Sloane, built this house and the neighboring Hammond House (see below) for their daughters on land purchased from Andrew Carnegie, whose own house was across the street (see No. 477) and who acquired a significant amount of property in the neighborhood in order to regulate its development. Warren & Wetmore provided Florence Sloane and her husband, James A. Burden, Jr. (son of the founder of the Burden Ironworks), with a grand, limestone-clad Beaux-Arts mansion with facades fronting both the street and the drive set between the two houses.

480 **John Henry and Emily Vanderbilt Sloane Hammond House,** now Consulate General of the Russian Federation in New York, 9 East 91st Street (Carrère & Hastings, 1902–03), designated 1974. This grand house, designed in the 16th-century Roman manner, and its neighbor, the Burden House (see above), were erected for the daughters and sons-in-law of William and Emily Vanderbilt Sloane on land that the Sloanes had purchased from Andrew Carnegie. The beautifully proportioned limestone-faced mansion is among the most impressive residential designs of Carrère & Hastings. The Hammonds' son John was a famous jazz promoter, and their daughter Alice married jazz great Benny Goodman. The house has been beautifully restored by the current owners.

481 **John B. and Caroline Trevor House,** now Consulate General of the Russian Federation in New York, 11 East 91st Street (Trowbridge & Livingston,

The Otto and Addie Kahn House (No. 478) was modeled on the 15th-century Palazzo della Cancelleria in Rome. Photo by Carl Forster.

1909–11), designated 1974. The Trevor House is the smallest of the four landmark town houses on the north side of East 91st Street. The simple French neoclassical residence is faced with limestone articulated by a trio of arched openings on the main floor and is crowned by a mansard roof.

482 Felix and Frieda S. Warburg House, now the Jewish Museum, 1109 Fifth Avenue (C. P. H. Gilbert, 1907–08), designated 1981. Gilbert, who specialized in mansions in the style of Francis I, designed similar limestone-faced, Loire Valley château–inspired houses for Isaac D. Fletcher (on Fifth Avenue at East 79th Street, now in the Metropolitan Museum Historic District), F. W. Woolworth (demolished), and the wealthy German-Jewish banker Felix Warburg. In 1944 Frieda Schiff Warburg donated the house as a permanent home for the Jewish Museum. An addition in 1990–93 by Kevin Roche that copied the design of the original house more than doubled the size of the museum.

■ **EAST OF MADISON AVENUE TO LEXINGTON AVENUE**

483 John S. and Catharine C. Rogers House, now the New York Society Library, 53 East 79th Street (Trowbridge & Livingston, 1916–17), designated 1967. The most impressive of the four landmark town houses on the north side of East 79th Street, the Rogers House was built for a wealthy lawyer and his wife. The limestone structure, whose design is based on Italian Renaissance prototypes, has housed the New York Society Library since 1937. Established in 1754, the library is the oldest in New York City and the fourth oldest in the country.

484 **John H. and Caroline Iselin House,** also known as the 59 East 79th Street House (Foster, Gade & Graham, 1908–09), designated 1981. The socially prominent lawyer John Iselin and his wife commissioned this house, which is stylistically unusual in its combination of Northern Renaissance and French classic forms, and lived here until 1919. It is one of four adjacent landmark town houses constructed early in the 20th century, when East 79th Street became an especially prestigious residential address.

485 **Thatcher and Frances Adams House,** also known as the 63 East 79th Street House (Adams & Warren, 1902–03), designated 1981. Lawyer Thatcher Adams commissioned this English neoclassical town house. The brick and limestone building is reminiscent of the urban dwellings of 18th-century London. The original mansard roof was replaced by the present fourth and fifth stories in 1945 (Elias K. Herzog, architect).

486 **George and Sarah Rives House,** also known as the 67–69 East 79th Street House, now the Greek Consulate General (Carrère & Hastings, 1907–08), designated 1981. Modeled on the late 17th-century town houses built on la place Vendôme in Paris, this house was commissioned by the lawyer, statesman (he was assistant secretary of state), and historian George Rives and his second wife, Sarah. Rives was an especially active supporter of New York's prominent institutions, serving on the boards of Columbia University (working closely with Seth Low in planning the Morningside Heights campus), the New York Public Library, and New York Hospital, as well as on the New York City Rapid Transit Commission, which guided construction of the New York City subway. In 1962 the Greek architect Pierre Zannettos altered the top two floors of the house and added a sixth story.

487 **Lewis Spencer and Emily Coster Morris House,** also known as the 116 East 80th Street House (Cross & Cross, 1922–23), designated 1967. The design of this house, the earliest of four adjoining landmark town houses, was based closely on

18th-century London residences. Especially notable features are the house's projecting central pedimented pavilion and the brick arches of the ground-floor windows. Lewis Spencer Morris traced his ancestry back to one of New York's most prominent colonial families. He was a lawyer, trustee of the Cathedral of Saint John the Divine, and a trustee of the New York Society Library.

488 **George and Martha Whitney House,** also known as the 120 East 80th Street House (Cross & Cross, 1929–30), designated 1968. The town house commissioned by George Whitney is the most elaborate of the four adjacent landmark houses on East 80th Street, all modeled on 18th-century London residences. Whitney was an internationally famous financier who served for many years as the head of J. P. Morgan & Co.

489 **Clarence and Anne Douglass Dillon House,** also known as the 124 East 80th Street House (Mott B. Schmidt, 1930), designated 1967. This four-story brick house, the last of the four large landmark town houses in the English neoclassical style erected on the south side of East 80th Street between 1922 and 1930, was commissioned by the financier Clarence Dillon and his wife, Anne. Their son, C. Douglas Dillon, would later serve as secretary of the Treasury. The Dillon House and its neighbor, the Vincent Astor House (see below), are fine examples of the sophisticated work of Mott B. Schmidt, a popular society architect who specialized in the design of residences in 18th-century revival styles.

490 **Vincent and Helen Astor House,** now the Junior League of the City of New York, 130 East 80th Street (Mott B. Schmidt, 1927–28), designated 1967. This grand limestone town house is closely modeled on Robert Adam's Society of Arts Building at the Adelphi in London. The house was erected by the millionaire real-estate owner and social reformer Vincent Astor, head of the American branch of the Astor family. Astor's fortune was used to establish the Vincent Astor Fund, which has benefited major social welfare projects in New York City and assisted such institutions as the New York Public Library.

491 **Church of Saint Ignatius Loyola (R.C.),** 980 Park Avenue (Schickel & Ditmars, 1895–1900), designated 1969. As is characteristic of Jesuit churches, the design of Saint Ignatius Loyola is modeled on the Jesuits' Renaissance churches in Rome. The symmetrically massed, limestone-faced structure rests on the rough stone base (visible on East 84th Street) of an earlier church, dedicated to Saint Lawrence O'Toole, that was begun in 1884 but never finished.

492 Regis High School, 55 East 84th Street (Maginnis & Walsh, 1913–17), designated 1969. Designed to harmonize in scale with the Church of Saint Ignatius Loyola (see above), across the street, Regis is an imposing five-story Classical Revival limestone building with street fronts on both East 84th and East 85th Streets. The school was founded by the Jesuits in 1912 to provide a liberal arts education to gifted Catholic men. The building was designed by a Boston firm that specialized in work for Roman Catholic institutions.

493 Lewis Gouverneur and Nathalie Bailey Morris House, 100 East 85th Street (Ernest Flagg, 1913–14), designated 1973. Flagg designed this idiosyncratic house for a descendant of a prominent colonial New York family. The town house is massed in three sections, all oriented toward East 85th Street: the main residential block, a rear wing with a garage at street level, and a stairway wing recessed behind a narrow court. The design combines American colonial detail with the massing and the free use of 18th-century forms favored by the English architect Richard Norman Shaw.

494 Reginald and Anna DeKoven House, 1025 Park Avenue (John Russell Pope, 1911–12), designated 1986. The light-opera composer Reginald DeKoven and his wife, the writer Anna DeKoven, commissioned this brick and limestone mansion from John Russell Pope, an architect best known for his austere classical buildings. The house was built after work was completed on the roofing of the Park Avenue railroad tracks. It was designed in the Jacobean Revival style, providing evidence of Pope's wide-ranging architectural talents.

495 120 and 122 East 92nd Street (No. 120, 1871; No. 122, attributed to Albro Howell, carpenter-builder, 1859), designated 1969. These two vernacular frame houses recall the period before intense

urbanization altered the semirural character of the Upper East Side. Each of the houses has a deep front porch, heavy window surrounds, and a bracketed cornice—all typical features of Italianate design. No. 122 was built by Adam C. Flanagan, a custom-house officer. In 1871 Flanagan sold adjacent land to John C. and Catherine E. Rennert. John Rennert, a wine merchant, commissioned No. 120.

496 George F. Baker, Jr., House Complex, now (in part) the Russian Orthodox Church Outside of Russia, 67, 69, and 75 East 93rd Street (No. 75, main house, 1917–18; No. 71–73, ballroom wing, 1928; No. 69, 1928–29; No. 67, 1931—all by Delano & Aldrich), designated 1969; No. 67, 1974. The main section of this complex, at the corner of Park Avenue and East 93rd Street, was commissioned by the financier Francis F. Palmer. Ten years after it was begun, the elegant town house was sold to George F. Baker, Jr., chairman of the First National Bank (now Citibank). Baker enlarged the house, first by the addition of a ballroom wing at No. 71–73 and garage (No. 69 East 93rd Street) and the creation of an open court to the west of the house, and later by the addition of 67 East 93rd Street, intended as a home for Baker's father, who died before the house was completed. The entire complex is a superb example of Delano & Aldrich's sophisticated handling of English and American 18th-century architectural forms. In 1958 the main house and its ballroom wing were converted for use as a Russian Orthodox church; a courtyard stairway was built to facilitate this new use.

497 Virginia Graham Fair Vanderbilt House, 60 East 93rd Street (John Russell Pope, 1930–31), designated 1968. Vanderbilt was a society leader, a racehorse breeder, the ex-wife of William K. Vanderbilt, and the daughter of Senator James Fair of Nevada, who made his fortune tapping the Comstock lode and the Big Bonanza mine. The limestone house resembles the great private *hôtels* built in Paris during the reign of Louis XV.

498 William Goadby and Florence Baker Loew House, now the Spence School, 56 East 93rd Street (Walker & Gillette, 1930–31), designated 1972. The scale and austere geometry of this monumental limestone mansion are reminiscent of late 18th-century English design. William Loew was a wealthy stockbroker and socialite with the financial resources to build this mansion during the Depression. The site was acquired soon after Loew's brother-in-law George Baker purchased a house across the street (see No. 496). The facade of the Loew House, with its concave front and refined fluted arches, is among the most unusual in New York. Following Loew's death in 1955, the house was acquired by theatrical producer Billy Rose, who lived here until his death in 1966.

499 **1321 Madison Avenue** (James E. Ware, 1890–91), designated 1974. This Queen Anne house with a towering pyramidal roof was originally the end building of a row of five brownstone-fronted dwellings. The brick facade on East 93rd Street has a prominent entrance set above a massive stone stoop.

■ EAST OF LEXINGTON AVENUE

HISTORIC DISTRICT

37 **Hardenbergh/Rhinelander Historic District,** designated 1998. The Rhinelander family played an important role in the development of the Carnegie Hill–Yorkville area. Most of their projects were well-designed private residences, including row houses and apartment buildings. The structures in the historic district were built on undeveloped lots in 1888–89. All were designed by Henry J. Hardenbergh, one of the period's most distinguished architects. Six identical row houses are aligned along Lexington Avenue, with a small apartment building on 89th Street. Clad in red brick and terra cotta, as well as brownstone, they incorporate picturesque details inspired by Northern Renaissance models. Above the ground story the facades are well preserved, embellished with terra-cotta panels and alternating pierced and pedimented parapets. The Rhinelander family owned these seven structures until 1948. In subsequent years, they were sold to private owners, including Andy Warhol, who lived at 1342 Lexington Avenue from 1960 to 1972.

38 **Henderson Place Historic District,** designated 1969. The twenty-four picturesque Queen Anne houses of this district survive from an enclave

of thirty-two houses built in 1881 by the developer John C. Henderson for "persons of moderate means." The architecture firm Lamb & Rich composed each blockfront as a unit, emphasizing the ends with small towers and creating lively street fronts. Henderson erected these modest houses as an investment, and most remained in his family until the 20th century. As is characteristic of the Queen Anne style, the massing is dynamic and the facades are richly textured. The houses are built of brick and rough stone and are enlivened by projecting bays and oriels, small-paned windows, and a roof line with an eccentric silhouette of gables, dormers, mansards, and stout towers with slate shingles.

INDIVIDUAL LANDMARKS

500 **157, 159, 161, 163, and 165 East 78th Street** (1861), designated 1968. These five brick houses with Italianate elements survive from a row of eleven erected by the builder Henry Armstrong at the time when the Upper East Side was just beginning to attract middle-class home owners. Nos. 163 and 165 have been combined into a single residence.

501 **208, 210, 212, 214, 216, and 218 East 78th Street** (1861–65), designated 1978. These six narrow Italianate row houses, surviving from a speculative venture that included the construction of fifteen identical red brick houses, were built just after the streets of Yorkville were opened in 1860. The unusual elliptically arched doors and windows on the facades lend a rhythmic pattern to the streetscape.

502 **East River Houses,** now the Cherokee Apartments, 507–523 East 77th Street and 508–522 East 78th Street (Henry Atterbury Smith, 1909–11), designated as the Shively Sanitary Tenements, 1985. The East River Houses were erected in response to two of New York City's most pressing social problems—a serious tuberculosis epidemic and the need for affordable housing. These "model tenements," sponsored by Mrs. William K. Vanderbilt, were intended to house working people, especially families in which a member suffered from tuberculosis. The idea for this complex was conceived by Henry Shively, a physician and an expert on consumption. The

Henderson Place Historic District (H.D. 38). Some of the twenty-four picturesque Queen Anne–style houses in the district. Photo by Peter Choy.

tenements were designed by architect and housing reformer Henry Atterbury Smith, with large central courts approached by passageways with Guastavino tile vaults, triple-sash windows, balconies with Guastavino tiles on the undersides, and open stair towers—all features maximizing the amount of sunlight and fresh air that reached each apartment. The buildings underwent an extensive exterior restoration in 1989–90.

503 **City and Suburban Homes Company, Avenue A (York Avenue) Estate,** 1470–1492 York Avenue, 501–555 East 78th Street, and 502–540 East 79th Street (Harde & Short, Percy Griffin, and

East River Houses (No. 502). These model tenements contained design features that maximized the amount of sunlight and fresh air that reached each apartment. Photo by Carl Forster.

Philip H. Ohm, 1900–13), designated 1990. The Avenue A Estate was, at the time of its completion, the largest "model tenement" complex ever built. It was a project of the City and Suburban Homes Company (see No. 465). The various buildings have different plans and room arrangements. All are clad in brick and feature modest amounts of ornament. Of special interest are the Potter Memorial buildings at 516 and 520 East 79th Street, designed in an appropriate neo-Gothic style as a memorial to the Episcopal bishop Henry C. Potter. The complex also included the Junior League Hotel for Women at 541–555 East 78th Street, erected to provide inexpensive accommodation for single working women, which has been converted into apartments.

504 New York Public Library, Yorkville Branch, 222 East 79th Street (James Brown Lord, 1902), designated 1967. The Palladian-inspired Yorkville Library was the first of numerous branch libraries throughout the city built as a result of An-

drew Carnegie's 1901 gift to the New York Public Library. This facility had been planned many years earlier by the New York Free Circulating Library, which explains the choice of James Brown Lord as architect; Lord had previously designed the Free Circulating Library's Bloomingdale Branch (see No. 419).

505 Sidewalk Clock (see No. 191), 1501 Third Avenue at East 84th Street (E. Howard Clock Company, late 19th century), designated 1981. This unusual sidewalk clock, designed in the form of a giant pocket watch, was erected by the jeweler Adolph Stern in front of his shop at 1508 Third Avenue. When the business relocated across the street in the 1920s, the clock was also moved. At some point after 1900, arms were placed above the watch fob; these once supported the three golden balls that are a traditional symbol of a pawnbroker.

506 Church of the Holy Trinity (Episcopal) Complex, 316–332 East 88th Street (Barney &

Chapman; Saint Christopher House, 1896–97; addition, 1897–99), designated 1967. Serena Rhinelander donated this church as a memorial to her father and grandfather, building it on land that had been in her family since 1798. Holy Trinity was planned as a settlement church, run by the affluent Saint James Parish on Madison Avenue, to minister to the poorer residents of Yorkville. The complex—consisting of the church, the parsonage, and Saint Christopher House, all of French Gothic inspiration—is faced with rich tawny brick with extensive terra-cotta trim and is set around a landscaped court anchored by one of New York's most beautiful towers. The church was built three years after Barney & Chapman designed the similarly styled but simpler Grace Chapel (see No. 169).

507 **Gracie Mansion,** East End Avenue at East 88th Street (attributed to Ezra Weeks, 1799–1804; Susan B. Wagner wing, Mott B. Schmidt, 1965–66), designated 1966. In 1793 the Scottish-born Archibald Gracie settled in New York, where he established a successful mercantile business. In 1798 Gracie began purchasing land on Horn's Hook, a small peninsula jutting into the East River at Hell Gate; here he erected a country house overlooking the river. The house was expanded in 1802–04. Gracie sold the property in 1823, and it had several owners before it was acquired by the city's Department of Parks in 1896. In 1924 the house was converted for use by the Museum of the City of New York. A major renovation was undertaken by the architect Aymar Embury II in 1934–36, following the museum's move to Fifth Avenue. Gracie Mansion became the official home of the mayor of New York City in 1942. Mott B. Schmidt added a wing to the house in 1965–66, and a major restoration was completed in 2003.

Gracie Mansion (No. 507). The official home of the mayor of New York City, Gracie Mansion was built between 1799 and 1804. Photo by John Barrington Bayley, c. 1965.

508 **Municipal Asphalt Plant,** now the Murphy Center at Asphalt Green, Franklin Delano Roosevelt Drive at East 90th Street (Kahn & Jacobs, 1941–44), designated 1976. The asphalt plant, built adjacent to the FDR Drive, was the first successful American use of the parabolic arch form in reinforced concrete. The radical design was based on principles that Robert Allan Jacobs had studied while working for Le Corbusier in France. The plant ceased operations in 1968 and the building was converted to a recreation center in 1984.

509 **146, 148, 150, 152, 154, and 156 East 89th Street** (Hubert, Pirsson & Co., 1886–87), designated 1979. Six houses survive from an original group of ten striking Queen Anne dwellings erected by William Rhinelander, whose family had acquired this land in 1812. The narrow houses were designed as a unit with richly textured facades, oriels, and a continuous mansard roof pierced by gables, dormers, and tall brick chimneys.

510 **160 East 92nd Street** (attributed to Albro Howell, carpenter-builder, 1852–53), designated 1988. One of the few residences to survive from the period when Yorkville was a country village, this vernacular frame house is surprisingly well preserved. The original Corinthian columns of the front porch were replaced around 1930.

Municipal Asphalt Plant (No. 508). This building was the first successful American use of the parabolic arch form in reinforced concrete. Photo by Carl Forster.

UPPER EAST SIDE AND EAST HARLEM, EAST 94TH TO EAST 106TH STREETS

MAP **16**

HISTORIC DISTRICT

Carnegie Hill Historic District. See Map 15.

INDIVIDUAL LANDMARKS

511 **Squadron A Armory,** Madison Avenue between East 94th and 95th Streets (John R. Thomas, 1893–95), designated 1966. The picturesque battlemented Madison Avenue facade is all that remains of the monumental Squadron A Armory, which once occupied the entire block between Madison and Park Avenues. The facade was saved when the remainder of the building was demolished in 1966, and it now serves as the entrance to the playground of the Hunter College High School.

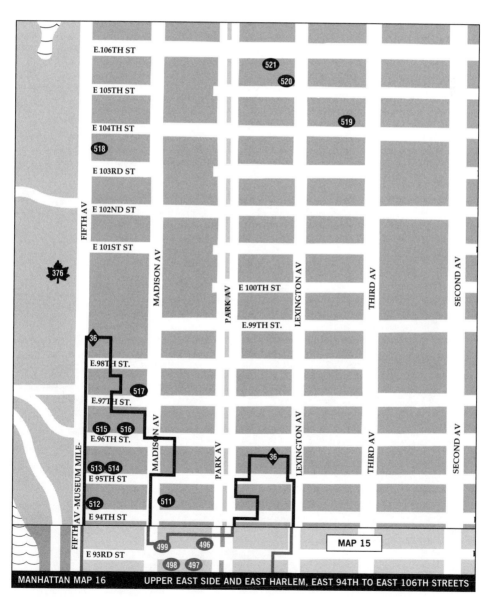

512 **Willard and Dorothy Whitney Straight House,** later the National Audubon Society and the International Center of Photography, 1130 Fifth Avenue (Delano & Aldrich, 1913–15), designated 1968. This imposing English Georgian Revival house was commissioned by Willard Straight, a diplomat and financier who specialized in Far Eastern affairs. While working as a Far East expert for J. P. Morgan & Co., Straight established India House (see No. 44), a club whose members were involved with foreign ventures. With the financial assistance of his wife, Straight later founded *The New Republic* and *Asia* magazines. The Straights' house is one of Delano & Aldrich's boldest designs. Of special note are the ocular windows on the upper story, which are modeled after similar windows on the wing of Hampton Court Palace in England designed by Christopher Wren. It is now a private residence.

513 **Mrs. Amory S. Carhart House,** 3 East 95th Street (Horace Trumbauer, 1913–16), designated 1974. Designed to resemble a Parisian town house from the era of Louis XVI, this elegant neoclassical limestone building is the work of the firm of the Philadelphia architect Horace Trumbauer. Mrs. Carhart commissioned the house a year after her husband's death but lived here only briefly before her own death in 1918.

514 **Ernesto and Edith Fabbri House,** now the House of the Redeemer, 7 East 95th Street (Egisto Fabbri and Grosvenor Atterbury, 1914–16), designated 1974. Edith Fabbri, great-granddaughter of Cornelius Vanderbilt, and her husband, the Italian count Ernesto Fabbri, built this L-shaped Italian Renaissance–inspired house; Count Fabbri's family's crest, an arm holding a hammer, is visible in the iron gate of the courtyard. Although Atterbury is the architect of record, it was apparently Count Fabbri's brother, the Italian architect and interior designer Egisto Fabbri, who was responsible for the actual design. In 1949 Mrs. Fabbri transferred the property to the House of the Redeemer, an Episcopal retreat center.

515 **Ogden Codman House,** now Manhattan Country School, 7 East 96th Street (Ogden Codman, 1912–13), designated 1967. Ogden Codman, one of the most important residential architects and interior designers of the early 20th century, designed this house for himself. Codman's advocacy of French design is reflected in the facade, which is modeled after that of an 18th-century Parisian town house.

516 **Lucy Dahlgren House,** later the Pierre Cartier House, 15 East 96th Street (Ogden Codman, 1915–16), designated 1984. The Dahlgren House is a companion to Codman's own house nearby (see above). This French neoclassical town house was built for the socially prominent and enormously wealthy heiress Lucy Drexel Dahlgren, who apparently spent little time here. For many years the house was occupied by Pierre Cartier, founder of the jewelry firm that bears his name.

517 **Saint Nicholas Russian Orthodox Cathedral,** 15 East 97th Street (John Bergesen, 1901–02), designated 1973. Saint Nicholas, the diocesan seat of the Russian Orthodox Church in North America, was built with funds collected throughout the Russian empire. The design of the building, with its five onion domes, polychromatic detail, and *kokoshniki* (ogival pediments), derives from 17th-century Baroque churches in Moscow. The "Moscow Baroque" style was revived in Russia in the late 19th century and was adapted for this New York site by an architect of Russian descent.

518 **Museum of the City of New York,** 1220–1227 Fifth Avenue (Joseph J. Freedlander, 1928–30), designated 1967. Designed in a Georgian colonial style—an appropriate choice for this museum, which specializes in local history—this brick building with a white marble base and trim is massed around a courtyard that opens onto Fifth Avenue and Central Park. The museum was incorporated in 1923 and was originally housed in Gracie Mansion (see No. 507). The city donated the site be-

Saint Nicholas Russian Orthodox Cathedral (No. 517). The design of this church derives from 17th-century Baroque churches in Moscow. Photo: Landmarks Preservation Commission collection.

tween East 103rd and East 104th Streets, but funds for construction were privately subscribed.

519 **28th Police Precinct House,** 177–179 East 104th Street (Nathaniel D. Bush, 1892–93), designated 1999. Among the last buildings planned for the New York City Police Department by Bush, this midblock structure recalls his earlier design for the 19th Police Precinct (see No. 457). Completed in 1893, it served as a general model for at least four subsequent police stations. Since 1981 it has been used by Hope Community, Inc., a nonprofit housing organization.

520 **Public School 72,** later P.S. 107, now Julio de Burgos Cultural Center, 1674 Lexington Avenue (David I. Stagg, 1879–82; annex, C. B. J. Snyder, 1911–13), designated 1996. Erected to serve a rapidly growing immigrant community, this neo-Grec-style brick building with stone trim is one of the oldest intact school structures in Manhattan. The building, extending along the entire Lexington Avenue blockfront between East 105th and East 106th Streets, is massed with a series of interlocking cubic forms capped by towers. Architects Lee Barrero and Raymond Plumey restored the former school in 1994–95, converting it for use as a cultural center.

521 **Saint Cecilia's Church (R.C.) and Regina Angelorum,** 112–120 East 106th Street (church, Napoleon Le Brun & Sons, 1883–87; Regina Angelorum, Neville & Bagge, 1907), designated 1976. Founded in 1873, Saint Cecilia's was one of the first Roman Catholic churches in East Harlem. The facade of this Romanesque Revival structure reflects the architects' masterful use of brick and terra cotta, especially evident in the arched panel depicting Saint Cecilia, the patron saint of music, playing an organ. The Regina Angelorum was designed to complement the church; its facade unified two earlier buildings, which were then used as a convent and a home for working girls (now a convent and day nursery).

Public School 72 (No. 520), dating from 1879–82, is one of the oldest intact school structures in Manhattan. Photo by Carl Forster.

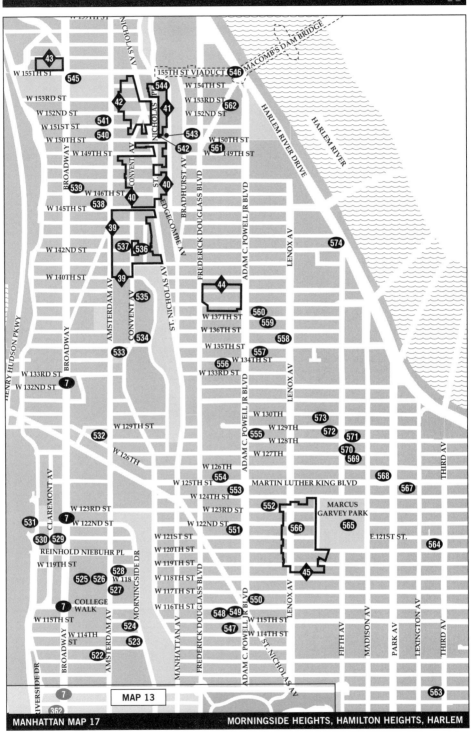

■ WEST OF FREDERICK DOUGLASS BOULEVARD

HISTORIC DISTRICTS

㊲ Hamilton Heights Historic District and Extension, designated 1974 and 2000. Located immediately north of City College (see No. 535) the Hamilton Heights Historic District is a neighborhood of row houses, apartment buildings, and impressive churches. The land was once part of Alexander Hamilton's estate, and Hamilton's own house is preserved at 287 Convent Avenue (see No. 536). The area remained largely undeveloped until the 1880s, when the new elevated rail line along Eighth Avenue brought it within commuting distance of Lower Manhattan. Speculative developers erected houses in a great variety of styles: Queen Anne residences lined Convent Avenue south of 144th Street, and some of the finest Northern Renaissance–inspired houses in the city were built at 453–467 West 144th Street. The block-long Hamilton Terrace, initially laid out as a private street, contains handsome brick and stone houses erected between 1895 and 1902. Deed restrictions limited construction in most of the district to row houses. However, the west side of Amsterdam Avenue was excluded, permitting construction of small apartment houses. Five to seven stories tall, these buildings were designed in various styles by Clarence True, Henry Andersen, and Neville & Bagge. When the deed restrictions expired in 1911, light-colored brick and limestone apartment houses were constructed to the east, such as Soundview Court at 260 Convent Avenue (George F. Pelham, 1911–12) and 270 Convent Avenue (Frank L. Norton, 1915–16). Architecturally the most significant religious structures are R. H. Robertson's St. Luke's Episcopal Church (1892–95) on Convent Avenue and West 141st Street, and Our Lady of Lourdes Church (see No. 537). The last building erected in the district, the Ivey Delph Apartments at 19 Hamilton Terrace, was designed in a Modernist style in 1948 by Vertner Tandy, the first black architect registered in New York State. Early residents of the district were mainly middle-class whites, both native and immigrant. During the 1920s and 1930s, many of the homes were sold to black families, and the neighborhood was commonly referred to as Sugar Hill. The celebrated musicians Billy Strayhorn and Mary Lou Williams lived in the district, as well as numerous writers and civic leaders.

㊵ Hamilton Heights/Sugar Hill Historic District and Extension, designated 2000 and 2001. This large district has residential buildings of great architectural and cultural merit. Built during a relatively short period, from the mid-1880s to the First World War, the area became known as Sugar Hill in the 1920s, when a large number of black professionals took residence. Celebrated in popular song and the media, the district was home to such notable figures as Adam Clayton Powell and Ralph Ellison. The earliest building in the district, a Queen Anne–style house at 8 St. Nicholas Place, was designed by Richard S. Rosenstock in 1885. The finest row houses were treated as block-long compositions in which materials and decorative features were arranged to create an unusually coherent streetscape, such as the Romanesque Revival row at 718–730 St. Nicholas Avenue (Arthur Bates Jennings, 1889–90), and a group of eleven neo-Renaissance houses at 757–775 St. Nicholas Avenue (Frederick P. Dinkelberg, 1894–95). Convent Avenue has many distinguished structures; at the corner of 148th Street are four groups of row houses, each designed by a different architect. A rare, if unplanned, urban ensemble, 421–431 Convent Avenue, 411–417 Convent Avenue, 420–430 Convent Avenue, and 408–418 Convent Avenue, is notable for the complementary materials, style, and scale. Henri Fouchaux was the district's most prolific architect. He was responsible for five groups of row houses, as well as 746 St. Nicholas Avenue (1901–02) and 772–778 St. Nicholas Avenue (1904–05). Dramatic in form and detailing, these Beaux Arts–style apartment buildings are among the finest in the district.

㊶ Hamilton Heights/Sugar Hill Northeast Historic District, designated 2001. Nearly all of the buildings in this historic district were constructed between 1905 and 1930, a period when developers ceased building single-family houses and began to build medium-size apartment buildings. These structures are located on uninterrupted block fronts that extend along St. Nicholas Place and Edgecombe Avenue, from 150th to 155th Streets. Most of the buildings are five or six stories tall and were designed by local architects who specialized in this type of structure, including Neville & Bagge,

Schwartz & Gross, and George F. Pelham. In several instances, these firms received multiple commissions, fashioning identical designs for as many eight contiguous lots. These buildings generally have brick and stone facades, reflecting popular neoclassical styles, especially Renaissance and Colonial Revival. Among the most notable examples are 385 Edgecombe Avenue (George F. Pelham, 1913), for its abundant glazed terra-cotta ornament, and 409 Edgecombe Avenue (see No. 544), a curved 12-story structure, near 154th Street. Beginning in the 1920s, the area became known as Sugar Hill. It attracted a large concentration of middle-class blacks, including many cultural figures. Among the buildings completed during this era were 66–74 St. Nicholas Place, a neo-Gothic building designed by

Horace Ginsbern (1930–31), and 379–381 Edgecombe Avenue (George F. Pelham, 1925–26), where Duke Ellington and family lived from 1929 to 1939.

42 Hamilton Heights/Sugar Hill Northwest Historic District, designated 2002. Speculative development transformed the blocks between 151st and 155th Streets during the last decades of the 19th century. Among the earliest row houses in the district are 411–423 West 154th Street and 883–887 St. Nicholas Avenue, built in 1883–84. Designed by James Stroud, they are sited behind raised gardens and feature decorative elements associated with the Queen Anne style. Subsequent groups were built in a succession of popular historical styles, including neo-Grec, neo-Renaissance, and

Many of the finest late 19th-century row houses in the Hamilton Heights/Sugar Hill Historic District (H.D. 40) are located on Convent Avenue, near 148th Street. Photo by Carl Forster.

HISTORIC STREET LAMPPOSTS

This early 20th century twin lamppost in the Hamilton Heights section of Harlem is located at the intersection of Amsterdam Avenue, Hamilton Place, and West 143rd Street. It is among approximately one hundred cast-iron lampposts in New York City that were designated by the Commission in 1997. Sixty-two lampposts and four wall bracket lamps are individually designated; the rest are located in historic districts or on specific landmark properties. The earliest example, dating from the mid-19th century, is a simple gas post on Patchin Place, just west of Sixth Avenue in the Greenwich Village Historic District (Manhattan H.D. 12). Electric lights were introduced along Broadway in 1880, but did not become widespread until the beginning of the 20th century. Of a group of fifty ornamental twin lampposts that were installed along Manhattan's Fifth Avenue in 1892, a single example survives in the Ladies' Mile Historic District (Manhattan H.D. 16) at the southeast corner of 17th Street. The "bishop's crook" was one of the earliest and most popular models and a significant number can be found throughout lower Manhattan and in City Hall Park. Other notable lamppost types that survive include the mast arm, reverse scroll bracket, lyre, and wall bracket fixtures. Especially fine ornamental posts can also be found near the intersection of Fifth Avenue and 23rd Street and at the entrance to the Harlem River Drive at Adam Clayton Powell, Jr., Boulevard. By the 1970s, the majority of cast-iron posts had been replaced with streamlined steel and aluminum designs. The largest number of designated lampposts is in Manhattan, followed by the Bronx, Brooklyn, and Queens.

Photo by Carl Forster

Beaux Arts. Many were produced by local architects who specialized in this type of work. However, a few were better known: C. P. H Gilbert, who designed 456–460 West 152nd Street (1890); and Clarence True, who was responsible for the charming Northern Renaissance row houses at 842–844 St. Nicholas Avenue (1894–95) and 43–57 St. Nicholas Place (1894–95). The earliest apartment building in the district, 468 West 153rd Street, was built in 1886 as a companion to three row houses. Designed by Henri Fouchaux in the Queen Anne style, it was one of the architect's first commissions. A large number of classically inspired apartment buildings were constructed over the next three decades, most notably 889 St. Nicholas Avenue (Neville & Bagge, 1906–07), 469 and 479 West 152nd Street (John P. Leo, 1895 and 1897), and 445 West 153rd Street (Schwartz & Gross, 1914). The last three examples have irregular footprints, reflecting the diagonal path of the Croton Aqueduct, constructed in the 1830s. By the mid-1920s, with construction of the IND subway, the neighborhood's residential population began to evolve. Most of the new residents were of African ancestry; while some were American-born, many came from the British or West Indies. In subsequent decades, the area was commonly called Sugar Hill.

43 **Audubon Terrace Historic District,** designated 1979. Established on the former estate of artist and naturalist John James Audubon, Audubon Terrace is one of America's first planned cultural centers. The complex was conceived by Archer M. Huntington, philanthropist, Spanish scholar, and heir to the Southern Pacific Railroad fortune. In 1904 Huntington founded the Hispanic Society of America and commissioned his cousin Charles P. Huntington to design a gallery and library for a site on West 155th Street, just west of Broadway. The Hispanic Society (1904–08) was soon joined by the American Numismatic Society (1907), the American Geographical Society (1911; now housing Boricua College), the Museum of the American Indian (1915–22), and the Spanish-language Church of Our Lady of Esperanza (1912), all designed by Huntington. Later the American Academy of Arts and Letters and the National Institute of Arts and Letters (now the American Academy and Institute of Arts and Letters) moved into a building designed by McKim, Mead & White (1921–23) at the west end of the

complex; Cass Gilbert designed an auditorium and art gallery addition for these organizations in 1928. The buildings share a unified Italian Renaissance style and are set around a plaza embellished with sculpture by Archer Huntington's wife, Anna Hyatt Huntington.

INDIVIDUAL LANDMARKS

522 **Fire Engine Company No. 47,** 500 West 113th Street (Napoleon LeBrun & Sons, 1889–90), designated 1997. Among the earliest civic structures built in Morningside Heights, this modest firehouse combines both Romanesque Revival and neoclassical elements. Occupied in 1891, it served as the model for Engine Company No. 18 at 132 West 10th Street (H.D. 12).

523 **Plant and Scrymser Pavilions for Private Patients, St. Luke's Hospital,** 401 West 113th Street and 400 West 114th Street (Ernest Flagg, 1904–06, 1926–28), designated 2002. Ernest Flagg was selected to design St. Luke's Hospital in 1892. His French Renaissance–inspired plan consisted of nine pavilions arranged symmetrically around a domed administration building. The first five pavilions were constructed in 1893–96. The sixth pavilion, financed by Margaret J. Plant, was dedicated in 1906. Facing Morningside Drive, this facility served wealthy private patients, and thus helped to subsidize other hospital programs. The adjoining (James Alexander) Scrymser pavilion, erected 1926–28, was the last of the eight Flagg-designed pavilions built.

524 **Eglise de Notre Dame (R.C.) and Rectory,** Morningside Drive at West 114th Street (Daus & Otto, 1909–10, and Cross & Cross, 1914; rectory, Cross & Cross, 1913–14), designated 1967. Daus & Otto's imposing limestone sanctuary, dedicated to Our Lady of Lourdes, was completed in 1910. The austere nave, front elevation, and rectory, designed by Cross & Cross, were completed four years later. The formal French neoclassical design, with its pedimented Corinthian portico, was originally intended to be crowned by a dome (never executed) modeled on that of the Pantheon in Paris.

Columbia University, Broadway at West 116th Street. In 1891 Columbia College announced that it would abandon its campus on East 49th Street and Park Avenue and move to the site of New York Hospital's Bloomingdale Insane Asylum. In December 1893 Charles F. McKim was chosen as architect of the new campus; designs were completed in 1894. McKim's axial plan, inspired by Beaux-Arts concepts, called for a central library symmetrically flanked by twelve classroom buildings (nine were constructed), a chapel, and an assembly hall, with a student center and memorial hall to the rear of the library (not built), all to be constructed on a raised platform. Much of this plan was completed, and several of the structures are now designated landmarks. As Columbia grew, land to the south and east was purchased, and McKim, Mead & White enlarged the campus plan.

525 **Low Memorial Library** (McKim, Mead & White, Charles F. McKim, partner in charge, 1894–97), designated 1966, interior 1981. Charles F. McKim's monumental domed library is at the heart of the Columbia campus. The building is raised above its surroundings on a series of

Low Memorial Library (No. 525). Modeled after the Roman Pantheon, this building is the centerpiece of the Columbia University campus. Photo by Peter Choy.

plazas linked by stairways and commands the main entrance to the academic precinct. Modeled on the Roman Pantheon, the library is the only building on the original Columbia campus that is faced entirely in stone. The library was a gift from Columbia president Seth Low as a memorial to his father, the China trader Abiel Abbot Low (see No. 49 and Brooklyn H.D. 4). The grandeur of the exterior is continued on the **interior,** which features a vestibule marked by a pair of Connemara marble columns and an enormous domed octagonal rotunda supported by four great piers and sixteen columns of green Vermont marble. The library's collections were relocated in 1934, and Low became an administrative center.

526 Saint Paul's Chapel (Howells & Stokes, 1904–07), designated 1966. Saint Paul's Chapel was a gift of Olivia and Caroline Phelps Stokes, in memory of their parents, and was designed by their nephew, I. N. Phelps Stokes. The building, a magnificent example of Northern Italian Renaissance design, is faced with burned brick, limestone, and marble trim and is surmounted by a tile roof. The Guastavino tilework used for the dome, vaults, and other elements is visible on the ceiling of the exterior portico.

527 Casa Italiana, 1151–1161 Amsterdam Avenue (McKim, Mead & White, William M. Kendall, partner in charge, 1926–27), designated 1978. Casa Italiana is located on Columbia's east campus. William M. Kendall appropriately styled this building to copy a 15th-century Roman palazzo. Constructed to house the university's center for Italian studies, Casa Italiana was primarily funded by wealthy New Yorkers of Italian descent, notably members of the Paterno family, leading real-estate developers.

528 Croton Aqueduct, West 119th Street Gatehouse, 432–424 West 119th Street (New York City Department of Public Works, 1894–95), designated 2000. Built as a replacement for an earlier gatehouse that impeded traffic along Tenth (now Amsterdam) Avenue, this rock-faced granite structure was constructed as part of the Croton Aqueduct system, delivering fresh water to a receiving reservoir in Cen-

tral Park. It remained in operation until 1990.

529 Union Theological Seminary, encompassing Brown Memorial Tower, James Tower, and James Memorial Chapel, Broadway at Reinhold Niebuhr Place (Allen & Collens, design, 1906–07; Brown Memorial Tower, base, 1908–10, tower, 1927–28; James Tower and James Memorial Chapel, 1908–10), designated 1967. This Protestant seminary, founded in 1836, followed Columbia University (see Nos. 525–527) to Morningside Heights, purchasing two entire square blocks along Broadway between West 120th (now Reinhold Niebuhr Place) and West 122nd Streets in 1905, primarily with money donated by D. Willis James, a businessman associated with the Phelps-Dodge Company. A 1906 design competition was won by the Boston firm Allen & Collens with its English Perpendicular Gothic–style entry. The landmark elements—the two tall towers and the chapel that faces onto Claremont Avenue—are the three most significant features of the campus. The complex is constructed of Manhattan schist quarried on the site and is trimmed in limestone.

530 The Riverside Church, 490–498 Riverside Drive and Claremont Avenue (Henry C. Pelton and Allen & Collens, 1928–30), designated 2000. Financed primarily by John D. Rockefeller, Jr., Riverside Church is one of the best-known religious structures in New York. Built during an era when most houses of worship were literally being overshadowed by corporate and residential skyscrapers, the 392-foot tower has a strong presence on the Upper West Side skyline. The architects loosely based their design on Chartres Cathedral, employing a limestone curtain wall to disguise the steel frame that was used to speed construction and support the immense weight of the 72-bell carillon.

531 General Ulysses S. Grant Tomb, now the General Grant National Memorial, Riverside Drive at West 122nd Street (John H. Duncan, 1891–97), designated 1975. Dramatically sited near the north end of Riverside Park, the Grant Tomb is among the most impressive Classical Revival monuments of its period. Begun six years after Grant's death in 1885, the tomb was erected at a time of increasing nostalgia for the Civil War era with money contributed by some ninety thousand people, including many African-Americans. Duncan's granite monument was modeled on reconstructions of one of the great classical tombs, the Mausoleum of Halicarnassus. The **interior,** incorporating a domed rotunda and dominated by a central crypt with twin sarcophagi (for Grant and his wife), was inspired by the Invalides, the final resting place of Napoleon, in Paris. A major restoration was completed in 1997.

532 **St. Mary's Protestant Episcopal Church, Parish House and Sunday School,** 517–523 West 126th Street (church, Theodore E. Blake, in association with Carrère & Hastings, 1908–09; parish house [originally the rectory], 1851; sunday school, George Keister, 1890), designated 1998. Built on land donated by Jacob Schieffelin, this Manhattanville parish complex has been in continuous use for more than 175 years. A large number of early constituents were poor, and in 1831 the congregation abolished pew fees—the first church in the city to do so. A gable-roofed porch provides entry to the complex, which features a neo-Gothic church with herringbone brickwork, a clapboard-covered parish house, and a garden.

533 **Croton Aqueduct, 135th Street Gatehouse,** West 135th Street at Convent Avenue (Frederick S. Cook, 1884–90), designated 1981. The granite and brownstone gatehouse is the most impressive local architectural feature of the new Croton Aqueduct (See Nos. 579 and 580). The building was erected to regulate the flow of water from both the new and the old Croton Aqueduct systems. Although relatively small, the building looms like an impregnable medieval fortress, symbolically protecting New York's vital water supply.

534 **New York Training School for Teachers and New York Model School,** now A. Philip Randolph Campus High School, 443–465 West 135th Street (William H. Gompert, 1924–26), designated 1997. The New York Training School was established in 1898 to provide the Board of Education with an adequate supply of elementary school teachers, most of whom were women. After operating in several locations, this Collegiate Gothic structure was completed in 1926, the first built expressly for the Training School. During the Depression the

school was abolished, and from 1933 to 1984 the building housed the High School of Music and Art, considered to be the first of its kind.

535 **City College,** now City College North Campus, City University of New York, Convent Avenue between West 138th and West 140th Streets (George B. Post and George B. Post & Sons, 1897–1930), designated 1981. What is now City College was founded as the Free Academy in 1847 and was located on Lexington Avenue near East 23rd Street. Renamed in 1866, the college purchased the site of its uptown campus along Convent Avenue in 1897. After Post won the design competition for the new campus, this Collegiate Gothic complex was erected. All the early campus buildings and the three original gates—at West 138th, 139th, and 140th Streets—were constructed of dark Manhattan schist, excavated on the site, and trimmed with contrasting white terra cotta. The buildings are Main Building (now Shepard Hall), 1902–07; Townsend Harris Hall, 1903–06; Chemistry Building (now Baskerville Hall), 1903–08; Mechanic Arts Building (now Compton Hall), 1903–08; Gymnasium (now Wingate Hall), 1903–08; and Technology Building (now Goethals Hall), 1928–30. A major restoration of the campus was undertaken in the 1990s.

536 **Alexander Hamilton House, the Grange,** now the Hamilton Grange National Monument, 287 Convent Avenue (John McComb, Jr., 1801–02), designated 1967. Alexander Hamilton's country house, designed in the Federal style, once stood on a 35-acre tract. In 1889, when development threatened its survival, it was given to Saint Luke's Church and moved from Convent Avenue and West 143rd Street to its present site and altered. The house was briefly used as a church and later as a rectory. It was purchased by a preservation organization in 1924, opened to the public nine years later, and donated to the U.S. Department of the Interior in 1962.

537 **Our Lady of Lourdes Church (R.C.),** 467 West 142nd Street (O'Reilly Brothers, 1902–04), designated 1975. This Roman Catholic church, one of the oddest buildings in New York, is composed of pieces salvaged from three of the city's most prominent mid-19th-century landmarks and combined by Cornelius O'Reilly. Much of the High Victorian

MANHATTAN

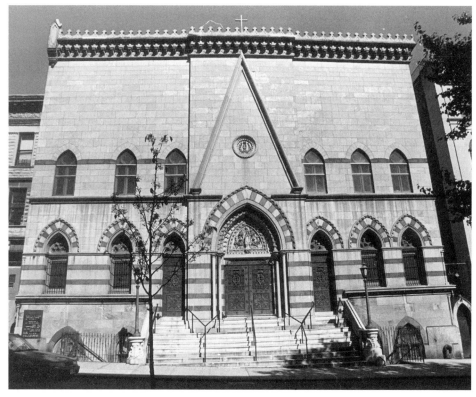

Our Lady of Lourdes Church (No. 537). Elements salvaged from three of the city's most prominent 19th-century structures were used to create this West 142nd Street church. Photo by Carl Forster.

Gothic facade is a reconstruction of Peter B. Wight's famous National Academy of Design (1863–65), which stood at Fourth Avenue and East 23rd Street. The rear of the church consists of the original east end of James Renwick, Jr.'s Saint Patrick's Cathedral (see No. 296), which was replaced in 1901–06 by a new lady chapel. The stone pedestals that flank the front steps come from the A. T. Stewart mansion (John Kellum, 1864–69), which stood at Fifth Avenue and 34th Street.

538 **New York Public Library, Hamilton Grange Branch,** 503 West 145th Street (McKim, Mead & White, Charles F. McKim, partner in charge, 1905–06), designated 1970. In the late 19th century, most of the city's public libraries were run by private organizations (see Nos. 157 and 419). The New York Public Library, founded in 1895, had an endowment devoted to its research facility and lacked the finan-

cial resources to organize and run a circulating system. Andrew Carnegie solved the problem in 1901 when he offered the New York Public Library a gift of more than $5 million for the construction of sixty-seven branch libraries. Because land in Manhattan was expensive, almost all the libraries were conceived as relatively narrow midblock structures, and a general plan was devised that could easily be adapted to most of these sites. Each library was to be three stories tall, with a Renaissance-inspired limestone facade. This basic arrangement had been successfully employed by the Free Circulating Library (these libraries were merged into the public library system). This branch library, built as a result of the Carnegie donation, has a beautifully proportioned rusticated facade with alternating triangular and segmental window pediments and elegant iron railing, features adapted from the Palazzo Farnese in Rome.

539 **Hamilton Theater,** 3560–3568 Broadway (Thomas W. Lamb, 1912–13), designated 2000. Built as a vaudeville house for B. S. Moss and Solomon Brill, in the late 1920s the Hamilton was one of the first movie theaters in New York to showcase "talking pictures." Located at the corner of West 146th Street, the imposing neo-Renaissance facades have large engaged Corinthian columns executed in terra cotta, and elaborate cast-iron caryatids. The theater closed in 1958.

540 **Joseph Loth & Company Silk Ribbon Mill,** 1828 Amsterdam Avenue (Hugo Kafka, 1885–86), designated 1993. One of New York's most exceptional industrial buildings is located on Amsterdam Avenue between West 150th and West 151st Streets. Established in New York in 1875, the Loth company manufactured Fair and Square brand silk ribbons. The factory, a rare example of an architect-designed mill structure, was planned in the shape of a K, which permitted the construction of interior spaces uninterrupted by columns and walls and maximized the light entering the building. The massing of the facades, with their brick facing and large windows separated by narrow pilasters, typifies mill design. The factory, which has undergone some additions and alterations, now houses a variety of industrial and commercial tenants.

541 **32nd Police Precinct Station House,** later the 30th Police Precinct Station House, 1854 Amsterdam Avenue (Nathaniel D. Bush, 1871), designated 1986. After Bush became the police department's first architect in 1862, he designed a series of Italianate and French Second Empire brick precinct houses. When the 32nd Police Precinct Station House was built, the area around it was still largely rural, and the structure, with its large mansard roof and handsome iron cresting, was among the most conspicuous in the vicinity. The building is currently used by Saint Luke's AME Church as the home of the African Methodist Episcopal Church Self Help Program.

542 **James A. and Ruth M. Bailey House,** now Blake Funeral Home, 10 Saint Nicholas Place (Samuel B. Reed, 1886–88), designated 1974. The circus impresario James A. Bailey (of the famed Barnum & Bailey Circus) commissioned this flamboyant Romanesque Revival limestone house with Flemish

gables. At the time of its construction, the house was located in a relatively undeveloped neighborhood and enjoyed fine views to the east, toward Long Island Sound.

543 **Nicholas C. and Agnes Benziger House,** 345 Edgecombe Avenue (William Schickel, 1890–91), designated 1999. This freestanding brick house sits on a ridge overlooking the Harlem Plain at 150th Street. Built for a successful publisher, manufacturer, and importer of articles used in Catholic worship, Schickel's picturesque design incorporates a flared mansard roof with gabled dormers. Sold in 1920, it has since been used as a hospital, nursery school, and housing for formerly homeless adults.

544 **409 Edgecombe Avenue** (Schwartz & Gross, 1916–17), designated 1993. Originally called the Colonial Parkway Apartments, this 12-story building set on a ridge overlooking central Harlem was the most prestigious address for African-American New Yorkers from the 1930s through the 1950s. Among the prominent tenants were singer and actor Julius C. Bledsoe (creator of the role of Joe in *Show Boat* and the first to sing "Ole Man River"); poet and critic William Stanley Braithwaite; pioneering black physician May Edward Chinn; painter Aaron Douglas; scholar and sociologist W. E. B. Du Bois, a leading civil rights activist and founder of the NAACP; bandleader Jimmie Lunceford; lawyer Thurgood Marshall, who became the first African-American Supreme Court justice; civil rights leader and NAACP executive Walter White; and White's successor as head of the NAACP, Roy Wilkins.

545 **Chapel of the Intercession (Episcopal),** now the Church of the Intercession Complex, Broadway at West 155th Street (Bertram Goodhue of the firm Cram, Goodhue & Ferguson, 1910–14), designated 1966. The Church of the Intercession, a chapel of Trinity Church until 1976, is a remarkable complex of English Gothic inspiration, consisting of the main church, with its gabled front and tall tower, and a full cloister, vicarage, vestry, and parish house to the rear. Intercession has been called the quintessential Goodhue church, and was the architect's own favorite; he is, in fact, buried in the north transept.

546 **Macomb's Dam Bridge and 155th Street Viaduct,** spanning the Harlem River between West

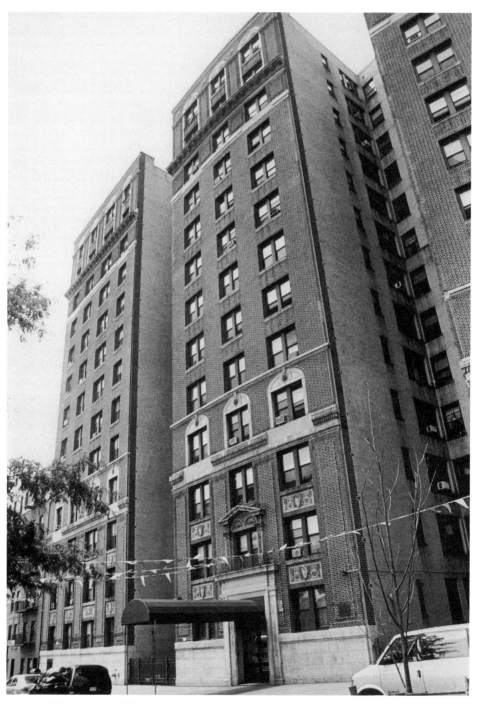

From the 1930s through the 1950s, 409 Edgecombe Avenue (No. 544) was the most prestigious address in Harlem. Photo by Carl Forster.

155th Street and Saint Nicholas Place, Manhattan, and Jerome Avenue and East 162nd Street, the Bronx (Alfred Pancoast Boller, consulting engineer, 1890–95), designated 1992. Known until 1902 as Central Bridge, this is the oldest metal truss swing bridge and the third-oldest bridge in the city. The ensemble consists of a swing bridge over the Harlem River with an intricate latticework of steel crowned with four finials; stone end piers capped by shelter houses; a camelback span over the railroad tracks in the Bronx; the long 155th Street steel viaduct with tall stairways in Manhattan; and a shorter steel approach road in the Bronx.

■ FREDERICK DOUGLASS BOULEVARD EAST TO LENOX AVENUE

HISTORIC DISTRICT

44 **Saint Nicholas Historic District,** designated 1967. This district is an outstanding example of late 19th-century urban design in New York City. The four blockfronts, each a unified streetscape, were conceived by the developer David H. King, Jr., in 1891, "on such a large scale," he wrote, "and with such ample resources as to 'Create a Neighborhood' independent of surrounding influences." King was a builder who had previously worked on many important local projects and was familiar with the city's leading architects. He hired three distinguished architectural firms to design the 146 row houses and three apartment buildings. James Brown Lord designed the red brick and brownstone Georgian-inspired row on the south side of West 138th Street; Bruce Price was responsible for the yellow brick Colonial Revival houses with white limestone and terra-cotta trim on the north side of West 138th Street and the south side of West 139th Street; and McKim, Mead & White partner Stanford White designed the elegant Italian Renaissance–inspired row in dark mottled brick with brownstone and terra-cotta trim on the north side of West 139th Street. The houses were equipped with up-to-date amenities and handsome woodwork and other details demanded by middle-class families. Service alleys, an extremely rare feature in New York City, run behind each row. Few houses were sold, and in 1895, dur-

ing an economic depression, the mortgagor, the Equitable Life Assurance Company, foreclosed on almost all the properties. Equitable retained most of the buildings until 1919–20, when they were sold to African-Americans. Many became rooming houses, but others were home to prominent members of New York's black community, including, on West 138th Street, surgeon Louis T. Wright (No. 218), composer Will Marion Cook (No. 221), singer and songwriter Eubie Blake (No. 236), and Harry Pace (No. 257), the founder of the Black Swan Record Company, a pioneer in recording African-American singers and musicians; and, on West 139th Street, architect Vertner Tandy (No. 221), musician W. C. Handy (No. 232), bandleader Fletcher Henderson (No. 228), and boxer Harry Wills (No. 245). During the 1920s these houses became known as Striver's Row, a reference to the aspirations of many of the black residents who had recently moved into the area.

INDIVIDUAL LANDMARKS

547 **Wadleigh High School for Girls,** now Wadleigh School, 215 West 114th Street and 226–250 West 115th Street (C. B. J. Snyder, 1901–02), designated 1994. The construction of Wadleigh High School, a result of the increasing demand for advanced education for girls around 1900, is named for Lydia F. Wadleigh, an early proponent of women's education. This was the first high school erected in New York City specifically for girls. The French Renaissance–style structure, with its picturesque dormers and tall tower, is one of the finest and most innovative designs of Superintendent of School Buildings C. B. J. Snyder. The seriously deteriorated building was restored in the early 1990s under the auspices of the New York City School Construction Authority.

548 **New York Public Library, 115th Street Branch,** 203 West 115th Street (McKim, Mead & White, Charles F. McKim, partner in charge, 1907–09), designated 1977. The 115th Street Branch Public Library was built as part of Andrew Carnegie's public library system (see No. 538). Many of the finest library buildings erected as a result of Carnegie's donation were designed by

Charles F. McKim of the firm McKim, Mead & White. Among the finest of McKim's branch libraries is this building on West 115th Street. The emphatic rustication on the facade is reminiscent of that on the Palazzo Strozzi in Florence. A flamboyant shield bearing the seal of New York is balanced by a pair of putti above the central window on the ground floor.

549 **Regent Theater,** now First Corinthian Baptist Church, 1910 Adam Clayton Powell, Jr., Boulevard (Thomas W. Lamb, 1912–13), designated 1994. One of the first elaborately designed movie theaters in America, the Regent represents the transition of movie theaters from undistinguished nickelodeons to luxurious palaces. The facade, clad almost entirely in glazed, polychromatic terra cotta, is a fanciful version of a Venetian palazzo, meant to catch the attention of passersby. The Regent is an early work by theater specialist Thomas W. Lamb, who designed many of the finest theaters in America (see Nos. 263, 265, 348). The theater was sold in 1964 to the First Corinthian Baptist Church, an African-American congregation established in Harlem in 1939.

550 **Graham Court Apartments,** 1923–1937 Adam Clayton Powell, Jr., Boulevard (Clinton & Russell, 1899–1901), designated 1984. Commissioned by William Waldorf Astor, whose family had owned this site in Harlem since the 1860s, Graham Court is one of the grandest courtyard apartment houses in New York and became the prototype for the Apthorp Apartments (see No. 396). The building, designed in the Italian Renaissance style, offers evidence of Harlem's early development as an affluent urban neighborhood.

551 **Washington Apartments,** 2034–2040 Adam Clayton Powell, Jr., Boulevard (Mortimer C. Merritt, 1883–84), designated 1993. The Queen Anne–style Washington Apartments, faced in red brick with terra-cotta trim and crowned by a pediment, is one of the oldest apartment houses in New York City and the earliest in Harlem planned specifically to house middle-class families. The construction of this building reflects the increasing popularity of Harlem as a residential community following the opening of elevated rail lines through northern Manhattan in the late 1870s.

552 **Saint Paul's German Evangelical Lutheran Church,** now Greater Metropolitan Baptist Church, 147 West 123rd Street (Schneider & Herter, 1897–98), designated 1994. This neo-Gothic church, designed by German immigrant architects, was erected late in the 19th century as the German community in the Mount Morris area increased in size and wealth. The street facade of the building is Vermont marble. Saint Paul's remained in this building until 1939, long after most white church congregations had left Harlem. For forty-five years, beginning in 1940, this was home to the 12th Church of Christ, Scientist. In 1978 the Greater Metropolitan Baptist Church split from the Metropolitan Baptist Church (see No. 555), and in 1985 it purchased the West 123rd Street building.

553 **Hotel Theresa,** now Theresa Towers, 2090 Adam Clayton Powell, Jr., Boulevard (George & Edward Blum, 1912–13), designated 1993. The Hotel Theresa is one of the most prominent buildings in Harlem, a major work of the architectural firm George & Edward Blum and a key landmark in the cultural history of Harlem as an African-American community. Erected as Harlem's most prestigious hotel, the Theresa's white brick and terra-cotta facades are adorned with the distinctive geometric ornament favored by the Blums. The Theresa remained a segregated establishment until 1940 when the discriminatory policy was dropped and it rapidly became what *Ebony* called the "Waldorf of Harlem," hosting black celebrities and the social events of Harlem's African-American community. The hotel also contained the offices of A. Philip Randolph's March on Washington Movement and Malcolm X's Organization of Afro-American Unity. The Theresa is now an office building.

554 **Apollo Theater,** originally Hurtig & Seamon's New (Burlesque) Theater, 253 West 125th Street (George Keister, 1913–14), designated 1983. The Apollo became famous in the 1930s when the theater began to feature black entertainers. Today it is world renowned as a stage for African-American performing artists. In recognition of the Apollo's importance in the history of American entertainment and, more specifically, its central role in the presentation of major African-American performers, both the exterior and the neoclassical **interior** of the theater have been designated as landmarks.

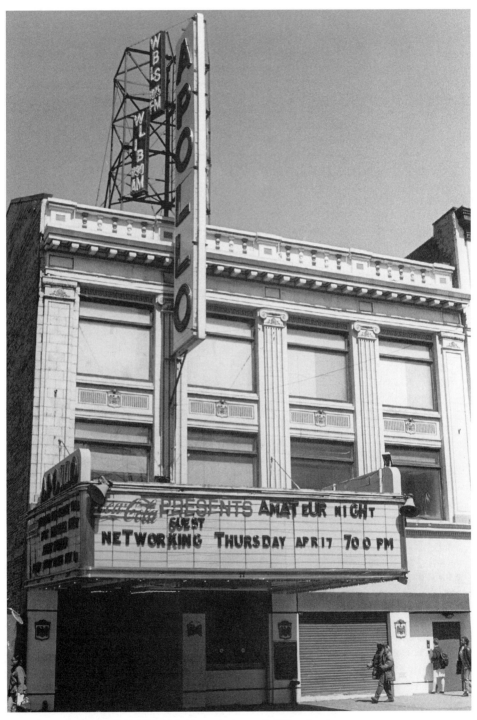

Apollo Theater (No. 480). The historic and world-renowned venue for African-American performing talent. Photo by Carl Forster.

OFF-BROADWAY

The largest group of theaters in New York is concentrated in Midtown Manhattan, particularly along West 44th, 45th, and 47th Streets. Many of these buildings and their interiors were designated as landmarks in 1987 to preserve the history of Times Square. Beyond Broadway, however, are numerous theaters that have contributed to the city's reputation as the nation's cultural capital. The oldest auditorium in New York is Carnegie Hall, completed in 1891 (Manhattan No. 357). The most famous concert hall in the United States, it owes its longevity to fine acoustics and the introduction of electricity, which diminished the likelihood of theater fires. Designed in the neo-Renaissance style by William B. Tuthill and originally incorporating three smaller halls, this complex anticipates the Brooklyn Academy of Music (BAM), which opened in 1908. Herts & Tallant were responsible for the latter's handsome neo-Renaissance design, which today includes an opera house, four-screen cinema, and restaurant/café (Brooklyn H.D. 8).

Radio City Music Hall, built as part of Rockefeller Center in 1932, was once the largest theater in the world. An Art Deco masterpiece, it consists of a series of magnificent interiors, including a huge theater inspired by Joseph Urban's egg-shaped auditorium at the New School, as well as an elegant vestibule leading to a soaring foyer decorated with murals by Ezra Winter. Radio City was planned as a venue for grand entertainment, but soon after opening it began to offer programs combining live shows and film (Manhattan No. 294 and H.D. 12, N).

The earliest movie palace in New York is the Regent Theater, at the corner of Adam Clayton Powell, Jr., Boulevard and 116th Street (Manhattan No. 549). In contrast to the modest nickelodeons that preceded it, the Regent was a serious work of architecture, loosely modeled on the Doge's Palace in Venice. Managed by movie theater impresario Samuel "Roxy" Rothafel, it set new standards in theater design and comfort. Other notable entertainment venues in Harlem include the legendary Apollo, which since the 1930s has launched the careers of numerous black entertainers, and the Hamilton, a pioneer in the presentation of movies with sound (Manhattan Nos. 554 and 539). Of the five "Wonder" theaters built for Loew's in the late 1920s, two are designated landmarks: the Paradise on the Grand Concourse and the Valencia in Jamaica (Bronx No. 28 and Queens No. 44). These large theaters were famous for their flamboyant decoration, and both feature richly embellished street facades. The Upper West Side has two theaters that deserve mention, the Midtown, with its polychrome terra-cotta facade, and the Beacon, designed by Walter Ahlschlager (Manhattan Nos. 393 and 418). The Beacon has an impressive lobby rotunda and interior inspired by classical and Renaissance sources. It should be noted that many designated theaters have been converted to new uses, including the Yiddish Art Theater, which has been a cinema since 1991 (Manhattan No. 161).

Adaptive reuse has increased the number of theatrical venues in New York. One of the earliest examples is the Cherry Lane, at 38 Commerce Street (Manhattan H.D. 12). Built as a silo in the early 19th century, it became a theater in 1914. Other notable conversions include the Astor Library, which Joseph Papp and architect Giorgio Cavaglieri transformed into the Public Theater in 1966; the Performing Garage at 33 Wooster Street, home to the Wooster Group since the early 1970s; and the former Union Square Savings Bank, now the Daryl Roth Theater (Manhattan No. 151, H.D. 9, and No. 208).

555 **Metropolitan Baptist Church,** originally the New York Presbyterian Church, 151 West 128th Street (John R. Thomas, 1884–85; additions, Richard R. Davis, 1889–90), designated 1981. Although built in two sections, this church reads as a single, unified structure. John R. Thomas was responsible for the chapel and lecture room on West 128th Street, while the main sanctuary on Adam Clayton Powell, Jr., Boulevard is attributed to the Harlem architect Richard R. Davis (who may have used Thomas's unexecuted design). The unusual building combines Romanesque-inspired massing and rough-textured stonework with such Gothic features as pointed arches and flying buttresses. In 1918 the building was sold to the Metropolitan Baptist Church, a reflection of the changing character of Harlem as it developed into America's most important African-American community. Metropolitan was one of the first black congregations established in Harlem and remains one of the most prestigious churches in the community.

556 **Saint Philip's Episcopal Church,** 214 West 134th Street (Tandy & Foster, 1910–11), designated 1993. This is the home of New York's oldest African-American Episcopal church congregation, established in 1818. Saint Philip's followed the city's black population north from Lower Manhattan to Mulberry Street, to West 25th Street, and finally to Harlem, where two of America's first African-American architects, Vertner Tandy and George W. Foster, Jr., designed a handsome neo-Gothic–style church building of Roman brick and terra cotta. Saint Philip's was an active supporter of the migration of New York's black community to Harlem, not only building an impressive new church but also purchasing apartment buildings that were rented to black households.

557 **Young Men's Christian Association Building, 135th Street Branch,** now Harlem YMCA, 180 West 135th Street (Architectural Bureau of the National Council of the YMCA, James C. Mackenzie, Jr., architect in charge, 1931-32), designated 1998. Since opening in 1932, this YMCA branch has played an important role in Harlem's recreational and cultural life. Though blacks were excluded from white YMCAs as late as 1946, this 11-story brick structure with neo-Georgian details was described as one of the largest and best-equipped branches in the county. Many area residents and visitors have benefitted from its athletic programs and affordable accommodations, including athletes, artists, musicians, writers, and civil rights leaders.

558 **New York Public Library, Schomburg Center for Research in Black Culture,** originally 135th Street Branch, 103 West 135th Street (McKim, Mead & White, Charles F. McKim, partner in charge, 1903–05), designated 1981. The 135th Street Branch was one of the first new libraries completed with money from the Carnegie grant (see No. 538). The building's design is loosely based on Michele Sanmicheli's Palazzo Canossa in Verona. Early in the 1920s, in response to changes in the surrounding Harlem neighborhood, the branch librarian Ernestine Rose began compiling a small collection of black literature and history books; in 1925 the branch was renamed the 135th Street Branch Division of Negro Literature. A year later the famed Schomburg Collection—a treasure trove of material on black culture and history, amassed by Arthur Schomburg—was purchased for the library. The facility was renamed for Schomburg in 1972, and eight years later a new building to house the research collection was completed on an adjacent site. The original building was restored in 1990.

559 **Mother African Methodist Episcopal Zion Church,** 140 West 137th Street (George W. Foster, Jr., 1923–25), designated 1993. Mother A.M.E. Zion is the oldest African-American church congregation in New York and, as its name connotes, the "mother" church of the A.M.E. Zion denomination. The congregation relocated to Harlem in 1914 and eleven years later moved into this neo-Gothic stone church. George W. Foster, Jr., was one of the first black architects in America and one of the first two African-American architects registered in the state of New Jersey. Mother A.M.E. Zion has a long history of social activism in the black community and continues to be one of the most dynamic congregations in Harlem.

560 **Abyssinian Baptist Church and Community House,** 132 West 138th Street (Charles W. Bolton & Son, 1922–23), designated 1993. The second-oldest African-American church in New York City, Abyssinian is famous for its prominent ministers, notably Adam Clayton Powell, Sr., and his son

MANHATTAN

Adam Clayton Powell, Jr., who became the first black congressman from New York City. Organized in 1808 by black worshipers who withdrew from the First Baptist Church, the congregation took a name associated with ancient Ethiopia. The neo-Gothic church complex was designed by a Philadelphia firm that specialized in church design.

561 **Dunbar Apartments,** West 149th Street to West 150th Street between Frederick Douglass and Adam Clayton Powell, Jr., Boulevards (Andrew J. Thomas, 1926–28), designated 1970. The Dunbar was the first major nonprofit cooperative apartment complex built specifically for African-Americans. Financed by John D. Rockefeller, Jr., the Dunbar con-

sists of six five- and six-story walk-up buildings set around a landscaped central courtyard. Named for the poet Paul Laurence Dunbar, the cooperative (now rental buildings) attracted many of the most prominent members of the Harlem community, including W. E. B. Du Bois, A. Philip Randolph, Paul Robeson, and Bill ("Bojangles") Robinson.

562 **Harlem River Houses,** West 151st to West 153rd Streets, Macombs Place to Harlem River Drive (Archibald Manning Brown, chief architect, 1936–37), designated 1975. Harlem River Houses was one of the first two federally funded housing projects in New York City. Built in 1936 as "a recognition in brick and mortar of the special and urgent needs of

Harlem River Houses (No. 562). The human scale, generous open space, and careful detailing of one of the first two federally funded housing projects in New York City set a standard for public housing that has rarely been matched. Photo by Carl Forster.

Harlem," the project was an attempt to provide high-quality housing for African-American working people. The four- and five-story buildings of the nine-acre complex are set around large open areas that are landscaped with walkways as wide as streets, recreation sites, and lawns. The human scale, generous open space, and careful detailing of the project set a standard for public housing that has rarely been matched. Among the architects of Harlem River Houses was John Louis Wilson, Jr., one of the first African-American architects registered in New York State.

■ EAST OF LENOX AVENUE

HISTORIC DISTRICT

45 **Mount Morris Park Historic District,** designated 1971. The streets of this district are lined with substantial masonry row houses interspersed with institutional buildings of exceptional quality, all reflecting Harlem's development as an affluent residential community following the extension of transit lines into the area around 1880. Initial construction in the neighborhood was closely linked to Mount Morris Park (renamed Marcus Garvey Park in 1973 in honor of one of the first black nationalist leaders) and wide, tree-lined Lenox Avenue. Almost every street in the district contains fine examples of row houses in the neo-Grec, Romanesque Revival, and neo-Renaissance styles, designed primarily by architects who specialized in the creation of speculative row houses. In addition, the affluent Protestant and German-Jewish residents of the neighborhood in the late 19th and early 20th centuries commissioned major institutional buildings. These include the masterful Holy Trinity Episcopal Church (now Saint Martin's Episcopal Church; see No. 491); the picturesque Lenox Avenue Unitarian Church (now Bethel Gospel Tabernacle; Charles Atwood, 1889–91); the Gothic Revival Reformed Low Dutch Church (now Ephesus Seventh Day Adventist Church; John R. Thomas, 1885–87), with its soaring tower; the imposing Classical Revival Temple Israel (now Mount Olivet Baptist Church; Arnold W. Brunner, 1906–07); and the Queen Anne–style Harlem Club (now Bethelite Community Church; Lamb & Rich, 1888–89), all on Lenox Avenue, and the eccentric Harlem Presbyterian Church (now Mount

Morris Ascension Presbyterian Church; Thomas H. Poole, 1905–06) on Mount Morris Park West. The evolving character of the area's population affected all these buildings. The Unitarian Church became an Orthodox synagogue in 1919 at a time when the area had a large immigrant Jewish population. In 1920, as Harlem was increasingly becoming the center of New York's black community, church congregations composed of African-Americans and Caribbean immigrants began to acquire these institutional buildings. Over the years many of the row houses were converted into rooming houses, while others remained single-family homes. Restoration work within the district has returned many buildings to their original character.

INDIVIDUAL LANDMARKS

563 **New York Public Library, Aguilar Branch,** 174 East 110th Street (Herts & Tallant, 1904–05), designated 1996. The Aguilar Free Library Society was founded in 1886 to serve the expanding population of Jewish immigrants and was named for Grace Aguilar, a popular early 19th-century English writer of Sephardic Jewish descent. The East Harlem branch was the society's fourth library. A building designed by Herts & Tallant was erected in 1898–99 and then totally redesigned and enlarged a few years later, after the Aguilar branches were incorporated into the New York Public Library system (see No. 538). The unusual Classical Revival facade consists of a grid of iron and glass framed by a pair of colossal limestone Ionic pilasters and a massive entablature.

564 **Harlem Courthouse,** 170 East 121st Street (Thom & Wilson, 1891–93), designated 1967. One of the most impressive buildings in East Harlem, the former Harlem Courthouse is an idiosyncratic Romanesque Revival brick structure with an octagonal tower and a four-faced clock. The building was erected to house the New York City Police Court and District Court, but since the reorganization of the court system in 1962, several other city agencies have used the building.

565 **Watch Tower,** Marcus Garvey Park (Julius Kroehl, 1855), designated 1967. Rising from a rocky outcropping in what was originally known as Mount Morris Park, this three-tiered cast-iron structure, with spiral staircase and octagonal lookout, is the only surviving fire tower in New York City. Use was discontinued in 1878, after the installation of fire alarm boxes.

566 **Saint Martin's Episcopal Church Complex,** originally Holy Trinity Episcopal Church, Rectory, and Parish House, 230 Lenox Avenue (William A. Potter, 1887–89), designated 1966. Known as Saint Martin's Episcopal Church since 1928, this prominent Harlem church is generally considered the finest Romanesque Revival religious complex in the city. The church and its related buildings have massive rough-hewn granite walls pierced by large rectangular and round-arched windows trimmed with brown sandstone. The complex was compactly planned; the parish house faces Lenox Avenue, and the sanctuary, with its tall square bell tower, and rectory are to the rear.

567 **Fire Hook and Ladder Company No. 14,** now Engine Company No. 36, 120 East 125th Street (Napoleon LeBrun & Sons, 1888–89), designated 1997. This firehouse was designed by Napoleon LeBrun, who served as the fire department's chief architect from 1880 to 1895. Built on the site of an earlier volunteer, and later suburban, company, the facade has Romanesque Revival details and rusticated brownstone trim.

568 **Mount Morris Bank Building,** 81–85 East 125th Street (Lamb & Rich, 1883–84, enlarged 1889–90), designated 1993. This prominently sited Romanesque Revival–style building on the corner of Park Avenue and East 125th Street is one of the most impressive structures in Harlem. Built of brick and red sandstone, the building originally housed a bank and six apartments. Lamb & Rich created a boldly scaled structure with massive arched entries, picturesque oriels, and exceptional terra-cotta detail. The same architecture firm designed the 1889–90 expansion of the building along Park Avenue. The Mount Morris Bank became a branch of the Corn Exchange Bank in 1913 and then merged with Chemical Bank in 1954.

569 **Langston Hughes House,** 20 East 127th Street (Alexander Wilson, 1869), designated 1981. Langston Hughes, one of the leading figures of the Harlem Renaissance, lived on the top floor of this Italianate brownstone from 1947 until his death in

1967. Hughes wrote many works while residing on East 127th Street, including his humorous pieces documenting the life of the common man in Harlem (as represented by Jess B. Semple) and a series of books exploring aspects of African-American culture.

570 **Saint Andrew's Church (Episcopal),** 2067 Fifth Avenue (Henry M. Congdon, 1872–73; enlargement, 1889–90), designated 1967. Saint Andrew's is one of the finest Victorian Gothic churches in New York City and one of the few 19th-century Protestant churches in Harlem that are still occupied by the original congregation. Henry Congdon designed Saint Andrew's for a site on East 127th Street between Park and Lexington Avenues, but by the late 1880s the congregation had outgrown the building. Congdon was rehired to dismantle the structure and supervise its reconstruction and enlargement on this more prestigious site at the corner of Fifth Avenue and East 127th Street.

571 **17 East 128th Street** (c. 1864), designated 1982. In the mid-19th century, northern Manhattan was dotted with hundreds of wooden houses, few of which survive. This French Second Empire example is one of a handful of buildings still standing that relate to Harlem's early history as a rural village. The house is remarkably well preserved; it retains its original stoop, decorated porch, double doors, shutters, and multicolored slate roof.

572 **12 West 129th Street** (c. 1863; alterations and additions: Edward Gustaveson, builder, 1882–83; Asbury Baker, 1896; c. 1920s), designated 1994. In the mid-19th century, modest suburban houses such as this residence were erected in increasing numbers in the village of Harlem. The house was originally a 2½-story structure erected around 1863. In 1882 piano merchant John Simpson Jr., leased the property and commissioned additions, including the complex Moorish-inspired porch with its perforated detail cut by scroll saws. In 1896 an order of Franciscan Sisters moved in, added a full third story, and, in the 1920s, stuccoed the facade.

573 **Astor Row,** 8–62 West 130th Street (Charles Buek, 1880–83), designated 1981. The twenty-eight houses of Astor Row were erected in three campaigns on land owned by William Astor. The coherent blockfront of brick houses with wooden porches is unique in New York City. Nos. 8–22 were built in freestanding pairs, while the remaining twenty houses are linked at their rear sections. Most of the houses in the row have been rehabilitated and their porches restored as part of an ongoing project undertaken with private and public funding.

574 **369th Regiment Armory,** 2360 Fifth Avenue (drill shed, Tachau & Vought, 1921–24; ad- ministration building, Van Wart & Wein, 1930–33), designated 1985. One of the last New York City armories to be constructed, the 369th Regiment was built in two campaigns. The massive administration building is unusual in its combination of the medieval motifs common to armory design and Art Deco features. The armory is the home of the renowned African-American regiment known as the Harlem Hell Fighters.

Astor Row (No. 573). The coherent blockfront of brick houses with wooden porches is unique in New York City. Photo by Carl Forster.

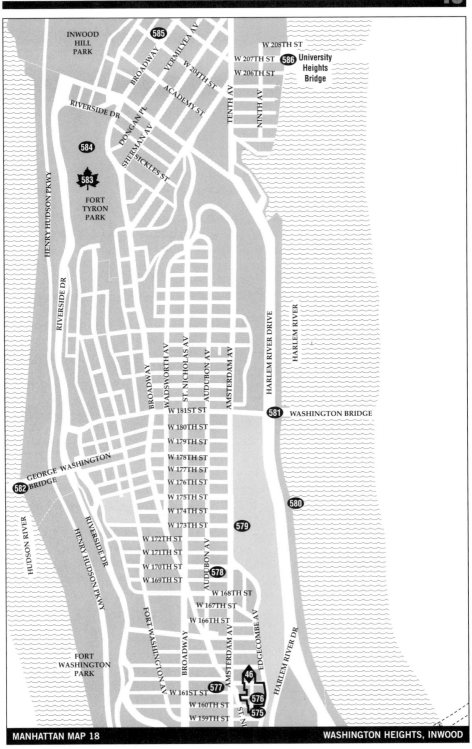

INWOOD HILL PARK

585

W 208TH ST

W 207TH ST 586 University Heights Bridge

W 206TH ST

BROADWAY

VERMILYEA AV

W 204TH ST

ACADEMY ST

TENTH AV

NINTH AV

RIVERSIDE DR

DONGAN PL

SHERMAN AV

SICKLES ST

584

583

FORT TYRON PARK

HENRY HUDSON PKWY

RIVERSIDE DR

BROADWAY

WADSWORTH AV

ST. NICHOLAS AV

AUDUBON AV

AMSTERDAM AV

HARLEM RIVER DRIVE

HARLEM RIVER

W 181ST ST

W 180TH ST

W 179TH ST

581 WASHINGTON BRIDGE

W 178TH ST

W 177TH ST

W 176TH ST

W 175TH ST

580

W 174TH ST

W 173TH ST

579

W 172TH ST

W 171TH ST

W 170TH ST

W 169TH ST

578

AUDUBON AV

GEORGE WASHINGTON

582 BRIDGE

HUDSON RIVER

HENRY HUDSON PKWY

RIVERSIDE DR

W 168TH ST

W 167TH ST

W 166TH ST

FORT WASHINGTON AV

BROADWAY

AMSTERDAM AV

EDGECOMBE AV

HARLEM RIVER DR

FORT WASHINGTON PARK

46

W 161ST ST 577

576

W 160TH ST 575

W 159TH ST

HISTORIC DISTRICT

46 **Jumel Terrace Historic District,** designated 1970. This small historic district consists largely of row houses erected adjacent to the Roger Morris House (see No. 576) after the former Morris estate was sold in 1882 by the heirs of Eliza Jumel. In that year the estate's carriage drive (now Sylvan Terrace) was built up with twenty two-story wooden houses (Albert Robinson Jr., 1882–83) that were initially rented to working-class civil servants and laborers. Restored in 1979–81, these houses are among the few surviving examples of the frame dwellings once common in northern Manhattan. The remainder of the district contains Queen Anne, Romanesque Revival, and neo-Renaissance row houses erected between 1890 and 1902.

INDIVIDUAL LANDMARKS

575 **555 Edgecombe Avenue** (Schwartz & Gross, 1914–16), designated 1993. When this building, known as the Roger Morris, was completed in 1916, the apartments were leased to white tenants. In 1939–40, as the population of the surrounding area was changing, the tenants of 555 became exclusively African-American, soon including jazz great Count

Jumel Terrace Historic District (H.D. 46). View of Sylvan Terrace about 1900. The houses were built in 1882. Photo: Landmarks Preservation Commission collection.

Basie, actor/producer Canada Lee, social psychologist Kenneth Clark, and actor/singer Paul Robeson and his wife, Eslanda, an anthropologist and author.

576 **Roger and Mary Philipse Morris House, Mount Morris,** also known as the Morris-Jumel Mansion, West 160th Street at Edgecombe Avenue (1765; remodeling, c. 1810), designated 1967, interior 1975. Mount Morris was built as a summer villa by the British military officer Roger Morris and his American-born wife, Mary Philipse Morris. The house is an early example of the use of Palladian forms in North America; the double-height portico with a triangular pediment was an especially innovative feature in 1765. Historically, the house is famed for having served as General George Washington's headquarters for more than a month in 1776. Later used by the British, the house was confiscated at the end of the war. In 1810 Stephen Jumel, a wealthy French immigrant merchant, purchased the property and moved in with his wife (formerly his mistress), Eliza Bowen. The Jumels undertook some remodeling, including the addition of the handsome entrance in the Federal style. The house was purchased by New York City in 1903 and converted into a museum; operations were handed over to a women's group known as the Washington Head-quarters Association. The mansion contains some of the finest Georgian **interiors** in America, including what is generally believed to be the country's first octagonal room.

577 **Fire Engine Company No. 384 and Hook & Ladder Company No. 34,** 513–515 West 161st Street (Francis H. Kimball, 1906–07), designated 1997. For nearly a century these fire companies have occupied this handsome Beaux Arts structure. Built as Washington Heights was being transformed from a rural area to a densely populated residential district, it features twin apparatus bays to serve each company. Kimball, a specialist in skyscraper design, used various two- and three-dimensional forms to animate each section of the facade, including overscaled scrolled keystones and an American eagle that crowns the parapet.

578 **Fire Engine Company No. 67,** 514 West 170th Street (Ernest Flagg and Walter B. Chambers, 1897–98), designated 2001. A hooded round arch, capped by an elaborate cartouche and bracketed cornice, gives this firehouse a strong presence on a mostly residential block in Washington Heights. Its Beaux Arts design anticipates Flagg & Chambers' subsequent (and larger) firehouse on Great Jones Street (see No. 146).

The Morris-Jumel Mansion (No. 576) is an early example of a Palladian villa in America. The principal facade was restored with funds from the Historic Preservation Grant Program of the Landmarks Preservation Commission in 2002. Photo by William Neeley Jr.

579 **High Bridge Water Tower,** High Bridge Park (John B. Jervis, 1866–72), designated as Water Tower, 1967. As the population of New York increased, the city's municipal water system was expanded to meet the growing demand. In 1872 the High Bridge Water Tower was constructed as part of a new northern Manhattan reservoir. This 200-foot-high granite tower was erected with a 47,000-gallon tank that provided gravity pressure for Manhattan's water supply, a necessity by the early 1870s as the use of flush toilets increased. Water was pumped into the tank from an adjacent reservoir, which was replaced by a public swimming pool in 1934. Fifteen years later the tower was removed from service. In 1989–90 the stonework was cleaned and restored, and the striking cupola, which had burned, was reconstructed.

580 **High Bridge,** spanning the Harlem River between West 170th Street, the Bronx, and High Bridge Park, Manhattan (John B. Jervis, 1838–48; addition, 1860; replacement of south piers, 1923), designated 1970. Prior to construction of the Old Croton Aqueduct, New York depended on private wells, water carts, rain barrels, and cisterns for its water supply. In 1842, amid great fanfare, the gravity-fed municipal system was inaugurated, providing New Yorkers with pure water brought from the Croton Reservoir in northern Westchester County. Water traveled more than forty miles from the Croton Dam to the Harlem River, where it passed over High Bridge (a temporary pipe served the system until the structure was completed) and followed the future course of Tenth (later Amsterdam) Avenue through cast-iron pipes to a large receiving reservoir at West 79th Street (now the Great Lawn, see No. 376) and finally to an Egyptian Revival distributing reservoir at Fifth Avenue and 42nd Street (the current site of the New York Public Library, see No. 278). Upon completion in 1848, High Bridge was hailed as a great feat of engineering. The soaring granite arches of the 1,450-foot-long bridge were modeled after ancient Roman aqueducts, such as the Pont du Gard in southern France. The aqueduct on the bridge carried the water via two 36-inch mains. In 1860 a 90-inch main was installed atop the earlier two, and the walls of the bridge were raised. In the mid-1920s five piers were replaced with a single steel arch to improve navigation on the Harlem

River. High Bridge is the oldest standing bridge in New York City and one of the oldest (in part) masonry bridges in the nation.

581 **Washington Bridge,** spanning the Harlem River between West 181st Street, Manhattan, and University Avenue, the Bronx (Charles C. Schneider and Wilhelm Hildenbrand, 1886–89; modifications, Union Bridge Company, William J. McAlpine, Theodore Cooper, and DeLemos & Cordes, with Edward H. Kendall, consulting architect; reconstruction, 1989–93), designated 1982. The Washington Bridge is an important monument of 19th-century American engineering; its complex design and construction history includes the contributions of many engineers and architects. The bridge consists of arcaded masonry approaches leading to a pair of steel arches supported by masonry piers. It was the first major link between Manhattan and the Bronx. A reconstruction of the roadway was undertaken in the late 1980s.

582 **Jeffrey's Hook Lighthouse,** also known as the Little Red Lighthouse, Fort Washington Park (1880; reconstruction, 1921), designated 1991. Erected in Sandy Hook, New Jersey, in 1880, this small conical iron lighthouse was moved to Jeffrey's Hook on Manhattan's Hudson River shore in 1921. The lighthouse, located beneath the George Washington Bridge, is best known as the subject of the children's book *The Little Red Lighthouse and the Great Gray Bridge,* written by Hildegarde Swift and published in 1942. Threatened with demolition after being taken out of service in 1951, the lighthouse was saved after an outcry from children led to its acquisition by New York City's Parks Department.

583 **Fort Tryon Park Scenic Landmark** (Olmsted Brothers, 1930–35), designated 1983. Fort Tryon Park is an outstanding example of the work of Olmsted Brothers, the successor firm to the one founded by Frederick Law Olmsted. The park occupies a portion of the site of the Revolutionary War Battle of Washington Heights; after the war the land was parceled into several country estates. John D. Rockefeller, Jr., began buying the estates in 1917 with the intention of creating a park. In 1935 he presented Fort Tryon Park to the city. The park contains varied landscape features, among them a magnificent heather garden, and takes full advantage of its spectacular setting overlooking the Hudson River and the Palisades. In addition to the parkland, Rockefeller purchased a collection of medieval art, housed at the time in a nearby building, and donated it to the Metropolitan Museum of Art. The museum built the Cloisters, located within the park, for display of the collection (see below).

584 **The Cloisters,** Fort Tryon Park (Charles Collens of Allen, Collens & Willis, 1934–39), designated 1974. The Cloisters, located in the midst of Fort Tryon Park (see above), was designed by the Boston architect Charles Collens to house a portion of the Metropolitan Museum of Art's medieval art collection and to incorporate fragments from various cloisters and other medieval buildings that had been collected by the sculptor George Gray Barnard and purchased for the museum by John D. Rockefeller, Jr. The building, designed to resemble a French Ro-

manesque abbey, has a tall tower that is an important focal point in the Fort Tryon Park landscape.

585 **Dyckman House,** Broadway at West 204th Street (c. 1785; restoration, Alexander M. Welch, 1915–16), designated 1967. The only farmhouse in the Dutch Colonial style surviving in Manhattan, the Dyckman House is constructed of fieldstone, brick, and wood and contains the gambrel roof, spring eaves, and porch typical of rural Dutch Colonial–style buildings. The house replaced an earlier building erected by the Dyckmans that was burned in the Revolutionary War. In 1915 when the house was threatened with demolition, two Dyckman sisters initiated a restoration project (under the architectural direction of the husband of one of the women) and presented the house to the city.

586 **University Heights Bridge.** See Bronx No. 27.

The Cloisters (No. 584). Besides housing a portion of the Metropolitan Museum of Art's medieval collection, the Cloisters incorporates parts of cloisters and other medieval buildings from Europe. Photo by John Barrington Bayley, c. 1965.

BROOKLYN

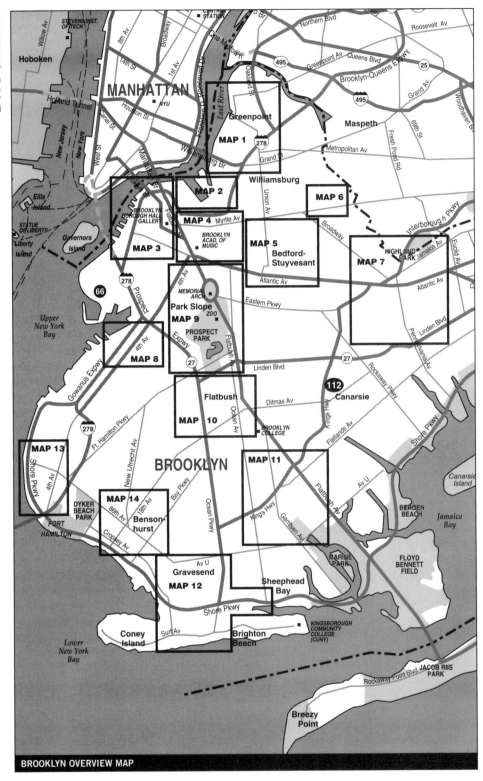

BROOKLYN

MANHATTAN

BROOKLYN OVERVIEW MAP

216

HISTORIC DISTRICT

1 **Greenpoint Historic District,** designated 1982. Unlike Brooklyn's other 19th-century residential historic districts, Greenpoint was not settled primarily by people who commuted to Manhattan. Rather, development in Greenpoint was closely linked to the prosperity of the nearby industrial waterfront. The district contains a wide variety of buildings, reflecting the varied income levels of the local residents. Houses range from early examples of flats to modest frame dwellings to impressive masonry row houses. Construction boomed in the 1860s and early 1870s, and it was during these decades that

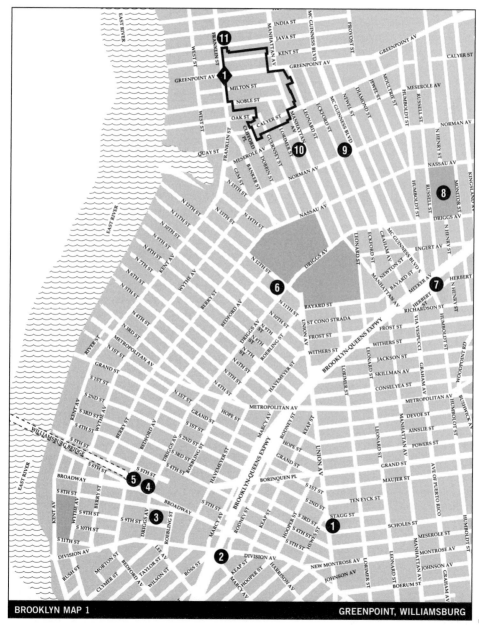

some of the district's finest houses were erected. Among them are a large number of Italianate brick row houses with cast-iron window lintels and door hoods that were probably cast in local Greenpoint foundries. The houses at 128–132 Noble Street and 114–124 Kent Street (1867–68) are particularly notable. Also within the district are some of the most impressive ecclesiastical buildings in eastern Brooklyn, reflecting the importance of religious life to Greenpoint's residents. Among the major churches are the English Gothic–inspired Episcopal Church of the Ascension (Henry Dudley, 1865–66) and the High Victorian Gothic Reformed Church of Greenpoint (now Saint Elias Greek Rite Roman Catholic Church, William B. Ditmars, 1869–70; Sunday School, W. Wheeler Smith, 1879), both on Kent Street. Also of interest are the German Gothic–inspired Saint John's Evangelical Lutheran Church (Theobald Engelhardt, 1891–92) on Milton Street and the Early Romanesque Revival First Baptist Church of Greenpoint (now Union Baptist Church, 1863–65) on Noble Street. Most prominent is Saint Anthony of Padua Roman Catholic Church (1875) on Manhattan Avenue, the most distinguished of Brooklyn resident Patrick C. Keely's many local Gothic Revival churches.

INDIVIDUAL LANDMARKS

1 **Colored School No. 3,** later Public School 69, 270 Union Avenue (Samuel B. Leonard, 1879-81), designated 1998. A reminder of Brooklyn's segregated past, this small school house was built for an exclusively black student body. Leonard, who served as superintendent of buildings for the Brooklyn Board of Education for two decades, enlivened the red brick facade with details based on classical and medieval sources. Transferred to the Public Works Commission in 1934, the building is now privately owned.

2 **Brooklyn Public Library, Williamsburgh Branch,** 240 Division Avenue (Richard A. Walker, 1903–05), designated 1999. Among twenty Brooklyn branches funded by Andrew Carnegie in 1901, the classically inspired Williamsburgh Branch was the second built and one of the most distinctive. Situated on a raised triangular plot, at the intersection of three streets, the library has an unusual Y-shaped plan with a rounded rear pavilion containing the book stacks.

3 **New England Congregational Church,** now Light of the World Church, 179 South 9th Street (Thomas Little, 1852–53), designated 1981. In the 19th century, numerous rural New Englanders settled in Brooklyn and built new Congregational churches. The former New England Congregational Church is one of these and is a rare example of an Italianate brownstone church building. The design and scale of the church, which occupies a midblock site, help to integrate the building into the surrounding urban fabric.

4 **Williamsburgh Savings Bank,** 175 Broadway (George B. Post, 1870–75; additions, Helmle, Huberty & Hudswell, 1905, and Helmle & Huberty, 1925), designated 1966, interior 1996. With its monumental arched entrance portico and towering dome, this early work by George B. Post is one of the first conscious expressions of the Italian Renaissance style erected in America. Post's design anticipates the explosion of interest in Renaissance and classical architecture that culminated in the World's Columbian Exposition of 1893. The Williamsburgh Savings Bank was founded in 1851 to serve the rapidly growing independent city of Williamsburgh. This building was the bank's third home and served as its headquarters until its new tower (see No. 44) was completed in 1929. The vast **interior,** with its open plan, marble pilasters, and decorative iron grilles, contains one of the rare surviving examples of a post–Civil War ornamental scheme. This was designed by architect Peter B. Wight, with extraordinary neo-Grec and neo-Renaissance polychromatic stencil decoration in the cast-iron dome.

5 **Kings County Savings Bank,** 135 Broadway (King & Wilcox, 1868), designated 1966. This former bank, built of light-colored sandstone, is one of New York's most magnificent French Second Empire buildings. The baroque quality of the design is accented by a projecting entrance portico, recessed loggias, a pair of projecting corner pavilions on the side facade, and beautifully executed carving on the ground floor.

Kings County Savings Bank (No. 5), one of the city's most magnificent French Second
Empire buildings. Photo: Landmarks Preservation Commission collection.

❻ Russian Orthodox Cathedral of the Transfiguration of Our Lord, Driggs Avenue at North 12th Street (Louis Allmendinger, 1916–21), designated 1969. The Greek cross plan and the impressive scale of the onion domes of this small yellow brick church typify design in the Russian Orthodox tradition. The cathedral itself stands as a symbol of the importance of Eastern European immigrants in the history of northeastern Brooklyn.

❼ 19th Police Precinct Station House and Stable, 43 Herbert Street and 512–518 Humboldt Street (George Ingram, 1891–92), designated 1993. In 1886 the Brooklyn Police Department began a campaign to expand the number of neighborhood precinct structures. George Ingram, the architect of this Romanesque Revival police station, with its bold arched entrance porch, prominent tower, and handsome ironwork, was the assistant engineer in the Brooklyn Department of City Works, where he developed the standard plan for Brooklyn's police station and stable complexes. Although no longer a precinct station, the building is still used by the Police Department.

❽ Winthrop Park Shelter Pavilion, now Monsignor McGolrick Park, bounded by Nassau and Driggs Avenues, Monitor and Russell Streets (Helmle & Huberty, 1910), designated 1966. For this small park in Greenpoint, Helmle & Huberty designed a curved pavilion that is reminiscent of such 17th- and 18th-century French garden structures as the Grand Trianon at Versailles. The use of Renaissance precedents can also be seen in other works by these architects, notably in the Brooklyn Central Office, Bureau of Fire Communications (see No. 77), and the Prospect Park Boathouse (see No. 82).

❾ Public School 34, also known as the Oliver H. Perry School, 131 Norman Avenue (Samuel B. Leonard, 1867; additions, Samuel B. Leonard, 1870, and James W. Naughton, 1887–88), designated 1983. Public education began in Brooklyn in 1816 and by the late 19th century had grown to the point that Brooklyn had one of the most extensive systems of public education in the country. As the population of Brooklyn increased and as more school buildings were needed, the office of superintendent of buildings was established. Samuel B. Leonard served as superintendent from 1859 to 1879 and was responsible for the design of many of Brooklyn's oldest surviving schools. He was succeeded by James W. Naughton, who retained the position until the Brooklyn school system was merged into that of the newly consolidated city in 1898 and New York's superintendent of school buildings, C. B. J. Snyder, took charge of school design and construction throughout the city. One of the oldest schools in continuous use in New York City, Greenpoint's P. S. 34 is an Early Romanesque Revival building that is similar in design to P. S. 9 (see No. 71).

❿ Sidewalk Clock, 753 Manhattan Avenue (early 20th century), designated 1981. This cast-iron sidewalk clock in Greenpoint is typical of the large clocks that were once commonly used to advertise jewelry stores and other businesses (see Manhattan No. 191).

⓫ Astral Apartments, 184 Franklin Street (Lamb & Rich, 1885–86), designated 1983. The Astral is a significant example of "model tenement" design. Erected by Charles Pratt and named for the "astral oil" manufactured by one of his companies in a nearby Greenpoint refinery, the building was planned as quality affordable housing for ninety-five families. Each apartment contained adequate windows, a toilet, hot and cold running water, and other amenities not usually provided to working-class families in the 19th century. The building was designed in the Queen Anne style by a Manhattan firm often engaged by the Pratt family.

The Russian Orthodox Cathedral of the Transfiguration of Our Lord (No. 6) is a symbol of the importance of Eastern European immigration in the history of northeastern Brooklyn. Photo by John Barrington Bayley.

HISTORIC DISTRICT

❷ **Vinegar Hill Historic District,** designated 1997. The three sections of this historic district—one of Brooklyn's oldest residential communities—are characterized by groups of brick and frame houses erected in the first half of the 19th century along the Brooklyn waterfront, just west of the Brooklyn Navy Yard. The area was named Vinegar Hill by John Jackson, one of its original developers, in commemoration of the Battle of Vinegar Hill of 1798, at which the English ended a rebellion by the Irish. Development began early in the 19th century, but the major period of residential construction was between the 1830s and early 1850s, when Greek Revival and Italianate houses were erected, including the impressive Greek Revival brick row at 237–249 Front Street and the frame houses with brick fronts at 51–59 Hudson Avenue, with Greek Revival and Italianate detail and ground-floor shop fronts. By the late 19th century, Vinegar Hill had so many residents of Irish background that it was often referred to as Irishtown. Industrial expansion along the waterfront replaced much of the surrounding residential community and is represented in the district by the factory building at 232–233 Front Street, designed by the prominent Brooklyn architect William Tubby in 1908 for Benjamin Moore & Co., paint manufacturers.

INDIVIDUAL LANDMARKS

Brooklyn Navy Yard. The Brooklyn Navy Yard was established in 1801 and rapidly grew into one of the busiest naval stations on the eastern seaboard. Some four hundred ships were fitted out at the navy yard during the Civil War, and during World War II the yard employed more than seventy thousand people. Although the navy yard is now an industrial center, most of its early buildings are extant.

❶❷ **Commandant's House,** Evans Street at Little Street (1805–06), designated 1965. The design of this frame house has often been attributed to the Boston architect Charles Bulfinch, working in association with John McComb, Jr., but there is no evidence to support this attribution. The house is among the most elegant structures in the Federal style in New York. Of special note are the porches supported by slender colonnettes and the pair of especially fine fanlighted entranceways. The house was the residence of Matthew Perry when he served as commanding officer of the shipyard in the 1840s.

❶❸ **Dry Dock #1,** Dock Street at the foot of 3rd Street (William J. McAlpine, chief engineer, 1840–51), designated 1975. The construction of Dry Dock #1 was one of the great feats of 19th-

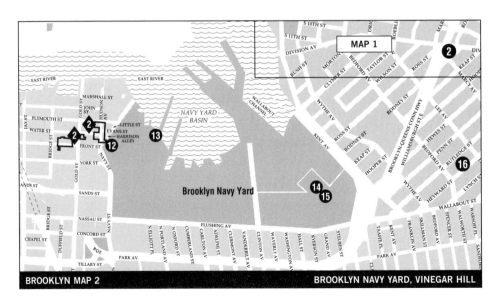

century American engineering. At a cost of more than $2 million, the dry dock was constructed of granite from Maine and Connecticut that was laid under the supervision of the master mason Thornton MacNess Niven.

⑭ Surgeon's House, Flushing Avenue opposite Ryerson Street (True W. Rollins and Charles Hastings, builders, 1863), designated 1976. This mansarded French Second Empire house, built for the chief surgeon of the nearby naval hospital (see below), was erected during the Civil War, a period when the Brooklyn Navy Yard experienced extensive growth.

⑮ U.S. Naval Hospital, Hospital Road (Martin E. Thompson, 1830–38; wings, 1840 and c. 1862), designated 1965. Designed by one of the most prominent architects of the pre–Civil War period, the former U.S. Naval Hospital is an austere yet impressive Greek Revival structure built of Westchester marble. It is distinguished by the eight square stone piers along its main facade.

⑯ Public School 71K, now the Beth Jacob School, 119 Heyward Street (James W. Naughton, 1888–89), designated 1981. This French Second Empire structure in Williamsburg is one of the most beautiful schools designed by Naughton. The building is massed with projecting, pedimented end pavilions and a central frontispiece capped by a mansard roof, and it is articulated by large expanses of finely proportioned windows that permit a maximum amount of light to enter the classrooms.

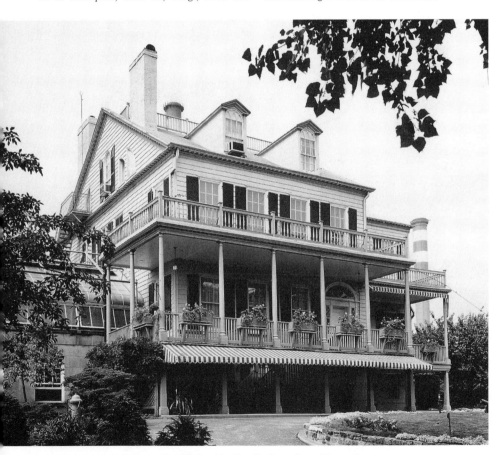

The elegant Commandant's House (No. 12), Brooklyn Navy Yard, was the residence of Matthew Perry when he commanded the shipyard in the 1840s. Photo by John Barrington Bayley, c. 1965.

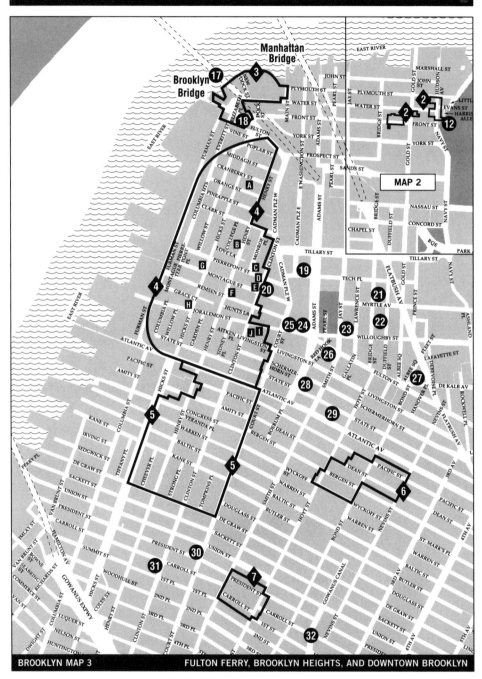

HISTORIC DISTRICTS

③ Fulton Ferry Historic District, designated 1977. The development of Fulton Ferry, Brooklyn's only commercial area designated a historic district, is closely related to the advent of steam-powered ferry service between Brooklyn and Manhattan in 1814. The success of the ferry and resultant commuter traffic led business owners to erect new commercial structures. Among the district's notable early buildings are the Greek Revival Long Island Insurance Company (1835) at 5–7 Front Street, thought to be New York City's earliest surviving office building; the row of Greek Revival stores at 7–23 Fulton Street, erected after the street was widened in 1835; the cast-iron Long Island Safe Deposit Company (William Mundell, 1868–69) at Fulton and Front Streets; and the Italianate Brooklyn City Railroad Building (see

The imposing Romanesque Revival Eagle Warehouse, Fulton Ferry Historic District (H.D. 3). Photo by Carl Forster.

No. 18). The most impressive building on Fulton Street is the former Eagle Warehouse (now apartments), a massive Romanesque Revival brick structure designed in 1893 by Frank Freeman. Throughout much of the 19th century, the district's waterfront was lined with stores and warehouses used for the storage of produce and other goods that were shipped through the port. The monumental Empire Stores at 53–83 Water Street (1869; Thomas Stone, 1885), with their round-arched openings and iron shutters, are among the handful of port warehouses that survive. The opening of the Brooklyn Bridge (see No. 17) in 1883 doomed the ferry and the economic life of Fulton Street, but the area began to revive in the 1970s through the rehabilitation and adaptive use of many of the buildings in the district.

❹ Brooklyn Heights Historic District, designated 1965. Brooklyn Heights, New York City's first historic district, is a rare example of a neighborhood where one can trace practically the entire history of urban residential design in New York City beginning in the 1820s. Following the establishment of the steam-powered Fulton Ferry in 1814, the Heights became the first area of Brooklyn to be urbanized. In the 1820s and early 1830s, elegant 2½-story houses in the Federal style were erected, primarily in the northern part of the Heights. Some of these were wooden buildings, notably the magnificent Eugene Boisselet House at 24 Middagh Street (c. 1829), with its detached carriage house, and 135 Joralemon Street (c. 1833), with its mid-19th-century iron veranda, while others were faced in brick laid in Flemish bond, notably the row of three at 155–159 Willow Street (c. 1826), each with an extraordinary doorway with elegant leaded sidelights and transom. By the 1830s and 1840s, large-scale speculative row-house construction was occurring in the Heights, and many three-story brick houses were erected in the Greek Revival style. These austere buildings generally have grand, often overscale brownstone entrance enframements, including those with massive pilasters, such as the long row at 35–75 Joralemon Street (c. 1844), others with eared enframements, such as the well-preserved row at 20–26 Willow Street (c. 1846), and a few with fluted columns, as at 173–175 Hicks Street (c. 1848). Brooklyn Heights also contains a rare surviving colonnaded row at 43–49 Willow Place (c. 1846), with monumental square piers, and the

Adrien Van Sinderen House (c. 1839) at 70 Willow Street, a four-bay-wide Greek Revival mansion that is among the largest houses of the style in New York City. Besides these noteworthy individual houses and rows, there are several streets lined with three-story and basement brick houses that indicate the character of urban neighborhoods in the 1840s; this is evident on Clinton Street between Livingston and State Streets and Henry Street between Joralemon and State Streets. Gothic Revival row houses also appeared in Brooklyn Heights in the 1840s. Although this style was never overwhelmingly popular for row houses, one of the largest collections of these buildings can be found in this neighborhood. Many of these are early examples of the use of brownstone, and all are embellished with such Gothic-inspired features as pointed-arch openings and drip lintels. Notable Gothic Revival row houses include the brick structures at 103–107 State Street (c. 1847), with their pointed-arch, cast-iron stoop and areaway railings and the quatrefoil-embellished iron balcony at No. 107; the unusual brick houses at 2–8 Willow Place (c. 1847), with their arched porticoes supported by clustered colonnettes; and the exceptionally well preserved brownstone rows at 118–122 Willow Street (c. 1845) and 131–135 Hicks Street (c. 1848). Also within the district is the George Hastings House at 36 Pierrepont Street, a large individual house with Gothic ironwork designed in 1846 by the prominent architect Richard Upjohn. By the time the brownstone-faced Italianate row house became popular in Brooklyn in the 1860s, much of Brooklyn Heights had already been developed, and there was little room for the long rows erected in neighborhoods such as Fort Greene and Clinton Hill (see Map 4). However, a few individual row houses were erected, and the neighborhood contains the two largest surviving Italianate mansions in New York, the Alexander M. White and Abiel Abbot Low houses (Frederick A. Petersen, c. 1857) at 2 and 3 Pierrepont Place. In the 1880s and 1890s, a few Queen Anne and Romanesque Revival row houses and mansions were erected. These include the exuberant Queen Anne row at 108–112 Willow Street (William Halsey Wood, 1880), the massive Romanesque Revival row at 262–272 Hicks Street (William Tubby, 1887), and one of the great masterpieces of Romanesque Revival design in New York City, the Herman Behr House (Frank Freeman, 1889) at 84 Pierrepont Street. The 1880s also mark

Brooklyn Heights Historic District (H.D. 4). Federal-style houses at the southeast corner of Middagh and Willow Streets in the city's first historic district. Photo by Caroline Kane Levy.

the beginning of the development of middle-class apartment buildings in Brooklyn, with some of the finest early examples on Montague Street—the Queen Anne–style Montague, Grosvenor, and Berkeley (Parfitt Brothers, 1885), at Nos. 103, 115, and 117, and the Arlington (Montrose Morris, 1887) at No. 62. By the 20th century, large numbers of apartment houses were built, generally replacing earlier structures. Beaux-Arts apartment houses appeared in the northern end of the Heights early in the 20th century. By the 1920s and 1930s, English Gothic-, Romanesque-, and Colonial-inspired apartment buildings were erected throughout the neighborhood, followed in the 1930s and 1940s by Art Deco structures. Brooklyn Heights also became a center for apartment hotels, with several of Brooklyn's most famous hotels erected early in the 20th century, including the Beaux-Arts Bossert (Helmle & Huberty, 1908–13) at 98 Montague Street with its famous rooftop restaurant, the Marine Grill, and the St. George on Clark Street between Hicks and Henry Streets, once New York's largest hotel (with what was reputed to be the world's largest saltwater

swimming pool), composed of many buildings, including a high-rise tower (Emery Roth, 1929–30). Even in the post–World War II era a few important buildings appeared in Brooklyn Heights, notably the modern row houses at 40, 44, and 48 Willow Place (Joseph & Mary Merz, 1965–66). Brooklyn Heights also contains some of the most important institutional buildings in New York City which are individually discussed below.

A **Plymouth Church (Congregational),** now Plymouth Church of the Pilgrims, Orange Street between Henry and Hicks Streets (Joseph C. Wells, 1849–50). After the organization of this congregation in 1847 as the third Congregational church in Brooklyn, Henry Ward Beecher was called to the ministry. Beecher was one of the most dynamic preachers of the 19th century, perhaps best known for his outspoken abolitionism. The church building is a simple barnlike structure with a seating plan consisting of pews arranged in arcs in front of the pulpit. Both the design and the plan became prototypes for churches erected by other evangelical

Protestant congregations throughout the country. The entrance porch and stained-glass windows were added early in the 20th century, and the adjoining church house and arcade were built in 1913 (Woodruff Leeming, architect). The statue of Beecher in the church garden is by Gutzon Borglum (best known for his work at Mount Rushmore; he also did sculpture on the New York Evening Post Building—see Manhattan No. 55).

B **First Presbyterian Church,** 124 Henry Street (William B. Olmsted, 1846). This bold but somewhat naive Gothic Revival church is dominated by an exceedingly wide 90-foot-tall crenellated tower punctuated by a large pointed-arch window. The design reflects a greater freedom in the use of Gothic forms among Protestant denominations in contrast to the more strictly medieval inspiration of many contemporary Episcopal churches such as Grace (see entry H, below). First Presbyterian was established in 1822 just as Brooklyn was beginning its urban development and affluent Presbyterians were settling in the Heights.

C **First Unitarian Church of Brooklyn, Church of the Saviour,** Pierrepont Street at Monroe Place (Minard Lafever, 1842–44). The New Englanders who arrived in Brooklyn in the 1830s and 1840s not only established many Congregational churches (see H.D. 4, entries A and F) but also founded this Unitarian church in 1833. The brownstone church in the Gothic Revival style is among architect Minard Lafever's masterpieces. The form, with a gabled end flanked by turrets, is loosely based on King's College Chapel, Cambridge. The corner lot is marked by an exceptionally fine Gothic cast-iron railing. In 1995 a major restoration of the facade was undertaken (Robert Meadows, architect). As part of the congregation's efforts to improve conditions among Brooklyn's working poor, the church established a mission on the waterfront in 1865. Ten years later the **Willow Place Chapel,** now Alfred T. White Community Center (Russell Sturgis, 1875–76), was erected at 26 Willow Place, under the direction of Alfred Tredway White, who was also about to begin work on his pioneering Home and Tower model tenements in the Cobble Hill Historic District (see H.D. 5) and would later also erect the Riverside Homes on Columbia Place in Brooklyn Heights, completed in 1890 (partially extant;

William Field & Son). Sturgis used a High Victorian Gothic style reflecting the ideas of English art theorist John Ruskin, as is evident in the chapel's brick facade with contrasting light-colored stonework, high clerestory, cusped arches, and dog-tooth detail.

D **Long Island Historical Society,** now the Brooklyn Historical Society, 128 Pierrepont Street (George B. Post, 1878–81). Organized in 1863, the Long Island Historical Society soon grew into a leading library and museum of local history. Fourteen architects entered a design competition for the society's building in 1878. Post's Renaissance-inspired design won, and the new building, the first in New York to exploit ornamental terra cotta extensively, was dedicated in January 1881. It contains one of New York's great 19th-century **interiors.** The second-floor Othmer Library (designated 1982) retains its original furnishings and stained-glass windows; outstanding architectural features include columns, a gallery railing, and other woodwork carved of black ash. The library houses an important collection of books, prints, photographs, and other material relating to Brooklyn. A major restoration of the building and library was completed in 2003.

E **Holy Trinity Church (Episcopal),** now Saint Ann and the Holy Trinity Episcopal Church, Clinton Street at Montague Street (Minard Lafever, 1844–47). Seven years after Holy Trinity parish was organized in 1837, construction began on this Gothic Revival church, chapel, and parish house funded by paper manufacturer John Bartow, who dreamed of erecting an Episcopal church in Brooklyn that would rival such New York City churches as Trinity (see Manhattan No. 1815). At its completion, this was the largest church in Brooklyn. Lafever planned a spire, but it was not until 1866 that a spire designed by Patrick C. Keely (architect for many of Brooklyn's Roman Catholic churches; see Greenpoint Historic District, H.D. 1) was built; it was removed in 1905. The windows, designed by William Jay Bolton and John Bolton, America.represent the first major program of stained glass made in America. A complete restoration of the exterior and windows was begun in 1979.

F **Church of the Pilgrims (Congregational),** now Our Lady of Lebanon Maronite Rite Roman Catholic Church, Henry Street and Remsen Street

(Richard Upjohn, 1844–46; rectory, Leopold Eidlitz, 1869). As Brooklyn was becoming urbanized in the pre–Civil War era, large numbers of New Englanders moved to the city, organizing many Congregational churches. This was the first Congregational church erected in Brooklyn and was a radical design. The church is the first round-arched, Early Romanesque Revival ecclesiastical building in America and became a model for many buildings erected by evangelical Protestant congregations in succeeding decades. The original corner steeple has been removed, as has the cap to the southern tower. In

First Unitarian Church of Brooklyn (Entry C). A Gothic Revival masterpiece by architect Minard Lafever. Photo by Caroline Kane Levy

1869 the church was expanded with a High Victorian addition that is one of the few surviving buildings by Leopold Eidlitz, a major figure in 19th-century American architecture. In 1944 the Church of the Pilgrims merged with Plymouth Church (see entry A, above), and this building was sold to a Lebanese Roman Catholic congregation. The medallions on the entrance doors, originally part of the main dining room doors on the French luxury liner *Normandie,* were purchased by Our Lady of Lebanon at an auction in 1945.

G **Heights Casino and Casino Mansions Apartments,** 75 Montague Street and 200 Hicks Street (Boring & Tilton, 1905, and William A. Boring, 1910). Most affluent residential neighborhoods in the 19th and early 20th centuries were home to private clubs that catered to residents' social needs. The Casino is one of the few such clubs in Brooklyn still in use. The building is a Dutch Renaissance–inspired structure with brick laid in diaper patterns to enliven the blank walls where squash courts preclude the use of windows. Iron tie rods on the walls take the form of squash rackets. In 1910 William Boring designed the neighboring apartment building, the Casino Mansions, in conformity with the design of the club. With two apartments per floor, this was one of Brooklyn's most luxurious apartment houses.

H **Grace Church (Episcopal),** Hicks Street at Grace Court (Richard Upjohn, 1847–49). Grace is one of the most mature Gothic designs in New York City by the prestigious architect Richard Upjohn, who was a resident of Brooklyn. Grace was organized in 1847 as an offshoot of Upjohn's own church, Christ Episcopal in the Cobble Hill Historic District (H.D. 5). The nave and chancel are clearly demarcated on the brownstone exterior, but a proposed corner tower was never built.

I **Packer Collegiate Institute For Girls,** now Packer Collegiate Institute, 170 Joralemon Street (Minard Lafever, 1853–56; additions, Napoleon Le Brun & Son, 1884 and 1886). The Brooklyn Female Academy, founded in 1844, burned in 1853, but Harriet L. Packer offered to reestablish the school in honor of her husband. Minard Lafever designed one of the finest Gothic Revival buildings of the 1850s, modeling his picturesque structure after college buildings at Oxford and Cambridge. The tall octago-

nal tower was originally capped and housed a telescope. Additions to the east and the west were designed by the Le Brun firm. Packer (now a coeducational school) has been a superb steward of its buildings and has carefully restored the brownstone facade and the Gothic cast-iron railings.

J **Saint Ann's Church (Episcopal),** now part of Packer Collegiate Institute, Clinton Street at Livingston Street (Renwick & Sands, chapel, 1866–67; church, 1867–69). The former Saint Ann's is not only a major work of James Renwick, Jr.'s, but one of the most important High Victorian Gothic churches in America. Saint Ann's was the first Episcopal congregation established in Brooklyn; this was its third home. The church is a complex Ruskinian building erected of contrasting Belleville sandstone from New Jersey with Cleveland stone trim from Ohio. It has a full tripartite horizontal massing with an arcade articulated by simple pointed-arch windows, a triforium with ornate tracery, and a clerestory with small windows set in horizontal frames. The roofline bristles with pinnacles and crockets. In the late 1960s Saint Ann's moved into the Holy Trinity Church (see entry E), and this building became the property of Packer Collegiate Institute (see entry I, above). It is currently used as classrooms.

5 **Cobble Hill Historic District and Extension,** designated 1969 and 1988. The inauguration in 1836 of service on South Ferry, linking Atlantic Avenue and Whitehall Street across the East River, led to the development of what at the time was farmland into a middle-class residential neighborhood. The row houses of Cobble Hill are primarily Greek Revival, Italianate, and Anglo-Italianate in style; most are faced with brick or brownstone and feature high stoops with exceptionally fine ironwork. The district also includes two "model tenement" complexes that are among the most significant housing erected in the United States in the 19th century. The Home and Tower buildings, on Hicks Street at Baltic Street, designed by William Field & Son in 1876 and 1878, respectively, were erected by the Brooklyn businessman Alfred T. White as decent affordable housing for working people. The apartments were designed to provide plumbing and sufficient light and air, amenities that are often taken for granted today. Behind the Tower Apartments, stretching along Warren Place (a one-block street extending from Warren Street to Baltic

BEYOND THE TENEMENT

New York was a workshop for innovative housing during the late 19th and early 20th centuries. Apartments, variously known as French flats and tenements, were built to house the city's growing population. Immigrants crowded in tenements, structures that maximized profits for developers while providing few of the amenities we take for granted today, such as light, air, and private bathrooms. Despite efforts to legislate minimum standards in 1867 and 1879, initially it was steps by private individuals that made decent housing affordable to the working class. One of the earliest examples, the Home Buildings at the corner of Hicks and Baltic Streets, was sponsored by the housing reformer Alfred T. White (Brooklyn H.D. 5). Designed by William Field & Son in 1877, it was called by the *New York Times* "the pioneer of all good tenement houses in New York." Luxurious by contemporary standards, each apartment had abundant light and air, running water, and a private water closet. Along with the Tower Buildings on Baltic and Warren Streets (1879), it served as inspiration for the Queen Anne–style Astral Apartments, sponsored by oil merchant Charles Pratt, and for White's second project, Riverside, located at 4–30 Columbia Place in Brooklyn Heights (Brooklyn H.D. 5, No. 11, and H.D. 4).

On Manhattan's Upper East Side, several "model" tenements were constructed at the beginning of the 20th century. The largest of these, the Avenue A (York Avenue) Estate, was built by the City and Suburban Homes Company, whose investors limited their profits to 5 percent (Manhattan No. 503). The adjoining complex, known as the East River Houses, was sponsored by Mrs. William K. Vanderbilt to serve families whose members suffered from tuberculosis (No. 502). Designed by the architect and housing reformer Henry Atterbury Smith, these neoclassical buildings provided residents with a living environment both beautiful and healthful.

Garden apartments came into vogue after 1900. Suburban in character, most examples were located in less-developed areas, where land was still cheap and new transit routes made them accessible. The largest group is located in Queens in the Jackson Heights Historic District (Queens H.D. 3). Built by the Queensboro Corporation, the finest examples—the Chateau and the Towers on 34th Avenue between 80th and 81st Streets—were erected around the perimeter of a single block and have beautifully landscaped courtyards. Cooperatively owned, they were the first apartment houses in New York planned for middle-class residents. Subsequent examples include Tudor City, straddling the east end of 42nd Street, and the "Coops," built by the United Workers Cooperative Association in two campaigns (Manhattan H.D. 23 and Bronx No. 39). The later buildings, designed by Herman Jessor in 1927, incorporate decorative features associated with European Modernism. In Harlem, the Dunbar Apartments were built in 1926–28 (Manhattan No. 561). Financed by John D. Rockefeller, Jr., this complex of walk-up apartments was the first major nonprofit cooperative complex built for residents of African descent. During the Depression, apartment complexes were mainly built with public funds. The first of these, aptly called the First Houses, was sponsored by the New York City Housing Authority in 1935–36 (Manhattan No. 165). Located in the East Village, the L-shaped complex incorporated both older tenements and new construction. Additional buildings that deserve mention include the Harlem River Houses and the Clinton Hill Houses (Manhattan No. 562 and Brooklyn H.D. 10). Designed by Harrison, Fouilhoux & Abramowitz, the latter complex, at 335–373 Clinton Avenue, served navy personnel and consists of a series of freestanding towers in a parklike setting.

Street between Henry Street and Hicks Street), White built two rows of 11-foot-wide houses facing onto a common garden. The district contains several religious structures designed by important New York architects—notably Christ Episcopal Church (1840–41) on the corner of Clinton and Kane Streets, an early Gothic Revival work by Richard Upjohn, and Minard Lafever's Gothic Revival Strong Place Baptist Church (now Saint Francis Cabrini R.C. Chapel; 1851–52) on the corner of Degraw Street and Strong Place.

⑥ Boerum Hill Historic District, designated 1973. Located just south of busy Atlantic Avenue, Boerum Hill is a homogeneous district composed primarily of row houses with brick or brownstone facades. Designed in the Greek Revival and Italianate styles, most of the houses were erected between the 1840s and the early 1870s. The district contains unusually long rows for this period, accenting the cohesive nature of the blockfronts. The quality of the blocks is further enhanced by the survival of many cast-iron stoop and areaway railings, original wood double doors, and bluestone sidewalks.

⑦ Carroll Gardens Historic District, designated 1973. This small district of row houses set behind deep front yards retains much of its 19th-century character. The impression of space is the result of the surveyor Richard Butts's plan, devised in 1846, which created building lots with especially deep front yards and a street pattern that protects President and Carroll Streets from through traffic. All the row houses in the district were erected between 1869 and 1884 by local builders, and most are brownstone-fronted buildings in the Italianate and neo-Grec styles.

INDIVIDUAL LANDMARKS

⑰ Brooklyn Bridge, spanning the East River between Cadman Plaza, Brooklyn, and City Hall Park, Manhattan (John A., Washington, and Emily Roebling, 1867–83), designated 1967. The Brooklyn Bridge, one of the great engineering feats of the 19th century, was the first physical link between the independent cities of Brooklyn and New York (they merged in 1898). It not only became the world's longest suspension bridge but was also an aesthetic

triumph, with its intricate web of cables and its bold Gothic-inspired piers serving as symbolic portals to the two cities. Conceived by a German immigrant engineer, John A. Roebling, who had previously designed suspension bridges in Cincinnati and Pittsburgh, the project was taken over by his son Washington after Roebling died from an injury sustained during construction. Even when Washington Roebling was later paralyzed by caisson disease, he continued, with the help of his wife, Emily, to oversee the project from the window of a house in Brooklyn Heights. In 1972–73 the bridge was repainted in historically accurate colors. The pedestrian walkway was rebuilt in 1981–83, and the cables have been rehabilitated.

⑱ Brooklyn City Railroad Company, 8 Cadman Plaza West (Old Fulton Street) (1860–61), designated 1973. Established in 1853, the Brooklyn City Railroad Company operated horse-car lines that brought people to and from the Fulton Ferry terminal. The company's headquarters building is an Italianate brick structure with granite trim and a cast-iron storefront. It has been converted into apartments.

⑲ United States Post Office and Court House, Brooklyn Central Office, 271–301 Cadman Plaza East (Washington Street) (Mifflin E. Bell, 1885–91; extension, 1930–33), designated 1966. The office of the supervising architect of the U.S. Treasury was responsible for the design of many Romanesque Revival post offices in the United States. This Brooklyn building is one of the few such post offices still standing and still in use. The construction began during Bell's brief tenure as supervising architect (1884–86); Bell's design was transformed into a boldly scaled Romanesque Revival work following his resignation. The complementary Depression-era addition was designed during James Wetmore's tenure as acting supervising architect.

⑳ Brooklyn Trust Company Building, 177–179 Montague Street (York & Sawyer, 1913–16), designated 1996. The Brooklyn Trust Company, established in 1866, was responsible for the construction of the most beautiful building on Brooklyn's "bank row." York & Sawyer created an elegant structure modeled on Italian Renaissance designs, drawing especially from the Palazzo della

Gran Guardia, often attributed to Veronese architect Michele Sanmicheli. The building set a precedent for the firm's largest Renaissance banks—the Central Savings Bank (see Manhattan No. 392) and the Federal Reserve Bank (see Manhattan No. 27). Both the exterior and the **interior** are magnificently crafted. The banking hall draws inspiration from ancient Roman and Italian Renaissance architecture. The monumentally scaled space has a vaulted, coffered ceiling with enormous chandeliers, grand arched windows, and a Cosmati-work floor of intricately patterned marble mosaic.

㉑ First Free Congregational Church, later the Bridge Street African Wesleyan Methodist Episcopal Church, now Polytechnic Institute, Wunsch Student Center, 311 Bridge Street (1846–47), designated 1981. A rare surviving Greek Revival church structure in Brooklyn, this building first served as a Congregational church. Just seven years after its completion, it was sold to Brooklyn's oldest African-American congregation, the African Wesleyan Methodist Episcopal (A.W.M.E.) Church. This congregation, which soon became known as the Bridge Street A.W.M.E. Church, occupied the building for eighty-four years before moving to Bedford-Stuyvesant. The building eventually became a factory and was rehabilitated by Polytechnic Institute after it acquired the property in 1968. A more extensive restoration, overseen by architect James Wong, was completed in 1996.

㉒ Duffield Street Houses, between Willoughby and Myrtle Avenues, designated 2001. Brooklyn was incorporated as a city in 1834, and during the years that followed a wave of speculative building transformed the blocks east of the new City Hall (see No. 24). Most of the houses were occupied by middle-class residents, including merchants, lawyers, brokers, builders, and teachers. In 1990, as part of the MetroTech redevelopment project, these four row houses were stabilized and moved from Johnson Street to the present site, where they adjoin St. Boniface Church. All share a uniform building line and small front gardens, an arrangement stipulated by Samuel R. Johnson, who erected three of the houses.

182 Duffield Street (c.1839–40). Originally located at the corner of Johnson and Lawrence Street, this brick house with Greek Revival features was not part of the original group.

184 Duffield Street (1847). Built as an investment property by Francis H. Chichester, this three-story brick row house displays simple Greek Revival details.

186 Duffield Street (c. 1835–38). Johnson built this frame house as a pair with 188 Duffield Street. Notable features include the dormer windows and a rare surviving example of a free-standing Greek Revival portico.

188 Duffield Street (c. 1835–38). Remodeled and enlarged in the 1880s, the clapboard siding was enriched with Queen Anne and Second Empire–style ornamentation, such as a bracketed hood and a richly detailed metal cornice.

㉓ Brooklyn Fire Headquarters, 365–367 Jay Street (Frank Freeman, 1892), designated 1966. The former headquarters of the Brooklyn Fire Department, designed by one of Brooklyn's most talented 19th-century architects, is a masterpiece of the Romanesque Revival. This powerful building is distinguished by its massive entrance arch and richly textured elevation, clad in rock-faced red sandstone and gold Roman brick and trimmed with terra cotta. The building is now an apartment house.

㉔ Brooklyn City Hall, now Brooklyn Borough Hall, 209 Joralemon Street (Gamaliel King, 1845–48; alterations, Vincent Griffith and Stoughton & Stoughton, 1898), designated 1966. Brooklyn City Hall is an imposing Greek Revival structure. The exterior of the Tuckahoe marble building, with its Ionic portico and crisp window enframements, remained unaltered until its original cupola was destroyed by fire in 1895. The architects Vincent Griffith and Stoughton & Stoughton designed a new cast-iron cupola in 1898, the same year that Brooklyn was consolidated into Greater New York and the building became Borough Hall. A restoration of the building was completed in 1989 under the direction of the architecture firm Conklin & Rossant; the copper shingles of the cupola were meticulously reconstituted by the French firm Les Metalliers Champenois (which also restored the Statue of Liberty), and a crowning figure of justice, planned in 1898, was finally installed.

Brooklyn City Hall (No. 24), built in 1845–48, when Brooklyn was an independent city.
Photo by Caroline Kane Levy.

㉕ Interborough Rapid Transit System Underground Station, Borough Hall. See Manhattan No. 7

㉖ Gage & Tollner Restaurant, 372 Fulton Street (building, c. 1875; restaurant design, 1892), designated 1974, interior 1975. One of Brooklyn's most celebrated restaurants, Gage & Tollner opened at a nearby location in 1879. The restaurant moved to this brownstone building in 1892, at which time a new wooden shop front was added and the **interior** was redesigned. The dining room retains an authentic 19th-century character, with cherry wood trim, original furnishings and mirrors, Lincrusta (an imitation leather) wall covering, and graceful gaslight fixtures. In 1996 the interior was completely refurbished to enhance its historic character.

㉗ Dime Savings Bank, 9 DeKalb Avenue (Mowbray & Uffinger, 1906–08; enlarged, Halsey, McCormack & Helmer, 1931–32), designated 1994. This is one of New York City's most monumental banks, and it typifies early 20th-century savings bank architecture, which used impressive design to attract large numbers of small depositors. In 1906 the Dime purchased an oddly shaped lot on a triangular block and erected an imposing Classical Revival building faced with marble. The building was substantially enlarged in 1931–32, creating the present domed, temple-fronted building. The spectacular, richly detailed **interior,** focusing on a rotunda supported by twelve red German marble columns with gilded capitals displaying Mercury dimes, was created at this time.

㉘ Friends Meeting House, 110 Schermerhorn Street (attributed to Charles T. Bunting, 1857), designated 1981. Consistent with Quaker taste, the Brooklyn Friends Meeting House is a beautifully proportioned but severely simple brick structure. It is articulated by tall multipaned windows that allow light to flood the second-floor meeting room.

㉙ State Street Houses, 291–299 and 290–324 State Street (1847–74), designated 1973. These twenty-three row houses between Smith and Hoyt Streets reflect the development of this formerly rural section of Boerum Hill into a prosperous urban residential neighborhood in the mid-19th century. The brick-and brownstone-fronted houses are Greek Revival and Italianate in style.

㉚ South Congregational Church Complex, 358–366 Court Street and 253–269 President Street (chapel, 1851; church, 1857; ladies' parlor, F. Carles Merry, 1889; rectory, Woodruff Leeming, 1893), designated 1982. Located on a prominent corner in the old neighborhood of South Brooklyn— now generally known as Carroll Gardens—South Congregational is a brick church articulated by a series of arches expressive of the finest Early Romanesque Revival design. To the rear are the chapel, the Romanesque Revival ladies' parlor, and the neo-Gothic rectory. The church congregation now worships in the former parlor, and the church and the chapel have been converted into apartments.

㉛ John Rankin House, also known as the 440 Clinton Street House, now the F. G. Guido Funeral Home (c. 1840), designated 1970. This handsomely proportioned Greek Revival brick structure was erected for a wealthy merchant at a time when the area now known as Carroll Gardens was still largely rural. One of Brooklyn's largest residences of the 1840s, the house has an especially fine granite entrance surround and granite newel posts.

㉜ Carroll Street Bridge, spanning the Gowanus Canal (Robert Van Buren, chief engineer; George Ingram, engineer in charge, 1888–89), designated 1987. One of the oldest bridges in New York City and the oldest of the four known American examples of a "retractile" bridge, the Carroll Street Bridge rolls horizontally onto land whenever a barge needs to pass along the Gowanus Canal. The superstructure was manufactured by the New Jersey Steel and Iron Company, a subsidiary of Cooper, Hewitt & Company, one of the country's foremost iron and steel producers. The bridge was restored in 1989 by engineers in the city's Department of Transportation.

Dime Savings Bank (No. 27). The monumental design and grand interior were intended to attract small investors. Photo: Landmarks Preservation Commission collection.

HISTORIC DISTRICTS

8 **Brooklyn Academy of Music Historic District,** designated 1978. This small district at the western edge of the Fort Greene neighborhood is composed of Italianate and Anglo-Italianate row houses erected primarily between 1855 and 1859 as residential development in Brooklyn was moving east across Flatbush Avenue. The streets are lined with row houses faced in either brick or brownstone and highlighted with fine wooden cornices, cast-iron railings, wood doors, and double-hung wood window sash. A small section of Fulton Street, Brooklyn's major 19th-century commercial thoroughfare, runs through the district and contains an unusual row of cast-iron buildings erected in 1882 that had stores on the ground floor and flats above. The three most prominent buildings in the district are the Williamsburgh Savings Bank's tower (see No. 44); the neo-Gothic Central Methodist Church (1929–31) on Hanson Place, designed by Halsey, McCormack, & Helmer, the same architecture firm responsible for the neighboring bank tower; and,

most significant, the Brooklyn Academy of Music. The Brooklyn Academy of Music was established in 1859. Soon after its home on Montague Street burned in 1903, a decision was made to move to a site that was near the center of Brooklyn's population and was convenient to railroad, subway, and streetcar lines. The noted theater architecture firm Herts & Tallant designed the Italian Renaissance–inspired building, which opened in October 1908. The academy is faced in textured, sand-blasted cream-colored brick with extraordinary polychromatic terra-cotta detail, including entrances adorned with putti singing and playing musical instruments, inspired by the work of Renaissance master Luca Della Robbia. The Brooklyn Academy of Music continues to be one of New York's most vital cultural institutions. A reproduction of the original cornice and a new marquee were installed in 2003.

9 **Fort Greene Historic District,** designated 1978. In the 1850s, as Brooklyn's population was expanding rapidly, middle-class residential development moved up the slope of Clinton Hill into the neighbor-

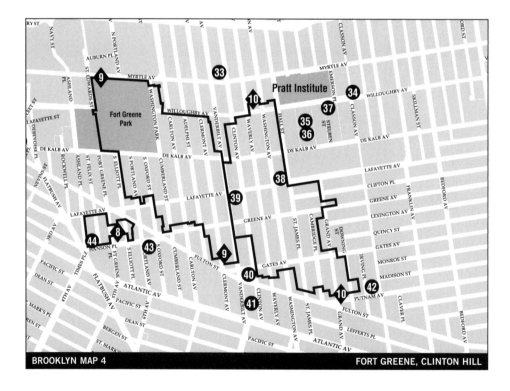

hood now known as Fort Greene. A number of the streets in the area were named for the great Regency terraces of London (Portland, Oxford, Cumberland, Carlton, and Adelphi), and between 1855 and the early 1870s these and nearby streets were lined with fine row houses. Many of the early houses are simple brick buildings in the Italianate or transitional Greek Revival/Italianate styles; heavy concentrations of such row houses are found on Cumberland and Carlton Streets. By the 1860s grander Italianate and French Second Empire rows with brownstone facades and ornate carved detail were erected. The Italianate houses on South Portland Avenue are especially elaborate, as are the long rows of French Second Empire houses with mansard roofs that line Washington Park and Clermont Avenue between Willoughby and DeKalb Avenues. One of the most intact blockfronts of brownstone-fronted row houses in Brooklyn is that on the west side of Vanderbilt Avenue between Greene and Gates Avenues, built in 1872–79. A few important churches were erected to minister to the needs of the neighborhood's new residents. The most famous of these is the Lafayette Avenue Presbyterian Church (Grimshaw & Morrill, 1861–62), a brownstone Early Romanesque Revival–style structure. The church was led by the Reverend Theodore L. Cuyler, one of New York's prominent mid-19th-century ministers. The focus of the new neighborhood was (and still is) Fort Greene Park, designed by Frederick Law Olmsted and Calvert Vaux in 1867 on the site of a Revolutionary War fort. In the center of the park is McKim, Mead & White's Prison Ship Martyrs' Monument of 1906–09, an enormous Doric column commemorating the American patriots who died on British prison ships in nearby Wallabout Bay during the Revolutionary War. A few single-family houses and apartment buildings were erected in the district later in the 19th century and in the early 20th century, and two prestigious institutions were built on Lafayette Avenue between Clermont and Vanderbilt Avenues—the Brooklyn Masonic Temple (Lord & Hewlett, 1906), a grand Classical Revival structure built of brick with exceptional polychromatic terracotta detail, and Queen of All Saints Roman Catholic Church and School (Reiley & Steinback, 1910), an imposing French Gothic structure built of cast stone. Even with these additions to the area, the character of the district remains one of cohesive mid-19th-century row houses.

⑩ Clinton Hill Historic District, designated 1981. Clinton Hill is unusual among Brooklyn residential neighborhoods in that it has undergone many periods of development and redevelopment, creating a varied character along the streets. Clinton Avenue, at the crest of Clinton Hill, was laid out in 1832 as a wide boulevard for large suburban residences; several of these survive, notably the wooden Gothic Revival house erected at No. 284 (Field & Correja, c. 1854, with later additions) and the brick and stone Italianate villa at No. 447 (c. 1850). In the 1860s long rows of Italianate brick or brownstone houses were erected. Grand Avenue, Cambridge Place, and Saint James Place contain some of New York's most intact mid-19th-century row houses. In the 1870s Clinton Avenue and Washington Avenue began to attract many of Brooklyn's wealthiest citizens. Charles Pratt erected a large but restrained neo-Grec mansion at 232 Clinton Avenue in 1874 (Ebenezer L. Roberts, architect), and he was followed in the next half century by other wealthy industrialists who established Clinton Avenue as Brooklyn's "Gold Coast." Some of these mansions were designed by prominent Manhattan architects, including Herts & Tallant (the Liebman House at 384 Clinton Avenue; 1907), Babb, Cook & Willard (the Frederick B. and George DuPont Pratt houses at 229 and 245 Clinton Avenue; 1895 and 1901), and Dwight James Baum (the Van Glahn House, 367 Washington Avenue; 1921–22), but other mansions and groups of late 19th-century row houses were the work of such talented Brooklyn architects as William B. Tubby (notably the Charles Millard Pratt House of 1890 at 229 Clinton Avenue) and Montrose Morris (the row houses at 285–289 and 282–290 DeKalb Avenue of 1889–90). In the late 19th century, small apartment houses were built in the neighborhood, and in the 1920s many larger six-story buildings were erected, often replacing mansions. Apartment-house construction culminated with the erection of the Clinton Hill Houses on Clinton Avenue (Harrison, Fouilhoux & Abramovitz), a group of towers planned during World War II for workers in the nearby Brooklyn Navy Yard (see Nos. 12–15). The mix of row houses, mansions, apartment buildings, and a few institutional structures (see Emmanuel Baptist Church, No. 38), designed in a variety of styles, contributes to the unique character of Clinton Hill's streets.

The Clinton Hill Historic District (H.D. 10) contains the magnificent mansions of the Pratt family, once Brooklyn's wealthiest citizens. Photo by Carl Forster.

INDIVIDUAL LANDMARKS

㉝ Lefferts Laidlaw House, 136 Clinton Avenue (c. 1836–40, south wing before 1855), designated 2001. This freestanding wood house was constructed at a time when many private residences were built close to the Brooklyn Navy Yard. Four fluted Corinthian columns support a pedimented gable roof, making it one of the finest examples of a temple-fronted Greek Revival structure in Brooklyn. The house was restored in the 1970s and 1980s.

㉞ Saint Mary's Episcopal Church, 230 Classon Avenue (Richard T. Auchmuty, 1858–59), designated 1981. One of New York's most original but least well known Gothic Revival churches, Saint Mary's was designed by a partner in the firm Renwick & Auchmuty. Executed in brownstone, the church was erected to minister to the population that settled near the bustling Brooklyn Navy Yard (see Nos. 12–15).

㉟ Pratt Institute: Main Building Complex, 215 Ryerson Street (Main Building, Lamb & Rich,

1885–87; South Hall, William B. Tubby, 1891; porch, William B. Tubby, 1894; Memorial Hall, John Mead Howells, 1926–27), designated 1981. Pratt Institute was founded in 1884 by the wealthy Brooklyn manufacturer Charles Pratt as a school to train men and women in the manual arts. Pratt recognized the growing need for skilled industrial workers, and he believed that the best way to help people was to teach them to help themselves. The institute buildings were erected only a few blocks from Pratt's home on Clinton Avenue and originally faced onto city streets; the current campus environment was not created until the 1950s. The Main Building is an imposing Romanesque Revival brick and stone structure that originally housed all institute functions. The bold arched entrance porch, perhaps the building's most striking feature, is an addition designed by Tubby in 1894. Tubby's South Hall is a modest Romanesque Revival work that was originally used as the Pratt Institute High School. The neo-Romanesque Memorial Hall, commemorating Charles Pratt's second wife, Mary Richardson Pratt, was planned as an assembly hall; the brick and stone building is adorned with sculpted figures by Rene

Chambellan. Memorial Hall was restored by H & H Building Consulting in 1996–97.

③⑥ Pratt Institute Library, 224–228 Ryerson Street (William B. Tubby, 1896; north porch, John Mead Howells, 1936), designated 1981. Charles Pratt organized Brooklyn's first free library, open to all citizens over the age of fourteen, as part of the institute. Originally located in the Main Building (see above), the library received its own home in 1896. This transitional Romanesque Revival/Renaissance Revival structure is one of many designed by Tubby for the Pratt family. When this library was removed from the Brooklyn Public Library system in 1940, it became the home of the Pratt Institute library.

③⑦ Pratt Row Houses, 220–234 Willoughby Avenue, 171–185 Steuben Street, and 172–186 Emerson Place (Hobart A. Walker, 1907), designated 1981. The Pratt family built a large number of row houses in the Clinton Hill neighborhood. These three rows, encompassing twenty-seven houses, survive from an original complex of thirty-eight houses that were planned for "people of taste and refine-

ment, but of moderate means." Of Northern Renaissance–inspired design, the complex was built with rear service alleys and a central heating plant. The houses soon became popular with people affiliated with Pratt Institute; they are currently used as faculty housing.

③⑧ Emmanuel Baptist Church, 279 Lafayette Avenue (Francis H. Kimball, 1886–87; chapel, Ebenezer L. Roberts, 1882–83; school, 1925–27), designated 1968. The construction of the imposing Emmanuel Baptist Church was financed largely by Charles Pratt, a Standard Oil vice president and Brooklyn's wealthiest citizen, who resided nearby. Built of a light-colored Ohio sandstone, the church recalls the medieval Gothic cathedrals of France. The complex consists of a towered chapel on Saint James Place; the sanctuary, which is Kimball's largest ecclesiastical design; and the neo-Gothic school building to the west of the church.

③⑨ Joseph Steele House, 200 Lafayette Avenue (c. 1850), designated 1968. Erected early in the 1850s, this frame house is a magnificent example of

Joseph Steele House (No. 39), an excellent example of a building containing Greek Revival and Italianate elements. Photo: Landmarks Preservation Commission collection.

a residence in a transitional style, combining Greek Revival and Italianate elements. Of special interest are the handsome Greek Revival entrance and the Italianate cupola. The small wing at the east side of the house may date from as early as 1812.

40 Royal Castle Apartments, 20–30 Gates Avenue (Wortmann & Braun, 1911–12), designated 1981. One of the earliest elevator apartment houses in Clinton Hill, the Royal Castle, faced in brick and limestone, is embellished by a series of fanciful corbels in the form of building masons. The building has a striking roofline with projecting arched gables reminiscent of early 20th-century Viennese architecture.

41 Saint Luke's Episcopal Church, now the Church of Saint Luke and Saint Matthew, 520 Clinton Avenue (John Welch, 1888–91), designated 1981. Saint Luke's, built at the time when Clinton Avenue was Brooklyn's "Gold Coast," is one of the grandest 19th-century ecclesiastical buildings in Brooklyn. The design of the church and its adjoining chapel is loosely based on the Romanesque churches of Northern Italy. The building is faced with six materials carefully modulated in color and texture to create a dramatic street facade.

42 Lincoln Club, now Mechanics Temple, Independent Order of Mechanics of the Western Hemisphere, 65 Putnam Avenue (Rudolph L. Daus, 1889), designated 1981. The former home of the Lincoln Club is a flamboyant Queen Anne brick, stone, and terra-cotta structure designed by one of Brooklyn's most original late 19th-century architects. The club was organized in 1878 by a group of affluent local gentlemen who sought to band together for social purposes and to further the interests of the Republican Party (political activities were soon dropped). The Lincoln Club disbanded in 1931. In the 1940s the clubhouse was acquired by the Mechanics. This is a rare example of a 19th-century clubhouse that still serves its original social function.

43 Hanson Place Baptist Church, now the Hanson Place Seventh Day Adventist Church, 88 Hanson Place (George Penchard, 1857–60), designated 1970. This unusual church building combines the austere round-arched brick forms of the Early Romanesque Revival, a style popular with Protestant denominations in the 1850s, with a grand Corinthian temple front. A restoration of both the exterior and the interior was undertaken in the late 1970s.

44 Williamsburgh Savings Bank Building, 1 Hanson Place (Halsey, McCormack & Helmer, 1927–29), designated 1977, interior 1996. In 1929 the Williamsburgh Savings Bank moved its headquarters from Broadway in Williamsburg (see No. 4) into Brooklyn's tallest building. The bank's new home consisted of a domed tower soaring 512 feet above Hanson Place. The skyscraper is famous for its monumental four-faced clock, the largest in the world at the time of the building's completion. At its base, the building is embellished with relief carving—much of it evoking themes related to saving and thrift, including figures of bees, pelicans, and squirrels—and metal grilles depicting four continents. The **interior** lobby and banking hall are among the finest 20th-century interiors in Brooklyn, finished in quality materials and ornamented with symbolic decoration. The lobby is divided into a series of groin vaults covered with blue mosaics highlighted with gold stars. The doors leading into the banking hall are ornamented with figures in metal by Rene Chambellan representing the working men who might deposit their savings at the bank. The basilica-like form of the banking hall gives this space the feel of a cathedral of thrift. Twenty-two marbles were employed on the interior, for the walls, floors, columns, and decorative trim. Ornament includes symbols of commerce, thrift, industry, education, and finance; a mosaic ceiling with signs of the zodiac by Angelo Magnenti; and a mosaic mural showing an aerial view of Brooklyn executed by Ravenna Mosaics of Berlin.

Williamsburgh Savings Bank Building (No. 44). Brooklyn's tallest building contains marvelous exterior and interior detailing and a monumental four-faced clock. Photo by Caroline Kane Levy.

HISTORIC DISTRICT

11 **Stuyvesant Heights Historic District,** designated 1971. This residential district is a part of the larger Bedford-Stuyvesant community. Early development in the district took place in the 1860s, when freestanding suburban houses were erected at 87 MacDonough Street (1863) and 97 MacDonough Street (1861). A few row houses were built in the early 1870s, but most of the district's row houses and mansions were built between about 1880 and the first years of the 20th century. Within the district are fine examples of French Second Empire, neo-Grec, Romanesque Revival, and neo-Renaissance houses, all designed by Brooklyn architects. There are also a number of early apartment houses for middle-class residents, most located on corner sites. As is true of most of Brooklyn's 19th-century residential neighborhoods, this district also contains several ar-

chitecturally distinguished churches: the Victorian Gothic–style Our Lady of Victory Roman Catholic Church (Thomas F. Houghton, 1891–95) and the neo-Gothic-style Saint Philip's Episcopal Church (Arni Delhi, 1899), both on MacDonough Street, and the handsome Embury Methodist Church (now Mount Lebanon Baptist Church), in the Romanesque Revival style, designed in 1894 by the prominent Brooklyn firm Parfitt Brothers and located on Decatur Street.

INDIVIDUAL LANDMARKS

45 **Antioch Baptist Church,** originally the Greene Avenue Baptist Church and Church House, 828 and 826 Greene Avenue (church, Lansing C. Holden and Paul F. Higgs, 1887–92; church house, Langston & Dahlander, 1891–93), designated 1990.

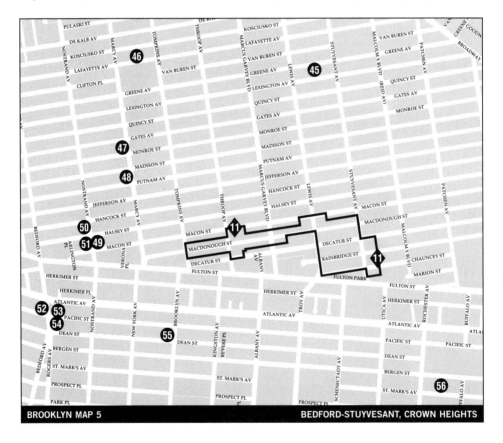

The Greene Avenue Baptist Church built this Romanesque Revival/Queen Anne building at a time when this section of Bedford-Stuyvesant was being rapidly developed as a row-house neighborhood. The manner in which the midblock church is massed to resemble a group of row houses reflects the architect's effort to design a building that would fit within its urban context. Holden prepared a design, but only the extant basement can definitively be attributed to him. The upper church is either a new design by Higgs or an adaptation by Higgs of Holden's original scheme. The church was sold in 1950 to the Antioch Baptist Church, an African-American congregation established in downtown Brooklyn in 1918. The church has hosted many leaders of the civil rights movement, including Martin Luther King, Jr., as well as many important politicians and notable African-Americans. The Romanesque Revival church house is one of a row of seven houses designed in 1891.

46 Magnolia Grandiflora and Magnolia Tree Earth Center, 677, 678, and 679 Lafayette Avenue (tree, c. 1885; houses, 1880–83), designated 1977. This magnificent tree, which grows at the northern edge of its species' range, was planted around 1885 from a slip brought from North Carolina. The preservation of the tree and the reuse of the three adjacent late 19th-century houses, now converted into a center for environmental education, were the inspiration of Hattie Carthen, who began a grassroots campaign to revitalize Bedford-Stuyvesant in 1969.

47 Saint George's Episcopal Church, 800 Marcy Avenue (R. M. Upjohn, 1887–88, and Sunday school, 1889), designated 1977. This late High Victorian Gothic design is a striking example of the vivid polychromy characteristic of the style. The building also reflects the idiosyncratic nature of R. M. Upjohn's work, notably at the entrance porch, with its stout dwarf columns, and the octagonal chimney tower. Upjohn, an architect of national prominence, lived in Cobble Hill, Brooklyn.

48 Boys' High School, now the Street Academy, Brooklyn Literacy Center, and Outreach Program, 832 Marcy Avenue (James W. Naughton, 1891–92; additions, C. B. J. Snyder, c. 1905–10), designated 1975. In the late 19th century, Boys' High School was considered one of the most important public schools in Brooklyn; its new home was therefore conceived as a major architectural monument visible throughout much of central Brooklyn. The focus of this Romanesque Revival building is its dynamic roofline, with gables, dormers, round tower, and lofty corner campanile, all modeled on the public buildings of Henry Hobson Richardson. The school initially housed 782 students in 22 classrooms; as enrollment increased, several additions were constructed early in the 20th century. Boys' High and the nearby Girls' High (see below) were organized in 1878 as separate departments of the Central Grammar School. The building has been restored by Beyer Blinder Belle, architect.

49 Girls' High School, now the Board of Education Brooklyn Adult Training Center, 475 Nostrand Avenue (James W. Naughton, 1885–86, and rear addition, 1891; Macon Street addition, C. B. J. Snyder, 1912), designated 1983. The roots of Girls' High School extend back to the organization of the Central Grammar School, Brooklyn's first public high school, in 1878. As the student population increased, a new school was erected on Nostrand Avenue between Halsey and Macon Streets. Only the Girls' Department of Central Grammar School moved to this facility; the Boys' Department later moved to Boys' High School (see above). The Nostrand Avenue building, popularly known as Girls' High School (the name was made official in 1891), is the oldest surviving structure in New York City erected as a high school. The design of the Victorian Gothic building focuses on the central entrance pavilion with its tall cupola. The building was restored by the School Construction Authority.

50 Renaissance Apartments, 488 Nostrand Avenue and 140–144 Hancock Street (Montrose Morris, 1892), designated 1986. The Renaissance was commissioned by the developer Louis F. Seitz, who was responsible for some of Brooklyn's finest late 19th-century apartment houses. The design of this pale yellow brick and terra-cotta structure is closely related to that of Morris's contemporaneous Imperial Apartments (see No. 54). The vacant and deteriorated building was rehabilitated for housing in 1995–96 by Anderson Associates, architect and developer.

51 Alhambra Apartments, 500–518 Nostrand Avenue and 29–33 Macon Street (Montrose Morris, 1889–90), designated 1986. The earliest of the three major apartment houses in the area designed by Morris for developer Louis F. Seitz (see Nos. 50 and 54) and an early example of a Brooklyn apartment house for affluent middle-class tenants, the Alhambra displays rich textural contrasts and is notable for its six towers, steep roof slopes, gables, loggias, arcades, and lively terra-cotta detail. The building was restored in 2000.

52 23rd Regiment Armory, 1322 Bedford Avenue (Fowler & Hough and Isaac Perry, 1891–95), designated 1977. Designed to resemble a medieval fortress, the 23rd Regiment Armory is a vast and impressive example of late 19th-century military architecture. With its corner tower rising 136 feet, its great arched entrance, and its enormous drill shed, this building is the most imposing of Brooklyn's 19th-century armories. Fowler & Hough were local architects responsible for several important late 19th-century Brooklyn buildings; Isaac Perry was the architect for

Boys' High School (No. 48). The grand design reflects the building's status as an important public school in Brooklyn in the late 19th century. Photo by Caroline Kane Levy.

New York State (the state financed the construction of most armories) and a specialist in armory design.

❸ Saint Bartholomew's Church (Episcopal), 1227 Pacific Street (George P. Chappell, 1886–90), designated 1974. Chappell, one of Brooklyn's most creative late 19th-century architects, was responsible for this quirky English-inspired Queen Anne design. The asymmetrically massed church, with its richly textured stone and brick walls, tile cladding, and picturesque tower, is set behind a garden that creates the illusion of a rural church in this urban neighborhood.

❹ Imperial Apartments, 1198 Pacific Street and 1327–1339 Bedford Avenue (Montrose Morris, 1892), designated 1986. The success of the Alhambra Apartments (see No. 51) led the developer Louis F. Seitz to commission this apartment house and the Renaissance (see No. 50) in 1892. The light-colored brick building, with its terra-cotta trim, metal bay windows, tall arcades, and round corner tower, is an important presence on Grant Square. This relatively early example of a prestigious apartment house in Brooklyn was built at a time when hundreds of handsome row houses were being erected on the surrounding streets of the Crown Heights neighborhood.

❺ John and Elizabeth Truslow House, 96 Brooklyn Avenue (Parfitt Brothers, 1887–88), designated 1997. Built for a prominent businessman and philanthropist, this residence was designed by the Parfitt Brothers, one of late 19th-century Brooklyn's most important firms. In this project, the architects used ornament sparingly, preferring to enliven the building's appearance through textural contrasts and asymmetrical massing.

❻ Weeksville Houses, 1698–1708 Bergen Street (1840–83), designated as the Houses on Hunterfly Road, 1970. These four small frame houses are all that remains of the 19th-century African-American community of Weeksville. Initially settled in the 1830s by free blacks, Weeksville grew by the 1870s into a community of several hundred, with its own public school, church, and other institutions. The surviving houses are located in the middle of a block, facing onto Hunterfly Road, a country road that predates Brooklyn's street grid. The houses have been restored by Li-Saltzman Architects to serve as a living museum of African-American history and culture.

The Weeksville Houses (No. 56) are the remnant of a 19th-century African-American community. The four houses are now a museum of African-American history and culture. Photo by Caroline Kane Levy.

INDIVIDUAL LANDMARKS

57 **Public School 86,** also known as the Irvington School, 220 Irving Avenue (James W. Naughton, 1892–93), designated 1991. Naughton's creative use of Romanesque Revival forms is evident on this relatively small school in Bushwick, with its rough stone base, trios of arched windows, and large central gable articulated by a massive semicircular arch and flanked by pedimented dormers. (see also No. 9)

58 **20th Precinct Police Station House and Stable,** later the 83rd Precinct Station House, now Brooklyn North Task Force, 179 Wilson Avenue (William B. Tubby, 1894–95), designated 1977. Tubby, one of Brooklyn's most inventive late 19th-century architects, designed this fanciful police station as a mock-medieval fortress, complete with crenellations and a round corner tower; the building is entered through an eccentric Doric entrance porch embellished by a beautifully carved frieze. An exceptional restoration by Ehrenkrantz & Eckstut returned the deteriorated building to active use in 1996.

59 **Public School 116,** 515 Knickerbocker Avenue (James W. Naughton, 1897–99), designated 2002. Among the last schools built in Brooklyn prior to the consolidation of the five boroughs, this handsome four-story building has served the children of Bushwick for over a century. Naughton, who designed numerous structures for the Broooklyn Board

of Education, embellished the red brick elevations with terra-cotta reliefs and an elaborate iron cornice.

60 **Reformed Church of South Bushwick,** 855–867 Bushwick Avenue (Messrs. Morgan, 1853; chapel and Sunday school, J. J. Buck, 1881; church enlargement, 1883), designated 1968. This imposing church is unusual in its combination of austere Greek Revival forms, still popular in the 1850s in outlying areas such as Bushwick, with the type of Georgian-inspired tower and steeple that had gone out of fashion in most areas more than twenty-five years earlier. The church's records note that the design was "drawn up by Messrs. Morgan"; just who these men were is not known.

BROOKLYN MAP 6 **BUSHWICK**

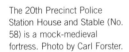

The 20th Precinct Police Station House and Stable (No. 58) is a mock-medieval fortress. Photo by Carl Forster.

INDIVIDUAL LANDMARKS

61 **Engine Company No. 252,** originally Fire Engine Company 52, later Engine Company 152, 617 Central Avenue (Parfitt Brothers, 1896–97), designated 1995. One of Brooklyn's most talented architecture firms created this whimsical brick, red sandstone, and terra-cotta firehouse for the Brooklyn Fire Department (the initials BFD are carved on the facade) at a time of major expansion. The Flemish Revival style, evident in the scrolled and stepped gables, links the building to Bushwick's history as a 17th-century Dutch settlement.

62 **Public School 73,** 241 MacDougal Street (James W. Naughton, 1888, and addition, 1895), designated 1984. The construction and rapid expansion of this school reflect the fact that the area where Bedford-Stuyvesant meets East New York underwent significant development following the opening of the elevated rail lines on Fulton Street and Broadway in the 1880s. The tall central tower of P.S. 73 is a focal point in the neighborhood; the school is ornamented with handsome terra-cotta detail. (See also No. 9)

63 **Public School 108,** 200 Linwood Street (James W. Naughton, 1895), designated 1981. The

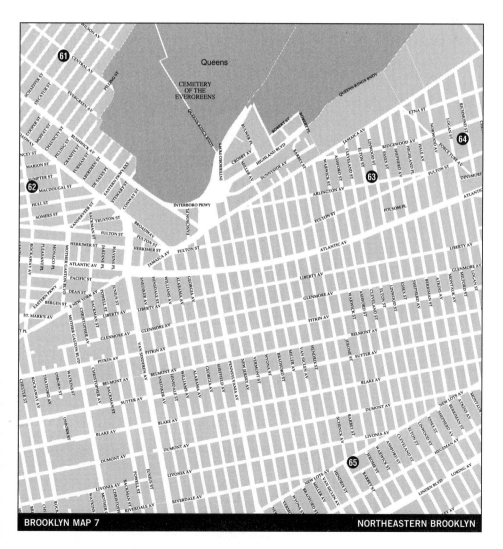

BROOKLYN MAP 7   NORTHEASTERN BROOKLYN

imposing yellow brick Romanesque Revival mass of P.S. 108 in Cypress Hills rises from a rough stone base to a steeply sloping roof that is punctuated by gables and dormers.

64 **Public School 65K,** 158 Richmond Street (Samuel Leonard, 1870; facade, James W. Naughton, 1889), designated 1981. The earliest part of P.S. 65K in Cypress Hills was built in 1870, but the unpretentious Romanesque Revival–style Richmond Street facade, with its striking Gothic-inspired detail was not constructed until 1889.

65 **New Lots Reformed Dutch Church,** now New Lots Community Church, 630 New Lots Avenue (1823–24), designated 1966. This simple wood building, with Gothic-inspired pointed win-

dows and a modest cupola, was erected to serve a small farming community. It has been transformed into an important historic presence in a struggling inner-city neighborhood.

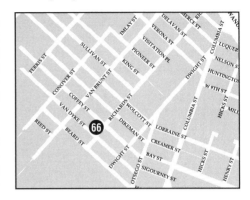

Engine Company No. 252 (No. 61). The Flemish Revival design reflects Bushwick's history as a 17th-century Dutch settlement. Photo by Andrew S. Dolkart.

INDIVIDUAL LANDMARKS

66 Brooklyn Clay Retort and Fire Brick Works Storehouse, 76–86 Van Dyke Street (1859), designated 2001. This exceptional industrial building was constructed in Red Hook to manufacture products used in the production of illuminating gas. Probably designed by the company's founder, Joseph K. Brick, the storehouse has basilicalike facades of local gray schist, detailed with brick and sandstone. The building was restored in the mid-1990s.

67 Weir Greenhouse, now McGovern-Weir Greenhouse, Fifth Avenue at 25th Street (G. Curtis Gillespie, 1895), designated 1982. Located across from the main entrance gates to Green-Wood Cemetery (see below), this structure is a rare surviving example of a 19th-century commercial greenhouse. Erected by James Weir, Jr., a member of a Brooklyn family long involved in horticulture, the greenhouse is a wood and glass structure with projecting corner pavilions and an octagonal dome. Since its completion, the greenhouse has catered to those seeking to purchase plants and flowers to embellish grave sites.

68 Green-Wood Cemetery Gate, Fifth Avenue at 25th Street (Richard Upjohn & Son, 1861–65), designated 1966. The design of this spectacular Gothic Revival gate is generally attributed to R. M. Upjohn, as opposed to his more famous father, Richard Upjohn. The two entrance arches with their soaring pinnacled gables and the adjoining pavilions are intricately carved from New Jersey brownstone. Above the arches are four panels of Nova Scotia sandstone carved with scenes evoking themes relating to death and resurrection; these are the work of John Moffit. A restoration of the gates was completed in 1996 (Platt, Byard & Dovell, architect).

69 18th Police Precinct Station House and Stable, later 68th Police Precinct House and Stable, now the Sunset Park School of Music, 4302 Fourth Avenue (George Ingram, 1890–92), designated 1983. This former police station is one of several station houses in Brooklyn designed by police department architect George Ingram (possibly with the assistance of Emile Gruwé) late in the 19th century to resemble a medieval fortress. The impregnable quality is emphasized by the presence of a massive

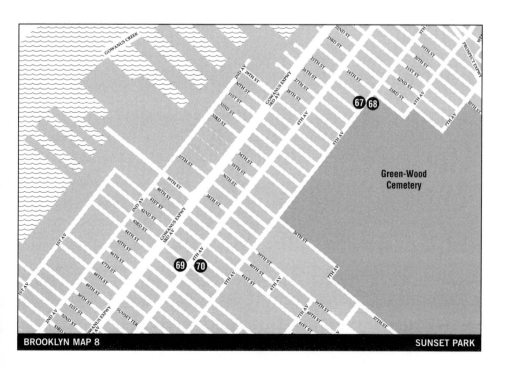

arched entry and a corner tower. The fortresslike design is offset by the use of such details as complex pointed-arch windows, exuberant iron tie rods, and fanciful carved heads. The stable and main building have been converted into a school of music.

70 **Sunset Park Courthouse,** 4201 Fourth Avenue (Mortimer Dickerson Metcalfe, 1930–31), des-

ignated 2001. This neoclassical structure was built as a neighborhood courthouse, serving both the magistrates' and municipal divisions. The imposing Ionic porticos that face 42nd and 43rd Streets originally served as entrances to the individual courts. Decorative quoins, capped by reliefs of American eagles, embellish the corners of the building. The courthouse was converted to nonjudicial use in 1962.

Clad in gray schist, Brooklyn Clay Retort and Fire Brick Works Storehouse (No. 66) recalls the first period of industrial development in Red Hook. Photo by Carl Forster.

The spectacular Green-Wood Cemetery Gate (No. 68) is carved with scenes relating to death and resurrection. Photo by Carl Forster.

HISTORIC DISTRICTS

⑫ Park Slope Historic District, designated 1973. Park Slope is situated along the western edge of Prospect Park (see No. 79). Located several miles from Brooklyn's 19th-century ferry terminals, Park Slope owes its development as a prestigious neighborhood to the opening of the Brooklyn Bridge in 1883; the convenience of commuting over the bridge permitted people to live in locations that were farther from Manhattan than previously developed areas. The Slope contains a mix of mansions,

row houses, apartment houses, and institutional buildings, almost all of which were erected in the final decades of the 19th century and the first years of the 20th century. These include many rows of brownstone houses as well as some of the most outstanding Romanesque Revival and Queen Anne residences in the United States. The brick and stone houses on Carroll Street and Montgomery Place designed by C. P. H. Gilbert in the late 1880s are especially distinguished, as is Montrose Morris's Henry Hulbert House, now the Poly Prep–Woodward School (1892) at 49 Prospect Park West. The dis-

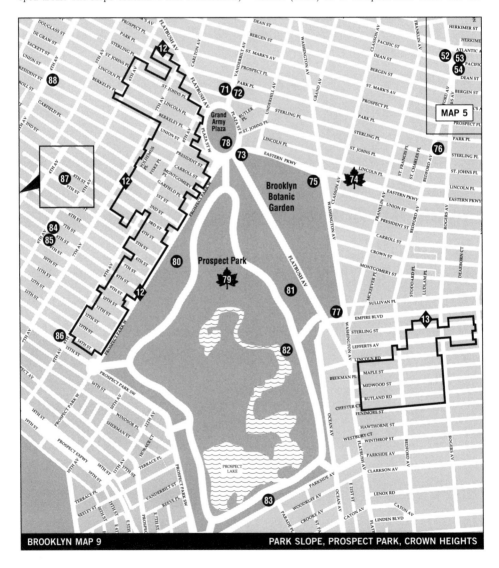

trict's fine institutional structures include a cluster of three Gothic-style churches at Saint John's Place and Seventh Avenue(Saint John's Episcopal (Edward T. Potter, 1889; nave, John Rochester Thomas, 1885), Grace Methodist (Parfitt Brothers, 1882–83), and Memorial Presbyterian (Pugin & Walter, 1882–83); the imposing Classical Revival Beth Elohim Synagogue (Eisendrath & Horowitz, 1908–10; Temple House, Mortimer Freehof and David Levy, 1928) on Eighth Avenue and Garfield Place; and the architect Francis H. Kimball's spectacular Venetian Gothic Montauk Club (1889–91) on Eighth Avenue and Lincoln Place, with its superb terra-cotta detail.

⑱ Prospect–Lefferts Gardens Historic District, designated 1979. At the time when suburban development was sweeping through Flatbush, the northern edge of the area was built up primarily with blocks of modest row houses. This movement was initiated in the 1890s by James Lefferts, who subdivided eight blocks of his family's ancestral farm (see No. 81) into Lefferts Manor, a development with restrictive covenants that required the construction of single-family houses. Between 1897 and the mid–1920s, row houses and a few freestanding houses were erected in Lefferts Manor and on some of the adjoining streets. Among the outstanding houses are the neo-Renaissance limestone rows on Maple and Midwood Streets designed by Axel Hedman in the first years of the 20th century and the Colonial Revival and neo-medieval brick houses from the 1920s that Slee & Bryson designed for sites on Fenimore and Midwood Streets and Rutland Road.

Park Slope Historic District (H.D. 12), Montgomery Place. The district contains some of the country's finest examples of Romanesque Revival and Queen Anne–style residences. Photo by Carl Forster.

INDIVIDUAL LANDMARKS

71 **Public School 9,** later Public School 111, now Public School 340, 249 Sterling Place (Samuel B. Leonard, 1867–68; additions, James W. Naughton, 1887), designated 1978. This early Romanesque Revival school was constructed in conjunction with the development of the surrounding Prospect Heights community in the 1860s. The focus of the building is a central gabled pavilion with fine brick arches (see also No. 9).

72 **Public School 9 Annex,** 251 Sterling Place (James W. Naughton, 1895), designated 1978. As the population of Prospect Heights increased in the late 19th century, P.S. 9 (see above) became overcrowded, and this handsome Romanesque Revival brick and stone annex with brownstone Renaissance-inspired detail was erected. The building has been converted into apartments.

73 **Brooklyn Public Library, Central Building,** Grand Army Plaza (Alfred Morton Githens and Francis Keally, 1935–41), designated 1997. Initially proposed when Brooklyn was an independent city in 1888, the central library is located on one of Brooklyn's most prominent sites, at the intersection of Flatbush Avenue and Eastern Parkway (see No. 74). Constructed on the foundations of an abandoned Beaux Arts scheme begun in 1911, this monumental library is a limestone-clad Modern Classical structure with impressive Art Deco reliefs by Thomas Hudson Jones and C. Paul Jennewein. The stair terrace and concave entrance facade were designed to reflect the elliptical configuration of the plaza. Passed by thousands each day, the library is one of Brooklyn's best known and most heavily used public buildings.

74 **Eastern Parkway Scenic Landmark,** between Grand Army Plaza and Ralph Avenue (Fred-

BLOCK BEAUTIFUL

Some of the most appealing streetscapes in New York are located in historic districts. Greater than the sum of their parts, the finest blocks are composed of private houses that are low in scale and create a gentle visual rhythm. A group of remodeled houses on Manhattan's East 19th Street, between Irving Place and Third Avenue, was given the name "Block Beautiful" in 1909 because of its charming and unified character. What follows is a subjective list of equally worthy examples. Greenwich Village has many attractive streets, particularly along Washington Square North, West 11th Street, and St. Luke's Place (Manhattan H.D. 12). The design of these row houses represents a shift in classical taste, from Federal and Greek Revival to the Italianate style. Lesser known is a block of mostly Italianate houses preserved in the Hunter's Point Historic District (Queens H.D. 2). Begun in the 1870s, these brick and marble-fronted structures recall the era when Long Island City was an important transit hub and this section of 45th Avenue was known as "white-collar row."

New York's street grid encouraged the proliferation of row houses. Edward S. Clark, who built the Dakota Apartments in 1880, also commissioned Henry Hardenbergh to build the houses that face it along the north side of West 73rd Street. Medieval in character, these buildings originally had high stoops with ornate railings. Two decades later, his grandson, Frederick Ambrose Clark, built eighteen buildings a block north on the south side of West 74th Street. In contrast to the earlier row, these dignified red brick dwellings were designed in the neo-Georgian style and incorporate street-level entrances (Manhattan H.D. 26). On West 78th Street, between Amsterdam and Columbus Avenues, are two groups of houses designed by Rafael Guastavino (Manhattan H.D. 25). Built for the developer Bernard S. Levy in the late 1880s, the facades incorporate unusual Moorish-inspired details. Another unique row is Sylvan Terrace, located in the Jumel Terrace Historic District (Manhattan H.D. 46). Completed in 1882, it is the only surviving block of attached frame dwellings in the city.

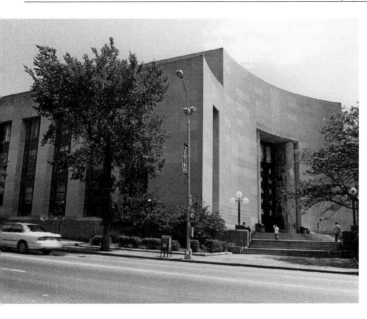

The Central Building of the Brooklyn Public Library (No. 73) is one of Brooklyn's best known and most heavily used public buildings. Photo by Carl Forster.

Many historic districts in Brooklyn feature fine row houses. Memorable examples can be found along Willow Street in Brooklyn Heights, where small groups of Federal, Gothic Revival, and Queen Anne–style houses are located, as well as at 181–209 McDonough Place in the Stuyvesant Heights Historic District (Brooklyn H.D. 4 and 11). Built in 1872, the McDonough Place brownstones are among the earliest rows in Bedford-Stuyvesant and feature deep front yards. Park Slope has many lovely streets, especially those adjoining Prospect Park (Brooklyn H.D. 12). Most date from the 1880s and 1890s and have Romanesque Revival, Queen Anne, and Renaissance Revival–style details. Montgomery Place is arguably the finest single block in the district. Developed by Harvey Murdock, both sides feature houses mostly designed by C. P. H. Gilbert that form a delightfully varied yet cohesive ensemble. In the Bronx, the earliest row dates from 1863–65 and is located along Alexander Avenue in Mott Haven. Other districts of note include the Longwood and Clay Avenue Historic Districts, which feature many Romanesque Revival and neo-Renaissance houses designed by Warren C. Dickerson (Bronx H.D. 2, 4, and 6).

After 1890, developers began to encourage architects to create unified ensembles that resemble private enclaves. The most celebrated example is found in the St. Nicholas Historic District (Manhattan H.D. 44). Known as Striver's Row, it consists of three distinct groups of neoclassical row houses on four block fronts. The corners of each block are enclosed by small apartment buildings, and the north block incorporates a service alley, a rare amenity in Manhattan. Additional landmarks that explore similar ideas include: the Albemarle-Kenmore Terraces Historic District, a pair of Colonial Revival cul-de-sacs; Pomander Walk, inspired by the popular play of the same name; and the Stockholm Street Historic District (Brooklyn H.D. 14, Manhattan No. 417, Queens H.D. 1). Built for working-class residents, the Queens block consists of mainly two-family houses flanking a rare surviving example of a street paved with brick.

BROOKLYN

erick Law Olmsted and Calvert Vaux, 1870–74), designated 1978. Eastern Parkway was part of a regional system envisioned by Olmsted and Vaux in 1866 as a means of introducing open space, fresh air, and greenery into the city's residential neighborhoods. The idea of a tree-lined boulevard with a central roadway flanked by access roads was new to the United States; Olmsted coined the term *parkway* in 1868 to describe this new type of urban thoroughfare. The 2.2 mile parkway begins near the entrance to Prospect Park and ends at Ralph Avenue. It was intended that the parkway would continue north to the East River and then, on the other side of the river, extend to Central Park and the Hudson River; to the south the system runs from Prospect Park, via Ocean Parkway (see No. 103), to the Atlantic shore. The parkway was beautifully restored in the 1990s.

75 Brooklyn Museum, now Brooklyn Museum of Art, 200 Eastern Parkway at Washington Avenue (McKim, Mead & White, 1893–1915; removal of front stairs, 1934–35), designated 1966. In 1893 McKim, Mead & White won a competition for the new home of the Brooklyn Institute of Arts and Sciences. The firm's winning entry proposed a monumental Classical Revival structure, only a small portion of which was eventually erected. The building

is enhanced by extensive sculptural embellishment undertaken by a group of artists supervised by Daniel Chester French. The museum was originally entered via a grand flight of stairs leading to the Ionic portico; these stairs were removed in 1934–35. Polshek Partnership Architects designed the glass entrance pavilion and plaza, completed in 2004. The museum, housing one of the country's finest art collections, is especially famous for its American, Egyptian, and African holdings.

76 Studebaker Building, 1469 Bedford Avenue (Tooker and Marsh, 1920), designated 2000. Following the introduction of the automobile, many showrooms were built along Bedford Avenue, including this neo-Gothic structure at the corner of Sterling Place. Clad in white terra cotta, the parapet is decorated with the manufacturer's trademark, a diagonal banner superimposed over the image of a wheel. Closed by Studebaker in 1939, the building was converted to residential use in 2000.

77 Brooklyn Central Office, Bureau of Fire Communications, 35 Empire Boulevard (Frank J. Helmle, 1913), designated 1966. Designed in a Florentine Early Renaissance style, this elegant building serves as a communications center for the New York

The upper stories of the Studebaker Building (No. 76) are embellished with the automobile manufacturer's logo. Photo by Carl Forster.

City Fire Department. Helmle was responsible for many of Brooklyn's finest early 20th-century Renaissance-inspired landmarks, including buildings in Prospect Park (see No. 79) and Winthrop Park (see No. 8) and several Roman Catholic churches.

⑦ Soldiers' and Sailors' Memorial Arch, Grand Army Plaza (John H. Duncan, 1889–92; alterations, McKim, Mead & White, 1894–1901), designated 1973. Designed in the tradition of Roman imperial arches, this Civil War memorial is the centerpiece of one of the finest formal civic design projects in the United States. The construction of Duncan's arch, the winning entry in a competition, was completed in 1892. Two years later Stanford White planned alterations to allow the addition of sculpture: heroic bronze groups representing the army and the navy, as well as the arch's crowning Victory quadriga, all by Frederick MacMonnies; a pair of bronze relief panels depicting Lincoln and Grant on horseback (the horses were modeled by Thomas Eakins, the figures by William O'Donovan); and carved spandrel figures by Philip Martiny.

⑦ Prospect Park Scenic Landmark, bounded by Flatbush Avenue, Parkside Avenue, Prospect Park West, and Prospect Park Southwest (Frederick Law Olmsted and Calvert Vaux, designed 1865; constructed 1866–73), designated 1975. Prospect Park is generally considered the masterpiece of designers Frederick Law Olmsted and Calvert Vaux. Planned as Brooklyn's counterpart to Central Park (see Manhattan No. 376), Prospect Park is a milestone in the movement to create naturalistic parks in America's cities as a response to the increasing industrialization and congestion of the urban environment. A Brooklyn park was initially authorized in 1859, but the Civil War delayed work. In 1864 James S. T. Stranahan, later known as the Father of Prospect Park, approached Vaux, who in turn persuaded Olmsted to assist with the design. Their plan, submitted in 1866, divided the park into three zones: meadows (notably the Long Meadow, which at ninety acres is the largest lawn in New York), forests, and water bodies. Vaux was responsible for a series of splendid structures, including several bridges, the Oriental Pavilion (restored, following a fire, by the New York City Department of General Services), and the terraces of the Concert Grove (designed in conjunction with Jacob Wrey Mould). The park's classical entrances, designed

between 1889 and 1907 by McKim, Mead & White in conjunction with prominent sculptors (notably Brooklyn-born Frederick MacMonnies), reflect a late 19th-century shift in ideas about landscape design away from the picturesque in favor of increased formality. In addition to the gates, classical pavilions were erected within the park based on designs by McKim, Mead & White and the local architecture firm Helmle & Huberty. Major restoration projects undertaken by the Parks Department and the Prospect Park Alliance since the late 1980s have focused on the entrances and Ravine section of the park.

⑧ Edwin Clarke and Grace Hill Litchfield House, Grace Hill, also known as Litchfield Villa, now the Brooklyn Headquarters of the New York City Department of Parks and Recreation, Prospect Park West at 5th Street (A. J. Davis, 1854–57), designated 1966. The lawyer and railroad financier Edwin Clarke Litchfield purchased a good deal of land in Brooklyn in the 1850s. At the crest of Prospect Hill, he erected one of the finest Italianate villas in the United States. Originally clad in stucco tinted to simulate stone, the building has a picturesque silhouette; its towers and projecting bays were planned to take advantage of views of the surrounding landscape and of New York Harbor. On the south side is a porch supported by columns with corncob capitals. Part of the grounds were incorporated into Prospect Park when the park site was acquired and the house was converted in 1913 for use by the Parks Department.

⑧ Peter Lefferts House, also known as the Lefferts Homestead, Flatbush Avenue near Empire Boulevard (1777–83), designated 1966. Peter Lefferts built this farmhouse in the traditional Dutch Colonial style to replace an earlier dwelling that was burned by American troops during the Battle of Brooklyn in 1776. Originally located on Flatbush Avenue between Maple and Midwood Streets, the house was moved to Prospect Park in 1918 to save it from destruction; it is now a museum specializing in children's educational programs.

⑧ Boathouse, Lullwater, now the Prospect Park Audubon Center (Helmle & Huberty, 1904), designated 1965. As is appropriate for a building located at water's edge, this white terra-cotta-clad pavilion was modeled on the Renaissance palaces that line the Grand Canal in Venice.

㉛ **Croquet Shelter,** near Parkside Avenue (McKim, Mead & White, 1904), designated 1968. The Croquet Shelter, also known as the Grecian Shelter, is a beautifully proportioned Corinthian temple reminiscent of 18th-century French neoclassical garden pavilions.

㉜ **Public School 39,** also known as the Henry Bristow School, 417 Sixth Avenue (Samuel B. Leonard, 1876–77), designated 1977. Located in

Park Slope, this building in the French Second Empire style displays typically French features—the projecting central frontispiece and end pavilions and the crowning mansard roof with iron cresting that were adapted by Leonard to the demands of public school design.

㉝ **Brooklyn Public Library, Park Slope Branch,** 431 Sixth Avenue (Raymond F. Almirall, 1906), designated 1998. Built at the urging of

neighborhood residents, this Classical Revival library is located on a prominent raised site at the corner of Sixth Avenue and Ninth Street. Clad in red brick and limestone, it features a projecting entrance portico and carved ornament that expresses the building's purpose. The architect was Raymond Almirall, a Brooklyn native, who designed four Carnegie branch libraries in the borough, as well as the original, though unexecuted, plan for the central library.

86 14th Regiment Armory, 1402 Eighth Avenue (William A. Mundell, 1891–95), designated 1998. Constructed by the State of New York for the 14th Regiment, which served with distinction during the Civil War, this well-preserved armory consists of an administration building and a vast barrel-vaulted drill shed. The structure's original function is powerfully articulated on the main facade, with corner bastions and a striking asymmetrical entrance pavilion crowned by machicolated brickwork. A bronze statue of a World War I doughboy, dedicated to the 14th Infantry, guards the entrance. In 1992 ownership was transferred to the City of New York.

87 William B. Cronyn House, also known as the 271 Ninth Street House (1856–57), designated 1978. This French Second Empire suburban villa was erected by a wealthy Wall Street merchant. The stucco-covered house is especially notable for its central cupola lit by a clerestory and its slate mansard roof with end pavilions and iron cresting. When the house was built, the surrounding area was largely open farmland, but by the end of the 19th century, the neighborhood had become industrialized and the house served as the headquarters for Charles M. Higgins's india ink company.

88 Public Bath No. 7, 227–231 Fourth Avenue (Raymond F. Almirall, 1906–10), designated 1984. Early in the 20th century, New York established an extensive system of public bathhouses in neighborhoods where most of the residences lacked indoor plumbing. This bathhouse on served the Gowanus community. The building is faced in brick and terra cotta with glazed white surfaces that connote cleanliness. Its ornamental forms evoke bathing and the sea. These include fish, tridents, shells, and streams of water, many of them in polychromatic terra cotta.

Prospect Park Scenic Landmark (No. 79). The masterpiece of renowned landscape architects and park designers Frederick Law Olmsted and Calvert Vaux. Photo: Landmarks Preservation Commission, from the collection of the Long Island Historical Society.

BROOKLYN

HISTORIC DISTRICTS

⑭ Albemarle–Kenmore Terraces Historic District, designated 1978. This small historic district, nestled behind the grounds of the Flatbush Reformed Dutch Church (see No. 89), consists of two culs-de-sac lined with houses designed by the local firm Slee & Bryson. Albemarle Terrace (1916–17) has charming Colonial Revival brick row houses, while the Garden City–inspired Kenmore Terrace (1917–18, with two houses 1919–20) is an early example of the influence of the automobile on American architecture; each house on the south side of Kenmore Terrace incorporates a garage into the ground story.

⑮ Prospect Park South Historic District, designated 1979. Prospect Park South, Brooklyn's most imposing suburban neighborhood, was a development scheme initiated by Dean Alvord, who sought "to create a rural park within the limitations of the conventional city block and city street." After purchasing approximately sixty acres of farmland in 1899, Alvord laid out all the utilities, erected brick gateposts, planned lawns and malls, and hired the Scottish landscape gardener John Aitkin to supervise

the plantings. Alvord also hired an architectural staff, which was headed by the talented John J. Petit, to design large, comfortable houses in a wide variety of styles. Petit was responsible for some of the finest houses in the district (as an alternative, owners could hire their own architects), including examples of the Colonial Revival (for example, 1510 Albemarle Road), neo-Tudor (183 Argyle Road), and Queen Anne (1423 and 1501 Albemarle Road) styles, as well as several more uncommon examples, most notably a Swiss chalet (100 Rugby Road) and a house modeled on a Japanese pagoda (131 Buckingham Road). Within a few years Alvord had created a community that, in his words, was "acceptable to people of culture with means equal to some of the luxuries as well as the necessities of life."

⑯ Ditmas Park Historic District, designated 1981. Following the success of Prospect Park South (see above) much of Flatbush was developed with freestanding suburban homes. Ditmas Park was a real-estate venture planned by the developer Lewis H. Pounds in 1902. Pounds graded the land, divided the area into lots, and planted the magnificent trees that still grace the streets. He then erected houses or

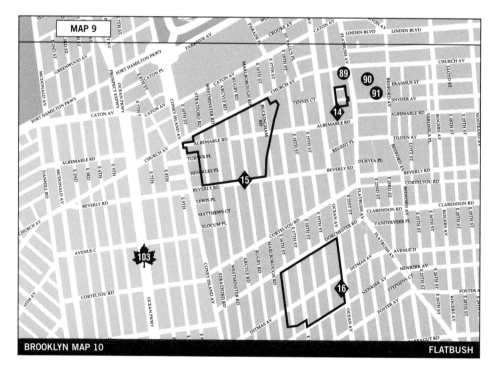

Prospect Park South Historic District (H.D. 15). Brooklyn's most imposing suburban neighborhood contains a varied mixture of architectural styles, including this idiosyncratic Japanese-style house at 131 Buckingham Road. Photo by Caroline Kane Levy.

sold lots to other builders. Most of the houses in the district are wood-frame structures in the Colonial Revival style, although there are also a few examples of neo-Tudor and neo-Renaissance design. Most were designed by local Brooklyn architects such as A. White Pierce, Arlington Isham, Benjamin Driesler, and Slee & Bryson who were responsible for residential work throughout Brooklyn in the early 20th century. The most unusual houses in the district are Arlington Isham's Arts and Crafts bungalows on East 16th Street, all built in 1909, and the romantic English cottage, designed in 1931 by Frank J. Forster and R. A. Gallimore for legendary baker Arthur Ebinger, located at 415 East 19th Street. The most prominent building in the district is the imposing neo-Georgian Flatbush Congregational Church, designed in 1910 by the Boston architecture firm Allen & Collens working in collaboration with the local architect Louis Jallade. The adjacent parish house, designed by Whitefield & King and built in 1899, is an unusual polygonal Shingle Style structure.

INDIVIDUAL LANDMARKS

89 Flatbush Reformed Dutch Church Complex, 890 Flatbush Avenue (church, Thomas Fardon, 1793–98; cemetery, first burial, 17th century; parsonage, at 2101–2103 Kenmore Terrace, 1853; church house, Meyer & Mathieu, 1923–24), designated 1979. This church, the third to be erected at this location, occupies the site in longest continuous use for religious purposes in New York City. The stone and brick building in the Federal style has an elegant clock tower and steeple. To the south and west is a cemetery that contains the graves of members of local families; familiar names include Vanderbilt, Lott, Lefferts, Cortelyou, and Bergen. The parsonage is an exceptional example of a vernacular house in a transitional style, with both Greek Revival and Italianate features. A Colonial Revival brick church house completes the complex.

90 Erasmus Hall Academy, in the courtyard of Erasmus Hall High School, 911 Flatbush Avenue (1786), designated as Erasmus Hall Museum, 1966. Erasmus Hall, the first secondary school chartered by the New York State Board of Regents, was originally a private school for boys. Founded with the assistance of Alexander Hamilton, Aaron Burr, John Jay, and others, the school was housed in this Federal-period wooden building until Erasmus Hall High School, the surrounding Collegiate Gothic complex, was erected early in the 20th century.

91 Flatbush Town Hall, 35 Snyder Avenue (John Y. Culyer, 1874–75), designated 1966. Designed in a High Victorian Gothic style by Culyer, an engineer, this brick and stone structure, with its prominent tower and gables, is a reminder of the period when Flatbush was an independent community. The building was restored in the late 1980s.

INDIVIDUAL LANDMARKS

92 Johannes Van Nuyse House, also known as the Van Nuyse–Magaw House, 1041 East 22nd Street (1800–03), designated 1969. With its wide gambrel roof, this house is an especially fine example of a traditional Dutch Colonial farmhouse. Moved to this site in 1916 from its original location several blocks to the south, the house was erected by Johannes Van Nuyse, the son of Joost Van Nuyse (see No. 93), and his bride, Nellie Lott. Between 1844 and 1909, the house and its surrounding farmland were owned by Robert Magaw and his descendants.

93 Joost and Elizabeth Van Nuyse House, also known as Coe House, 1128 East 34th Street (before 1792), designated 1969. Joost Van Nuyse is recorded as having died in this building in 1792. With its characteristic Dutch Colonial design, the house is the sole remnant of Joost's 85-acre Flatlands farm.

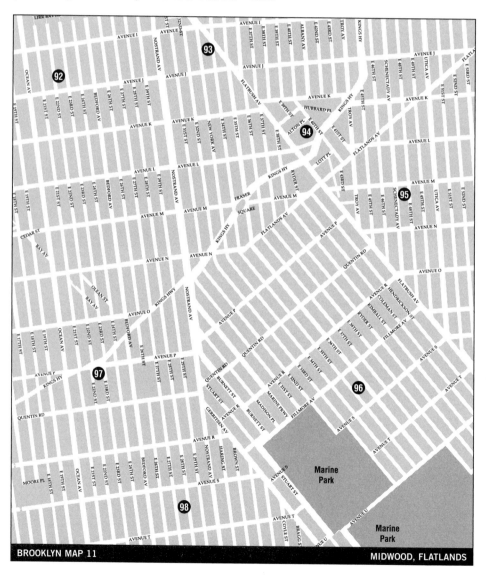

BROOKLYN MAP 11
MIDWOOD, FLATLANDS

94 **Flatlands Dutch Reformed Church,** Kings Highway at East 40th Street (1848), designated 1966. With its simple clapboard siding, multipaned windows, and tall steeple, the Flatlands church is a notable example of rural Greek Revival design. The church, which is the third building to occupy this site, was restored after a fire in 1977.

95 **John and Altje Baxter House,** also known as Stoothoff-Baxter-Kouwenhoven House, 1640 East 48th Street (wing, c. 1747; main house, 1811), designated 1976. The small wing of this house was probably erected by Wilhelmus Stoothoff. His granddaughter Altje married John Baxter, and in 1811 they moved the small building, connecting it to a new, larger house. The entire house was reoriented on the lot around 1900. The steeply pitched roof, projecting eaves, and end chimneys are typical features of Dutch Colonial design.

96 **Hendrick I. Lott House,** 1940 East 36th Street (east wing, 1720; main section and west wing, 1800), designated 1989. The Lott family first settled in what is now Brooklyn in 1652. In 1720 Johannes Lott erected a small house in the village of Flatlands. Eighty years later his grandson Hendrick built a new house that incorporated the earlier building as its east

wing. The house, designed in traditional Dutch Colonial style, remains on its original site and is virtually unaltered on the exterior, retaining its gambrel roof, spring eaves, and shingled siding. The large site gives a sense of the house's original setting.

97 **Henry and Abraham Wyckoff House,** also known as the Wyckoff-Bennett Homestead, 1669 East 22nd Street (c. 1766), designated 1968. Built by Henry and Abraham Wyckoff, this house is generally considered to be the most beautiful of the surviving Dutch Colonial farmhouses in Brooklyn. During the Revolutionary War, Hessian soldiers were quartered on the premises. In 1835 the house was sold to the Bennett family, and it remained in their possession until the 1980s. The house has a long porch sheltered by a curved roof that rests on columns, and it retains its original double Dutch door. It was reoriented on the site in the 1890s.

98 **Elias Hubbard Ryder House,** 1926 East 28th Street (1834), designated 1976. An extremely late example of a house designed in the Dutch Colonial style, the Ryder House displays such characteristic features as a sloping roof and deep projecting eaves. The house was slightly altered when it was moved to its present site in 1929.

The Henry and Abraham Wyckoff House (No. 97) is generally considered the most beautiful Dutch Colonial farmhouse in Brooklyn. Photo by Caroline Kane Levy.

INDIVIDUAL LANDMARKS

99 Gravesend Cemetery, Gravesend Neck Road at McDonald Avenue (c. 1650s), designated 1976. Gravesend was the first English settlement in the New Netherlands and the first European community in the New World established by a woman—Lady Deborah Moody. This small cemetery of 1.6 acres may date back to the 1650s, but all the gravestones predating the 18th century have been lost.

100 Parachute Jump, Riegelmann Boardwalk at West 16th Street (James H. Strong, inventor; Elwyn E. Seelye & Co., engineers, 1939), designated 1989. Originally constructed at the New York World's Fair of 1939–40, the Parachute Jump was rebuilt in 1940 at Coney Island's Steeplechase Park, where it continued to thrill riders for twenty-eight years. Although the jump has long been closed, the tapered steel structure with its radiating crown remains one of the borough's most visible landmarks.

101 Wonder Wheel, 3059 West 12th Street (Charles Herman, inventor; Eccentric Ferris Wheel

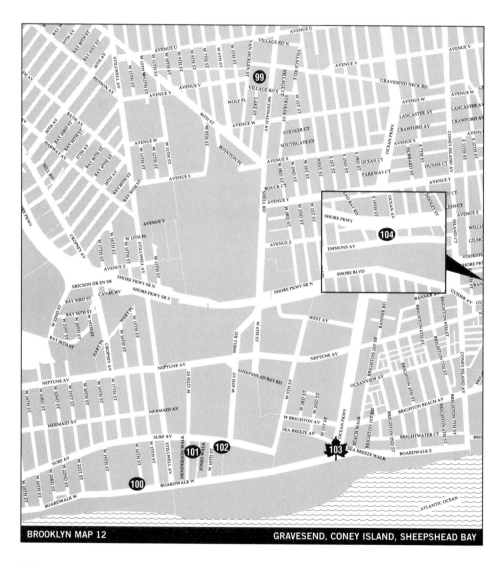

Amusement Co., manufacturer, 1918–20), designated 1989. The Wonder Wheel is a variant of the typical Ferris wheel. The 150-foot-tall, 200-ton steel wheel has 24 passenger cars and can hold up to 160 passengers. While 8 cars are stationary, the remaining 16 are swinging cars that slide along serpentine tracks. The Wonder Wheel has excited Coney Island visitors since the park opened on Memorial Day in 1920.

102 The Cyclone, 834 Surf Avenue (Harry C. Baker, inventor; Vernon Keenan, engineer, 1927), designated 1988. The Cyclone at Coney Island, one of America's most famous roller coasters (it has been called the world's best), is one of a vanishing breed of wood-track coasters. The Cyclone is a gravity ride. A chain pulls the three-car train to the top of the first plunge; the train then runs on its own momentum, reaching a speed of up to 68 miles per hour as it proceeds through nine drops and six curves.

103 Ocean Parkway Scenic Landmark, south of Prospect Park extending from Church Avenue to Seabreeze Avenue (Frederick Law Olmsted and Calvert Vaux, 1874–76), designated 1975. Ocean Parkway was planned as part of an extensive system of parkways

that would extend the rural beauty of Prospect Park into Brooklyn's residential neighborhoods and that were eventually to connect with Manhattan's Central Park. The 5½-mile road—with its central drive, landscaped malls, bridle path (now paved), pedestrian promenade, and narrow access roads—originally ran from the park to Coney Island and was a companion to Eastern Parkway (see No. 74). The northernmost section was destroyed in the 1950s for the construction of the Prospect Expressway.

104 F.W.I.L. Lundy Brothers Restaurant, 1901–1929 Emmons Avenue (Bloch & Hesse, 1934), designated 1992. Lundy's, one of New York's best-loved seafood palaces, is a major cultural and architectural presence in the waterfront community of Sheepshead Bay. The Spanish Colonial Revival–style restaurant, thought to be the largest restaurant in the country at its completion, was erected by Frederick Lundy at the time when the federal government was investing in the reconstruction of the area's waterfront. The restaurant boomed during the 1950s, serving fifteen thousand people on holidays such as Mother's Day. The restaurant closed in 1979 but reopened in 1996 after major restoration.

The Parachute Jump (No. 100) was moved to Coney Island in 1940. Photo by Carl Forster.

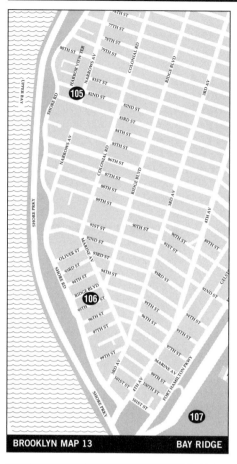

105 **Howard E. and Jessie Jones House** (J. Sarsfield Kennedy, 1916–17), designated as 8200 Narrows Avenue House, 1988. Arts and Crafts design is rare in New York City, but this house built of boulders is a striking example of the type. Erected in Bay Ridge for a successful shipping merchant, the house is set on a large landscaped plot and contains a series of homey details, including an asphalt roof designed to simulate thatch.

106 **Bennett–Farrell Feldman House,** 119 95th Street (c. 1847, moved 1913), designated 1999. Fashionable summer estates lined Shore Road during the mid-19th century, including this handsome Greek Revival villa. Built for Joseph Bennett, the 2½-story frame house retains many of its original details, including a columned front porch that extends the length of the street facade. The Feldman family purchased the house from executors of the James P. Farrell estate in 1912. Moved the following year, it stands within the original boundaries of the Bennett estate.

The Howard E. and Jesse Jones House (No. 105) is a rare example of the Arts and Crafts style in New York City. Photo by Carl Forster.

107 **Fort Hamilton Casemate Fort,** now the Officers' Club, Whiting Quadrangle (1825–31), designated 1977. Fort Hamilton and its companion, Fort Richmond (see Staten Island No. 29), were erected to protect the Narrows at the entrance to New York Harbor. The granite casemate fort, erected as part of the Totten system of seacoast fortifications, is an impressive example of 19th-century military architecture. The fort was altered in 1937–38 when it was converted for use as an officers' club.

Bennett–Farrell Feldman House (No. 106). This Greek Revival residence survives from the era when fashionable vilas lined Shore Road overlooking the Narrows. Photo by Carl Forster.

108 New Utrecht Reformed Dutch Church and Parish House, 18th Avenue, from 83rd to 84th Streets (church, 1828; parish house, Lawrence B. Valk, 1892), designated 1966 and 1998. Constructed with rubble ballast salvaged from the earlier church on the site, the New Utrecht Reformed Dutch Church has Georgian and Gothic elements, including a pedimented front elevation with pointed arches. South of the church is the brick parish house, a Romanesque Revival structure with gabled elevations and pyramidal roofs. Valk specialized in church design, and examples of his work can be found throughout Brooklyn. These buildings, along with the Liberty Pole, first erected in 1783, are sited on a large wooded lot.

109 New Utrecht Reformed Dutch Church Cemetery, adjacent to 16th Avenue, from 84th to 85th Streets (c. 1653), designated 1998. Gravestones and memorials, dating from the 18th through 20th centuries, are found in this one-acre cemetery. Established by 1653, it is located two blocks from the New Utrecht Reformed Dutch Church and contains the remains of some of the community's earliest settlers. There are also unmarked graves of American Revolutionary War soldiers and early church members of African descent.

110 Fire Engine Company 253, originally Engine Company 53, 2425–2427 86th Street (Parfitt Brothers, 1895–96), designated 1998. This section

Magen David Synagogue (No. 111) was constructed in 1920–21 for New York's flourishing Syrian-Jewish Community. Photo by Carl Forster.

of Bensonhurst, originally known as New Utrecht, was annexed by Brooklyn in 1894. To symbolize this new relationship and to provide fire protection, Fire Engine Company 53 was built, designed by one of Brooklyn's most prominent firms. Clad in tawny brick with complementary brownstone details, the main facade has twin apparatus bays and a corner tower embellished with stepped gables. These Dutch Renaissance Revival features recall the area's roots as one of the oldest settlements in Kings County.

111 **Magen David Synagogue,** 2017 67th Street (Maurice Courland, 1920–21), designated 2001. Syrian Jews from the Lower East Side and Williamsburg built this neo-Romanesque synagogue. The simply treated elevations are enlivened with patterned brickwork, round-arched windows, and various motifs associated with the congregation's Middle Eastern roots. While the tight-knit Syrian-Jewish community now lives primarily outside the area, many return here for funerals because of the important role this synagogue has played in their history.

OTHER BROOKLYN LANDMARKS

112 **Pieter Claesen Wyckoff House,** 5816 Clarendon Road at Ralph Avenue (c. 1652; additions, 1740 and 1820), designated 1965. The Pieter Claesen Wyckoff House includes the oldest surviving built structure in New York City; fittingly, the house was the first New York City landmark to be designated after the establishment of the Landmarks Preservation Commission in 1965. The west wing of the Wyckoff House appears to have been built around 1652, with the main section added around 1740. Owned by Wyckoff descendants until 1901, the house was repurchased by the Wyckoff Family Foundation in 1961, and donated to the city in 1969. It has been largely reconstructed (Oppenheimer, Brady & Vogelstein, architect) and is now a museum.

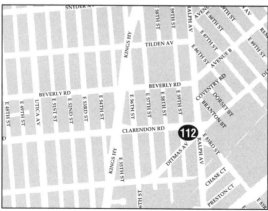

In 2001 the exterior of the Pieter Claesen Wyckoff House (No. 112) was restored with funds from the Historic Preservation Grant Program of the Landmarks Preservation Commission. Photo by William Neeley Jr.

QUEENS

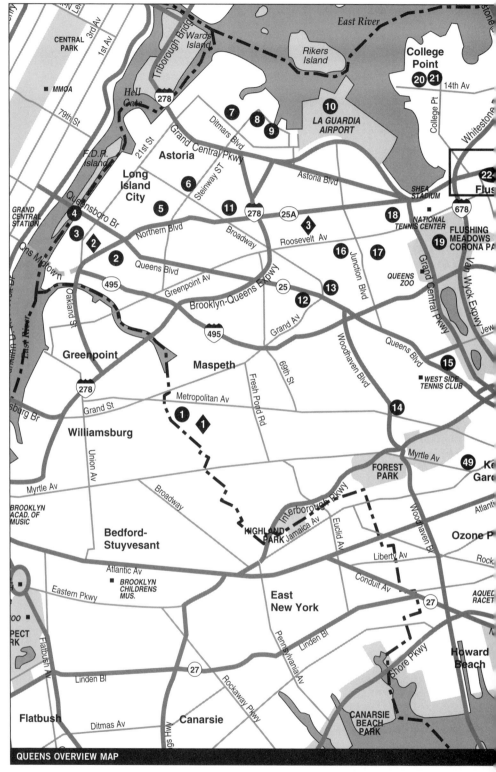

QUEENS

CENTRAL PARK

MMOA

East River

Rikers Island

College Point

20 21

14th Av

College Pt

Whitestone

F.D.R. Island

Astoria

Long Island City

GRAND CENTRAL STATION

Hell Gate

Triborough Bridge

278

Grand Central Pkwy

Ditmars Blvd

7

8 9

10

LA GUARDIA AIRPORT

Astoria Blvd

SHEA STADIUM

22

Flus

678

6

Steinway ST

11

278

25A

3

18

NATIONAL TENNIS CENTER

19

FLUSHING MEADOWS CORONA PA

5

Queensboro Br

4

Northern Blvd

Broadway

Roosevelt Av

16

17

Junction Blvd

QUEENS ZOO

Grand Central Pkwy

3

2

2

Cns Midtown

Oakland St

Queens Blvd

495

Greenpoint Av

25

12

13

Grand Av

Woodhaven Blvd

Queens Blvd

Van Wyck Expwy

Jew

East River

Greenpoint

278

Williamsburg

sburg Br

Grand St

Brooklyn-Queens Expwy

495

Maspeth

Metropolitan Av

1

1

Fresh Pond Rd

69th St

15

WEST SIDE TENNIS CLUB

14

Myrtle Av

FOREST PARK

Myrtle Av

49

Ke Gard

Union Av

Broadway

Interborough Pkwy

HIGHLAND PARK

Jamaica Av

Euclid Av

Woodhaven Bl

Atlant

Ozone P

BROOKLYN ACAD. OF MUSIC

Myrtle Av

Bedford-Stuyvesant

Atlantic Av

BROOKLYN CHILDRENS MUS.

Eastern Pkwy

East New York

Liberty Av

Conduit Av

27

Rock

AQUED RACET

OO

PECT RK

Flatbush Av

Linden Bl

27

Pennsylvania Av

Linden Bl

Rockaway Pkwy

gs Hwy

Howard Beach

Shore Pkwy

Flatbush

Ditmas Av

Canarsie

CANARSIE BEACH PARK

QUEENS OVERVIEW MAP

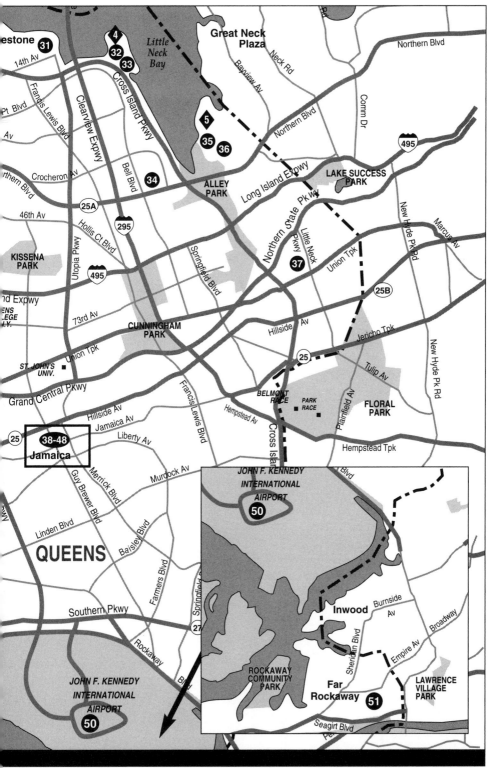

estone ③①
④ ③② ③③
Little Neck Bay
14th Av
Pt. Blvd
Francis Lewis Blvd
Clearview Expwy
Cross Island Pkwy
Great Neck Plaza
Bayview Av
Neck Rd
Northern Blvd
Comm Dr
Av
rthern Blvd
Crocheron Av
⑤
⑤⑤ ⑤⑥
Bell Blvd
③④
ALLEY PARK
Long Island Expwy
Northern Blvd
LAKE SUCCESS PARK
④⑨⑤
New Hyde Pk Rd
Marcus Av
②⑤A
46th Av
Hollis Ct Blvd
②⑨⑤
KISSENA PARK
Utopia Pkwy
Springfield Blvd
Northern State Pkwy
Little Neck Pkwy
③⑦
Union Tpk
②⑤B
d Expwy
ENS
LEGE
N.Y.
④⑨⑤
73rd Av
CUNNINGHAM PARK
Hillside Av
Jericho Tpk
New Hyde Pk Rd
ST. JOHN'S UNIV.
Union Tpk
②⑤
Tulip Av
Grand Central Pkwy
Francis Lewis Blvd
Hempstead Av
BELMONT RACE
PARK RACE
Plainfield Av
FLORAL PARK
Hillside Av
Jamaica Av
Liberty Av
②⑤ ③⑧-④⑧ **Jamaica**
Hempstead Tpk
Murdock Av
Cross Island Pkwy

Guy Brewer Blvd
Merrick Blvd
Baisley Blvd
QUEENS
Linden Blvd
Farmers Blvd
JOHN F. KENNEDY INTERNATIONAL AIRPORT
⑤⓪
JOHN F. KENNEDY INTERNATIONAL AIRPORT
⑤⓪
Blvd
Burnside Av
Inwood
Southern Pkwy
Springfield
②⑦
Rockaway Blvd
Sheridan Blvd
Empire Av
Broadway
JOHN F. KENNEDY INTERNATIONAL AIRPORT
⑤⓪
ROCKAWAY COMMUNITY PARK
Far Rockaway
⑤①
LAWRENCE VILLAGE PARK
Seagirt Blvd

LANDMARKS AND HISTORIC DISTRICTS

❶ Adrian and Ann Wyckoff Onderdonk House, 1820–1836 Flushing Avenue, Ridgewood (c. third quarter 18th century), designated 1995. This is a rare example of a surviving farmhouse built of stone in the Dutch Colonial, or "Dutch American," tradition. The gambrel-roofed structure faces Flushing Avenue, a colonial-era road connecting the Dutch town of Bushwick and the English settlement of Newtown. The house was built for members of the Van Ende family and was sold to the Onderdonks in 1821. The building was reconstructed by architect Giorgio Cavaglieri in 1980–82 following a disastrous fire.

◆ Stockholm Street Historic District, Ridgewood, designated 2000. Nearly all of the buildings in this small historic district were erected between 1907 and 1910. Flanking either side of Stockholm Street, between Woodward and Onderdonk Avenues, this modest enclave in western Queens is notable for its architectural coherence and as a well-preserved example of early 20th-century working-class housing.

Built by local developer Joseph Weiss, most of the houses contained two apartments, and the majority were owned or leased to occupants who were German-born, or of German ancestry. They were designed by Louis Berger & Company, a Ridgewood architect, and have iron-spot brick facades produced by

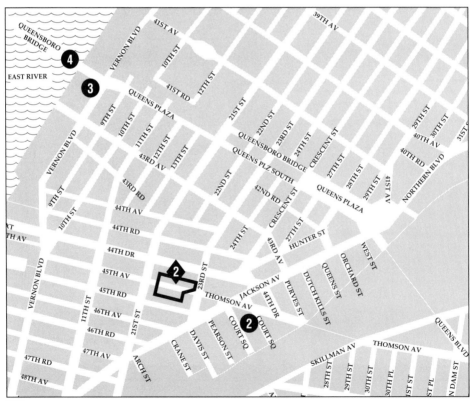

the Kreischer Brick Manufacturing Company of Staten Island (see Staten Island Nos. 71, 72), as well as painted wood porches and uninterrupted cornice lines. One of the most unique features is the road bed, entirely paved in brick. Once common in Queens and other parts of the city, this type of pavement survives in Ridgewood only in this historic district.

2 **Hunter's Point Historic District,** designated 1968. This district, extending along facing blockfronts, is an unusual example of 19th-century middle-class row-house construction in Queens. The urbanization of Hunter's Point followed the 1861 inauguration of ferry service between 34th Street in Manhattan and the nearby Long Island Railroad terminus. Development began in the historic district in the early 1870s and continued until 1890. Among the earliest houses are ten faced with Tuckahoe (or Westchester) marble, at 21-12–21-20 and 21-21–21-29 45th Avenue (1871–72). This material, common on mid-19th-century commercial buildings, was rarely used for entire row-house facades.

2 **New York State Supreme Court, Queens County, Long Island City Branch,** 25-10 Court Square, Long Island City (George Hathorne, 1872–76; reconstruction, Peter M. Coco, 1904–08), designated 1976. In 1870 the seat of Queens County was moved from Jamaica to Long Island City; shortly thereafter a new courthouse was erected. Following a disastrous fire in 1904, the building was rebuilt and enlarged in a Beaux-Arts manner by local architect Peter M. Coco. A parking garage was built at the rear of the courthouse in 1988–90 (Skidmore, Owings & Merrill, architect), replacing two jail structures.

3 **New York Architectural Terra Cotta Company Building,** 42-10–42-16 Vernon Boulevard, Long Island City (Francis H. Kimball, 1892), designated 1982. The New York Architectural Terra Cotta Company was one of the leading manufacturers of ornamental terra cotta between 1886, when the firm was founded, and 1928, when it went bankrupt. The company manufactured the terra cotta for such landmarks as the Ansonia Hotel (see Manhattan No. 390) and Carnegie Hall (see Manhattan No. 357). This small office building displays the range and potential of the products manufactured by the company. Its architect was a pioneer in the use of ornamental terra

cotta, as can be seen, for example, at his Montauk Club (1889–91) in Park Slope (see Brooklyn H.D. 12), with its Venetian-inspired terra cotta, also fabricated by this New York firm.

4 **Queensboro Bridge,** spanning the East River between 11th Street and Bridge Plaza North and Bridge Plaza South, Queens, and East 59th Street, Manhattan (Gustav Lindenthal, engineer; Henry Hornbostel, architect, 1901–08), designated 1974. Inspired by the Pont Mirabeau in Paris, the Queensboro Bridge is a "through-type" cantilevered structure; that is, the roadway runs between the structure's piers and trusses. As the third bridge to span the East River and the first to connect Queens and Manhattan, it was a potent influence on the development of the borough of Queens. The heavy steel towers and frame rest on stone piers. Beneath the bridge are tall vaulted spaces faced with Guastavino tiles.

5 **Famous Players–Lasky Studio,** now Kaufman's Astoria Motion Picture and Television Center, 35-11 35th Avenue, Astoria (Fleischman Construction Company, 1919–21), designated as Paramount Studios Building No. 1, 1978. Built at a time when New York City was a major center for motion picture production, the former Famous Players–Lasky Studio is once again one of America's most active film and television production centers. Between 1921 and 1927, more than 110 silent features were filmed here, including movies starring Gloria Swanson, Rudolph Valentino, W. C. Fields, and Dorothy Gish. Following the introduction of sound, films such as the Marx Brothers' *Animal Crackers* and Paul Robeson's acclaimed version of Eugene O'Neill's *The Emperor Jones* were shot at the studio.

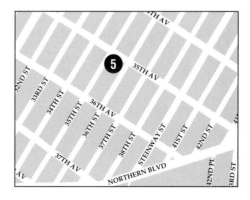

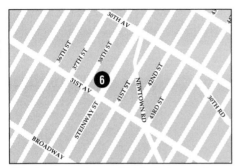

6 **Sidewalk Clock: 30-78 Steinway Street** (1922), designated 1981. Many of New York's commercial streets were once graced by cast-iron sidewalk clocks, generally erected as advertisements by local banks and stores. This clock, one of two in Queens (see No. 43), was erected by Wagner's Jewelers in 1922. It was purchased secondhand by Edward Wagner and moved from Manhattan to its present site.

7 **Lawrence Family Graveyard,** southeast corner of 20th Road and 35th Street, Steinway (1703–1975), designated 1966. This small private cemetery is the resting place of eighty-nine members of the distinguished Lawrence family, including twelve high-ranking American military officers. Oliver Lawrence, who died in 1975, was the last family member buried at the site.

8 **Benjamin T. Pike House,** 18-33 41st Street, (c. 1858), designated as Steinway House, 1967. Pike, a manufacturer of scientific instruments, erected this magnificent Italianate stone villa, with its tall square tower and cast-iron porches, on what at the time was a beautiful riverfront site. The house was purchased in 1870 by William Steinway, whose piano factory is still located nearby.

9 **Abraham Lent House,** also known as the Lent Homestead, 78-03 19th Road, Steinway (c. 1729), designated 1966. One of the few surviving dwellings in Queens built in the Dutch Colonial tradition, the Abraham Lent House has walls of rough stone and contrasting wooden shingles and a steeply sloping roof with deep front and rear overhangs.

10 **Marine Air Terminal, La Guardia Airport** (Delano & Aldrich, 1939–40), exterior and interior designated 1980. The Art Deco Marine Air Terminal evokes the glamour of early air travel. It was a principal feature of Mayor Fiorello La Guardia's plan to build a major airport in New York City. North Beach Airport (as La Guardia was originally called) was the largest single undertaking financed by the Works Progress Administration (WPA). The Marine Air Terminal was built for Pan American's luxurious transatlantic seaplanes, known as clipper ships.

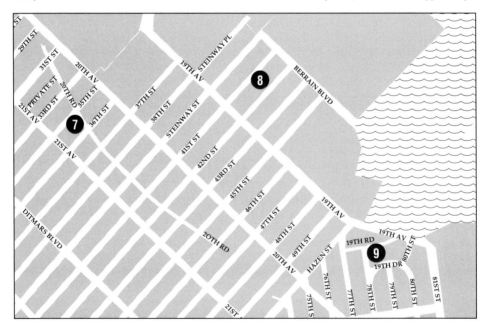

Benjamin T. Pike House (No. 8), a magnificent Italianate stone villa.
Photo by Stephen Senigo.

IN TRANSIT

From clipper ships and horsecars to bridges and airports, transportation has played an important role in the development and integration of the five boroughs. In the South Street Seaport Historic District, rows of brick counting houses and other nautical structures recall the city's origins as a bustling port (Manhattan H.D. 3). To guide ships safely into harbor, lighthouses were constructed on Staten and Roosevelt Islands and at Jeffrey's Hook on the Hudson River (Staten Island No. 43, Roosevelt Island No. 1, and Manhattan No. 582). The last of these, located beneath the east end of the George Washington Bridge, was made famous by the 1942 children's story *The Little Lighthouse and the Great Gray Bridge*. In Lower Manhattan, two historic piers have been preserved—Pier A, built by the Department of Docks and Harbor Police in 1884–86, and the Beaux-Arts Whitehall Ferry Terminal, completed in 1909 (Manhattan Nos. 2 and 4).

To monitor the port, the United States Custom Service has occupied three designated landmarks in Lower Manhattan (Nos. 36, 39, and 6). The last of these, now the National Museum of the American Indian, has a magnificent oval rotunda embellished with murals by Reginald Marsh. Installed in 1936–37, these paintings depict the arrival of a ship in New York harbor. Throughout the 19th and early 20th centuries, many shipping companies were located on lower Broadway, most notably the International Mercantile Marine Company at 1 Broadway and the Cunard Company, which built an imposing headquarters at 25 Broadway in 1917–21 (Manhattan Nos. 12 and 14). The Cunard building's spectacular domed ticketing hall, now a post office, was modeled on Raphael's Villa Madama.

Among the various bridges recognized by the Commission, the earliest example was not built to carry people and vehicles, but water. The High Bridge, completed in 1848, was constructed as part of the Croton Aqueduct system. Spanning the Harlem River at West 170th Street, the massive stone arches recall the work of Roman engineers (Manhattan No. 580). Subsequent landmarks that span this body of water include the Macomb's Dam Bridge at West 155th Street, the Washington Bridge at West 181st Street, and University Heights Bridge at West 207th Street (Manhattan Nos. 546, 581, and Bronx No. 27). Of the three, the last exhibits the most decoration, incorporating four sidewalk shelters and ornate iron railings. In Central Park is a significant group of bridges designed by Calvert Vaux and Jacob Wrey Mould, including five of the oldest cast-iron bridges in the United States (Manhattan No. 376, various locations). The Brooklyn Bridge, once the world's longest suspension bridge, soars across the East River. Opened with much fanfare in 1883, the raised central promenade offers pedestrians and cyclists spectacular views (Brooklyn No. 17). The Carroll Street Bridge, which connects Carroll Gardens

La Guardia
Airport

10

with Park Slope, is one of the city's most unusual. Built in 1888–89, it is the oldest of four known "retractile" bridges in the United States (Brooklyn No. 32). Also designated is Carrère & Hastings' monumental entrance to the Manhattan Bridge, completed in 1915 (Manhattan No. 120).

Prior to the introduction of subway service, many New Yorkers traveled by trolley. Several structures recall this mode of transportation, including the 1861 headquarters of the Brooklyn City Railroad Company which operated horsecars to and from the Fulton Ferry terminal; a pair of neoclassical tempietti at the Grand Army Plaza entrance to Prospect Park that sheltered waiting passengers; and McKim, Mead & White's Cable Building (1893), at the northwest corner of Broadway and Houston Street, which functioned as the powerhouse and headquarters of the Broadway & Seventh Avenue Railroad (Brooklyn Nos. 18 and 79, Manhattan H.D. 13). The basement of the last originally housed 32-foot wheels that carried the cables that pulled the cars from 15th Street to the Battery.

Grand Central Terminal is one of the city's most visible and important landmarks (Manhattan No. 280). Located on 42nd Street at the intersection of Park Avenue, the Beaux-Arts facade is crowned by Jules-Felix Coutan's statue of Mercury, messenger of the Roman gods. Nearby is the ornate New York Central Building, built above the tracks by the railroad's owner, and the Park Avenue Viaduct, an elevated road system that was conceived by the architects Reed & Stem to move traffic along and around the massive terminal (Manhattan Nos. 331 and 279). This steel and granite viaduct was one of the earliest roads in the United States built for the exclusive use of automobiles.

Service on the IRT subway began between City Hall and 155th Street in 1904. Many structures associated with the system are designated, including two control houses, the Manhattan Valley Viaduct from West 122nd to 135th Street, and numerous station interiors, many of which feature terra-cotta and faience plaques designed by Heins & La Farge (Manhattan No. 7). These stations became important transit hubs, and many new office buildings were planned to provide direct access to them, including the Equitable Building and Woolworth Building (Manhattan Nos. 23 and 57).

Most subsequent transit landmarks are located in Queens, where the expansion of subway service and construction of the Queensboro Bridge promoted the creation of such neighborhoods as Jackson Heights and Douglaston (Queens No. 4, H.D. 3 and 5). New York's major airports are located in the borough, and both feature dazzling transportation buildings and interiors, most notably the Art Deco Marine Air Terminal at La Guardia Airport, and the Trans World Airlines Flight Center at Kennedy Airport, one of Eero Saarinen's most celebrated works (Queens Nos. 10 and 50).

The terminal is massed around a central circular core, with a rectangular entrance pavilion and two symmetrically disposed wings. Its exterior ornament includes a polychromatic terra-cotta frieze of flying fish. The **interior** consists of a small foyer and vestibule with stainless steel detail and a spectacular central rotunda encircled with James Brooks's *Flight*, a 12-foot-high, 237-foot-long mural commissioned by the WPA. The mural, which was painted over in the 1950s, was restored by Alan Farancz in 1980. In 1996 Beyer Blinder Belle, architect, undertook a restoration of other interior features as well as the exterior.

3 Jackson Heights Historic District, designated 1993. The Jackson Heights Historic District celebrates the innovative garden apartment and garden home development undertaken by the Queensboro Corporation on the former farm fields of north central Queens, primarily in the 1910s and 1920s. The opening of the Queensboro Bridge (see No. 3) in 1909 and the inauguration of service on the ele-

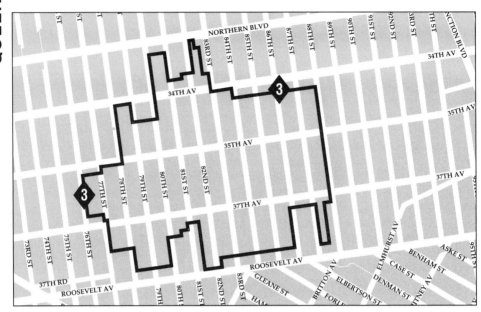

Jackson Heights Historic District
(H.D. 3), an innovative development
in the early 20th century, contains
garden apartments like the Chateau,
pictured here, at 34-06 81st Street.
Photo: Landmarks Preservation
Commission collection, 1993.

vated Interborough Rapid Transit line (now the No. 7 train) in 1917 made this outlying region of Queens County a prime location for the construction of homes for middle-class New Yorkers. The Queensboro Corporation began purchasing land in 1910 and erected a few traditional row houses and apartment buildings, such as the row at 37-46–37-60 83rd Street (Charles Peck, 1911) and the Laurel Court apartments (George H. Wells, 1913–14) at 33-01–33-21 82nd Street. Beginning in 1917, with the construction of architect George H. Wells's Greystone Apartments on both sides of 80th Street between 35th and 37th Avenues, the Queensboro Corporation pioneered in the design of garden apartment complexes with five- and six-story buildings erected in groups. They had large landscaped gardens at the rear that increased light and air and created a suburban atmosphere within the neighborhood's gridded urban street pattern. The most interesting of the apartment complexes were those erected on a single block with shared, undivided rear gardens. This plan was initiated by architect Andrew J. Thomas at Linden Court (1919–21) on 84th and 85th Streets between 37th and Roosevelt Avenues and reached its peak at Jackson Heights's most spectacular apartment complexes, including Wells's Cambridge Court (1922–23) on 85th and 86th Streets and Thomas's Chateau (1922) and Towers (1923–25), both of which line 80th and 81st Streets. The apartment complexes were designed, primarily by Wells and Thomas, in eclectic and conservative styles, including English Gothic/Tudor (Greystone), French Gothic (Chateau), neo-Georgian (Cambridge Court), and Italian Romanesque/Renaissance (Towers). To attract middle-class households that might otherwise have moved out of New York City to single-family suburban homes, the Queensboro Corporation organized its apartments as cooperatives, so that residents would also be owners. These are among the first cooperatives in New York City planned for the middle class. In addition to apartment buildings, the Queensboro Corporation built attached and semidetached single-family houses (some were planned so they could easily be converted into two-family units) in picturesque ensembles with brick facades and traditional American Colonial and English Tudor detail. These rows had combined rear yards or rear alleys leading to garages designed in the same style as the houses. Mostly erected in the mid-1920s, these houses can be seen

between 84th and 88th Streets. The depressed economic conditions of the 1930s led the Queensboro Corporation to build more traditional six-story apartment houses on its vacant sites, including neo-Georgian, Mediterranean, and neo-Tudor buildings designed by apartment-house specialists, many with offices in Brooklyn, such as Cohn Brothers and Seelig & Finkelstein. An exception was Dunolly Gardens, Thomas's last garden apartment complex (1939), on the block between 78th and 79th Streets and 34th and 35th Avenues, which was given a modernistic architectural treatment. Small-scale apartment-house construction continued into the 1950s, by which time almost all the vacant land in the neighborhood was filled with an extraordinary array of high-quality middle-class housing. The southern intersection of 37th Avenue, the commercial spine of the district, and 82nd Street is distinguished by a group of picturesque neo-Tudor commercial buildings dating from between the World Wars. These complement the residential buildings in their design.

⓫ Moore-Jackson Cemetery, Woodside (c. 1733–), designated 1997. Located midblock between 31st and 32nd Avenues, this small private cemetery extends from 51st to 54th Streets at what was once was the outskirts of the village of Newtown. A rare example of a colonial-era burial ground with visible headstones in Queens, it was established by Samuel and Charity Hallet Moore and continued to be used by family members until at least 1868. From the fifty-one burials that took place here, fifteen grave markers survive.

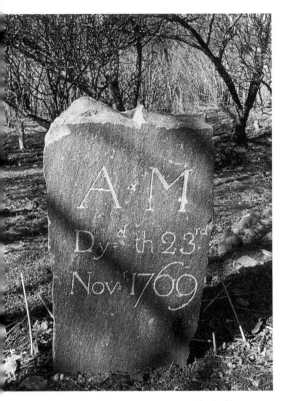

This well-preserved headstone, located in the Moore-Jackson Cemetery (No. 11), marks the grave of Augustine Moore. Photo by Carl Forster.

⑫ Benevolent and Protective Order of Elks, Lodge Number 878, 82-10 Queens Boulevard, Elmhurst (The Ballinger Company, 1923–24), designated 2001. After the First World War, the Elks grew at a rapid rate, and many new lodges were constructed. This imposing brick clubhouse was designed by the Ballinger Company, a Philadelphia-based firm, in the style of an Italian Renaissance palazzo. It features carved limestone details, a broad front terrace, and outside the main entrance, a large bronze elk by sculptor Eli Harvey.

⑬ Reformed Dutch Church of Newtown and Fellowship Hall, 85-15 Broadway, Elmhurst (church, 1831; hall, 1860), designated 1966. This wooden church building displays a late use of the Georgian style; its cupola is a prominent feature of the Elmhurst community. Fellowship Hall, originally a chapel designed in the Greek Revival style, was moved to the site in 1906.

⑭ Remsen Cemetery, adjacent to 69-43 Trotting Course Lane, Forest Hills (c. 1790–), designated 1981. The Remsens, among the earliest settlers of Queens, may have established this private cemetery in the mid-18th century, although the earliest extant gravestone dates from 1790. The main focus of the small plot is a World War I memorial with a flagpole and two statues of doughboys.

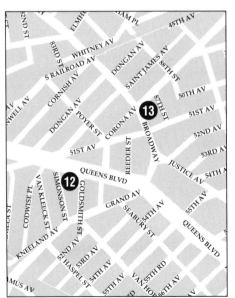

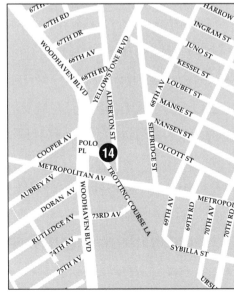

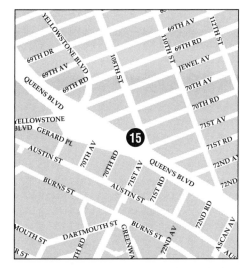

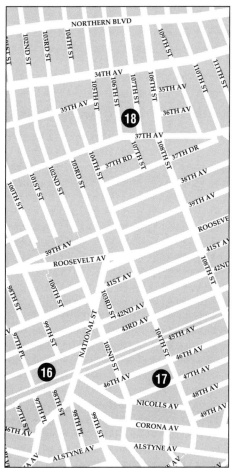

⑮ Ridgewood Savings Bank, Forest Hills Branch, 107-55 Queens Boulevard (Halsey, McCormack & Helmer, 1939–40), designated 2000. Designed to fit closely into a small triangular lot, this dignified neighborhood bank was built to serve Forest Hill's growing population. Faced in smooth limestone over a low granite base, the building has crisp stylized ornament, suggesting both Art Deco and classical sources.

⑯ Fire Engine Company 289, Ladder Company 138, 97-28 43rd Avenue (Satterlee & Boyd, 1912–14), designated 1999. Following the consolidation of Greater New York, an ambitious campaign was begun to bring professional fire fighting to Queens. This Corona station house was one of the finest erected in Queens and among the earliest in the city designed to accommodate motorized vehicles. Inspired by French Renaissance models, the broad main facade has side-by-side apparatus bays, tapestry brick walls, and a steeply pitched mansard roof with limestone dormers.

⑰ Edward E. Sanford House, Corona (c. 1871), designated as the 102-45 47th Avenue House, 1987. This small two-story house is one of the last intact 19th-century frame houses in Queens. Designed in a vernacular Italianate style, the house is especially notable for its decorative porch, gable, and fence, all of which display fanciful wooden detail.

⑱ Louis Armstrong House, 34-55 107th Street, Corona (Robert W. Johnson, 1910), designated 1988. One of the world's most renowned jazz musicians and entertainers purchased this modest house in 1943 and occupied it until his death in 1971. Armstrong—or Satchmo, as he was commonly known—gained world fame as a jazz trumpeter and bandleader onstage (notably at the Savoy Ballroom and other Harlem nightspots), in recordings, and in Hollywood films. In 1983 Armstrong's widow, Lucille, willed the house and its contents to New York City for the creation of a museum and study center devoted to Armstrong's career and the history of jazz.

⑲ Unisphere and Surrounding Reflecting Pool, Flushing Meadows–Corona Park (Gilmore D. Clarke, landscape architect; United States Steel Company, engineering and fabrication, 1963–64),

Louis Armstrong House (No. 18). Home of famed jazz trumpeter Louis Armstrong, the house is now a museum devoted to Armstrong's career and the history of jazz. Photo by Carl Forster.

designated 1995. The Unisphere, symbolizing peace through understanding, was the centerpiece of the 1964–65 New York World's Fair. The monumental steel globe surrounded by satellite rings stands in the center of a reflecting pool with fountains spraying water twenty feet into the air. It was fabricated and donated to the fair by the U.S. Steel Corporation. The city restored the ensemble in 1993–94.

⑳ Poppenhusen Institute, 114-04 14th Road, College Point (Mundell & Teckritz, 1868), designated 1970. The Poppenhusen Institute was established by the German-born Conrad Poppenhusen, founder in 1853 of the U.S. hard-rubber industry, as a vocational school for the workers in his nearby plant. What is thought to have been the first American free kindergarten for the children of working

mothers was housed in this French Second Empire structure. The building was designed by a Brooklyn architecture firm that specialized in institutional work. The institute, which still occupies the premises, continues to provide services to the community.

㉑ Queens Borough Public Library, Poppenhusen Branch, 121-23 14th Avenue (Heins & La Farge, 1904), designated 2000. Built on a corner site donated by the citizens of College Point, this Classical Revival structure was the only Carnegie branch designed by this noted architectural firm. Stairs lead to a projecting arched entrance, which is flanked by stone cartouches carved with images of open books. The nearby Poppenhusen Institute (see above) donated the library's original book collection.

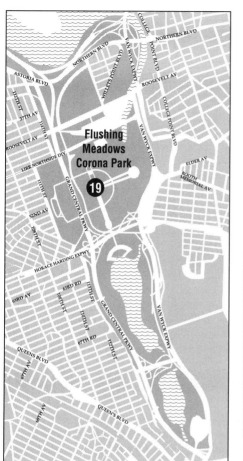

The Unisphere (No. 19), from the east.
Photo by Carl Forster.

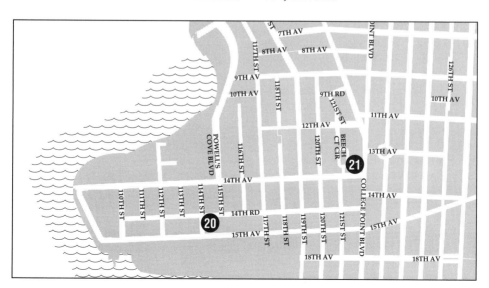

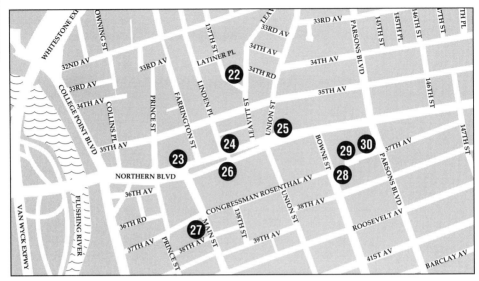

㉒ Lewis H. Latimer House, 34-41 137th Street, Flushing (c. 1887–89), designated 1995. The renowned African-American inventor Lewis H. Latimer lived in this house from 1902 until his death in 1928. Latimer was a specialist in electric lighting and invented the long-lasting carbon filament, which made possible the production of affordable electric lightbulbs. During his long career, Latimer worked with Alexander Graham Bell and Thomas Alva Edison and was active in civil rights and black history organizations. Threatened with demolition, the house was moved to its present site from Holly Avenue, west of Kissena Boulevard, in 1988.

㉓ RKO Keith's Flushing Theater (interior), 135-29–135-45 Northern Boulevard, Flushing (Thomas Lamb, 1927–28), designated 1984. The ticket lobby, grand foyer, promenade, and lounges of the former RKO Keith's Flushing Theater, designed in a fanciful Mexican Baroque style, are a reminder of the grandeur of movie palaces in the 1920s.

㉔ Flushing Town Hall, now Flushing Council on Culture and the Arts, 137-35 Northern Boulevard, Flushing (1862), designated as Flushing Municipal Courthouse, 1968. Before the consolidation of Greater New York in 1898, each town in the region had its own governmental center. This Early Romanesque Revival masonry building is one of the few such town halls still standing. The German-

inspired design is striking in its use of round-arched forms for windows and doors, its entrance portico, and its corbeled cornice. The Flushing Council on Culture and the Arts acquired the building in 1991.

㉕ Flushing High School, 35-01 Union Street (C. B. J. Snyder, 1912–15), designated 1991. Flushing High School, incorporated in 1875, is the oldest public secondary school in New York City. Its present home is an impressive Collegiate Gothic structure designed by the city's superintendent of school buildings. Like Snyder's earlier Curtis High School (see Staten Island No. 9) on Staten Island, Flushing High School was given a campus setting. The choice of style and setting evokes the great Gothic colleges of Oxford and Cambridge.

㉖ Friends Meeting House, 137-16 Northern Boulevard, Flushing (1694; additions, 1716–19), designated 1970. The eastern third of the Friends Meeting House in Flushing is New York City's oldest structure in continuous use for religious purposes. In its proportions and framing system, this austerely simple wooden building offers evidence of the survival of medieval building techniques in the American colonies.

㉗ St. George's Church (Episcopal), Old Parish House and Graveyard, 38-02 Main Street (Wills & Dudley, 1853–54; chancel, J. King James,

St. George's Episcopal Church (No. 27) is situated in the heart of downtown Flushing. Photo by Carl Forster.

1894; Old Parish House, Charles C. Haight, 1907–08), designated 2000. St. George's Church is one of the most impressive 19th-century structures in downtown Flushing. Designed in the Gothic Revival style, it has handsome walls of randomly laid granite rubble, fine stained-glass windows, and a lofty tapered spire that rises 150 feet. Subsequent additions to the complex, including the chancel and parish house, were executed in a sensitive manner,

with complementary materials and ornament. A masonry wall encloses the churchyard, which contains gravestones and memorials dating to the 18th and early 19th centuries.

❷❽ Bowne House, 37-01 Bowne Street, Flushing (1661; additions, 1680, 1696, and c. 1830), designated 1966. The kitchen wing of the Bowne House is the oldest surviving structure in Queens and one

Bowne House (No. 28). The house is significant as an example of 17th-century colonial construction and as a monument to religious freedom. Photo by Carl Forster.

of the oldest in New York City. The house is significant both as an example of 17th-century colonial construction and as a monument to religious freedom. John Bowne was arrested in 1662 for permitting the Quakers to hold meetings in the house. After appealing to the Dutch government in Holland, Bowne was acquitted, thus establishing the right to freedom of worship.

㉙ Kingsland Homestead, 143-35 37th Avenue, Flushing (1785), designated 1965. This vernacular frame house, the second oldest in Flushing, was erected by Charles Doughty shortly after the Revolutionary War. The house is named for Doughty's son-in-law, Joseph King, who purchased the property in 1801. Moved from 40-25 155th Street to its current site in 1968, the Kingsland Homestead is now the headquarters of the Queens Historical Society. The building was restored in 1996 by the Department of Parks.

㉚ Weeping Beech Tree, Weeping Beech Park, 37th Avenue between Parsons Boulevard and Bowne Street, Flushing (1847), designated 1966. Samuel Parsons, the owner of a large nursery in Flushing and the supplier of original plant stock to both Central and Prospect Parks, planted a weeping beech on this site in 1847. Acquired in Belgium as a tiny shoot, it matured into a magnificent specimen. Although the original tree died in 1998, a circle of pendulous offspring have taken root around it.

㉛ Arthur and Dorothy Dalton Hammerstein House, Wildflower, 168-11 Powells Cove Boulevard, Beechhurst (Dwight James Baum, 1924 and pre-1930), designated 1982. Although not as well known as his father, Oscar Hammerstein I, or his nephew, Oscar Hammerstein II, Arthur Hammerstein was a successful theatrical producer who sponsored twenty-six Broadway shows, including works by Victor Herbert, George Gershwin, and Jerome

Kern (see Hammerstein's Theater, Manhattan No. 351). Following the success of the musical *Wildflower* in 1923, and his marriage to the actress and film star Dorothy Dalton, Hammerstein purchased a waterfront plot in Queens and erected this sprawling neo-Tudor house, which was enlarged prior to 1930. The house is one of many mansions erected along the north shore of eastern Queens and adjacent sections of Long Island in the early decades of the 20th century.

◆ Fort Totten Historic District, designated 1999. Established in 1857 as the Fort at Willets Point, this large historic district was once part of the defense system of New York Harbor. Strategically situated on a peninsula extending into Long Island Sound, the unfinished fortifications were planned as a counterpoint to Fort Schuyler (see Bronx No. 60) on Throgs Neck in the Bronx. Most of the defense buildings were constructed between 1885 and 1914. In addition to upgrading the fortifications and batteries, installing torpedo buildings, and reconfiguring the parade grounds, the army built about eighty structures, mostly to house soldiers and officers. Named in 1898 for Maj. Gen. Joseph G. Totten, who helped develop the nation's coastal defense system prior to the Civil War, the post was used primarily for military and medical research, as well as for the advanced training of army engineers. The majority of facilities at Fort Totten have been turned over to the City of New York and are now operated by the Fire and Parks Departments, as well as the Historic House Trust. The earliest surviving structure, known as Building 211, was constructed for the Willets family in 1829. It was remodeled in the Gothic Revival style as living quarters for the fort's commanding officer during the late 1860s. The next phase of development was associated with construction of the fort. Notable structures include: the Battery (see No. 32), Quartermaster's Wharf (1864), torpedo storehouse (1871–79), and the Queen Anne–style photography laboratory (1882–83). The Army Corps of Engineers supervised many improvements during the 1890s that served officers and enlisted men, such as barracks and storehouses. During the early 20th century, the fort's expansion continued, resulting in a large group of brick structures in variants of the Colonial Revival style, including the monumental Commanding Officer's Quarters (1909). Circular drives follow the peninsula's elevated terrain, offering views of Long Island Sound and access to the parade ground. Oriented east to west, this large central space is flanked by many of the district's most noteworthy structures.

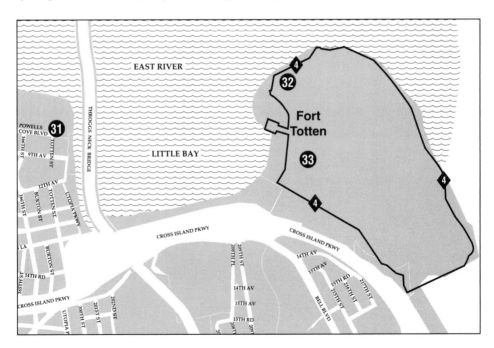

QUEENS

㉜ Fort Totten Battery (William Petit Trowbridge, engineer, 1862–64), designated 1974. This massive battery consists of two tiers of gun emplacements set into the hillside on the East River shoreline at Willets Point. The seaward wall is constructed of beautifully cut rough granite blocks with small square openings.

㉝ Fort Totten Officers' Club (c. 1870; enlargement, 1887), designated 1974. Originally a one-story building, this picturesque Gothic Revival frame structure was enlarged in 1887. Its mock-medieval features include a crenellated roofline, a pointed-arch portico, and drip lintels.

㉞ Lawrence Graveyard, 216th Street at 42nd Avenue, Bayside (1832–1925), designated 1967. The land on which this cemetery is located was given to the Lawrence family in 1645. Used for many years as a picnic ground, the plot became a

▶ The Fort Totten Battery (No. 32) was constructed during the Civil War. Photo by Carl Forster.

▼ Built in 1887, this Gothic Revival structure is now the headquarters of the Bayside Historical Society (No. 33). Photo by Carl Forster.

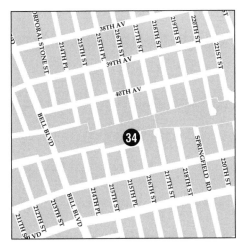

graveyard in 1832. Forty-eight members of the Lawrence family, including one mayor of New York, were interred at the site between 1832 and 1925.

5 **Douglaston Historic District,** designated 1997. Winding landscaped streets and picturesque freestanding residences give this large historic district its unique character. Located on a narrow mile-long peninsula that extends into Little Neck Bay, near the northeastern edge of Queens, the Douglaston Historic District contains more than 600 houses. The majority were constructed as part of the planned suburb of Douglas Manor, acquired by George Douglas in 1835 and redeveloped by the Rickert-Finlay Company after 1906. Among the historical styles employed, the Colonial Revival was the

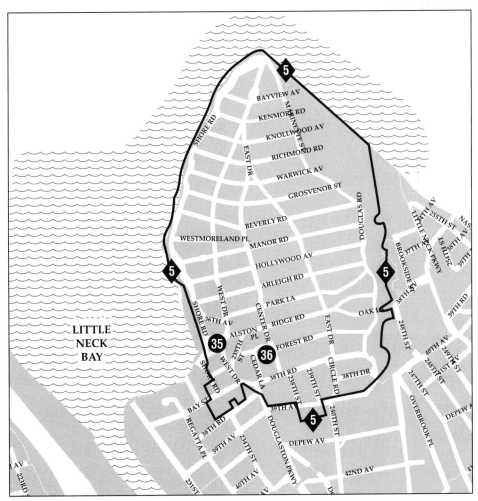

111 Hollywood Avenue, a fine example of the Craftsman style, is located in the Douglaston Historic District (H.D. 5). Photo by Carl Forster.

most popular, reflecting both contemporary taste and such earlier local structures as the Cornelius Van Wyck House (see No. 35), the Van Zandt Manor House (begun 1819) at 600 West Drive, and the Benjamin P. Allen House (see No. 36). To preserve the district's suburban atmosphere, fences were prohibited and the houses were required to be set back 20 feet from the street. Most were designed and built by Queens architects, including many from Douglaston itself. Alfred Scheffer, John C. W. Cadoo, and Albert Humble were among the most prolific firms. The more substantial residences tend to line Shore Road, while less expansive houses are located farther east. Of particular note are eight houses designed by Josephine Wright Chapman, one of America's earliest successful women architects, and several Arts and Crafts houses influenced by Gustav Stickley and his popular magazine *The Craftsman*. The surrounding landscape includes many impressive trees, mostly planted in the mid-19th century, as well as the white oak at 233 Arleigh Road, believed to be 600 years old.

35 Cornelius Van Wyck House, 37-04 Douglaston Parkway (126 West Drive), Douglaston (c. 1735; addition, mid-18th century), designated 1966. Set at the edge of Little Neck Bay, this house, built by the farmer Cornelius Van Wyck in the traditional Dutch Colonial mode with hand-hewn scalloped shingles, is one of the finest residences of its type on Long Island. A Georgian-style extension was added to the west and south at some point before 1770. Additions were also made early in the 20th century when the structure served as a clubhouse, but these were removed during a restoration, early in the 1920s, by the architect Frank J. Forster.

36 Benjamin P. Allen House, 29 Center Drive, Douglaston (c. 1848–50), designated as the Allen-Beville House, 1977. Allen acquired property in Douglaston in 1847 and is thought to have erected this house shortly thereafter. The house, one of the few surviving 19th-century buildings in Queens constructed as a farm dwelling, was designed in a transitional style; the basic form is Greek Revival, but the cornices on the main house and its porches display Italianate brackets.

37 Jacob Adriance Farmhouse, now the Queens County Farm Museum, 73-50 Little Neck Parkway, Floral Park (1772; additions, c. 1835 and later), designated as the Creedmoor (Cornell) Farmhouse, 1976. The Adriance House is a rare example of a New York City farmhouse that is still set in a rural landscape. The original house, with Dutch and English Colonial features, was greatly enlarged in the 19th century, giving the structure the Greek Revival character now evident.

38 First Reformed Church of Jamaica, 153-10 Jamaica Avenue, Jamaica (Sidney J. Young, 1858–59; addition, Tuthill & Higgins, 1902), designated 1966. The bold massing and complex use of arched motifs mark this red brick building as one of the finest Early Romanesque Revival churches in New York. It was designed by master carpenter Sidney J. Young, a member of the congregation, who had visited other local churches for inspiration, possibly including the Church of the Pilgrims (see Brooklyn H.D. 4, entry F) and South Congregational (see Brooklyn No. 30) in Brooklyn. This was the third church on this site of a congregation established in 1702.

39 Rufus King House, now King Manor Museum, Jamaica Avenue and 150th Street, King Park, Jamaica (1733–55; additions, 1806, 1810, and c. 1830s), designated as King Mansion 1966, interior 1976. Rufus King—Massachusetts delegate to the Continental Congress, antislavery advocate, and three-term senator from New York—purchased a modest gambrel-roofed farmhouse and adjacent

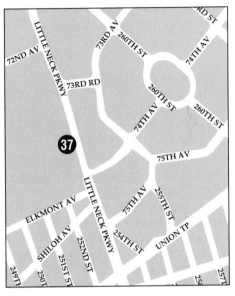

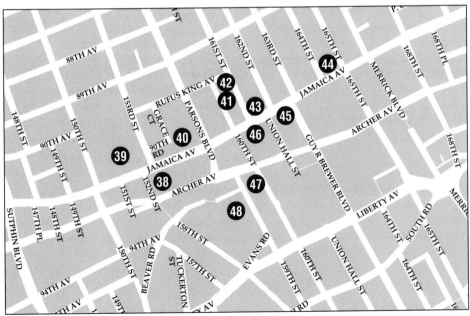

La Casina (No. 41), a jazzy, streamlined nightclub from the 1930s. Photo by Carl Forster.

acreage in Jamaica in 1805. King immediately added a kitchen wing to the house; in 1810 he undertook major alterations, including the addition of a new dining room with chambers above and the construction of a new front elevation. Rufus King's heir, John Alsop King, was probably responsible for the Greek Revival additions, notably the front porch supported by four Doric columns. After 1896, when the last member of the King family died, the house became the property of New York City. In 1989–90 the city undertook a major restoration of the exterior and the **interior,** which features fine plasterwork, woodwork, and marble mantels.

40 **Grace Episcopal Church and Graveyard,** 155-03 Jamaica Avenue, Jamaica (Dudley Fields, 1861–62; chancel, Cady, Berg & See, 1901–02; graveyard, c. 1734–), designated 1967. Grace Church was founded in 1702 as the official church of the British colonial government. The congregation has worshiped at this site on the main street of Jamaica since 1734. The present church, a rough-cut brownstone Early English Gothic–inspired structure with a tall spire, is the third at this location. The early 20th-century chancel complements the design of the original building. Among those buried in the graveyard are Rufus King, whose house (see above) still stands 200 yards to the west.

41 **La Casina,** (also known as La Casino), now Jamaica Business Resource Center, 90-33 160th Street, Jamaica (c. 1933), designated 1996. A rare surviving example of Streamlined Moderne design, this metal and stucco facade was designed for a nightclub and restaurant and reflects the jazzy, streamlined motifs fashionable for Depression-era nightspots. Erected in the heart of Jamaica's commercial center, the building was restored by Li-Saltzman Architects in 1994–95.

42 **Suffolk Title and Guarantee Company Building,** 90-04 161st Street (Dennison & Hirons, 1929), designated 2001. This distinctive office building was constructed as the headquarters of the short-lived Suffolk Title and Guarantee Company. Designed in the popular Art Deco style, it features continuous brick piers and a series of graceful setbacks above the sixth floor. While the zoning resolution of 1916 required this solution in taller buildings, in this case it was chosen for aesthetic reasons. Sculptor Rene Chambellan, who frequently worked with Dennison & Hirons, created the brightly colored terra-cotta panels above the second-story windows as well as the reliefs that decorate the crown.

43 **Sidewalk Clock, 161-11 Jamaica Avenue** (1900), designated 1981. This handsome clock, one of two surviving in Queens (see No. 6), was probably erected by a jewelry store. The clock is crowned by a Greek-inspired acroterion (see Manhattan No. 198).

44 Loew's Valencia Theater, now Tabernacle of Prayer for All People, 165-11 Jamaica Avenue (John Eberson, 1928), designated 1999. The first of five so-called "Wonder Theaters" built by the Loew's chain outside Midtown Manhattan during the late 1920s, the Valencia's design was inspired by Spanish and Mexican architecture of the Baroque or "Churrigueresque" period. Particularly notable is the yellow brick frontispiece, which is encrusted with elaborate terra-cotta reliefs. Loew's donated the theater to the Tabernacle of Prayer in 1997.

45 J. Kurtz & Sons Store, 162-24 Jamaica Avenue, Jamaica (Allmendinger & Schlendorf, 1931), designated 1981. The former J. Kurtz & Sons furniture store is one of the finest examples of Art Deco architecture in Queens and a building of great prominence on the commercial thoroughfare of Jamaica Avenue. As one of the architects recalled, the brick building, with its black-and-white glazed tile pylons, polychromatic terra-cotta panels, and prominent vertical sign, was designed to be as "modern and colorful" as the contemporary furniture displayed inside.

46 The Register, now the Jamaica Arts Center, 161-04 Jamaica Avenue, Jamaica (A. S. Macgregor, 1898), designated 1974. An excellent example of a public building in the neo–Italian Renaissance style, the former deeds registry, designed by a Queens architect, was erected in the year that Queens became a part of New York City.

47 Saint Monica's Church (R.C.), 94-20 160th Street, Jamaica (Anders Peterson, builder, 1856–57), designated 1979. Erected by the master mason Anders Peterson under the supervision of the Reverend Anthony Farley, Saint Monica's is one of the oldest surviving examples of Early Romanesque Revival architecture in New York, and one of the few Roman Catholic churches in the city executed in this style. Following the collapse of the sanctuary and apse in 1998, the main facade and campanile were stabilized with plans for future reuse.

48 Prospect Cemetery, 159th Street at Beaver Road, Jamaica (c. 1668–), designated 1977. This four-acre plot is the oldest cemetery in Queens. Established before 1668, the cemetery is the final resting place of many Revolutionary War veterans as well as members of such prominent Queens families as the Sutphins, Van Wycks, and Merricks. A small Romanesque Revival chapel was erected in 1857 by Nicholas Ludlum in memory of his three daughters.

49 Richmond Hill Republican Club, 86-15 Lefferts Boulevard (Henry E. Haugaard, 1908), designated 2002. Almost domestic in scale, this former clubhouse was designed in the Colonial Revival style to serve the social, political, and recreational needs of the Richmond Hill community. Haugaard, a local architect and builder, expressed the building's civic function by embellishing the principal facade with various classical elements, including a large wood pediment and Ionic columns.

50 Trans World Airlines Flight Center at New York International Airport, John F. Kennedy International Airport (Eero Saarinen & Associates, 1956–62), exterior and interior designated 1994. The former TWA Terminal is one of the great masterpieces of expressionistic modern design and is a major work by Eero Saarinen (with codesigner Kevin Roche), one of the leading modern architects in the United States. Built of carefully engineered concrete and glass, the distinctive winged form of the building reflects Saarinen's desire "to interpret the sensation of flying." The terminal was among the first planned with the satellite gates, jetways, and baggage carousels now common in airports. The dynamism of the design continues on the **interior,**

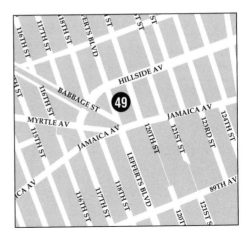

where the terminal is massed with a powerful series of curved concrete forms on the walls, stairs, balconies, and ceiling vaults of the main hall, jetways, and satellite gates.

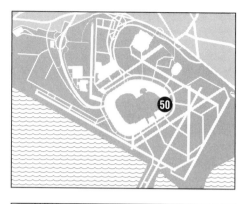

51 Richard Cornell Graveyard, adjacent to 1463 Gateway Boulevard, Far Rockaway (18th to 19th centuries), designated 1970. Named for the first European settler in the Rockaways, this small graveyard was established early in the 18th century and was used by the Cornell family into the 19th century.

Trans World Airlines Flight Center at John F. Kennedy International Airport (No. 50), one of the great masterpieces of expressionistic modern design. Photos by Carl Forster.

THE BRONX

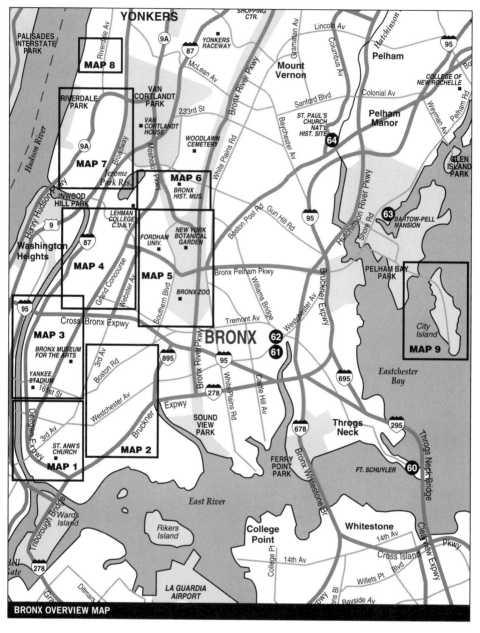

THE BRONX

BRONX OVERVIEW MAP

298

HISTORIC DISTRICTS

1 **Bertine Block Historic District,** designated 1994. This small historic district centers on a row at 414–432 East 136th Street, called the Bertine Block. These ten Queen Anne–style houses form one of the most exceptional late 19th-century residential groups in New York City. The houses, erected in 1891 by developer Edward D. Bertine (who moved into No. 416), were designed by Manhattan architect George Keister, who was responsible for several important landmark buildings (see Manhattan Nos. 256, 257, and 554). The narrow houses are faced with tawny brick with brownstone trim and massed with a diverse array of window openings, gables, mansards, corbeled cornices, and tall chimneys. Development in this district began in 1877 with a trio of neo-Grec row houses at Nos. 408–412 designed by Rogers & Browne, but further construction awaited the opening of a rail line in 1886, connecting the Mott Haven area to business districts in Manhattan. Following the completion of the centerpiece Bertine Block, Edward Bertine erected two other rows—the Romanesque Revival single-family houses at Nos. 415–425 designed in 1892 by John Hauser and the two-family neo-Renaissance houses at Nos. 434–440 designed by Adolph Balschun, Jr. Finally, eight tenements were erected in the district, between 1897 and 1899, all designed by local Bronx architect Harry T. Howell.

2 **Mott Haven Historic District,** designated 1986. This district, named for Jordan Mott, who established the Mott Iron Works at East 134th Street

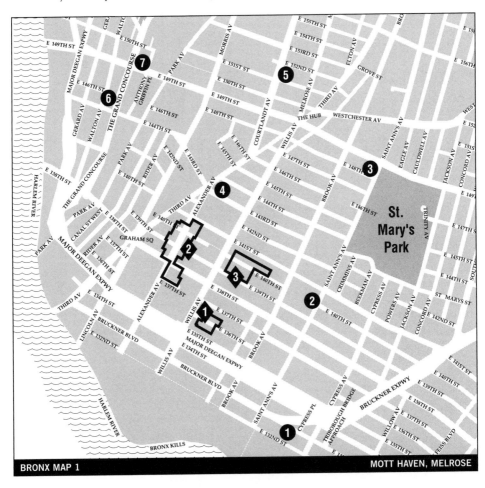

The Mott Haven East Historic District (H.D. 3), East 140th Street between Willis and Brook Avenues, contains the finest 19th-century row houses in the Bronx. Photo by Katherine Khan Reed.

and the Harlem River in 1828, contains the finest 19th-century row houses in the Bronx. Of particular note are two rows of brick houses on Alexander Avenue between East 139th and 140th Streets: a ten-house unit on the east side, built in 1863–65, that is among the earliest row houses in the Bronx; and a twelve-house row across the street, designed in 1881 by Charles Romeyn. The district also includes two imposing churches—Saint Jerome's Roman Catholic (Delhi & Howard, 1898) and the Third Baptist (Frank Ward, 1901)—a Carnegie public library branch (Babb, Cook & Willard, 1905; see Manhattan No. 538), and a police station (Thomas O'Brien, 1924).

3 Mott Haven East Historic District, designated 1994. This small district, facing onto East 139th and 140th Streets, exemplifies urban residential development in the southern part of the Bronx in the final years of the 19th century and the first years of the 20th century as new mass transit lines made this area accessible to working- and middle-class New Yorkers. The earliest buildings in the district are single-family neo-Grec row houses erected by architect/builder William O'Gorman in 1887–92 at 403–445 East 139th Street and 406–450 East 140th Street. An additional row, built by O'Gorman in 1897–1900 at 409–427 East 140th Street, has picturesque facades with Romanesque and Renaissance detail designed by Walter Hornum. By the late 1890s, speculative builders were erecting tenements, rather than row houses, in Mott Haven. O'Gorman and Hornum were responsible for a tenement at 407 East 140th Street. The remaining nine tenements in the district were designs of two of the most prolific apartment-house architects in New York City—George Pelham (Nos. 441–461 East 140th Street, 1902–03) and Neville & Bagge (Nos. 465–481 East 140th Street, 1901–02). Many of the early residents of the district were of German birth or descent. They commissioned the Second Saint Peter's German Evangelical Lutheran Church, a neo-Gothic complex designed by Louis Allmendinger and built in 1911 at 435 East 140th Street.

INDIVIDUAL LANDMARKS

❶ Bronx Grit Chamber, 158 Bruckner Boulevard (McKim, Mead & White, 1936–37), designated 1982. The Bronx Grit Chamber is a primary component of the Ward's Island Sewage Treatment Works, New York City's first major project to alleviate water pollution. The exterior of the building, a late work of McKim, Mead & White, is within the tradition of the monumental public buildings designed by the firm and is evidence of the fact that even the most utilitarian buildings were deemed worthy of impressive architectural expression.

❷ Saint Ann's Church (Episcopal) and Graveyard, 295 Saint Ann's Avenue (1840–41), designated 1967. The oldest surviving church in the Bronx, Saint Ann's was erected on the country estate of Gouverneur Morris, Jr., as a memorial to his mother. The Morrises, for whom the neighborhood of Morrisania is named, were a prominent colonial family. (Gouverneur Morris, Sr., was one of the framers of the Constitution.) The simple vernacular fieldstone church is articulated by Gothic windows and is capped by a Greek Revival steeple. The cemetery contains the graves of many members of the Morris family.

❸ Public School 27 (Saint Mary's Park School), originally Public School 154, 519 Saint Ann's Avenue (C. B. J. Snyder, 1895–97), designated 1995. One of the earliest designs of C. B. J. Snyder, then superintendent of school buildings, this limestone, brick, and terra-cotta school was designed with a combination of elements derived from Dutch and English colonial sources, including scrolled gables and an octagonal bell tower. The school is representative of the impressive neighborhood buildings

erected by the city as symbols of the importance of education to New York's citizens.

❹ Fire Hook and Ladder Company 17, also now Engine Company 60, 341 East 143rd Street (Michael J. Garvin, 1906–07), designated 2000. Mott Haven became part of New York in 1874, and soon after one of the earliest paid fire companies in the Bronx was established here. Garvin, who served as the first commissioner of buildings in the borough, designed this firehouse in the prevailing neoclassical style, embellishing the monumental facade with rusticated piers and carved stone ornament.

❺ 614 Courtlandt Avenue Building (1871–72), designated 1987. Erected by the saloon keeper Julius Ruppert as a saloon and meeting hall serving the German community of Melrose South, this building is a simple French Second Empire structure with cast-iron window lintels and a handsome two-story mansard roof.

❻ Public School 31, 425 Grand Concourse (C. B. J. Snyder, 1897–99), designated 1986. Public School 31 is one of a large number of schools erected in the Bronx to accommodate the waves of people moving to the borough from other parts of New York City and abroad. A relatively early work of the school architect C. B. J. Snyder, Public School 31 was one of the first Collegiate Gothic public schools in New York, and it set the stage for Snyder's better-known examples of the style, including Morris High School (see No. 10 and H.D. 5).

❼ Bronx Post Office, 560 Grand Concourse, at East 149th Street (Thomas Harlan Ellett, 1935–37), designated 1976. The Bronx Post Office, the largest of New York's twenty-nine Depression-era post offices, was designed by Thomas Harlan Ellett as part of a Department of the Treasury program to employ out-of-work architects. Almost as soon as it was completed, the gray brick edifice was proclaimed a "significant example of an evolving American style, a new classicism free of dependence on the works of antiquity." Important works of art were commissioned for many of the post offices of this period. On the exterior of the Bronx Post Office are a pair of limestone panels, *The Letter* by Henry Kreis and *Noah* by Charles Rudy; the lobby contains a significant series of murals by Ben Shahn on the theme of America at work.

HISTORIC DISTRICTS

❹ Longwood Historic District (and Extension), designated 1980 and 1983. The Longwood Historic District, located in the Morrisania section of the South Bronx, was almost entirely developed by George B. Johnson, who purchased the land in 1898. The cohesive character of the area can be traced to the fact that the majority of houses were designed by the same architect, Warren C. Dickerson. Most of the

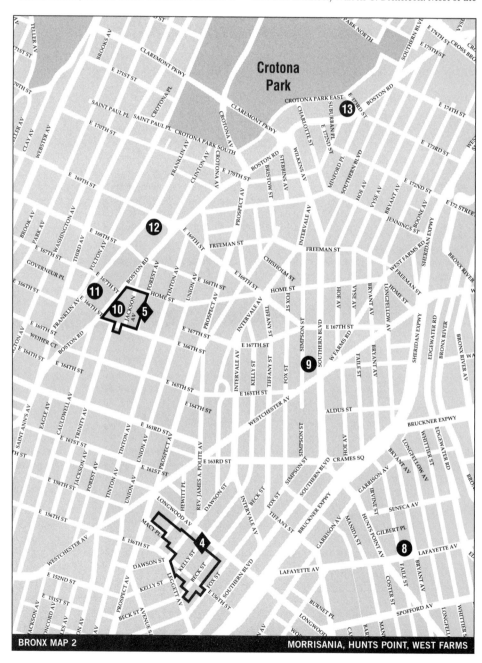

Longwood Historic District (H.D. 4), Beck Street between Longwood Avenue and East 156th Street. The cohesive character of the district is the result of the work of Bronx architect Warren C. Dickerson. Photo by Paul Sachner.

houses in the historic district are semidetached two- and three-family neo-Renaissance structures. Especially fine examples line Dawson, Kelly, Beck, and East 156th Streets. Among the distinctive features are the use of Roman brick and the roofs with false mansards capped by polygonal or cone-shaped peaks. Also in the district are a series of simple single-family houses on Hewitt Place, designed by the Bronx architect Charles S. Clark; several apartment houses; a church; and a former synagogue.

5 Morris High School Historic District, designated 1982. The Morris High School Historic District focuses on the architect C. B. J. Snyder's masterful Collegiate Gothic school building (1900–04; see No. 10) but also contains rows of neo-Renaissance houses on Jackson and Forest Avenues that were erected in this section of Morrisania around the same time as Morris High. The houses were designed by four local Bronx architects. The majority are the work of the prolific Warren C. Dickerson, with additional designs by John H. Lavelle, Harry T. Howell, and Hugo Alden. Construction in the district responded to the rapid population growth in the southwest Bronx in the early 20th century as subway and elevated train lines began to link this area to Manhattan. The district contains one survivor from Morrisania's rural past—the High Victorian Gothic red brick Trinity Episcopal Church of 1874.

INDIVIDUAL LANDMARKS

8 Peter S. Hoe House, Sunnyslope, later Temple Beth Elohim, now the Bright Temple A.M.E. Church, 812 Faile Street (c. 1860), designated 1981. This picturesque Gothic Revival villa is an extraordinary survivor from the mid-19th century. Built for Peter S. Hoe, a member of the firm R. M. Hoe & Co., manufacturers of printing equipment, Sunnyslope was part of a 14.6-acre estate in rural West Farms. Although the architect is not known, this compact, asymmetrical stone house is in the style of Calvert Vaux and may have been inspired by one of the designs Vaux published in his 1857 book *Villas and Cottages.* Most of the other country houses in West Farms were destroyed as the area was urbanized after 1900, but Sunnyslope was saved when it was converted into a synagogue in 1919.

9 62nd Police Precinct Station House, later 41st Police Precinct Station House, 1086 Simpson Street (Hazzard, Erskine & Blagden, 1912–14), designated 1992. As the West Farms neighborhood rapidly developed in the early 20th century, new civic structures were required, and the police department erected this imposing limestone-fronted Italian Renaissance–inspired precinct house. The design reflects the City Beautiful notion of erecting sophisticated buildings to ennoble the civic sector and to provide beauty for all citizens.

10 Morris High School Auditorium (interior), East 166th Street at Boston Road (C. B. J. Snyder, 1900–04; 1926), designated 1982. The Collegiate Gothic Morris High School, located within the Morris High School Historic District (see H.D. 5), was the first major public secondary school in the Bronx and is one of the masterpieces of the New York City school architect C. B. J. Snyder. The auditorium (now Duncan Hall), a high churchlike space with a balcony, is perhaps the finest interior in any city school. The room contains elaborate Gothic plasterwork, steel-ribbed vaults set within Tudor arches, stained-glass windows, and a series of organ pipes. It is decorated with several murals, most prominently the French artist Auguste Gorguet's monumental 1926 World War I memorial entitled *After Conflict Comes Peace.* The New York City School Construction Authority restored the auditorium in 1991.

11 Second Battery Armory, 1122 Franklin Avenue (Charles C. Haight, 1906–11; addition, Benjamin W. Levitan, 1926–28), designated 1992. This boldly massed brick structure is the earliest permanent armory erected in the Bronx. The building, with its crenellated roofline and restrained Gothic detailing, was designed by Charles C. Haight, one of New York's leading architects and a specialist in the use of Gothic design. The narrow wing on Franklin Avenue contains offices and company rooms (a story was successfully added in 1926–28) with a vast drill shed behind.

12 New York Public Library, Morrisania Branch, originally the McKinley Square Branch, 610 East 169th Street (Babb, Cook & Willard, 1907–08), designated 1998. A petition drive by local residents led to the establishment of this public

Sunnyslope (No. 8), a picturesque mid-19th-century Gothic Revival villa.
Photo by Carl Forster.

library in 1908. The fourth library built in the Bronx with funds from Andrew Carnegie, the T-shaped structure occupies a curved lot beside Franklin Avenue. The architects, who designed eight Carnegie branches and the philanthropist's Manhattan mansion (see Manhattan No. 477), embellished the red brick facade with handsome neoclassical details executed in limestone.

🔞 **Herman Ridder Junior High School,** 1619 Boston Road (Walter C. Martin, 1929–31), designated 1990. Herman Ridder was the first "modernistic" Art Deco public school in New York City and one of the first schools erected specifically for use as a junior high. The building, faced with limestone and yellow brick enlivened by subtle polychromatic trim, has dramatically massed vertical buttresses and an entrance tower capped by setbacks modeled on the form of contemporary skyscrapers. The ornamentation incorporates abstract Art Deco elements and such iconographic features as stylized figures of male and female students, open books, and lamps of knowledge.

HISTORIC DISTRICT

◆ **Clay Avenue Historic District,** designated 1994. The two blockfronts of Clay Avenue between East 165th and 166th Streets make up one of the most unified and harmonious streetscapes in the Bronx. The district contains thirty-two residential buildings—twenty-eight semidetached two-family houses designed by Bronx architect Warren C. Dickerson in 1901, a single-family house erected for hardware merchant Francis Keil in 1906 (Charles S. Clark, architect), and three corner apartment buildings de-

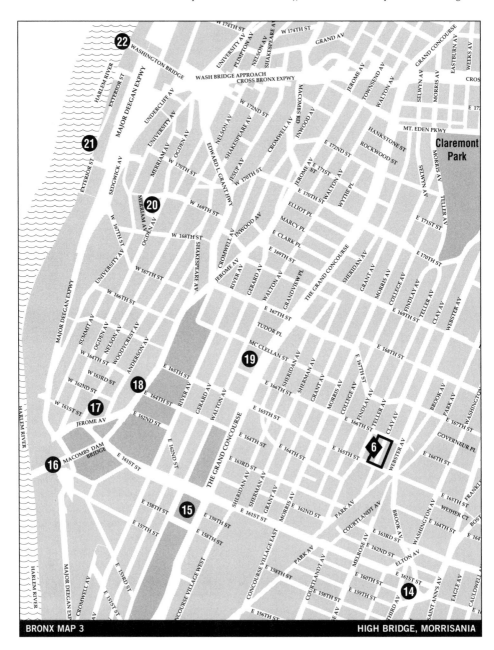

signed by Neville & Bagge in 1909–10. Dickerson's houses are a picturesque group of transitional Romanesque Revival/neo-Renaissance dwellings with brick facades, limestone trim, and a variety of peaked and scrolled gables and angled and rounded towers. The district is located on the site of Fleetwood Park, a trotting-horse park that ceased operations in 1898 just as this section of Morrisania was being intensively developed as a residential neighborhood.

INDIVIDUAL LANDMARKS

⑭ Bronx Borough Courthouse, East 161st Street at Third Avenue (Oscar Bluemner and Michael J. Garvin, 1905–15), designated 1981. The former Bronx Borough Courthouse was erected to serve the judicial needs of the rapidly growing borough. Garvin, a close political associate of the borough president, received the commission for the building, but he retained Bluemner to undertake the actual design work. Bluemner, who was trained as an architect in Europe and designed only a few buildings in New York, is best known as a pioneer of modern American painting. The Beaux-Arts courthouse is a massive granite structure embellished with overscaled French-inspired detail.

⑮ Bronx County Building, also known as the Bronx County Courthouse, 851 Grand Concourse (Max Hausle and Joseph H. Freedlander, 1931–35), designated 1976. This monumental limestone-faced structure is an impressive example of the austere classicism popular for public edifices in the 1930s. Its sculptural program is especially striking. The carved detail includes Charles Keck's frieze of heroic figures symbolically engaged in various modes of productive employment (e.g., agriculture, industry, the arts). Eight freestanding groups of figures carved in pink Georgia marble (two flanking each of the four entrances) represent such themes as achievement, progress, and the majesty of law. The sculptor Adolph Weinman carved two of these compositions and also supervised the work of three other artists: Edward F. Sanford, George H. Snowden, and Joseph Kiselewski. The building was restored by the New York City Department of General Services.

⑯ Macomb's Dam Bridge and 155th Street Viaduct, see Manhattan No. 546.

⑰ American Female Guardian Society and Home for the Friendless Woody Crest Home, 936 Woodycrest Avenue (William B. Tuthill, 1901–02), designated 2000. Toward the end of the 19th

American Female Guardian Society (No. 17). Photo by Carl Forster.

century, many charitable institutions moved to the Bronx, including the American Female Guardian Society, which acquired this property in suburban Highbridge to serve needy children. Designed by the architect of Carnegie Hall (see Manhattan No. 357) to resemble a large Beaux-Arts mansion, it features an arched entrance, elaborate window surrounds, and a mansard roof pierced by dormers and chimneys. In 1991 the building was converted to a residential care facility for families and individuals with AIDS.

⑱ Park Plaza Apartments, 1005 Jerome Avenue (Horace Ginsberg and Marvin Fine, 1929–31), designated 1981. As one of the first and most prominent Art Deco apartment houses in the Bronx, the Park Plaza ushered in the style that was to change the face of much of the borough. The facade was designed by Marvin Fine, who noted the direct stylistic influence of the new Chrysler and American Radiator Buildings (see Manhattan Nos. 326 and 275). The orange brick structure contains fine polychromatic terra-cotta ornament, including panels that depict an architect presenting a model of his building to the Parthenon.

⑲ Andrew Freedman Home, 1125 Grand Concourse (Joseph H. Freedlander and Harry Allan Jacobs, 1922–24; wings, David Levy, 1928–31), designated 1992. At his death in 1915, Andrew Freedman left most of his money for the establishment of a home for the elderly, with the unusual proviso that it care for poor people who had once been affluent. Freedman was a wealthy capitalist and Tammany Hall leader who was involved in financing the construction of the IRT subway and was, from 1894 to 1902, the controversial owner of the New York Giants baseball team. The design of the limestone-clad building is a free interpretation of Italian Renaissance architecture, combining the balanced rectilinearity of urban palazzi with the setting and terraces of a rural villa. The building continues to serve the elderly but now draws its residents from a broader spectrum of the community.

⑳ Public School 91, now Public School 11, 1257 Ogden Avenue (George W. Debevoise, 1889; additions, C. B. J. Snyder, 1905, and Walter C. Martin, 1930), designated 1981. As the population of the West Bronx rapidly increased late in the 19th century, the New York City Board of Education planned several new schools. Former Public School 91, one of the few surviving early school buildings in the borough, is a Romanesque Revival structure with a massive stone base, brick upper stories, and a mansard roof. The Ogden Avenue wing was added in 1905; the gymnasium/auditorium wing was built along Merriam Avenue in 1930.

㉑ High Bridge, see Manhattan No. 580.

㉒ Washington Bridge, see Manhattan No. 581.

Park Plaza Apartments (No. 18), one of the first and most prominent Art Deco apartment houses in the Bronx. Photo: Landmarks Preservation Commission collection.

HISTORIC DISTRICT

7 **Morris Avenue Historic District,** designated 1986. This one-block-long historic district is a notable example of a uniformly planned streetscape, developed by a single speculative builder working with one architect. In 1906–07 August Jacob purchased both sides of Morris Avenue between East Tremont Avenue and East 179th Street. John Hauser designed the two- and three-story neo-Renaissance two-family brick row houses with their projecting, full-height, angled or rounded bays; all the houses were built before 1910. Hauser was also responsible for the pair of tenements at the Tremont Avenue end of the street.

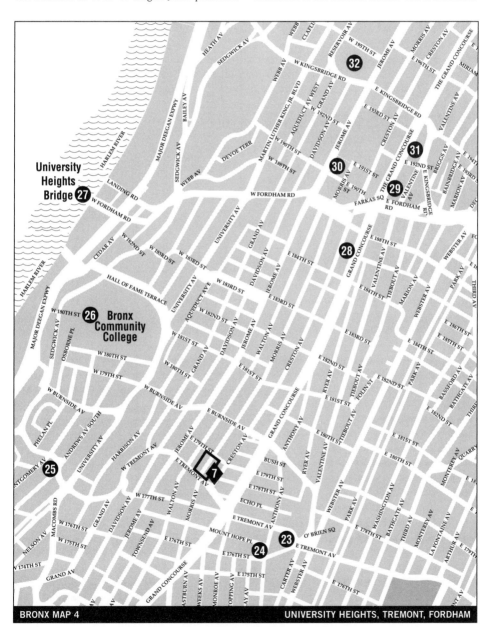

THE BRONX

INDIVIDUAL LANDMARKS

㉓ **Tremont Baptist Church,** 324 East Tremont Avenue (William H. Birkmire, 1904-06, 1911-12), designated 2000. Birkmire's design for the Tremont Baptist Church took full advantage of an unusual site, resulting in a picturesque structure with intersecting gables that follow the sloping curve of East Tremont Avenue, as well as a square tower that rises above the polygonal sanctuary. Inspired by early English Gothic sources, the exterior is clad in gray marble ashlar. Completed in 1913, the church remains an important social and physical presence in the Mount Hope neighborhood.

㉔ **Edwin and Elizabeth Shuttleworth House,** also known as the 1857 Anthony Avenue House (Neville & Bagge, 1896), designated 1986. One of the few surviving suburban residences in the southern Bronx, this house was built for a prosperous stone dealer and his wife. While the firm Neville & Bagge was responsible for the basic design, it is probable that Shuttleworth specified the use of one of the varieties of stone that he sold (stone houses were uncommon in the Bronx) and commissioned the sculpted detail from one or more of his most talented carvers. The idiosyncratic ornament, including male and female figures, marine elements, and portrait busts, survives as a monument to the anonymous stone carvers who created some of New York's finest architectural detail.

㉕ **Messiah Home for Children,** 1771–1777 Andrews Avenue South (Charles Brigham, 1905–08), designated 1997. Towers, turrets, and elaborately curved Flemish gables embellish the brick and stone facades of this former orphanage. Henry H. Rogers, a leading industrialist who was responsible for the development of the Standard Oil Company, financed the acquisition of the property and the building's construction.

㉖ **New York University,** now Bronx Community College of the City University of New York, Hall of Fame Terrace at Sedgwick Avenue (McKim, Mead & White, Stanford White, partner in charge; plan, 1892–94; construction, 1894–1912). Dramatically sited on a terrace placed at the crest of a steep ridge overlooking the Harlem River, with the Hudson River and the New Jersey Palisades beyond, the for-mer Bronx campus of New York University is a triumph of late 19th-century American architecture. In 1892 NYU decided to move its undergraduate school from its urbanized Washington Square site to a more rural location "suggestive of academic seclusion." White laid out the new campus and designed its classical and Renaissance-inspired buildings, all constructed of yellow Roman brick with terra-cotta and limestone trim. NYU left the campus in 1973, and it was acquired by the City University of New York.

Gould Memorial Library (1894–99), designated 1966, interior 1981. One of White's greatest buildings, this library is both the physical and the symbolic center of the campus. The library, with its temple front and dome, was clearly modeled on the Roman Pantheon. Set at the edge of the terrace, the building was designed to blend with, rather than overpower, its spectacular site. The importance of this design in White's work was recognized in 1919 when his peers chose to create a pair of bronze doors for the library as a White memorial. The Gould Memorial Library contains monumental **interior** spaces. Richly detailed in marble, stone, mosaic, wood, and bronze, with Tiffany glass highlights, the interior was planned as a single unified whole. A long Renaissance-inspired staircase rises from the entrance to the rotunda of the library's main reading room. The rotunda has sixteen columns of green Irish Connemara marble; sculpted, classically garbed figures; and a coffered dome.

Hall of Fame (1900–01), designated 1966. White initially designed an ambulatory at the rear of the library that would take advantage of the superb views to the west; in 1900 the university chancellor, Henry MacCracken, suggested instead the creation of a Hall of Fame commemorating great Americans. White's magnificent colonnade was dedicated in 1901, although construction was not completed until 1912. The open terrace with Guastavino vaults and a tile roof contains the busts of noted scientists, writers, educators, and others who have made their mark on American culture.

Hall of Languages (1892–95) **and Cornelius Baker Hall of Philosophy** (1892–1912), desig-

Gould Memorial Library (No. 26). This late masterpiece by Stanford White is the physical and symbolic center of the former New York University campus, now Bronx Community College. Photo: Landmarks Preservation Commission collection.

nated 1966. Although completed seventeen years apart, these twin classroom buildings, standing to either side of the library, complete the west range of White's 1892 campus plan. They are simpler than the library and serve as foils for that structure, accentuating its grandeur.

Begrisch Hall (Marcel Breuer & Associates, 1956–61), designated 2002. This remarkable trapezoidal structure was designed by Marcel Breuer, architect of the Whitney Museum of American Art (see Manhattan H.D. 33), as part of an expansion of the University Heights campus. Executed in exposed reinforced concrete, this daring modern design stands near the southwest corner of the campus and features a pair of sloping cantilevers that appear to defy gravity. These forms reflect specific programmatic requirements, enclosing a pair of steep-floored lecture halls. The principal facades are decorated with intersecting channels that divide the textured east and west walls into triangles, trapezoids, and rectangles.

Begrisch Hall, Bronx Community College (No. 26). Photo by Carl Forster.

㉗ University Heights Bridge, spanning the Harlem River between West Fordham Road, the Bronx, and West 207th Street, Manhattan (William H. Burr, consulting engineer, with Alfred P. Boller and George W. Birdsall, 1893–95; relocation and extension, Othniel F. Nichols, chief engineer, 1905–08; widening and reconstruction, 1987–92), designated 1984. The University Heights Bridge is a steel-truss structure consisting of a central revolving swing span, three masonry piers, and steel approach spans. The central span and two flanking approach spans were originally located at Broadway (at the northern tip of Manhattan Island) and made up the Harlem Ship Canal Bridge. In 1905–08 the bridge was floated south to its present location, and a second west approach span was constructed. The bridge is especially notable for the aesthetics of its design, a particular concern of the engineer Alfred P. Boller. It has a graceful curved profile, two stone pavilions, four sidewalk shelters with cast-iron piers, and ornate iron railings.

㉘ Loew's Paradise Theater, 2401–2419 Grand Concourse (John Eberson, 1928–29), designated 1997. An elaborate frontispiece, faced in glazed terra cotta and neon letters, advertises the entrance to what was once the largest and most famous movie palace in the Bronx. Designed by John Eberson, who created the "atmospheric theater" type, this Italian-Baroque confection is considered to be one of his most important commissions. The theater closed in 1994.

㉙ Dollar Savings Bank, 2516–2530 Grand Concourse (Halsey, McCormack & Helmer, Adolph L. Muller, architect in charge, 1932–33; additions, 1937–38 and 1949–52), designated 1994, interior 1994. The former Dollar Savings Bank's building grew in three stages from a small granite structure in a Modern Classical style into one of the most impressive buildings on the Grand Concourse. Organized in 1890, the Dollar was the first savings bank chartered in the Bronx. When the bank decided to open a branch near the busy corner of the Grand Concourse and Fordham

Road, it hired a firm that specialized in savings bank design. The Dollar prospered and expanded its branch in 1937–38 and then erected a ten-story tower with a four-faced clock for its headquarters. On the **interior,** the rectangular banking hall is boldly detailed in marble, limestone, terra cotta, bronze, and gold- and silver-leafed plaster, and contains five murals by Angelo Magnanti depicting scenes from early Bronx history.

❸⓿ Saint James Episcopal Church and Parish House, 2500 Jerome Avenue (church, Henry M. Dudley, 1864–65; parish house, Henry F. Kilburn, 1891–92), designated 1980. Designed for a rural parish in what at the time was part of Westchester County, Saint James is a major work by Dudley, one of the leading Gothic Revival church architects of the mid-19th century. It is noteworthy for its straightforward use of materials (fieldstone, red sandstone, wood, and slate) and for the expression of interior spaces (nave, side aisles, transepts, chancel, and porch) on the exterior massing. The Gothic-inspired parish house complements the church building.

❸❶ Poe Cottage, Poe Park, 2640 Grand Concourse (c. 1812), designated 1966. In 1846 Edgar Allan Poe moved from New York City to this small cottage lo-

The Dollar Savings Bank (No. 29), one of the most impressive buildings on the Grand Concourse, contains fine details, including this bronze door. Photo by Carl Forster.

cated in the village of Fordham. He lived in the house until 1849; it was while he resided here that he wrote such masterpieces as "Annabel Lee" and "The Bells." As development swept through Fordham later in the century, the house was slated for demolition, but a public outcry led to its preservation in 1902. In 1913 this shrine to one of America's great writers was moved by the city from its original location across the street to its present site at the north end of Poe Park. The cottage is operated as a house museum by the Bronx County Historical Society.

32 **Eighth Coastal Artillery Armory,** later the Eighth Regiment Armory, 29 West Kingsbridge Road (Pilcher & Tachau, 1912–17), designated as Kingsbridge Armory, 1994. Pilcher & Tachau's design, centering on two tall round towers, was inspired by French architect Eugène-Emmanuel Viollet-le-Duc's mid-19th-century reconstruction of the great French medieval castle at Pierrefonds. At the time of its completion, the armory boasted the world's largest drill hall; measuring 300 by 600 feet, the hall is set beneath a vaulted roof supported by a double-truss steel frame.

CITY BEAUTIFUL

Inspired by the success of the World's Columbian Exposition in Chicago in 1893, many New York architects (several of whom played a prominent role in the fair) reembraced the classical tradition. In subsequent decades, a significant group of monumental civic structures and complexes were commissioned, many of which subscribed to the ideals of the City Beautiful movement. The Bronx has two important examples: the unfinished campus of New York University (now Bronx Community College), planned prior to the fair by McKim, Mead & White, and Baird Court at the Bronx Zoo, designed by Heins & La Farge (Bronx Nos. 26 and 35). The plan of the latter project is symmetrical and longitudinal, terminating at the south end with a monumental domed Elephant House. This and other structures in the court are decorated with sculpted heads and reliefs illustrating the various animals that were originally housed in each building.

In Manhattan, one of the most ambitious examples of the City Beautiful movement is Audubon Terrace (Manhattan H.D. 43). Designed by Charles P. Huntington, the museums and research institutions that form the Washington Heights complex are notable for their unified style and cultural purpose. Other outstanding examples from this period include the Appellate Division Courthouse, the New York Public Library, and the gateway to the Manhattan Bridge (see Manhattan Nos. 193, 278, 120), all of which have elaborate stonework and statuary. In Brooklyn, the movement's impact was most strongly expressed in a series of new entrances to Prospect Park, located at Grand Army Plaza, 3rd Street, 15th Street, and Ocean Avenue, and in the partially completed design of the Brooklyn Museum of Art (Brooklyn Nos. 79 and 75).

When the incorporated villages of Richmond became Staten Island and joined the city in 1898, a new civic center was proposed for the waterfront in St. George. This ambitious plan was never fully realized. However, two neoclassical buildings by Carrère & Hastings were built: Staten Island Borough Hall and the Richmond County Courthouse (Staten Island Nos. 13 and 12). Subsequent additions to the complex were designed in a complementary manner, including the former 120th Police Precinct House and the Family Court (Staten Island Nos. 11 and 10). The movement's impact was also felt in residential areas, particularly in the design of neighborhood libraries, schools, police precincts, and firehouses.

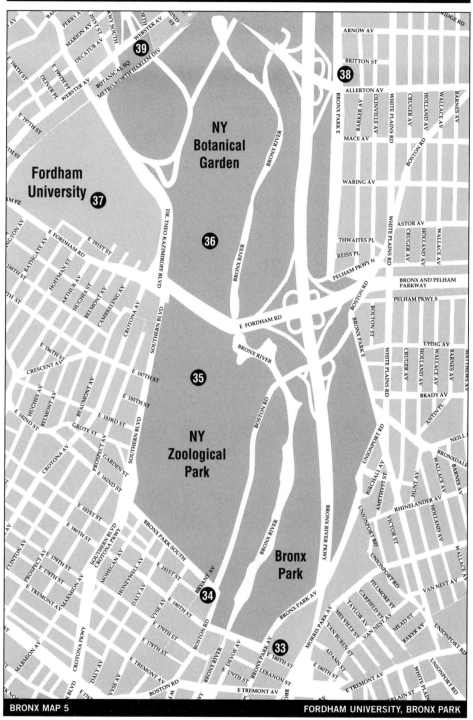

INDIVIDUAL LANDMARKS

㉝ New York, Westchester & Boston Railroad, Administration Building, now the East 180th Street (No. 2 and No. 5) Subway Station, 481 Morris Park Avenue (Fellheimer & Long and Allen H. Stem, 1910–12), designated 1976. The short-lived New York, Westchester & Boston Railroad ran from Manhattan, through the Bronx, to White Plains and Port Chester, from 1912 until 1937. The stations, designed by a nationally known firm of railroad architects, were modeled after Florentine villas. The 180th Street building, which served as both station and offices, has an arcade, arched windows, and two square towers. In 1941, the section of "the Westchester" located within city limits was incorporated into the IRT system.

㉞ Old West Farms Soldiers' Cemetery, 2103 Bryant Avenue (1815–), designated 1967. Situated in a modest landscaped enclosure, this cemetery is the oldest public veterans' burial ground in the Bronx. It serves as the last resting place of veterans of four wars—the War of 1812, the Civil War, the Spanish-American War, and World War I.

㉟ New York Zoological Park (The Bronx Zoo), Bronx Park, south of East Fordham Road. The New York Zoological Park (now Wildlife Conservation Society) was established in 1895. Under its first director, William T. Hornaday, the society assumed control of approximately 261 unspoiled acres in the southern half of Bronx Park. Construction began in 1898 and the zoo, originally consisting of wood structures and outdoor pens, formally opened to the public in November 1899.

Paul J. Rainey Memorial Gates, park entrance at East Fordham Road (Paul Manship, sculptor, and Charles A. Platt, architect, 1929–34), designated 1967. This pair of monumental bronze gates is one of the finest examples of Manship's

New York Zoological Park (No. 35), Paul J. Rainey Memorial Gates. One of the finest examples of Paul Manship's sculpture, at the world's first zoological research center. Photo by Joseph Brooks.

One of the most impressive buildings in the New York Zoological Park is the former Elephant House (No. 35), designed by Heins & La Farge. Photo by Carl Forster.

elegant public sculpture. The work consists of two gates with stylized plant and animal motifs. The gates were set within Platt's architectural framework. They were a gift of Grace Rainey Rogers in memory of her brother, Paul Rainey, a big-game hunter and supporter of the zoo.

Rockefeller Fountain, inside East Fordham Road entrance (Heins & La Farge, 1910), designated 1968. A gift of William Rockefeller, this 18th-century-style Italian fountain is set onto an exuberant basin designed by Heins & La Farge.

Baird Court, now Astor Court, south of East Fordham Road entrance (1899-1910, 1922), designated 2000. Modeled on the "Court of Honor" at the World's Columbian Exposition in Chicago in 1893, Baird Court consists of five neoclassical animal houses designed by Heins & La Farge, and a sixth building by Henry D. Whitfield. The plan is symmetrical and longitudinal, anchored at the ends by the domed Elephant House and a grand Italian Renaissance–inspired stair terrace. Animal sculptures decorate the animal houses, including figures and reliefs by Eli Harvey, Charles R.

Knight, and Alexander Phimster Proctor. Landscape architect Harold A. Caparn designed the grounds, fashioning the surrounding woodlands into animal habitats.

36 New York Botanical Garden, Bronx Park, north of East Fordham Road. The organization of the New York Botanical Garden in 1891 was inspired by the success of the Royal Botanic Garden at Kew, England. The garden and nearby New York Zoological Park (see above) were founded shortly after New York City acquired Bronx Park in 1884. The parkland had been part of the Lorillard estate, and the Botanical Garden incorporates the former Lorillard Snuff Mill. The 250-acre Botanical Garden was planned in 1895–96, but landscape and construction work did not actually begin until 1899.

Conservatory, now the Enid A. Haupt Conservatory, Kazimiroff Boulevard (Lord & Burnham, William R. Cobb, architect in charge, 1896–1902), designated 1973. The magnificent conservatory consists of a central domed rotunda (known as the Palm House) and ten connecting greenhouses. Cobb is credited with the design and the structural system, which was originally steel, cast iron, wood, and glass and was inspired by mid-19th-century exposition halls and horticultural structures, notably the Palm House at Kew. The conservatory was rehabilitated in 1976–78 under the direction of the architect Edward Larrabee Barnes and was renamed for the philanthropist who provided much of the funding. In 1997 a more extensive rehabilitation project was completed by Beyer Blinder Belle, architect, which entailed the disassembly of the building and the replacement of the wooden framing with aluminum, as well as a complete upgrading of the technical systems.

Lorillard Snuff Mill, Bronx River (c. 1840), designated 1973. One of the rare surviving examples of early industrial architecture in the city, this fieldstone and brick mill used the water power of the Bronx River to grind tobacco into snuff. The mill was in operation until 1870, when the Lorillard company moved to New Jersey. The building was rehabilitated in the 1950s.

37 Fordham University, East Fordham Road at East 191st Street. Fordham University, originally known as Saint John's College, received its first students in 1841. The campus is located on the former Rose Hill estate of the Brooklyn merchant Horatio S. Moat, which was purchased by Bishop John Hughes (later New York's first Catholic archbishop) in 1839.

Horatio Shepheard Moat House, now the Administration Building (1836–38; additions, 1907), designated as Rose Hill, 1970. The central part of this fieldstone building was originally a freestanding country house erected on the Rose Hill estate by Horatio S. Moat. It is a superb example of the Greek Revival style, distinguished by a fine Ionic entrance portico and an octagonal cupola. The building became the nucleus of Saint John's College, later Fordham University; the wings were added by the university in 1907.

Alumni House, (c. 1840), designated 1981. Although a stone plaque clearly dates this small fieldstone building to 1840, the exact date that construction began and what the building's original use was are not known. The austere rectilinear structure is a vernacular example of Greek Revival design, notable for the simplicity of its massing and fenestration.

Saint John's Church, now University Church (William Rodrigue, 1841–45; enlargement, Emile Perrot, 1928–29), designated as Fordham University Chapel, 1970. Rodrigue, a teacher at Saint John's College, as well as the brother-in-law of Bishop John Hughes, designed this Gothic Revival stone church with its tall pinnacled tower as the focal point of the campus of this new Catholic university. The chapel and nearby residence hall form the northern arm of the U-shaped complex known as Queen's Court (formerly the "Old Quad"). The chapel was enlarged in 1928–29 with the addition of the large transept.

Saint John's Hall, Queen's Court (William Rodrigue, 1841–45), designated 1970. This fieldstone building was the first dormitory on the Fordham campus. It was designed in a Gothic Revival style that is reminiscent of English collegiate architecture.

38 **52nd Police Precinct Station House,** 3016 Webster Avenue (Stoughton & Stoughton, 1904–06), designated 1974. This romantic red brick police station was modeled on the Italian Renaissance villas of Tuscany, as is especially evident in the gabled roof slopes and the square four-faced clock tower. The modestly scaled civic structure gains stature from the architects' exploitation of inexpensive materials—brickwork laid in a diaper pattern, terra-cotta plaques, and blue tile window spandrels.

39 **United Workers Cooperative Colony (The "Coops"),** 2700–2774 Bronx Park East (Springsteen & Goldhammer, 1925–27) and 2846–2870 Bronx Park East (Herman Jessor, 1927–29), desig-

nated 1992. The United Workers Cooperative Association was founded by left-wing secular Jewish garment workers who purchased land across from Bronx Park to erect high-quality housing with large apartments and plenty of fresh air and light. The earliest buildings form a neo-Tudor complex set around a large garden. The multiple entrances are ornamented with smoking factories, a hammer and sickle, and other details consistent with the group's beliefs. Architecturally, the second complex is more radical, adapting the expressive brickwork employed on contemporary workers' housing in Vienna and elsewhere in Europe. While the cooperative failed during the Depression, the buildings survive as a testament to a commitment to quality housing for all people.

United Workers Cooperative Colony (No. 39). The brickwork reflects contemporary European designs for workers' housing. Photo by Carl Forster.

INDIVIDUAL LANDMARKS

40 Bedford Park Congregational Church, 2988 Bainbridge Avenue (Edgar K. Bourne, 1891–92), designated 2000. Built to serve the recently developed railroad suburb of Bedford Park, this charming rustic church was designed by Edgar K. Bourne, son of the congregation's founder. Clad in rough-dressed fieldstone, the building's character is eclectic, combining forms and features inspired by the Shingle, Queen Anne, and Romanesque Revival styles.

41 Williamsbridge Reservoir Keeper's House, 3400 Reservoir Oval (New York City Department of Public Works, 1889–90, George W. Birdsall, chief engineer), designated 2000. To provide an adequate supply of fresh water to the western section of the Bronx, New York City built the Bronx and Byram River water systems during the 1880s. At Williamsbridge, a large oval reservoir was completed in 1889, along with the keeper's house to oversee maintenance. The reservoir was drained in 1925, and in 1946 the house became a private residence. Constructed from rock-faced gneiss with granite trim, this L-shaped structure was acquired by the Mosholu Preservation Corporation in 1998.

A timber-framed Queen Anne–style porch serves as the entrance to the Bedford Park Congregational Church (No. 40). Photo by Carl Forster.

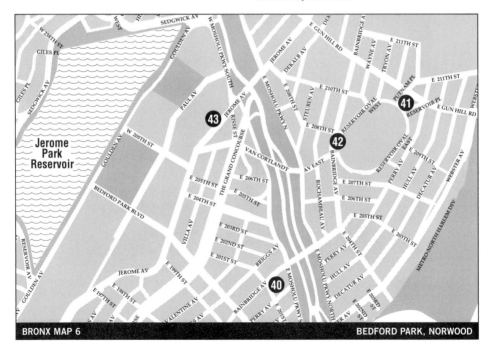

㊷ High Pumping Station, 3205 Jerome Avenue (New York City Department of Water Supply, Gas & Electricity, 1901–06, George W. Birdsall, chief engineer), designated 1981. The High Pumping Station, constructed as part of the Jerome Reservoir complex, pumped water to consumers throughout the Bronx, providing the necessary pressure to permit water to reach the upper floors of the borough's many new apartment houses. Although Birdsall oversaw construction of the project, it is not known whether he was responsible for its Romanesque Revival design. The building has a utilitarian form enlivened by expressive brick detail.

㊸ Isaac Valentine House, now the Valentine-Varian House, 3266 Bainbridge Avenue (1758), designated 1966. This pre–Revolutionary War vernacular Georgian house, constructed of fieldstone, was built for the blacksmith and farmer Isaac Valentine and was sold in 1791 to Isaac Varian. Saved from demolition when it was moved in 1965 onto city-owned property, the house has been restored and is owned and operated by the Bronx County Historical Society as the Museum of Bronx History.

In 2001 the Reservoir Keeper's House (No. 41) was renovated with funds from the Historic Preservation Grant Program of the Landmarks Preservation Commission. Photo by William Neeley Jr.

Issac Valentine House (No. 43). Constructed before the Revolutionary War, the building is now home to the Museum of Bronx History. Photo: Bronx County Historical Society.

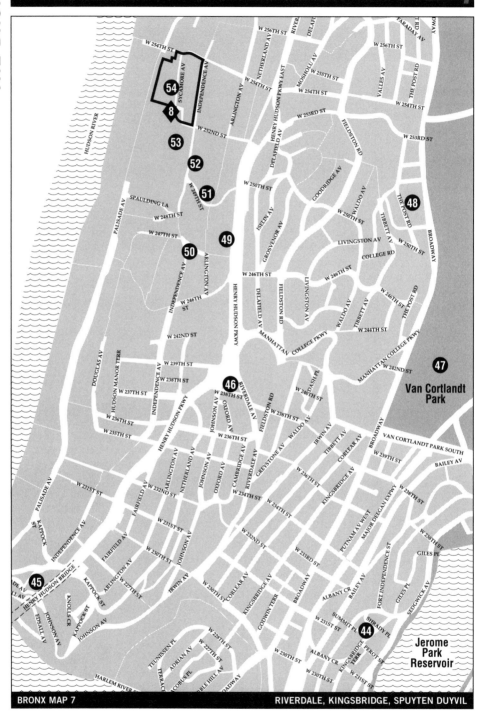

HISTORIC DISTRICT

8 **Riverdale Historic District,** designated 1990. Encompassing approximately fifteen acres of sloping land overlooking the Hudson River, the Riverdale district includes thirty-four buildings on landscaped sites. It is the nucleus of the parcel purchased in 1852 by five wealthy and influential businessmen who intended to create a suburban summer community named Riverdale that could be reached conveniently from Manhattan by the Hudson River Railroad. Riverdale was the first railroad suburb in New York City. The district includes seven original estates linked by a carriage alley (now Sycamore Avenue) and one parcel subdivided from the adjacent Wave Hill estate (see No. 53). All the estates, including that of William and Ann Cromwell (see No. 54), were developed in the 1850s. Several early estate houses in the Italianate and French Second Empire styles remain, as do stables and carriage houses (now converted for residential use), stone walls, iron fences, and important landscape elements. Notable among the carriage houses are that of the Cromwell estate (c. 1856–58) at 5286 Sycamore Avenue, designed in an Italianate style that matches that of the mansion, and, from a later period, the Queen Anne–style example at 5286 Sycamore Avenue, designed by Frederick Clarke Withers (1886) for William S. Duke. Later residences in the district illustrate the changing nature of suburbanization from the mid-19th century to the present. From the 20th century are a series of Colonial Revival houses, including examples by such prominent suburban home designers as Dwight James Baum (5200 Sycamore Avenue, 1922–24) and Julius Gregory (5249 Sycamore Avenue, 1937; and 5294 Sycamore Avenue, 1938).

INDIVIDUAL LANDMARKS

44 **40th Police Precinct Station House,** later the 50th Police Precinct Station House, 3101 Kingsbridge Terrace (Horgan & Slattery, 1901–02), designated 1986. This former police station is a small-scale Beaux-Arts structure with a dramatic curved corner and bold sculptural detail. It reflects the explicit intention of New York's leaders at the beginning of the 20th century to erect civic buildings throughout the five boroughs that would symbolize the importance of municipal government.

45 **Riverdale Presbyterian Chapel,** now Edgehill Church of Spuyten Duyvil (United Church of Christ), 2550 Independence Avenue (Francis H. Kimball, 1888–89), designated 1980. The Edgehill Church, originally built as a chapel of the nearby Riverdale Presbyterian Church (see No. 49), is a survivor from the period when Spuyten Duyvil was a sparsely populated area at the northern edge of New York City. Kimball's masterful design for this small, asymmetrical church nestled into a hillside combines elements from the Romanesque Revival, neo-Tudor, and Shingle styles in an extremely picturesque manner.

46 **Christ Church (Episcopal),** 5040 Riverdale Avenue (R. Upjohn & Son, 1865–66), designated 1967. As might seem appropriate for a church built in the suburban community of Riverdale, this High Victorian Gothic stone structure was designed to resemble a medieval English rural parish church. With its clearly delineated nave, transepts, chancel, and porch, its steep polychromatic slate roof (restored in 1991), its bell cote, diminutive crossing tower, and pointed-arch openings, Christ Church is among the most beautiful early designs of R. M. Upjohn, son of Richard Upjohn, architect of Trinity Church, Manhattan (see Manhattan No. 18).

47 **Frederick and Frances Jay Van Cortlandt House,** also known as the Van Cortlandt Mansion, Van Cortlandt Park, Broadway at West 242nd Street (1748–49), designated 1966, interior 1975. Solidly built of locally quarried fieldstone with contrasting brick trim, Frederick Van Cortlandt's mansion is one of the handsomest Georgian manor houses of the era. The formidable size of the house and the quality of its interiors are evidence of the great wealth amassed by a few prominent 18th-century New York families. The **interior** combines the formal elegance of the Georgian style with features typical of the older, more conservative Dutch Colonial tradition. The mansion was saved thanks to the creation of Van Cortlandt Park, and it has been maintained since 1896 by the National Society of Colonial Dames.

THE BRONX

48 Hadley House, 5122 Post Road (center section, 18th century; north wing, second quarter of the 19th century; south wing and remodeling by Dwight James Baum, 1915–16), designated 2000. The central stone portion of this house is one of the oldest residential structures in the Bronx. Dwight James Baum moved his practice to Fieldston in 1915, and the remodeling of the Hadley House was one of his earliest commissions here. In addition to designing the frame wing and breakfast porch to the south, he emphasized the structure's historic character by preserving many of the original features while incorporating new elements associated with American colonial architecture.

49 Riverdale Presbyterian Church and Manse, 4765 Henry Hudson Parkway (James Renwick Jr., 1863–64), designated 1966. Renwick's English-inspired Gothic Revival stone church was built in 1863 with funding provided by local estate owners, including William E. Dodge Jr., whose Renwick-designed house, Greyston (see below), was under construction nearby. In the adjoining stone manse, now known as Duff House, Renwick combined Gothic Revival forms with a French-inspired mansard roof.

50 William E. and Melissa Phelps Dodge House, Greyston, 690 West 247th Street (James Renwick Jr., 1863–64), designated 1970. Riverdale-on-Hudson became a popular country retreat for wealthy New Yorkers during the 1860s. William E. Dodge, Jr., who together with his father-in-law founded the mining firm Phelps, Dodge & Co., was among the first to build here, commissioning this stone villa from the prominent architect James Renwick, Jr. The angular detail, quirky silhouette, and polychromatic slate roof mark this house as one of Renwick's earliest High Victorian Gothic designs and reflect Renwick's understanding of contemporary English design ideas. In 1961 the Dodge family gave the property to Columbia University Teachers College, which used it as a conference center until the late 1970s, at which time it was sold to a Zen Buddhist community. Having undergone extensive rehabilitation by architect Joseph Pell Lombardi, the house is now once again a private home.

51 Anthony Campagna Estate, now Yeshiva of Telshe Alumni School, 640 West 249th Street (Dwight James Baum, 1929–30; landscape, Vitale & Geiffert), designated 1993. Anthony Campagna, a prominent Italian-born builder of apartment houses in the early decades of the 20th century, erected this vast Tuscan-inspired villa for his own family. It is a major design of Dwight James Baum, an architect whose career centered on the design of historically inspired homes,

Riverdale Presbyterian Chapel (No. 49), a picturesque amalgamation of architectural styles. Photo by Carl Forster.

Donated to the City of New York in 1960, Wave Hill (No. 53) has spectacular views of the Hudson River and Palisades. Photo: Landmarks Preservation Commission collection.

many in the Riverdale area. Baum's limestone and stucco house with sloping tile roof is perched on a site overlooking the Hudson River and is set amid a formal Italian Renaissance–inspired landscape.

㊾ Spaulding Estate Coachman's House, 4970 Independence Avenue (Charles W. Clinton, 1880), designated 1981. This small Stick Style cottage was built as the coachman's residence for Parkside, the estate of the businessman Henry Foster Spaulding. Lively and varied textures are created by board-and-batten siding on the first floor, crossed sticks above, dormer windows with jigsaw ornament, and a slate roof with overhanging eaves.

㊿ Wave Hill, William Lewis Morris House, 675 West 252nd Street (1843–44; later additions), designated 1966. This imposing stone mansion, the focus of a magnificent estate overlooking the Hudson, is operated as an educational-cultural center with an arboretum, greenhouses, art galleries, and a sculpture garden on the grounds. The original (central) section of the house was built for the jurist William Lewis Morris in 1843–44 using locally quarried Fordham gneiss. In 1866, following Morris's death, the house was sold to the publisher William

Henry Appleton. George W. Perkins, one of America's leading financiers, purchased the property in 1893. Between the time of his acquisition of Wave Hill and his family's donation of the estate to New York City in 1960, the side wings and main entrance enframement were constructed and the grounds relandscaped. In 1932 Perkins's tenant, Bashford Dean, built the armor hall at the north end of the house (Dwight James Baum, architect); Dean's armor collection is now at the Metropolitan Museum of Art.

㊾ William D. and Ann Cromwell House, Stonehurst, later the Robert Colgate House, 5225 Sycamore Avenue (1856–58), designated 1970. The importer William Cromwell was one of the original investors who helped to establish Riverdale as a suburban enclave in 1852 (see H.D. 7). He sold his interest a year later, then purchased another plot of land in 1856 for the construction of this villa. After Cromwell's death in 1859, his widow sold the property to the paint manufacturer Robert Colgate. Stonehurst is one of the most elegant mid-19th-century country houses along the Hudson and is unusual within the Italian villa tradition for its classical symmetry. The house derives its name from the beautifully dressed gray stone used in its construction.

INDIVIDUAL LANDMARKS

55 Fonthill, the Edwin Forrest House, now the Admissions Office of the College of Mount Saint Vincent, West 261st Street at Palisade Avenue (1848–52), designated 1966. Located on a bluff overlooking the Hudson, Fonthill is a country house designed to resemble a medieval castle. The building consists of six interlocking octagonal units of varying height, which culminate in a tall, slender tower. Fonthill was erected for the famed Shakespearean tragedian Edwin Forrest (see Manhattan No. 248) by a local builder, Thomas C. Smith, and was named for the English house Fonthill Abbey, built in 1796–1812. In 1856 Forrest sold the property to the Sisters of Charity of Saint Vincent-de-Paul, who have used the house at various times as administrative offices, a chaplain's residence, and a library. Fonthill's stone **carriage house/stable,** now Boyle Hall, and its **cottage** (c. 1848–52, both designated 1981) combine Gothic and Italianate features in a manner representative of the finest in 19th-century rural design.

56 Mount Saint Vincent Academy, now the Administration Building, West 261st Street at Palisade Avenue (Henry Engelbert, 1857–59; additions, 1865, 1883, and 1906–08), designated 1979. The main building on the campus of the College of Mount Saint Vincent is dramatically situated on a hill commanding a sweeping view of the Hudson River and the Palisades. With its complex round arches, tall tower, beautifully articulated brickwork, and two-story verandas, the building is a masterpiece of the Early Romanesque Revival. The expansive structure houses a wide variety of college activities.

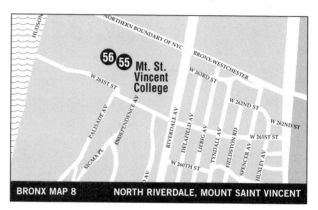

BRONX MAP 8   NORTH RIVERDALE, MOUNT SAINT VINCENT

Fonthill (No. 55), consisting of six interlocking octagonal units and designed to resemble a medieval castle, was built for the famed Shakespearean actor Edwin Forrest. Photo by Carl Forster.

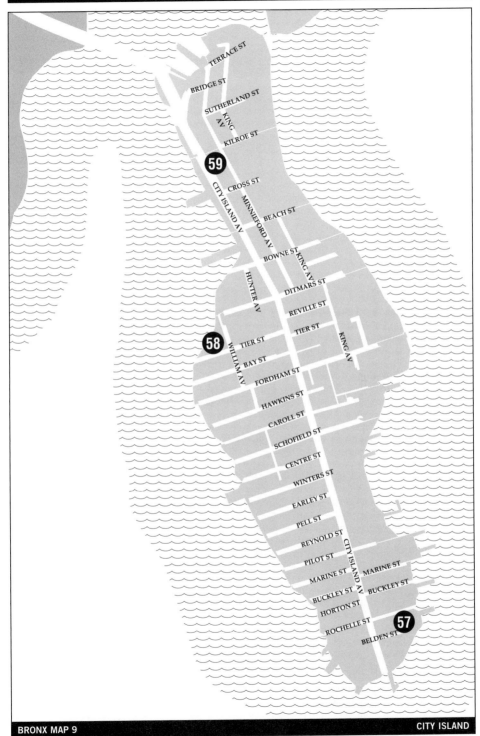

THE BRONX

57 **175 Belden Street** (c. 1880), designated 1981. This small clapboard house, with its superb jigsaw-cut struts and brackets and a slate roof, is one of the finest picturesque cottages in New York City. Although the exact date of construction is not documented, the house was erected during City Island's heyday as a maritime community supported by fishing, shellfishing, sail-making, and shipbuilding.

58 **21 Tier Street** (Samuel Booth, builder, 1896), designated 2000. Built as a summer retreat for Lawrence Delmour, a politician who made his fortune in real estate, and his wife Mary, this waterfront residence faces Eastchester Bay. A rare exam-

ple of the Shingle style in the Bronx, the house has many picturesque elements, including a large covered porch and a corner tower crowned by a conical roof.

59 **Samuel Pell House,** 586 City Island Avenue (c. 1876), designated 2002. Oysterman Samuel Pell constructed this large freestanding frame residence when oyster farms and yacht building were the chief industries on City Island. Designed in the Second Empire style, it has a spacious front porch with curved wood braces, as well as an elaborately detailed mansard roof that retains the original polychrome shingles.

Samuel Pell built this freestanding City Island residence c. 1876 (No. 59). Photo by Carl Forster.

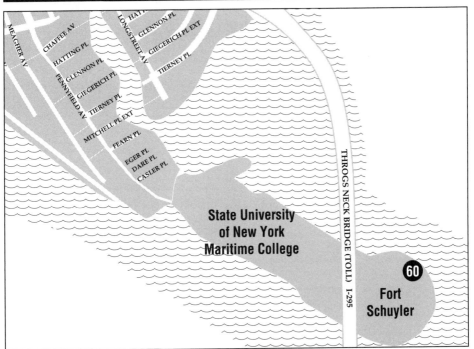

60 Fort Schuyler, now the State University of New York Maritime College, east of the Throgs Neck Bridge (Captain I. L. Smith, 1833–56), designated 1966. Fort Schuyler and its companion across Long Island Sound, Fort Totten (see Queens H.D. 4), were erected to protect the eastern entrance to New York Harbor from Long Island Sound. The massive fort, built of Connecticut granite, has walls up to 11 feet thick and once mounted more than 300 guns. The fort was abandoned in 1870. In 1934 the Works Progress Administration (WPA) rehabilitated the structure for use as a school. The architect William A. Hall converted the gun galleries into a library in 1966–67.

61 Saint Peter's Church (Episcopal), West-chester, Complex and Cemetery, 2500 Westchester Avenue (church, Leopold Eidlitz, 1853–55; alterations, Cyrus L. W. Eidlitz, 1879; Sunday school and chapel building, Leopold Eidlitz, 1867–68; cemetery, 1702–), designated 1976. Saint Peter's congregation was established in the village of Westchester in 1693. Leopold Eidlitz's impressive Gothic Revival stone edifice was the third church building on the site. In its straightforward use of materials and its

emphasis on structural clarity, the building is characteristic of the work of Eidlitz, who was one of the most talented and influential American architects of the 19th century. After part of Saint Peter's was destroyed by fire in 1877, the church was rebuilt and somewhat altered by Leopold's son Cyrus in 1879. Leopold's nearby Sunday school and chapel building (now called Foster Hall) is a superb example of High Victorian Gothic design. The cemetery contains many 18th-century gravestones.

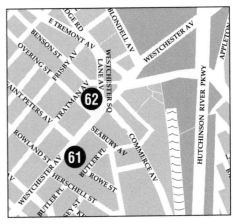

THE BRONX

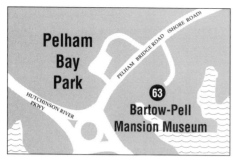

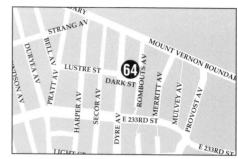

62 Van Schaick Free Reading Room/Huntington Free Library and Reading Room, 9 Westchester Square (Frederick Clarke Withers, 1882–83; addition, William Anderson, 1890–92), designated 1994. In 1882 local philanthropist Peter C. Van Schaick built a free noncirculating library for the village of Westchester, twelve years before it became part of the City of New York. He commissioned a picturesque little brick building from Frederick Clarke Withers, one of the most prominent American architects of the time. The citizens of Westchester rejected the gift, and the building remained vacant until railroad magnate Collis P. Huntington purchased, enlarged, endowed, and renamed the structure. The institution continues to serve as a noncirculating library open to the public.

63 Robert and Marie Lorillard Bartow House, now the Bartow-Pell Mansion Museum, Shore Road, Pelham Bay Park (1836–42), designated 1966, interior 1975, site expanded 1978. Located near Long Island Sound, on land that was once part of the Manor of Pelham, this magnificent neoclassical country seat was built by Robert Bartow, who was descended from the Pell family. The house was purchased by the city in 1888, and after several decades of neglect, restoration was undertaken in 1914 by the International Garden Club under the direction of the architecture firm Delano & Aldrich. The elegant stone house faces a terraced garden dating from 1914–16. The exceptionally fine Greek Revival **interiors** were designed in the manner of Minard Lafever. The site includes an original stone stable/carriage house, later walled gardens, and a small family memorial plot.

64 Public School 15, 4010 Dyre Avenue (Simon Williams, 1877), designated 1978. At the time of its construction, Public School 15—a rare example in New York City of the rural red brick schoolhouse—was largely surrounded by an undeveloped section of Westchester County. The Victorian Gothic building, with its paired gables supported by large brackets and its central bell tower, was designed by Simon Williams, who became the school's principal.

Bartow House (No. 63), now the Bartow-Pell Mansion Museum, a neoclassical country manor house. Photo by John Barrington Bayley, c. 1965.

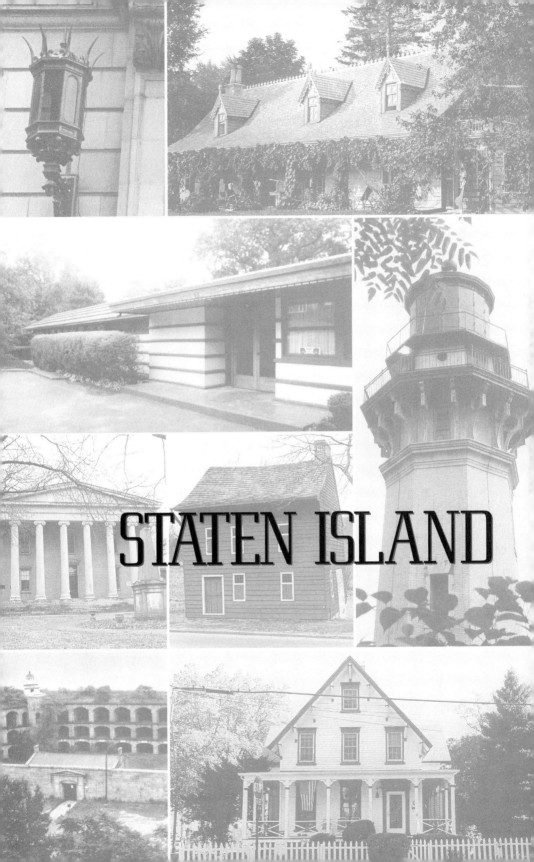

STATEN ISLAND

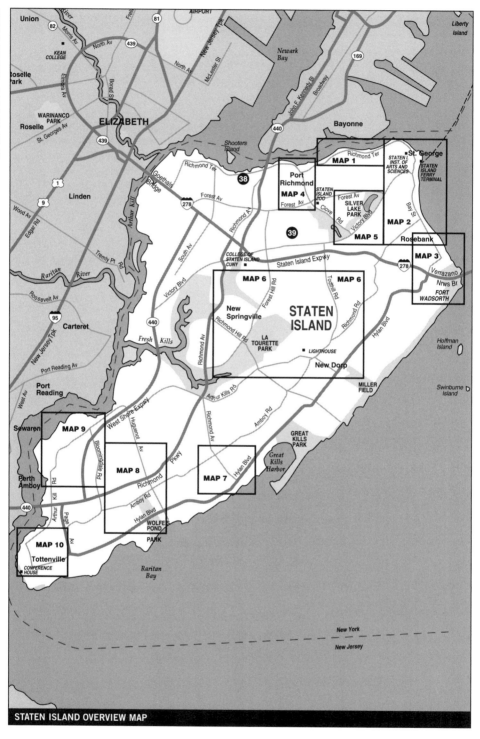

STATEN ISLAND

Union
KEAN COLLEGE
Roselle Park
Roselle
WARINANCO PARK
ELIZABETH
Linden
Carteret
Port Reading
Port Reading
Sewaren
Perth Amboy
Tottenville
CONFERENCE HOUSE

AIRPORT
Newark Bay
Bayonne
Liberty Island

Shooters Island
Port Richmond
MAP 1
MAP 4
Forest Av
St. George
STATEN I. INST. OF ARTS AND SCIENCES
STATEN ISLAND ZOO
SILVER LAKE PARK
MAP 5
MAP 2
Rosebank
MAP 3
STATEN ISLAND FERRY TERMINAL
Verrazano Nrws Br
FORT WADSORTH

COLLEGE OF STATEN ISLAND CUNY
Staten Island Expwy

MAP 6
MAP 6
STATEN ISLAND
New Springville
LA TOURETTE PARK
LIGHTHOUSE
New Dorp

MILLER FIELD
Hoffman Island
Swinburne Island

MAP 9
MAP 8
MAP 7
GREAT KILLS PARK
Great Kills Harbor

WOLFES POND PARK

MAP 10

Raritan Bay

New York
New Jersey

STATEN ISLAND OVERVIEW MAP

INDIVIDUAL LANDMARKS

❶ Cornelius Cruser House, also known as the Kreuzer-Pelton House, 1262 Richmond Terrace (1722; additions, 1770 and 1836), designated 1967. Three construction phases are clearly visible on the exterior of this house. Cornelius Van Santvoord, minister of the Dutch Reformed Church in Port Richmond, erected the original one-room section in the Dutch Colonial tradition. The steep-roofed central wing was added by Cornelius Cruser, and the two-story brick end section in the Federal style was built by Daniel Pelton.

❷ 69 Delafield Place House, also known as the Samuel MacKenzie Elliott House (possibly Calvin Pollard, c. 1850), designated 1967. This beautifully proportioned stone house was built as a real-estate investment by Samuel MacKenzie Elliott, a prominent oculist and eye surgeon and a vocal abolitionist. Elliott, who began purchasing property in northern Staten Island in 1839, built so many suburban houses in the vicinity that the area became known as Elliottville. The Scottish-born doctor/developer is known to have commissioned several designs from the prestigious New York City architect Calvin Pollard, and this Gothic Revival house may be one of them.

❸ Sailors' Snug Harbor, now the Snug Harbor Cultural Center, 914–1000 Richmond Terrace. Sailors' Snug Harbor was established with an 1801 bequest from the merchant Robert Randall, who left a large plot of land north of Washington Square in Manhattan for the establishment of an institution for

the care of "aged, decrepit and worn-out sailors." Randall's bequest was challenged in court, and it was not until 1830 that the case was settled, by which time the Washington Square area was being developed as a prestigious residential neighborhood. Realizing that their Manhattan property was extremely valuable, the trustees of Sailors' Snug Harbor leased the land and in 1831 purchased a large farm on the north shore of Staten Island, where they proceeded to erect a complex of buildings. Sailors' Snug Harbor housed retired seamen at this location until 1976, when it moved to North Carolina. Following a series of court challenges that upheld the validity of landmarks regulation and devised tests to determine its effects on property devoted to charitable purposes, the Sailors' Snug Harbor facility was sold to New York City. The complex is now a cultural center.

Main Buildings, Buildings A through E (Administration Building, Minard Lafever, 1831–33; interior renovation, 1884; dormitories, Minard Lafever, 1831–41, and Richard P. Smyth, 1879–81), designated 1965, interior of Building C, 1982. The centerpiece of the Sailors' Snug Harbor complex is the former Administration Building (Building C), Minard Lafever's earliest surviving work. This magnificent Greek Revival structure, with its monumental Ionic portico, was constructed of Westchester marble. It originally housed all of the institution's functions except for cooking. The plan of the **interior** is Lafever's, but the retangular hall, second-floor gallery, and elliptical dome were redecorated in 1884 with stained glass, murals, and other

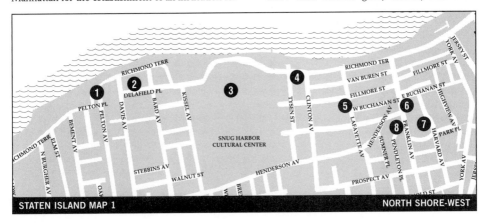

STATEN ISLAND MAP 1 — NORTH SHORE-WEST

painted details in the neo-Grec style. The murals were painted by the New York firm Artman & Fechteler and restored in 1993 by the Ever-Greene Painting Studios. As the number of residents at Sailors' Snug Harbor increased, new dormitory buildings were erected. The pavilions (Buildings B and D) that flank the main building were designed by Lafever in 1831 in a simplified Greek Revival style but were not built until 1839–41. The end pavilions (Buildings A and E), designed by Richard Smyth, echo the form of the central building. Together the buildings form a masterpiece of the Greek Revival.

Chapel, now Veterans Memorial Hall (James Solomon, 1854–56; interior renovation, 1873; addition, 1883), designated 1965, interior 1982. The Manhattan builder James Solomon erected this Italianate chapel in 1855–56; the bell tower that he had recommended was not built until

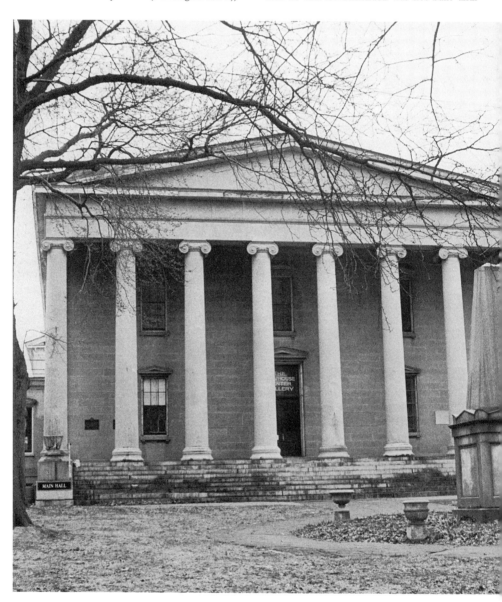

1883. The chapel was an important aspect of life at Sailors' Snug Harbor, since daily attendance was mandatory for all residents. The **interior** of this deconsecrated chapel has a simple rectangular layout with three aisles, a raised platform and shallow apse, and a balcony supported by cast-iron columns. In 1873 the decorator Charles Berry refurbished the chapel, adding trompe l'oeil architectural elements that include the recently restored pilasters and entablature.

Fence (Frederick Diaper, 1841–45), designated 1973. This monumental iron fence, erected to keep residents from unauthorized excursions, extends for more than a third of a mile along Richmond Terrace. The fence was designed by the British-born Diaper, who derived inspiration from the Cumberland Gates in Hyde Park, London; the fence was fabricated by William Alexander of Manhattan.

North Gatehouse (Richard P. Smyth, 1873), designated 1973. The Italianate gatehouse, with its arched central tunnel and diminutive cupola, gave access to the main building complex from Richmond Terrace. It was one of four gatehouses erected in an effort to prevent liquor from being brought onto the property illicitly.

4 **Tysen-Neville House,** also known as the Neville House and the Old Stone Jug, 806 Richmond Terrace (c. 1800), designated 1967. The builders of this exceptional farmhouse of rough sandstone (now whitewashed) were probably Jacob and Mary Tysen. Rehabilitation work on the facade in 1991 revealed that the unusual two-story veranda, which was added at an unknown date, perhaps in the late 19th century, assumed its present configuration around 1910, and that the hexagonal cupola was added at that time. For part of the 19th century, the house was used as a tavern, known as the Old Stone Jug, which was frequented by residents of Sailors' Snug Harbor (see No. 3). The building is often referred to as the Neville House, after Captain John Neville, a retired naval officer who purchased the property in the 1870s.

5 **New Brighton Village Hall,** 66 Lafayette Avenue (James Whitford, 1868–71), designated 1965. This small but impressive French Second Empire brick building was erected at a time when the northern Staten Island village of New Brighton was the suburban home of many prominent New Yorkers. Whitford was a local architect who arrived in Staten Island from England in 1852.

Sailors' Snug Harbor (No. 3). Established as a home for "aged, decrepit, and worn-out sailors," Sailors' Snug Harbor contains a group of exquisite 19th-century Greek Revival buildings. Photo by Carl Forster.

STATEN ISLAND

❻ 105 Franklin Avenue, also known as Hamilton Park Cottage (Carl Pfeiffer, c. 1864), designated 1970. Hamilton Park (originally known as Brighton Park) was one of the earliest suburban residential parks on Staten Island and one of the first self-contained, limited-access suburban subdivisions in the United States. Laid out around 1851–52 by Charles Hamilton, Hamilton Park had dwelling sites set on curving drives amid a naturalistic landscape. Development proceeded slowly; only three or four houses were erected in the 1850s, but in the 1860s the German-born architect Carl Pfeiffer designed twelve additional residences. The Hamilton Park cottages were among Pfeiffer's first American commissions. Somewhat simpler and less picturesque than the earlier Harvard Avenue House (see below), this Italianate brick building has a magnificent arcaded loggia.

❼ 66 Harvard Avenue, also known as the Pritchard House (c. 1853), designated 1968. This Italianate stuccoed house, with its stone trim and its notable wooden porch, balcony, and projecting window hood, is the only intact survivor of Hamilton Park's original suburban residences, which predate the houses designed by Carl Pfeiffer in the 1860s (see above).

❽ 22 Pendleton Place, also known as the W. S. Pendleton House (attributed to Charles Duggin, c. 1855), designated 1969. This Gothic Revival house—with its tower, oriel, varied windows, and steeply pitched gables—commands a high elevation above the Kill van Kull. The house was one of a number of suburban dwellings in New Brighton built as rental units by William S. Pendleton. Several of these houses are known to have been designed by the English-born and -trained architect Charles Duggin, and although there is no specific documentation for this house, it is probably one of his buildings.

The 105 Franklin Avenue House (No. 6) is located in one of the first limited-access suburban developments in America. Photo by Peter Choy.

HISTORIC DISTRICT

◆ Saint George/New Brighton Historic District, designated 1994. The genesis of this district extends back to the 1835 creation of New Brighton, one of the earliest planned suburban communities in

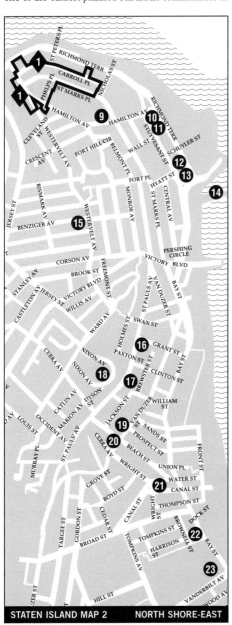

the New York area. New Brighton was established by Thomas E. Davis, an English immigrant who named his projected summer retreat for the famous English seaside resort. Davis erected several houses, including the district's earliest building, the Greek Revival house at 404 Richmond Terrace (c. 1835), before selling the property to a group of investors who laid out the curving streets that survive to this day. A few houses were erected in the late 1830s, but a financial panic in 1837 eventually led to a foreclosure action. Over the next several decades, scattered development occurred in New Brighton, notably a group of semidetached French Second Empire–style houses, such as those at 36–38 and 60–62 Westervelt Avenue, probably dating from the late 1860s. The establishment of a unified ferry terminal at Saint George and the opening of the Staten Island Rapid Transit's rail lines in the mid-1880s led to major development in the northern portion of Staten Island as an increasing number of middle-class families moved there. A real-estate boom in the late 1880s and 1890s, including the construction of a group of Queen Anne, Shingle Style, and Colonial Revival houses, established the dominant character of the district. Most notable are those designed by Edward A. Sargent, Staten Island's leading architect of the late 19th century, who was responsible for such superb Shingle Style dwellings as the Rodewald House (c. 1890) at 103 Saint Marks Place and the Camman House (1895) at No. 125. In the early 20th century, suburban residential development continued with several fine Colonial Revival houses, such as 65 Westervelt Avenue (Thomas C. Perkins, 1908). The district also contains one important institutional complex, Saint Peter's Roman Catholic Church and Rectory. Saint Peter's is the oldest Catholic parish on Staten Island. The neo-Romanesque church, with its soaring tower visible from a distance, was designed by Harding & Gooch in 1900 to replace an earlier building that had burned.

INDIVIDUAL LANDMARKS

❾ Curtis High School, 105 Hamilton Avenue at Saint Marks Place (C. B. J. Snyder, 1902–04; additions, 1922, 1925, and 1937), designated 1982. Staten Island's first secondary school building, Curtis High School was built following the consolidation of

Saint George/New Brighton Historic District (H.D. 1). The district contains several groups of Shingle Style houses on Westervelt Avenue. Photo by Caroline Kane Levy.

Greater New York. It was part of a plan to erect a major high school in each of the outlying boroughs—Erasmus Hall in Brooklyn, Morris (see Bronx No. 10), and Flushing (see Queens No. 25) High Schools were the other three. The school is named for the nationally prominent writer and orator George W. Curtis, who lived nearby. The Collegiate Gothic school is situated in an appropriate campuslike setting.

⑩ Staten Island Family Courthouse, originally Staten Island Children's Courthouse, 100 Richmond Terrace (Sibley & Fetherston, 1929–31), designated 2001. Built to hear spousal and child support cases as part of a larger campaign to decentralize the municipal court system, this neoclassical structure was designed to complement earlier buildings in Staten Island's civic center. Perched on an elevated site overlooking the harbor, the terra-cotta clad court-

house is notable for its human scale and restrained ornamentation.

⑪ 120th Police Precinct Station House, originally 66th Police Precinct Station House and Headquarters, 78 Richmond Terrace (James Whitford, Sr. 1920–23), designated 2000. Set on a raised terrace at the north side of the civic center, this neo-Renaissance station house was designed by a leading figure in Staten Island's civic and business affairs during the early 20th century. Clad in terra cotta treated to resemble limestone, the entrances are surmounted by wrought-iron balconies and figures displaying the seal of New York City.

⑫ Richmond County Courthouse, 12–24 Richmond Terrace (Carrère & Hastings, 1913–19), designated 1982. Shortly after Staten Island became a part of New York City, a new civic center was

120th Police Precinct Station House (No. 11). This impressive neo-Renaissance building is located at the north end of Staten Island's civic center. Photo by Carl Forster.

planned. This impressive temple-fronted L-shaped limestone courthouse and the Staten Island Borough Hall (see below) are the only two major features of the plan that were erected. Carrère & Hastings, one of the preeminent early 20th-century American architecture firms, received the commission for both civic center buildings, probably because John M. Carrère was a resident of Staten Island.

⓭ Staten Island Borough Hall, 2–10 Richmond Terrace (Carrère & Hastings, 1904–06), designated 1982. Borough Hall is the most prominent feature of Staten Island's governmental center and one of the great early 20th-century civic monuments of New York City. Carrère & Hastings designed Borough Hall in a style reminiscent of the brick-and-stone châteaux erected in France during the early 17th century. This is especially evident on the east elevation, facing New York Harbor, where the facade consists of a central pavilion flanked by projecting wings, all crowned by a mansard roof. The massing creates a courtyard reached by a long flight of stairs. A tall clock tower, visible from the harbor, rises from the center of the west elevation.

⑭ U.S. Light-House Service, Third District, Staten Island Depot Office Building, later the U.S. Coast Guard Station Administration Building, 1 Bay Street (Alfred B. Mullett, c. 1865–71; wings, 1901), designated 1980. The relatively small but boldly detailed granite and red brick office building is one of the few surviving examples of the French Second Empire buildings designed by A. B. Mullett during his tenure as supervising architect of the Treasury. The Staten Island lighthouse depot complex was established for the storage of materials destined for East Coast lighthouses and as an experimental station for the testing of new materials and methods of lighthouse operation. The office building was constructed, beginning in 1868, as a fireproof facility for the storage of the depot's records.

⑮ August and Augusta Schoverling House, 344 Westervelt Avenue (1880–82), designated 2001. This picturesque brick house is a distinguished but late example of the Second Empire style. Built by a prosperous firearms merchant, it features a deep timber porch that extends along two facades, as well as angled bay windows to provide views of New York harbor. The house was converted to apartments during the 1930s.

⑯ Public School 15 (Daniel D. Tompkins School), 98 Grant Street (Edward A. Sargent, 1897–98), designated 1996. This former district school commissioned by Middletown Township was completed just as Staten Island became a part of New York City and was renamed P.S. 15. The picturesque building, with its chamfered pavilions, Queen Anne detail, and tall clock tower, was designed by Staten Island's most talented late 19th-century architect, many of whose residential works are in the Saint George/New Brighton Historic District (H.D. No. 1).

⑰ Saint Paul's Memorial Church (Episcopal) and Rectory, 217–225 Saint Pauls Avenue (Edward T. Potter, 1866–70), designated 1975. Saint Paul's Memorial Church and Rectory form one of the finest High Victorian Gothic religious complexes in New York City. The noted architect Edward T. Potter created a dynamic work using a dark gray stone with lighter-colored Connecticut brownstone banding and polished granite dwarf columns on the entrance porch. The church was damaged by fire in 1940 and again in 1985; restoration took place following both fires. The rectory, resembling a rural English parish house, complements the church.

⑱ Caleb T. Ward House, 141 Nixon Avenue (Seth Geer, c. 1835), designated 1978. Located at the crest of Ward's Hill, with a magnificent view of New York Harbor, this monumental mansion is the finest Greek Revival country house surviving in New York City. The house has brick walls stuccoed to simulate stone and an impressive two-story portico. Geer, the builder of La Grange Terrace (see Manhattan No. 152), was involved in a number of Staten Island building projects.

⑲ 364 Van Duzer Street (c. 1835), designated 1973. This house is a fine example of Staten Island vernacular construction that combines the trad-tional curved overhanging eaves of the Dutch Colonial style with a two-story Greek Revival portico. It is one of three dwellings erected by Robert M. Hazard, an early Stapleton developer, shortly after he purchased the site in 1834.

⑳ 390 Van Duzer Street, designated 1973. This house of indeterminate history no longer occupies its original site. The house is thought to be an 18th-century structure onto which a Greek Revival porch, possibly salvaged from another house, was added.

㉑ Edgewater Village Hall, 111 Canal Street in Tappan Park (Paul Kühne, 1889), designated 1968. This Romanesque Revival brick building with a square central tower was erected to house the civic functions of the village of Edgewater. It is one of only two village halls built on Staten Island (see No. 5).

㉒ Dr. James R. Boardman House (1848), designated as the 710 Bay Street House, 1982. Boardman, the resident physician at the nearby Seaman's Retreat hospital (see below) built this wood-frame Italianate house atop a steep bluff overlooking the

Saint Paul's Memorial Church (Episcopal) and Rectory (No. 17). One of the finest High Victorian Gothic religious complexes in New York City. Photo: Landmarks Preservation Commission collection.

Narrows. In 1894 the house was purchased by Captain Elvin Mitchell with money received from the Cunard Lines in recognition of his heroism in saving the lives of all 176 people aboard the SS *Oregon,* which sank off Fire Island.

㉓ Seaman's Retreat, now part of Bayley-Seton Hospital, 75 Vanderbilt Avenue. The Seaman's Retreat was founded by the New York State Legislature in 1831 to care for sick and disabled merchant seamen. The institution served seamen for 150 years. Run by the state until 1883, the facility became a U.S. Marine Hospital and then a U.S. Public Health Service Hospital; government use ceased in 1981. As befits a hospital for sailors, the Seaman's Retreat enjoys a waterfront location with fine harbor views. The retreat's physicians were in the forefront of medical research and reform, campaigning for improved conditions for sailors on ship and in port and undertaking bacteriological research that laid the groundwork for the public health endeavors later carried out by the National Institutes of Health.

Main Building (Abraham Maybie, builder, 1834–37; additions, 1848, 1853, and 1911–12), designated 1985. This imposing Greek Revival hospital, constructed of granite ashlar, originally consisted of a central pavilion (with Doric entrance portico) projecting forward from flanking wings with two-story porches. As the hospital expanded, matching end pavilions were constructed in 1848 and 1853, and an additional story was added to the flanking wings in 1911–12.

Physician-in-Chief's Residence (Staten Island Granite Company, builder, 1842), designated 1985. Designed to harmonize with the nearby hospital building, this house is a severe granite structure in the Greek Revival style.

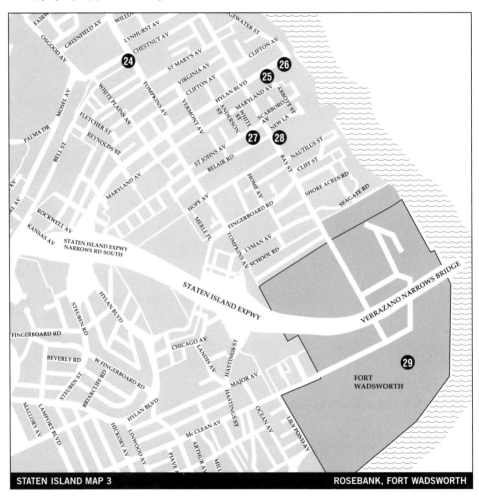
INDIVIDUAL LANDMARKS

㉔ Garibaldi-Meucci Museum, 420 Tompkins Avenue (c. 1845), designated 1965. This small house is preserved by the Sons of Italy as a memorial to two great Italians. Giuseppe Garibaldi, the liberator of Italy, lived in the house in 1851–53 while in exile in the United States. Garibaldi was a guest of Antonio Meucci, one of the early developers of the telephone.

㉕ Henry McFarlane House, later the New York Yacht Club, also known as the McFarlane-Bredt House, 30 Hylan Boulevard (c. 1841–45; additions, c. 1860, c. 1870s, and c. 1890s), designated 1982. The site of this villa adjoining the Alice Austen House (see No. 26) property enjoys commanding views across the

harbor. The house has had many owners and has been substantially enlarged since the original cottage was constructed, apparently by the merchant Henry McFarlane. The earliest addition was built around 1860 when the dry goods merchant Henry Dibblee doubled the size of the dwelling, copying the original detail so that the house appeared to be a single structure. Between 1868 and 1871, the house served as the headquarters of the New York Yacht Club (see Manhattan No. 285); it was during its tenancy that the club first successfully defended the America's Cup.

㉖ Alice Austen House, 2 Hylan Boulevard (c. 1700–50; remodeling, 1846, c. 1852, and 1860–78), designated 1971. This picturesque house overlooking the Narrows was the home of Alice Austen

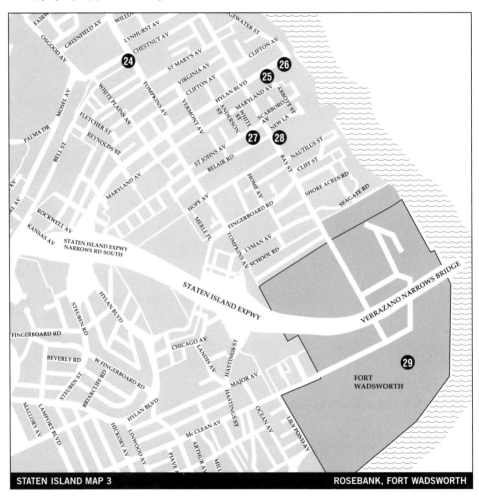

Alice Austen House (No. 26). The picturesque home of one of America's outstanding early photographers is now a museum. Photo courtesy of the Staten Island Historical Society.

(1866–1952), one of America's outstanding early photographers. The original one-room Dutch Colonial house was erected in the early 18th century and gradually enlarged. In 1844 Alice Austen's grandfather purchased the property, renamed it Clear Comfort, and remodeled it in the Gothic Revival style. The house was restored by New York City and is now a museum commemorating Alice Austen's artistry.

㉗ Woodland Cottage, also known as the 33–37 Belair Road (c. 1845; addition, c. 1900), designated 1982. In the 1830s Staten Island's farms began to undergo suburban development. Woodland Cottage, which was built as a rental unit, is one of the few surviving examples of the picturesque Gothic Revival houses that were quite common in Clifton in the early years of the area's suburbanization. The original cross-gabled section has steep roof slopes outlined by bargeboards; the house features diamond-paned casement windows with drip moldings. Between 1858 and 1869, the cottage served as the rectory of Saint John's Church (see below).

㉘ Saint John's Church (Episcopal), 1331 Bay Street (Arthur D. Gilman, 1869–71), designated 1974. Arthur D. Gilman's Gothic Revival granite structure, whose tall spire serves as a prominent landmark to ships arriving in New York Harbor, was planned to resemble a medieval English parish church. The design reflects 19th-century theories of Episcopal church architecture, especially in its clear delineation of such building parts as nave, side aisles, transepts, chancel, and tower. Gilman was a well-known architect in Boston before moving to Staten Island and receiving the commission for this church,

which replaced an 1844 wooden church building.

㉙ Fort Richmond, now Battery Weed (Joseph G. Totten, 1845–61) and **Fort Tompkins,** Hudson Road (1858–76), now Fort Wadsworth, part of Gateway National Recreation Area, designated 1967 and 1974. Built at a crucial site on the edge of the Narrows at the entrance to New York Harbor, Fort Richmond was designed in 1845 by the army's chief engineer, but construction did not begin until two years later. Due to inadequate funding, work dragged on until 1861. The trapezoidal granite building, named for General Stephen Weed after his death at Gettysburg in 1863, is a magnificent example of military architecture. Fort Tompkins, a pentagonal granite structure, is set on a hill above Fort Richmond. The fort contained gun emplacements that were burrowed into the hill.

Fort Tompkins at Fort Wadsworth (No. 29). A magnificent example of military architecture. Photo: Landmarks Preservation Commission collection.

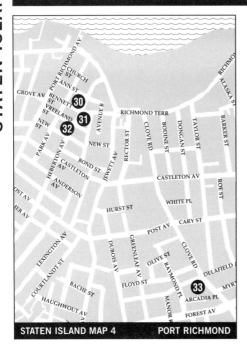

30 New York Public Library, Port Richmond Branch, 75 Bennett Street (Carrère & Hastings, 1904–05), designated 1998. Of four libraries built on Staten Island with funds donated by Andrew Carnegie, the Port Richmond branch was the second to open. In contrast to many libraries in New York, this building has a suburban feel, set back on a spacious lawn planted with trees. The projecting center entrance suggests a classical temple, with large stone columns supporting a wood cornice, frieze, and pediment.

31 121 Heberton Avenue (James G. Burger, c. 1859–61), designated 2002. The character of this frame dwelling was inspired by popular mid-19th-century pattern books. It has a spacious veranda, ornamental brackets, and a broad gable—features often associated with English rustic cottages. The earliest owner was Captain John J. Housman, a prosperous oysterman and noted abolitionist.

32 Northfield Township District School 6, later Public School 20 Annex, now Parkside Senior

The Port Richmond Branch of the New York Public Library (No. 31) was designed by Carrère & Hastings. Photo by Carl Forster.

Housing, 160 Heberton Avenue (1891; addition, James Warriner Moulton, 1897–98), designated 1988. This structure is among the most impressive of the public school buildings erected on Staten Island before its consolidation with New York City. The Romanesque Revival school, which has a wealth of sculptural ornament, was built in two sections, each with a tower that is visible throughout the neighborhood. In 1993–94 the architecture firm Diffendale & Kubec converted the vacant building to low-income housing for the elderly.

③③ 752 Delafield Avenue House, also known as the Scott-Edwards House, 752 Delafield Avenue (early 18th century; remodeling, 1840), designated 1967. The original one-story brownstone house on this site was probably erected in the first part of the 18th century, possibly by Captain Nicholas Manning. At a later date the second story was added; the Greek Revival portico was most likely placed on the building in the 1840s, perhaps by Ogden Edwards, the first New York State supreme court justice from Staten Island, shortly after he purchased the house.

The picturesque design of 121 Heberton Avenue (No. 32) was inspired by 19th-century pattern books. Photo by Carl Forster.

34 **Julia Gardiner Tyler House,** originally the Elizabeth Racey House, also known as the Gardiner-Tyler House, 27 Tyler Street (c. 1835), designated 1967. This Greek Revival mansion with a portico supported by four Corinthian columns was purchased by Juliana and David Gardiner and given to their daughter Julia, the wife of President John Tyler. Julia did not occupy the house until 1868, after her husband's death, when she moved to Staten Island with her seven stepchildren.

35 **John King Vanderbilt House,** 1197 Clove Road (c. 1836), designated 1987. A representative example of Greek Revival design on Staten Island, this house reflects the transition of the northern part of the island from a rural area into a region of suburbs and villages. The building was restored in 1955 by Dorothy Valentine Smith, who lived next door (see below) and who was a descendant of the original owner.

36 **John Frederick Smith House,** later the Dorothy Valentine Smith House, 1213 Clove Road (1893–95), designated 1987. The prominent local banker and insurance dealer John F. Smith erected this house in a restrained version of the Queen Anne style. The house was the lifelong home of Smith's daughter Dorothy, the author of several books and articles on Staten Island's history and a founder of Historic Richmond Town (see No. 47).

37 **Louis A. and Laura Stirn House,** 79 Howard Avenue (Kafka & Lindenmeyr, 1908), designated 2001. This large mansion is prominently located on Grymes Hill, where it commands spectacular views of New York Harbor. Stirn was a silk merchant, and his wife, an expert on horticulture, was the grand-daughter of bridge builder John Roebling. While the overall form recalls an Italian Renaissance villa, the stained glass and polychrome terra-cotta details were inspired by the Arts and Crafts movement.

Louis A. and Laura Stirn House (No. 37). Sited on Grymes Hill, this large neo-Renaissance mansion incorporates details associated with the Arts and Crafts movement. Photo by Carl Forster.

OTHER NORTH SHORE LANDMARKS

38 **Stephen D. Barnes House,** 2876 Richmond Terrace (c. 1853), designated 1976. One of the few survivors on "Captain's Row," which runs along the shore road opposite the Kill van Kull, this large Italianate brick house was erected by Stephen D. Barnes, a prosperous oysterman.

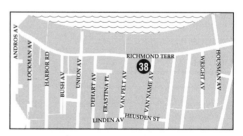

39 **Peter Housman House,** 308 Saint John Avenue (c. 1730; addition, c. 1760), designated 1970. The small one-room stone wing of this 18th-century vernacular house was erected around 1730 on the Dongan estate. (Shortly after his appointment as royal governor of New York in 1683, Thomas Dongan acquired approximately 5,100 acres on Staten Island.) Thirty years later Peter Housman, a prosperous millwright, erected a large clapboard extension. With its steep roof and unusually deep overhang, the addition matches the architectural form of the original building.

HISTORIC DISTRICT

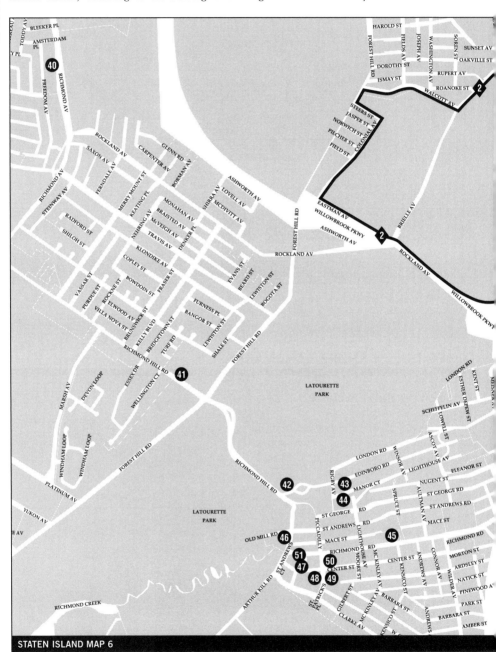

❷ **New York City Farm Colony–Seaview Hospital Historic District,** designated 1985. This historic district, consisting of the buildings and grounds of two municipal institutions, illustrates the commitment made by New York City at the start of the 20th century to improve social and health-care services for the needy. Construction began at the Farm Colony in 1904 on a series of

STATEN ISLAND MAP 6

MAP 6

STATEN ISLAND

striking Colonial Revival dormitories and other structures built of local rubble stone. These buildings, designed by Renwick, Aspinwall & Owen, set the style for buildings by other architects erected during the following ten years. The New York City

Farm Colony was established in 1902 by the New York City Department of Public Charities. Able-bodied paupers were sent to the facility to learn discipline and self-sufficiency, raising vegetables for themselves and for other public institutions. Between 1930 and

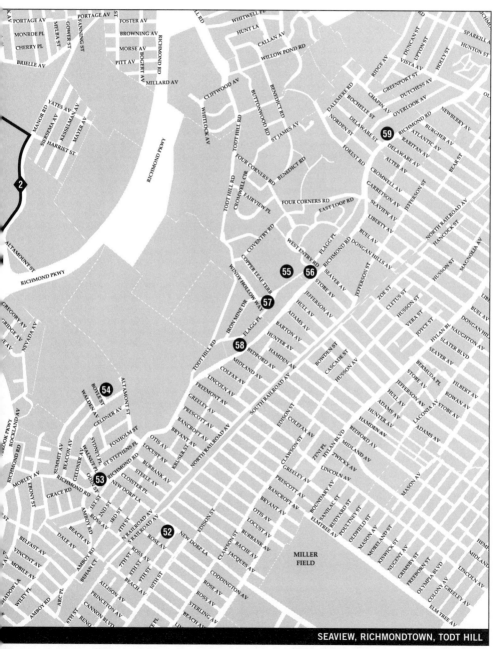

SEAVIEW, RICHMONDTOWN, TODT HILL

1934, the capacity of the farm colony was doubled with the construction of a series of Colonial Revival brick structures designed by Charles B. Meyers. The entire complex is bordered by fields that were farmed by the colony's residents. Separated from the farm colony by Brielle Avenue, Seaview Hospital was founded in 1905 for the treatment of tuberculosis. The architect Raymond F. Almirall conceived the plan for the hospital and designed the original facility. Later additions include Renwick, Aspinwall & Tucker's two groups of small open-air pavilions designed in 1917 for ambulatory patients. The hospital buildings were all set within a therapeutic environment that provided abundant fresh air and landscaped vistas. Most of the buildings are no longer in use.

INDIVIDUAL LANDMARKS

40 Asbury Methodist Church, now Son-Rise Interfaith Charismatic Church, 1970 Richmond Avenue (1849; remodeling, 1878), designated 1968. This church was named for Francis Asbury, a preacher sent to America by John Wesley, the founder of Methodism. Asbury, who was consecrated in 1784 as the first bishop of the American Methodist Episcopal Church, preached on Staten Island for forty-five years. This simple vernacular brick church building, constructed by a mason named Riker and the carpenter J. L. Richards, follows in the traditions of Federal architecture. The front was rebuilt and the tower added in 1878.

41 Decker Farmhouse, 435 Richmond Hill Road (c. 1810; expansion, c. 1840), designated 1967. This simple clapboard building is typical of the small farmhouses that once dotted Staten Island. The modest early 19th-century house was expanded in 1840 when the front porch and other additions were constructed. The building is now a farm museum operated by Historic Richmond Town (see No. 47).

42 David Latourette House, now the Latourette Park Golf Course Club House, Latourette Park, Richmond Hill Road (c. 1836; alterations, 1936), designated 1968. The Latourette House, an especially imposing example of a Greek Revival residence, is one of the few early 19th-century brick country houses on this scale to survive in New York City. In 1928 the Latourette farm was sold to the city for use as a park and golf course. The Parks Department subsequently undertook a series of alterations that included the removal of dormer windows; the reconstruction of the four tall chimneys; the replacement or reconstruction of the floor, cornice, and railings at the original front porch; and the extension of the porch along the south elevation.

43 Staten Island Lighthouse, Edinboro Road (1912), designated 1968. This octagonal brick tower rising from a rusticated limestone base houses a 350,000-candlepower beacon that guides ships into New York Harbor.

44 William and Catherine Cass House, The Crimson Beech, 48 Manor Court (Frank Lloyd Wright, 1958–59), designated 1990. The only residence in New York City designed by Frank Lloyd Wright, this house is an example of the prefabricated houses Wright initially designed in 1956 for the builder Marshall Erdman of Madison, Wisconsin. These prefabs were the last of Wright's many attempts at designing moderate-cost housing. The components were shipped from Madison and assembled on Lighthouse Hill under the supervision of Wright's associate Morton H. Delson.

45 Reverend David Moore House, also known as the Moore-McMillen House, 3531 Richmond Road (1818), designated 1967. This frame farmhouse with a gambrel roof and an elegant entranceway is one of the few buildings in the Federal style on Staten Island. The house was built by Saint Andrew's Church (see below) for its minister, David

The Staten Island Lighthouse (No. 43). Lighthouse Hill takes its name from this handsome structure. Landmarks Preservation Commission collection, 1968.

William and Catherine Cass House, The Crimson Beech (No. 44). The only residence in the city designed by noted architect Frank Lloyd Wright, the house is an example of Wright's attempts to design moderate-priced housing. Photo by Carl Forster.

Moore. Moore served the church for forty-eight years and was eventually given the house; his descendants occupied the premises until 1943. In the following year the prominent Staten Island historian Loring McMillen purchased the property and lived here until his death in 1990.

㊻ Saint Andrew's Church (Episcopal), Old Mill Road at Arthur Kill Road (attributed to George Mersereau, 1872), designated 1967. This stone edifice housing Staten Island's oldest Episcopal congregation is located just outside Historic Richmond Town (see below). Construction of the original church began in 1709. This structure burned in 1867 and again in 1872; surviving sections of the original walls are encased in the present stonework.

With its rounded windows and carefully delineated nave, tower, and entrance porch, the church resembles the Norman parish churches erected in 12th-century England.

㊼ Historic Richmond Town, Richmond Road, Richmondtown. Due to its central location, the town of Richmond became the seat of county government on Staten Island in 1729. Richmondtown's importance declined after Staten Island joined New York City in 1898, although its courthouse remained in use until the Richmond County Courthouse (see No. 12) opened. In 1939 the Staten Island Historical Society inaugurated the preservation of Richmondtown, including the restoration of historic village buildings and the relocation of endangered buildings from other Staten Island sites. The museum village, which is owned by New York City and operated by the historical society, recalls three centuries of life on Staten Island.

Basketmaker's House (c. 1810–20), designated 1969. Originally located in New Springville, this modest clapboard Dutch Colonial cottage was erected for the basketmaker John Morgan.

Bennett House (c. 1839; addition, c. 1854), designated 1969. This clapboard house with Greek Revival elements is located on its original site. Built as a residence with a cellar bakery, the house belonged to the shipping merchant John Bennett and his family from the late 1840s through the early 20th century.

Boehm-Frost House, now Boehm House (c. 1750; addition, c. 1840), designated 1969. This extremely simple pre–Revolutionary War clapboard house, the home of the teacher Henry M. Boehm from 1855 to 1862, was moved to this site from Greenridge.

Britton Cottage (c. 1670; additions, c. 1755, c. 1765, and c. 1800), designated as Cubberly-Britton Cottage, 1976. Built in four stages, this wood and stone farmhouse was moved from New Dorp Beach in 1967. The central stone section, which was probably built around 1670, may have served as Staten Island's first government building. The Britton family owned the house from 1695 to 1714 and again from 1895 to 1915.

Christopher House (c. 1720; addition, 1730), designated 1967. Originally a one-room-and-attic structure on the Dongan estate (see Peter Housman House, No. 39), this vernacular stone house was the home of the patriot Joseph Christopher during the Revolutionary War and is said to have been the meeting place of the American Committee of Safety. It was moved to Richmondtown in 1969.

Eltingville Store, now Print Shop (c. 1860), designated as Grocery Store, 1969. This modest board-and-batten commercial building was origi-

nally a one-room grocery store in the village of Eltingville.

Guyon-Lake-Tysen House (c. 1740; additions, c. 1820 and c. 1840), designated as Lake-Tysen House, 1969. A superb Dutch Colonial–style house erected in the New Dorp–Oakwood area by the Huguenot settler Joseph Guyon, this building was moved to Richmondtown in 1962. The gambrel roof, spring eaves, and front porch are especially notable. The kitchen wing was added around 1820 and the dormer windows twenty years later.

Historical Museum, originally the County Clerk's and Surrogate's Office (1848; additions to c. 1918), designated 1969. This simple brick building, constructed in the tradition of the Federal style, served the county government until around 1920, when civic functions moved to Saint George. The building was converted into a museum in 1934.

Kruser-Finley House (c. 1790; additions, c. 1820 and c. 1850–60), designated as Cooper's Shop, 1969. Endangered by the construction of the Willowbrook Parkway, this modest clapboard building was moved from Egbertville in 1965. Originally a one-room house, the structure was extended around 1820 and again around 1850–60, when a shop, thought to have been used by a cooper, was added.

Parsonage (c. 1855), designated 1969. Located on its original site, this vernacular Gothic Revival clapboard building with gingerbread detail was originally the parsonage of the Reformed Dutch Church of Richmondtown.

Rezeau–Van Pelt Cemetery (1780s to 1860s), designated 1969. A rare surviving 18th-century private graveyard, this cemetery was used by two families who occupied the Voorlezer's House (see below) in the 18th and 19th centuries, after the house ceased to be used as a school.

Stephens-Black House (c. 1838–40), designated as Stephens House and General Store, 1969. Stephen D. Stephens erected this simplified Greek Revival house, and his family lived

STATEN ISLAND

YE OLDE NEW YORK

Farmhouses, cemeteries, and street patterns serve as poignant reminders of the colonial origins of New York. While most examples are located outside Manhattan, two landmarks in the financial district recall the colonial era: the street plan of New Amsterdam, which took its present form below Wall Street in the mid-17th century, and Trinity Church graveyard, where burials date as early as the 1680s (Manhattan Nos. 1 and 18). Farming was, of course, integral to the settlement of the metropolitan area. The largest concentration of surviving farmhouses is located in Flatlands, in southeast Brooklyn. Most are modest frame buildings constructed in the Dutch or English style, including the Pieter Claesen Wyckoff House, which is probably the oldest structure in New York City and one of the oldest in the state (Brooklyn No. 112). Built in c. 1652 on land purchased from the Canarsie Indians, it remained in the Wyckoff family until 1901. Other examples in the vicinity include the beautiful Henry and Abraham Wyckoff House, the Joost and Elizabeth Van Nuyse House, once part of an 85-acre farm, and the Hendrick I. Lott House (Brooklyn Nos. 97, 93, and 96). The major reminder of the first English settlement in New York is Gravesend Cemetery (Brooklyn No. 99). This small burial ground, established by Lady Moody and other English settlers in the 1650s, was part of one of the earliest planned communities in the nation.

In downtown Jamaica are a number of landmarks that document the colonial heritage of Queens. These include the picturesque Prospect Cemetery, the earliest burial ground in the borough, and the King Manor Museum (Queens Nos. 48 and 39). Built as a farmhouse in the 1730s, this gambrel-roofed structure was acquired by the statesman and signer of the Declaration of Independence Rufus King in 1805. Close by is Grace Episcopal Church, which was founded as the official church of the British colonial government. Although the building itself dates from the 1860s, the surrounding graveyard was opened in 1734 and contains King's final resting place (Queens No. 40). In Flushing, two frame structures from the second half of the 17th century are closely associated with the struggle for religious tolerance in the American colonies: the John Bowne House and the Friends Meeting House (Queens Nos. 28 and 26). English Quakers first settled northeastern Queens during the 1650s, and the latter structure continues to serve its original function. Several structures in the Bronx were built before the American Revolution, including the Van Cortlandt Mansion, the Isaac Valentine House, and the center section of the Hadley House (Bronx Nos. 47, 43, and 48).

Staten Island, which retained much of its rural character into the 20th century, has many designated properties from this era. A large number, some of which were moved, are on the grounds of Historic Richmond Town, a museum village near the center of the island. They include the Britton Cottage, a wood and stone farmhouse begun in 1670, and the Voorlezer's House, the oldest elementary school building in the nation (Staten Island No. 47). Two designated landmarks on Staten Island are located on sites that still suggest their original rural settings and enjoy waterfront views: the Conference House, dating from the late 17th century, where a fruitless peace conference was convened in 1776, and the Alice Austen House, home to the famed photographer. As built by a Dutch merchant in c. 1700, it was a modest one-room house, but like many residences from this era the Austen House grew in stages, reflecting the needs and tastes of a succession of 18th- and 19th-century owners (Staten Island Nos. 26 and 76).

here until 1870, operating the one-story general store (reconstructed in 1964) that was added to the rear at some point after the main house was completed.

Third County Courthouse, now Visitors Center (1837), designated 1969. With its Doric portico and square cupola, this Greek Revival courthouse was the centerpiece of Richmondtown during its period as a governmental center. The courthouse remained in use until 1919.

Treasure House (c. 1700; additions, c. 1740, c. 1790, and c. 1860), designated 1969. Still on its original site, this modest clapboard building was the house and workshop of Samuel Grasset, a tanner and leatherworker. The Treasure House derives its name from the local legend that a $7,000 cache of British coins was found hidden in its walls around 1860.

Voorlezer's House (c. 1695), designated 1969. Built by the Reformed Dutch Church as a school, church, and home for the "voorlezer," or lay reader and teacher, this two-story clapboard structure is the oldest surviving elementary school in the country and the oldest surviving building from the settlement of Richmondtown. Its restoration in 1939–42 was Richmondtown Restoration's first project.

Historic Richmond Town (No. 47), a museum village, contains historic buildings that were relocated from other parts of the island. Pictured is the Voorlezer's House, the oldest surviving elementary school building in the United States. Photo by Carl Forster.

48 **Public School 28,** 276 Center Street (C. B. J. Snyder, 1907–08), designated 1998. Built to educate the children of Richmondtown, this brick schoolhouse is notable for its small scale and rural setting. Snyder, who served as superintendent of buildings for the Board of Education for more than three decades, designed few facilities of this type, and this is the only example to survive. Tudor Revival elements, including a half-timbered gable and covered porches, reinforce the building's suburban character. Closed in 1965, it now houses the offices and library of the Staten Island Historical Society.

49 **Saint Patrick's Church (R.C.),** 45 Saint Patrick's Place (1860–62), designated 1968. Located across the street from Historic Richmond Town (see No. 47), Saint Patrick's is an integral part of the old community of Richmondtown. The church is a dignified example of the Early Romanesque Revival style.

50 **Stephens-Prier House,** 249 Center Street (c. 1857–59), designated 1999. This painted clapboard house is one of the best-preserved mid-19th-century dwellings in central Staten Island. Restored in 1977–86, the facades incorporate Greek Revival and Italianate elements, including projecting porches and a cross-gabled roof with shallow pediments. In 1991 it became the administrative headquarters of Historic Richmond Town.

51 **Edwards-Barton House,** 3742 Richmond Road (1869), designated 2001. Webley Edwards, a businessman and public official, built this frame house when Richmondtown was Staten Island's county seat. A well-preserved example of a common mid-19th-century rural house type, the main facade incorporates modest Italianate and Second Empire–style details, as well as a front porch and center gable.

52 **Lane Theater (interior),** 168 New Dorp Lane (John Eberson, 1937–38), designated 1988. Designed by one of the preeminent theater architects of the 20th century, the Art Moderne foyer, lounge corridor, and auditorium of the Lane Theater make up one of the last surviving historic theater interiors on Staten Island.

53 **Gustave A. Mayer House,** originally the David R. Ryers House, 2475 Richmond Road (1855–56), designated 1989. With its boxy massing, arcaded porch, deep bracketed eaves, round-arched openings, and square cupola, this house, built for David R. Ryers, epitomizes the Italian villa form that became popular in the United States in the 1850s. In 1889 the property was purchased by Gustave A. Mayer, the confectioner who invented the Nabisco sugar wafer. Mayer used the basement of the villa as a workshop to experiment with novelties for his business. The house was occupied by members of the Mayer family for one hundred years.

54 **New Dorp Light,** 25 Boyle Street, New Dorp Heights (c. 1854), designated 1967, site expanded 1973. Now converted into a residence, this vernacular clapboard cottage with a tall square tower served for almost ninety years as a beacon to ships entering New York Harbor.

55 **Ernest Flagg House, Stone Court,** now the Scalabrini Fathers of Saint Charles and the Copperflagg Residential Development, 209 Flagg Place (Ernest Flagg, 1898 to c. 1917), designated 1967, site expanded 1983. Stone Court was built as the country estate of the prominent American architect Ernest Flagg. Flagg was introduced to Staten Island in 1897, and a year later he began to purchase land in a section of Todt Hill with splendid ocean views. Here he erected a large house that was indebted to the form of Staten Island's early Dutch Colonial–style dwellings, with their steep, sloping gambrel roofs and deep eaves (the roof slope was somewhat altered when the house was enlarged in 1907–09). Flagg extensively landscaped his grounds and also erected a series of other structures, including the extant gatehouse, stable, water towers, retaining wall, gardener's cottage, palm house, garage, and storage house, all of which were originally faced with whitewashed fieldstone. Much of the estate is now occupied by a complex of large suburban houses designed by Robert A. M. Stern and built in the 1980s.

56 **Ernest Flagg Estate Cottage: Bowcot,** 95 West Entry Road (Ernest Flagg, 1916–18), designated 1987. Flagg not only built his own large estate on Todt Hill, but he also used the area to experiment with the construction of innovative low-cost dwellings of modular design that embodied his pioneering vision of affordable middle-class housing. Although Flagg erected only a few cottages, his ideas were widely disseminated through popular magazines and his book *Small Houses*. Three of the houses are landmarks. Bowcot was the earliest of Flagg's experimental stone cottages. Built into a curved section of the stone wall of his estate (thus the name Bowcot, a diminutive for "bowed cottage"), the small house is carefully integrated with its setting. Among Flagg's innovations was the use of "mosaic rubble," a technique of setting rubble stone into a concrete wall.

⑤⑦ Ernest Flagg Estate Cottage: Wallcot, also known as House-on-the-Wall, 285 Flagg Place (Ernest Flagg, 1918–21), designated 1987. Wallcot is a simple dwelling erected in conjunction with flanking walls. Both the cottage and the walls were built of Flagg's mosaic rubble. The house has the picturesque sloping roofs and dormers that Flagg favored for their evocation of "home."

⑤⑧ Ernest Flagg Estate Cottage: McCall's Demonstration House, 1929 Richmond Road (Ernest Flagg, 1924–25), designated 1987. In 1924–25 Flagg built a model house for the benefit of the readers of *McCall's* magazine. A series of articles detailing the construction of this cottage served to popularize Flagg's ideas on residential design. When the house was completed, he leased it to his secretary.

⑤⑨ Pierre Billiou House, also known as the Billiou-Stillwell-Perine House, 1476 Richmond Road (c. 1660s; additions, c. 1680 to c. 1830), designated 1967. The original stone section of this house was erected by Pierre Billiou in the 1660s, shortly after the first permanent settlement was founded in the region known as Olde Dorp. Constructed according to medieval building traditions, the house is the oldest surviving building on Staten Island. Billiou's daughter married Thomas Stillwell, and they built the first of several additions to the house. For 150 years, beginning in 1764, the house was owned by members of the Perine family. In 1919 this became the first site on Staten Island to be acquired by a historical society for use as a house museum.

Ernest Flagg Estate, Stone Court (No. 55). The country estate of the prominent American architect Ernest Flagg contains an impressive estate house as well as a myriad of experimental and model buildings. Photo by Andrew S. Dolkart

INDIVIDUAL LANDMARKS

60 Saint Alban's Episcopal Church, originally the Church of the Holy Comforter (Episcopal), 76 Saint Alban's Place (R. M. Upjohn, 1865; enlargement, R. M. Upjohn, 1872), designated 1980. Saint Alban's in Eltingville, a rare example of board-and-batten construction in New York City, is one of the city's finest rural Gothic Revival wood-frame buildings. The church was built in 1865; in 1872 it was moved to its present site and enlarged by the insertion of transepts between the nave and chancel. In 1951 the Holy Comforter parish merged with Saint Anne's, Great Kills, to form Saint Alban's. In 1990 the church completed a restoration (Li-Saltzman Architects) that included repainting in historically accurate colors.

61 Frederick Law Olmsted House, also known as the Poillon House, 4515 Hylan Boulevard (early 18th century; additions, 1830s), designated 1967. The high stone base of the present house was probably erected in the early part of the 18th century and used as a barn. The building appears to have been converted into a residence by the addition of the frame upper stories in the 1830s. In 1839 the house and surrounding land were purchased by Samuel Akerly, a renowned agricultural reformer. Nine years later the young Frederick Law Olmsted bought the property; over the next few years he relandscaped the site and undertook a variety of agricultural experiments. In 1853 Olmsted moved to Manhattan, where he would eventually embark on a career as America's first landscape architect.

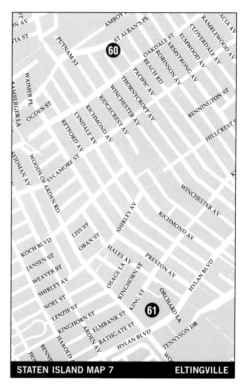

STATEN ISLAND MAP 7   ELTINGVILLE

Saint Alban's Episcopal Church (No. 60), one of New York City's finest rural Gothic Revival wood-frame buildings. Photo: Andrew S. Dolkart.

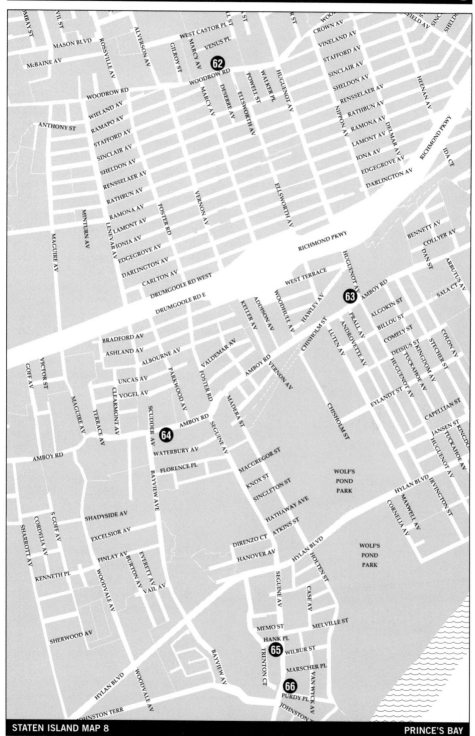

STATEN ISLAND

INDIVIDUAL LANDMARKS

62 Woodrow United Methodist Church, 1075 Woodrow Road (1842), designated 1967. This simple Greek Revival country church was built in 1842 on the site of Staten Island's first Methodist church. The tower was added in 1876.

63 Memorial Church of the Huguenots, now the Reformed Church of Huguenot Park, 5475 Amboy Road (Ernest Flagg, 1923–24; assembly hall, James Whitford, Jr., 1954–55; library, 1903–05), designated 1990. Dedicated in 1924 as the National Monument of the Huguenot–Walloon–New Netherlands 300th Anniversary of Religious Freedom, this stone church is both a testament to a significant as-

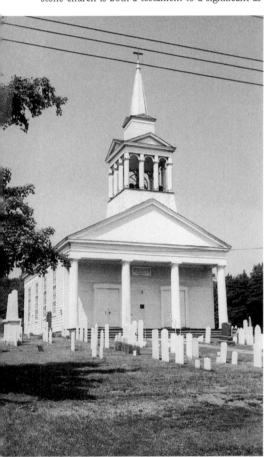

Woodrow United Methodist Church (No. 62). Photo: Landmarks Preservation Commission collection.

pect of Staten Island's early history and an important late work by Ernest Flagg (see No. 55). The design, reminiscent of the vernacular Norman architecture of England and northwestern France, offers evidence of Flagg's interest in medieval design and his experimentation with economical means of construction. Like the Ernest Flagg Estate Cottages (see Nos. 56–58), the building is a concrete structure set with rubble stone (quarried on Flagg's nearby estate) and built on the modular system first used at the estate cottages. The site also includes an assembly hall that was added to the west side of the church in 1954–55 and a small wooden public library built in 1903–05 and moved to this site shortly thereafter. The former library was once the smallest branch of the New York Public Library system.

64 Abraham J. Wood House, also known as the 5910 Amboy Road House (c. 1840), designated 1974. This house was erected by the farmer and oysterman Abraham Wood shortly after he purchased the property in 1840. The main section of Wood's new Greek Revival house may have been an addition to an earlier building (now part of the west wing). The house, which has many features typical of vernacular Greek Revival design on Staten Island, is notable for its entranceway.

65 Joseph H. Seguine House, 440 Seguine Avenue (1837), designated 1967. This sophisticated Greek Revival country house is located at the highest point on the Seguine family's ancestral farm. The farmer, shipping merchant, and industrialist Joseph Seguine, born in the nearby Manee House (see below) belonged to the fifth generation of his family to live on Staten Island.

66 Abraham Manee House, also known as the Manee-Seguine Homestead, 509 Seguine Avenue (late 17th to early 19th centuries), designated 1984. Located on Prince's Bay near the southern tip of Staten Island, this house has a complex building history that may extend back to the construction of a one-room dwelling by Paulus Regrenier in the late 17th century. A major rubble-stone addition was constructed early in the 18th century by Abraham Manee. Further additions were made early in the next century by the Seguine family, who acquired the property in the 1780s.

INDIVIDUAL LANDMARKS

67 **Sleight Family Graveyard,** also known as the Rossville or Blazing Star Burial Ground, Arthur Kill Road at Rossville Road (1750–1850), designated 1968. This small graveyard, which served the village of Rossville, is one of the earliest community cemeteries on Staten Island.

68 **Rossville A.M.E. Zion Church Cemetery,** Crabtree Avenue (1852–), designated 1985. This cemetery is a major surviving element of Sandy Ground, a 19th-century settlement of free black oystermen and their families who moved to Staten Island from Maryland. The cemetery contains the burial sites of members of at least thirty-four African-American families, some of whose descendants still reside in the area.

69 **Westfield Township School No. 7,** later Public School No. 4, 4210–4212 Arthur Kill Road, Charleston (1896; enlarged, C. B. J. Snyder, 1906–07),

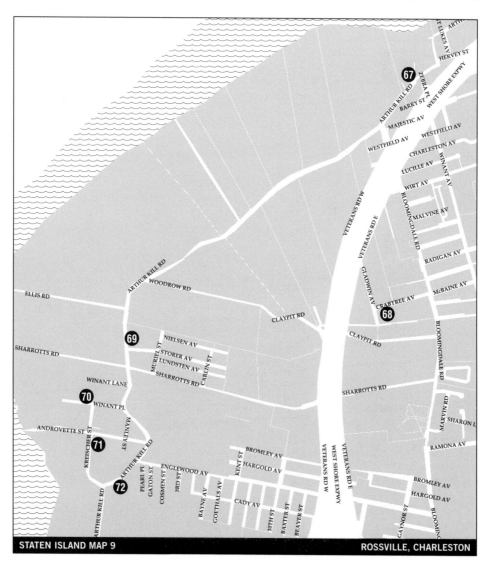

designated 1995. Kreischerville, or Charleston, the seventh school district of Westfield Township, erected this school during the years of peak employment at the Kreischer Brick Works and accompanying village development. The association with the company is evident on the front facade, which employs two colors of ironspot brick and uses brick to spell out the name and date of the building. It remains in use as Public School 25, Annex D, under the jurisdiction of the Board of Education's Division of Special Education.

(70) **Saint Peter's German Evangelical Reformed Church of Kreischerville,** now Free Magyar Reformed Church, Parish Hall, and Rectory, 19–25 Winant Place, Charleston (church, Hugo Kafka, 1883; parish hall, 1898; rectory, Royal Daggett, 1926), designated 1994. This small wooden church complex reflects the immigrant history of the Kreischerville area. The church was a gift of Balthasar Kreischer, owner of the Kreischer Brick Works, to the many German workers in his factory. By the early 20th century, the work force was increasingly Hungarian, and in 1919 the Carpenter Gothic church and parish hall were sold to the Magyar Reformed Church.

(71) **Kreischerville Workers' Houses,** 71–73, 75–77, 81–83, and 85–87 Kreischer Street, Charleston (c. 1890), designated 1994. These four identical pairs of houses are rare surviving examples of their type. Built by prominent local landowner Peter Androvette as housing for workers in the adjacent Kreischer Brick Works, they, along with the nearby Kreischer House (see below), reflect the evolution of a Richmond County hamlet into a company town. Although the houses are clad in wood shingles, the sidewalks are paved in Kreischer brick.

(72) **Charles Kreischer House,** 4500 Arthur Kill Road (attributed to Palliser & Palliser, c. 1888), designated 1968. In 1854 Balthasar Kreischer established the Kreischer Brick Company in southwestern Staten Island. He built a villa at the top of a hill overlooking his factory, and around 1888 a pair of houses was erected at a lower elevation for his two sons. One of the houses was this exuberant Stick Style structure built for Charles Kreischer; it is the only one of the Kreischer family houses that survives. The Kreischer Brick Company was an important late 19th-century Staten Island industry, producing a variety of architectural materials, including terra-cotta ornament and many types of bricks.

The Kreischerville Workers' Houses (No. 71) are remnants of this once bustling company town. Photo by Carl Forster.

INDIVIDUAL LANDMARKS

73 New York Public Library, Tottenville Branch, 7430 Amboy Road (Carrère & Hastings, 1903–04), designated 1995. With Andrew Carnegie's $5 million gift, the New York Public Library erected branches in Manhattan, the Bronx, and Staten Island. This handsome Classical Revival building is the oldest public library on Staten Island and was the work of Carrère & Hastings (John Carrère was a resident of the island), architect of the main Fifth Avenue Library (see Manhattan No. 278).

74 Westfield Township District School No. 5, now Public School 1 Annex, Yetman Avenue and Academy Avenue (1878; enlarged, Pierce & Brun, 1896–97), designated 1995. Prior to becoming a borough of New York City, Staten Island had its own school system organized by township. Westfield, the southernmost town on the island, had seven districts; Tottenville was No. 5. This modest neo-Grec school of brick with stone trim was originally capped

by an open belfry. It is the oldest school building on Staten Island remaining in use. An addition was erected in 1896–97 for a two-year high school.

75 Henry Hogg Biddle House, 70 Satterlee Street (late 1840s), designated 1990. The Biddle House, overlooking the Arthur Kill, exemplifies an unusual aspect of vernacular design on Staten Island—the combining of Dutch Colonial–style spring eaves with Greek Revival columned porticoes. This structure is the only extant local house with two-story porticoes and spring eaves on both the front and rear elevations. These elements add a sense of grandeur to the relatively small waterfront dwelling.

76 Conference House, also known as Bentley Manor, the Christopher Billopp House, 7455 Hylan Boulevard (c. 1675), designated 1967. This house is historically significant as the site of a conference on September 11, 1776, between three delegates of the Continental Congress—Benjamin Franklin, John Adams, and Edward Rutledge—and the British Ad-

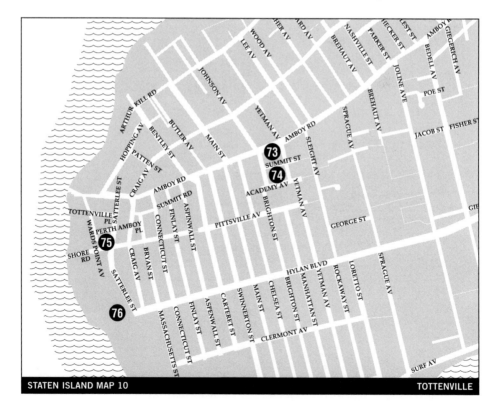

miral Lord Howe that proved an unsuccessful effort to avert the Revolutionary War. The house was built by naval captain Christopher Billopp, who was granted a patent on sixteen hundred acres of south-ern Staten Island in 1676. Because of its historical importance, efforts were made to preserve the site as early as 1888, but it was not until 1926 that it was acquired by the city and restoration began.

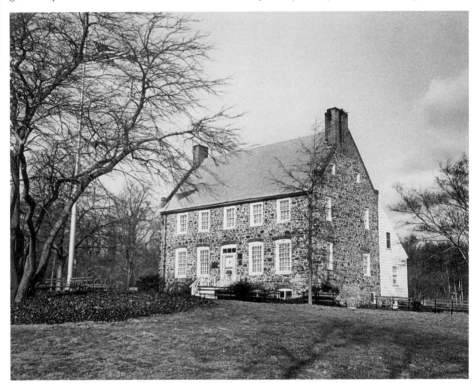

▲ The Conference House (No. 76). Photo: Landmarks Preservation Commission collection.

▶ Henry Hogg Biddle House (No. 75), a vernacular design that has an unusual combination of Dutch Colonial and Greek Revival elements. Photo by Carl Forster.

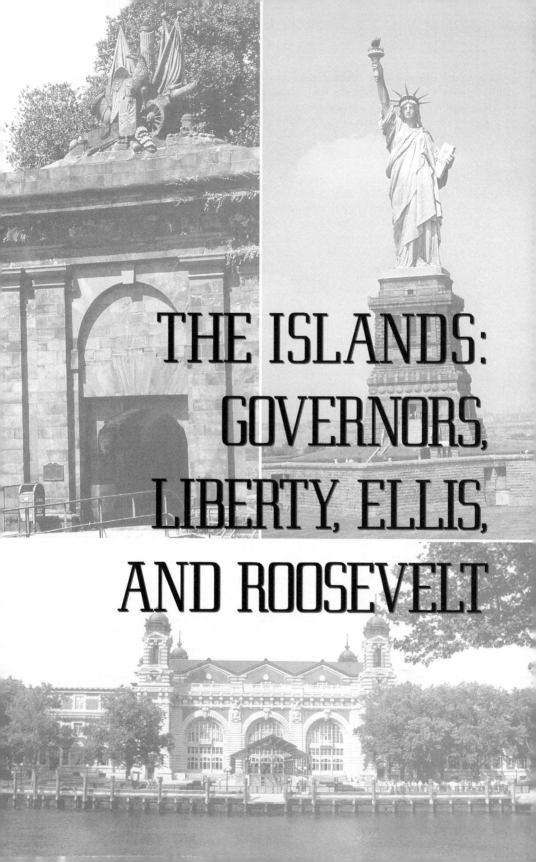

THE ISLANDS: GOVERNORS, LIBERTY, ELLIS, AND ROOSEVELT

Governors Island Historic District, designated 1996. Governors Island, located one-half mile from Manhattan in New York Harbor, was used by the United States military for almost two hundred years. In 1637 the island, called Pagganck by the Canarsee Indians and Nutten by the Dutch, became the private property of Wouter Van Twiller, the director general of the New Netherlands. It remained in the hands of succeeding Dutch and English governors, thus accounting for its name. The island was initially fortified by American and later British troops during the Revolutionary War. The first permanent fortifications were erected by the United States government in 1794–96 and named Fort Jay in 1798. In 1800 the island was ceded by New York City to the federal government, along with Ellis and Bedloe's (now Liberty) Islands (see below). Between 1807 and 1811, as tensions between the United States and Britain increased, a series of fortifications were built in New York Harbor, including Fort Columbus, to re-

place Fort Jay (the name Fort Jay was later restored; see below), and Castle William (see below). As the importance of the island in the defense of New York Harbor waned in the mid-19th century, the island was adapted for other army uses, notably as an arsenal. Twelve buildings were erected for the arsenal, including seven that survive. Barracks, a hospital, officers' housing, and other buildings in the Greek Revival style were also built for troops stationed at Fort Columbus. Under the command of General Winfield Scott Hancock, the island became an army administrative center, and a series of officers' quarters, including a group of picturesque clapboard houses set around Nolan Park (1878–1902), and large brick houses, known as Regimental Row (1893–1917), were erected. Also dating from this period is the Chapel of Saint Cornelius the Centurion, a neo-Gothic church designed by Charles C. Haight in 1905. In the early 20th century, the island was enlarged through landfill, and Charles F. McKim of the

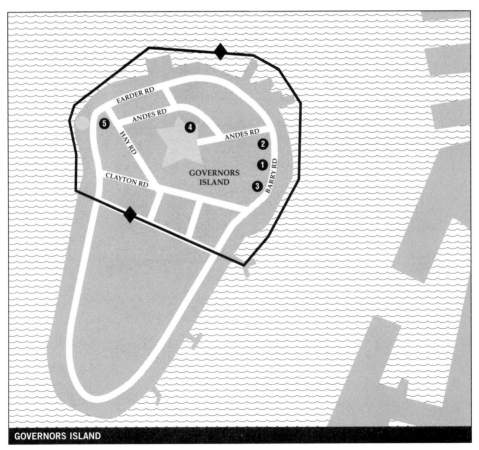

GOVERNORS ISLAND

The impressive French-inspired entrance to Fort Jay on Governor's Island. Photo by John Barrington Bayley, c. 1965.

firm of McKim, Mead & White was hired to plan for additional troop facilities. It was not until 1928 that work began on the first buildings designed by the McKim, Mead & White firm. These include a neo-Georgian-style model barracks (Building 400) that was the longest military building in the world at the time of its completion and a similarly styled officers' quarters (Building 12) built with a U-shaped plan in seven sections. The construction of neo-Georgian-style buildings in the 1930s, some according to McKim's plan, included quarters for officers and their families and nurses' quarters designed by Rogers & Poor; the First United States Army headquarters building, designed by Lorimer Rich; and Public School 26, designed by Eric Kibbon. In 1966, after over 150 years on Governors Island, the army left the island and the United States Coast Guard es-tablished it as the Atlantic Area headquarters. In Jan-uary 2003 the federal government sold Governors Island to New York City and New York State.

Prior to the designation of the Governors Island Historic District, which incorporates the portion of the island northeast of Division Road, five buildings were designated as individual landmarks; in recent years much new information has come to light on these buildings, based on an extensive study in

WAR AND PEACE

In 1776, British troops fought local patriots for control of New York City. Acts against the crown helped spark the American Revolution, most notably the destruction of an equestrian statue of King George III at Bowling Green (Manhattan No. 11). Battles took place in Brooklyn, especially at what is now called Battle Pass in Prospect Park, and then Manhattan, and in the Hamilton Heights/Sugar Hill Historic Districts (Brooklyn No. 79 and Manhattan H.D. 39–42). The latter clash was especially significant. General George Washington had established his headquarters in Mount Morris (Manhattan No. 576) and led the Continental Army to a modest victory over their much better-trained adversary. A fruitless peace conference was convened at a private home on Staten Island (Staten Island No. 76) during September, attended by Benjamin Franklin, John Adams, and Edward Rutledge. The conflict ended at Yorktown in 1783, and it was in Manhattan at Fraunces Tavern (Manhattan No. 46) that Washington said good-bye to his officers. Subsequent landmarks associated with American wars include structures built to protect the city, to prepare for conflicts overseas, and to remember those who served. These include the impressive fortifications that defended the Battery, Narrows, and mouth of the East River (Manhattan No. 3, Staten Island No. 29, Brooklyn No. 107, Bronx No. 60, and Queens No. 32). Located in all five boroughs, most of these early 19th-century complexes have been decommissioned and now serve civilian uses. The Brooklyn Navy Yard (Brooklyn No. 12–15), established in 1801, played an important role in American wars, producing such legendary vessels as the *Maine, Arizona*, and the *Missouri*—where the peace treaty with Japan was signed ending the Second World War in September 1945.

The earliest tribute to an American war hero is located on the east facade of St. Paul's Chapel. Dedicated to General Richard Montgomery, who died at the Battle of Quebec in 1775, it was commissioned by the Continental Congress and installed in 1787. Other notable monuments associated with the American Revolution include the Soldier's Monument in the graveyard of Trinity Church and the Prison Ship Martyrs' Monument at the summit of Fort Greene Park (Manhattan No. 18 and Brooklyn H.D. 9). Significant monuments can also be found within scenic landmarks, such as the Maryland 400 Monument in Prospect Park (Brooklyn No. 79), designed by Stanford White in 1895; Attilio Picarelli's Maine Monument of 1913, at the southwest corner of Central Park (Manhattan No. 376) the General Ulysses S. Grant Tomb (Manhattan No. 531) in Riverside Park; and the Soldiers and Sailors Monument in Grand Army Plaza (Brooklyn No. 78), which has statuary groups by Frederick MacMonnies and a pair of bas-reliefs with horses modeled by Thomas Eakins. It should also be noted that many designated cemeteries and churchyards contain burials associated with American wars.

archival documents by the Historic American Buildings Survey:

❶ Commanding Officer's Quarters, Nolan Park, west of Barry Road (Martin E. Thompson, 1843; south wing, 1886; porch, c. 1893–1918), designated as the Admiral's House, 1967. This building served as the home of the island's commanding officer from the time of its completion until the summer of 1996. The building was originally a rectangular Greek Revival–style structure with a porch. A wing was added to the south in 1886, and sometime between 1893 and 1918 the original front porch was altered to incorporate the present slender Tuscan columns with a balustrade above. With funding from the Works Progress Administration in 1936–37, Charles O. Cornelius redesigned the rear of the house and embellished the building with ironwork, giving it an "early American" character. The house was the site of a historic 1988 luncheon meeting between President Ronald Reagan and President Mikhail Gorbachev of the Soviet Union.

❷ Governor's House (originally a guardhouse), Nolan Park, corner of Barry Road and Andes Road (c. 1805–13), designated 1967. Previously thought to have been erected around 1708, this Georgian-style house was actually built in the early 19th century and was originally Governors Island's main guardhouse. In 1824 the building became the quarters of the island's commanding officer. By 1839 the roof slope had been altered to the present combination of hipped and gabled slopes. The building later served again as a guardhouse and then as the post headquarters, and in the 1920s it became the residence of the army's post commander. A one-story addition was added at the rear in the 1930s. The entrance portico with Ionic columns and pilasters may also date from this period.

❸ Post Hospital, Nolan Park, northwest of Barry Road (1839), designated as the Block House, 1967. This two-story Greek Revival building with a fieldstone base and granite entrance enframement served as a hospital until 1878 and was later used as an army headquarters building and as apartments. The austerity of the

design has led to its being popularly named the Block House. The building originally had a flat roof, but this had been replaced by 1863 (or earlier) with the present shallow hipped roof to prevent damage from leaks.

❹ Fort Columbus, Andes Road (Lieutenant Colonel Jonathan Williams, 1806–09), designated as Fort Jay, 1967. In 1794–96 an earthen fortification, known as Fort Jay, was erected on this site as part of the earliest attempt to fortify New York Harbor. In 1806 this was replaced by Fort Columbus, an impressive star-shaped structure inspired by French fortifications; only a few sections of the earlier fort were saved and incorporated into the new structure. Lieutenant Colonel Jonathan Williams, who designed this and other contemporary forts, had lived in France in 1776–85 under the auspices of his great-uncle Benjamin Franklin; there he gained familiarity with French military design. The sandstone structure has four bastions enclosed by a dry moat. The impressive French-inspired entrance is crowned by a large sandstone trophy sculpture with an eagle and military symbols. The interior of the fort contains Greek Revival barracks with impressive colonnaded porticoes that were constructed in 1834–36. The fort was renamed for John Jay in 1904.

❺ Castle Williams, Hay Road (Lieutenant Colonel Jonathan Williams, 1807–11), designated 1967. Castle Williams is a massive bastion forming three-fifths of a circle, with a two-story entrance pavilion filling in the remainder of the form. Erected to support more than one hundred cannons, it is one of a series of forts, including Castle Clinton (see Manhattan No. 3), just across New York Harbor, built to fortify New York as tensions rose between America and the British in the early 19th century. At the time of its construction, it served as a prototype for seacoast fortifications in America, and it is today one of the best examples of its type in existence. The imposing three-tiered fort was constructed of red Newark sandstone with walls that are eight feet thick at the base and seven feet thick at the top. During the Civil War, the fort served as a prison for Confederate soldiers; it was later used as quarters for new recruits, as a military prison, and for storage.

THE ISLANDS

Liberty Island. Known as Bedloe's Island until 1956, this island was the site of Fort Wood, a structure in the shape of an eleven-pointed star, erected in 1806–11 to fortify the entrance to New York Harbor. The fort was incorporated into the plans for the base of the Statue of Liberty. Although located within New Jersey's territorial waters, the island itself has been considered a part of New York City since the late 17th century. An agreement of 1834 provides that the island is in New York above the mean low-water mark and in New Jersey below it.

Statue of Liberty (Frédéric Auguste Bartholdi, sculptor, and Gustave Eiffel, engineer, 1871–86; base, Richard Morris Hunt, 1881–86), designated 1976. This portrait of Liberty, famed the world over as a symbol of the United States of America, was a gift from the people of France. The idea for the statue originated with a group of French intellectuals who advocated republican rule in France during the Second Empire. They hoped that inspiration provided by the ideals associated with the construction of the statue would lead to the expansion of democracy in France. It was not until 1903, when Emma Lazarus's famed poem "The New Colossus" was inscribed on a tablet at the base of the pedestal, that the Statue of Liberty became the symbol of American immigration. The Alsatian sculptor Frédéric Auguste Bartholdi started work on the statue in 1871 and by 1875 was ready to begin construction. Money was raised in France for the casting of the colossal piece. The beaten copper exterior was placed on a wrought-iron armature designed by Gustave Eiffel to support the statue's weight and to provide bracing against the winds that would batter the statue at the mouth of New York Harbor. Construction of the base was the responsibility of the United States. Appropriately, the design was undertaken by the French-trained architect Richard Morris Hunt, with money raised through contributions encouraged by Joseph Pulitzer in his newspaper, the *New York World*. In 1885 the statue arrived from France in hundreds of crates and was assembled under the supervision of General Charles P. Stone, an army engineer. A major

restoration of the statue was completed in time for its centennial in 1986. This work was directed by Swanke Hayden Connell, architect, with the engineering firm Ammann & Whitney; the French metalworkers Les Metalliers Champenois also contributed their expertise.

Ellis Island Historic District, designated 1993. The Ellis Island Historic District commemorates the significance of immigration to the history of the United States. Beginning in 1892, when Ellis Island first became an immigrant station, more than twelve million poor immigrants from all over the world came through Ellis Island before settling in New York City or continuing their journeys to every corner of the nation. Ellis Island had been a fort (Fort Gibson) before it was converted into an immigrant arrival station, replacing Castle Clinton (see Manhattan No. 3) as the site for the federal registration of immigrants. After the original wooden facility burned in 1897, the present Beaux-Arts-style complex was erected to the designs of the New York City architecture firm Boring & Tilton (1897–1900). The immigration station focuses on the main building, a monumental brick and limestone structure with prominent corner towers where the immigrants were received, registered, and examined, where their baggage was stored, and where some were de-

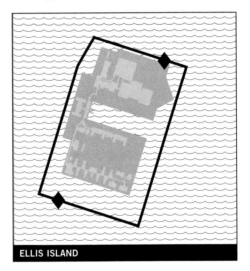

ELLIS ISLAND

The Statue of Liberty. Photo courtesy of the National Park Service.

tained in dormitories. Most of those who came to Ellis Island were soon sent on their way, but a small percentage of prospective immigrants were held on the island or sent back to their place of embarkation. The most prominent space on the **interior** of the main building is the double-height Registry Room on the second floor. The vast open space, lit by natural light entering from large windows, was originally divided by iron railings into alleys where immigrants lined up for inspection. The railings were replaced by benches in 1911. In 1916 an explosion in New Jersey, caused by German saboteurs, damaged the building, and in 1918 the damaged plaster ceiling and asphalt floor were replaced by a spectacular Guastavino tile arched ceiling and a floor of red Ludowici tile. Adjoining the main building are Boring & Tilton's kitchen and laundry building (1898–1901) and powerhouse (1900–01) and a baggage and dormitory building designed by Supervising Architect of the Treasury James Knox Taylor (1907–09). Boring & Tilton was also responsible for the original hospital (1901–09) located across the ferry slip from the main building. To accommodate the increasing number of immigrants arriving at Ellis Island, the island

was enlarged through landfill, and many new buildings were erected. The hospital was enlarged, and a contagious disease complex was built early in the 20th century, all to designs by James Knox Taylor. The passage of restrictive immigration legislation in 1924 and the institution of immigration checks at United States consulates changed the use of Ellis Island. It became largely a center for the deportation of aliens, usually illegal immigrants. In 1934–36 the Public Works Administration allocated funds for the construction of additional buildings, including another immigration building, ferry house, and recreation building, all designed in a Modern Colonial idiom by architect Chester H. Aldrich of the firm Delano & Aldrich. In 1954 the island was closed, but eleven years later President Lyndon B. Johnson made it a part of the Statue of Liberty National Monument. A restoration undertaken by Beyer Blinder Belle began in the 1980s, and in 1990 the main building at Ellis Island reopened as a museum of immigration history that is now one of the most popular sites in New York City. The remainder of the island, including the majority of the buildings, awaits restoration and reuse.

Ellis Island, gateway to America. Photo by Carl Forster.

On May 26, 1998, the United States Supreme Court ruled on a dispute between the State of New Jersey and the State of New York over the ownership of Ellis Island. The lawsuit was the latest skirmish in a boundary dispute between the two states that commenced soon after the Revolutionary War. The court found that New York owned only the original three-acre island as it existed in 1834 (including most but not all of the main building and parts of the baggage and dormitory building, kitchen and laundry building, and bakery and carpentry building that were subsequently built there), and that all filled portions of the existing 27½-acre island belonged to New Jersey. This decision means that most of the Ellis Island Historic District is now situated in the Garden State.

Roosevelt Island. The six landmark structures on Roosevelt Island, dating from the late 18th century to the early 1890s, illustrate the transformation of this 107-acre island from a farm to the home of several large institutions. In 1676 the Blackwell family took possession of the island, and it remained in their hands until it was purchased by the city in 1828 for the construction of hospitals, asylums, and a prison. Long known as Blackwell's Island, the name was changed to Welfare Island in 1921 and to Roosevelt Island in 1973. The island now houses several institutions as well as a planned residential community that opened in 1975. In conjunction with the residential development, several of the older buildings were restored or stabilized by Giorgio Cavaglieri.

❶ Lighthouse (James Renwick, Jr., supervising architect, 1872), designated 1976. The 50-foot-tall lighthouse was erected on what was once a separate tiny island. The octagonal shaft, faced with rough stone blocks of gray gneiss quarried on the island by convict labor, is enlivened by Gothic detail, notably a gabled entrance and a band of foliate ornament.

❷ New York City Lunatic Asylum (A. J. Davis, 1835–39; alterations, Joseph M. Dunn), designated as Octagon Tower, 1976. The Octagon Tower—the sole surviving portion of the city's insane asylum—was originally the central section of a larger structure planned by Davis in 1835–36. As completed in 1839, the complex consisted of the octagon and two patient wings. In 1879 the

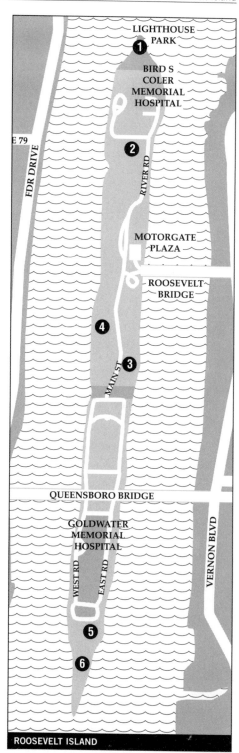

wings were enlarged and a dome was added. The tower is now badly deteriorated but is scheduled to be restored and incorporated into a residential building that recalls the earlier structure.

❸ **James Blackwell House** (between 1796 and 1804), designated 1976. This simple Georgian-vernacular clapboard farmhouse, the oldest building on the island, was erected by descendants of the island's original European settlers.

❹ **Chapel of the Good Shepherd,** now Good Shepherd Community Ecumenical Center (Frederick Clarke Withers, 1888–89), designated 1967. Withers's design for this late Victorian Gothic chapel combines the traditions of English parish churches with the demands of an unusual commission. The chapel was a gift of the banker George M. Bliss to the Episcopal City Mission Society and was intended for use by inmates of the nearby city institutions. The stone building has a

RARE & UNUSUAL

Most landmarks are residences, commercial buildings, and houses of worship. These categories, however, don't cover all designated properties. The Commission has designated the colonial street plan of Lower Manhattan (Manhattan No. 1), the land associated with the Commons laid out by the Dutch government of New Amsterdam, and the site of the 18th-century African Burial Ground (Manhattan H.D. 4), two tree-lined boulevards in Brooklyn conceived by Olmsted & Vaux—Eastern and Ocean Parkways (Brooklyn Nos. 74 and 103)—as well as lampposts and sidewalk clocks. Installed to promote local businesses, four of these freestanding clocks survive on Manhattan streets (Nos. 191, 289, 428, and 505), two in Queens (Astoria and Jamaica, Nos. 6 and 43), and one in Brooklyn (Greenpoint No.10). A pair of historic iron fences have also been designated, located at Bowling Green and at Sailors' Snug Harbor (Manhattan No. 11 and Staten Island No. 3)

Many of the more unusual landmarks are great feats of engineering. Dry Dock #1 is located at the Brooklyn Navy Yard. Completed in 1851, this monumental granite-walled facility has served many oceangoing vessels, including the *Monitor* and the *Niagara,* which laid the first trans-Atlantic cable (Brooklyn No. 13). A cast-iron watchtower at the summit of Marcus Garvey Park is the only surviving fire tower in New York City; the 200-foot-tall granite High Bridge Water Tower was built to increase water pressure in Manhattan; and the Carroll Street Bridge, spanning the Gowanus Canal, is the oldest retractable bridge in America (Manhattan Nos. 565 and 579, Brooklyn No. 32). Other civic structures with unusual origins include the Bronx Grit Chamber, part of an early sewage-treatment project designed by McKim, Mead & White, and the Municipal Asphalt Plant, a soaring parabolic structure of reinforced concrete (Bronx No. 1 and Manhattan No. 508).

Some buildings, though historic, are not exactly what they appear to be. Fraunces Tavern, where George Washington bade farewell to his officers in 1783, is an early 20th-century reconstruction designed by William H. Mersereau, and the Theodore Roosevelt Birthplace, demolished in 1916, was rebuilt in 1923 by Theodate Pope Riddle to honor the 26th president's memory (Manhattan Nos. 46 and 187). Several landmarks are partial fragments of what were originally much larger structures: La Grange Terrace, also known as Colonnade Row; Squadron A Armory; and Riverside, a model tenement located at 4–30 Columbia Place in Brooklyn Heights (Manhattan Nos. 152 and 511, Brooklyn H.D. 4).

clearly delineated nave, chancel, and tower, as well as a pair of entrance porches—for male and female inmates, respectively.

❺ Strecker Laboratory (Withers & Dickson, 1892; third floor, William Flanagan, 1905), designated 1976. This small Romanesque Revival gray-stone and orange-brick building was originally a pathology laboratory for the nearby Charity Hospital.

❻ Smallpox Hospital (James Renwick, Jr., 1854–56; south wing, York & Sawyer, 1903–04; north wing, Renwick, Aspinwall & Owen, 1904–05), designated 1976. Now a picturesque ruin that was stabilized in the 1970s, this Gothic Revival stone structure was built for the treatment of smallpox patients. In 1903–05, by which time the hospital served as a nurse's residence, the facility was enlarged to form a U-shaped structure.

At the south end of Roosevelt Island is the Smallpox Hospital. Designed by James Renwick Jr. in 1854–56 and later expanded, the shell of this Gothic Revival structure survives as a highly visible and picturesque ruin (Roosevelt Island No. 6). Our Lady of Lourdes Church, completed in 1904, is composed of elements saved from earlier structures—the National Academy of Design, the east end of St. Patrick's Cathedral, and the Fifth Avenue mansion of A. T. Stewart (Manhattan No. 537). Another major building incorporating elements from an earlier structure is the monumental National City Bank Building on Wall Street. Two separate building campaigns are skillfully expressed on the main facade; while the lower floors feature an Ionic colonnade that dates from 1836–42, the upper stories, added by 1910, are screened by Corinthian columns (Manhattan No. 39). The two columns that flank the corner entrance to the Delmonico's Building have an interesting provenance. Reputedly ancient artifacts that were brought from Pompeii to New York by the restaurant's founder, they were salvaged from the restaurant's original 1835 building on this site (Manhattan No. 42). In Central Park, two structures have unusual origins: Cleopatra's Needle, an ancient Egyptian obelisk near East 81st Street, and the Swedish Cottage, at West 79th Street. Commissioned by the Swedish government for display at the Centennnial Exposition in Philadelphia in 1876, this wooden schoolhouse was moved to the park shortly after the fair's closing and has been used as a children's theater since 1947. Also of note is the Vanderbilt Gate at East 105th Street, rescued from the Cornelius Vanderbilt II house that originally stood at Fifth Avenue, between 57th and 58th Streets (Manhattan No. 576).

In Coney Island, three memorable amusement rides have been recognized by the Commission, two of which still operate—the Wonder Wheel, a 150-foot-tall Ferris wheel, and the Cyclone, considered one of the world's most thrilling roller coasters (Brooklyn Nos. 101 and 102). Several blocks away is the recently restored Parachute Jump (Brooklyn No. 100). Although the colorful tapered steel structure no longer welcomes riders, it remains one of Brooklyn's most cherished landmarks.

Among the rarest of individual landmarks are trees. Two specimens have been designated: the Weeping Beech, planted in Flushing by nurseryman Samuel Parsons in 1847 and now consisting of an impressive group of offspring, and the Magnolia Grandiflora, which grows and flowers in Bedford-Stuyvesant (Queens No. 30 and Brooklyn No. 46). Planted around 1885, this beautiful tree flourishes at the northern edge of its species' range.

Appendix:
What is the New York City Landmark Preservation Commission?

What does the Landmarks Preservation Commission do?

The Landmarks Preservation Commission is the New York City agency that is responsible for identifying and designating local landmarks and historic districts. The Commission also regulates changes to designated properties.

Who are the Landmarks Commissioners?

According to the Landmarks Law, the eleven Commissioners that make up the Commission must include at least three architects, one historian, one city planner or landscape architect, and one realtor. There must be at least one resident of each borough on the Commission. Ten Commissioners serve part-time and receive no salary; the Chairman is a full-time, paid Commissioner. The Commissioners are appointed by the Mayor for three-year terms. The Chairman and the Vice-Chairman are designated by the Mayor.

What are the Commissioners' duties?

The Commissioners meet several times a month for public hearings and public meetings. On these occasions, they address Commission policies; review, discuss, and vote on landmark designations and applications to make changes to designated properties; and establish guidelines for future alterations to designated buildings. Sub-committees of Commissioners are sometimes created to review particular items and to make recommendations to the full Commission. There is, for instance, a Designation Committee, as well as committees to review particular Parks Department applications or specific applications from the public.

Who are the Commissions's staff members?

The agency's staff, headed by the Executive Director, includes architects, architectural historians, restoration specialists, planners, and archaeologists, as well as administrative, legal, and clerical personnel. Although it is one of the smallest New York City agencies, the Commission is the largest municipal preservation agency in the United States.

What does the Commission's staff do?

The Research Department carries out research and makes presentations to the Commissioners on the history and significance of proposed landmarks and historic districts. Members of the public can request the Commission to consider designating a particular building or area as a landmark or historic district.

The Preservation Department is the regulatory arm of the agency. It works with applicants who propose alterations or additions to designated properties or new construction in historic districts, and issues permits for changes that the Commission has found to be appropriate.

The Commission also administers the Historic Preservation Grant Program, which awards restoration grants to low and moderate-income homeowners and not-for-profit organizations.

When was the Commission established?

The Landmarks Preservation Commission was established in 1965 when Mayor Robert Wagner signed the local law creating the Commission and giving it its power.

Why was the Landmarks Law enacted?

The Landmarks Law was enacted in response to New Yorkers' growing concern that important buildings and other physical elements of the city's history were being lost despite the fact that these structures could be reused or adapted for other uses. Events like the demolition of the architecturally distinguished Pennsylvania Station in 1963 increased public awareness of the need to protect the city's architectural, historical, and cultural heritage.

Why is it important to designate and protect landmarks and historic districts?

As the Landmarks Law explains, protection of these resources serves the following important purposes:

- safeguarding the city's historic, aesthetic and cultural heritage;

- helping to stabilize and improve property values in historic districts;

- encouraging civic pride in the beauty and accomplishments of the past;

- protecting and enhancing the city's attractions for tourists, thereby benefiting business and industry;

- strengthening the city's economy; and

- promoting the use of landmarks for the education, pleasure, and welfare of the people of the city.

What is a landmark?

A landmark is a building, property, or object that has been designated by the Landmarks Preservation Commission because it has a special character or special historical or aesthetic interest or value as part of the development, heritage, or cultural characteristics of the city, state or nation.

Landmarks are not always buildings. A landmark may be a bridge, a park, a water tower, a pier, a cemetery, a building lobby, a sidewalk clock, a fence, or even a tree. A property or object is eligible for landmark status when at least part of it is thirty years old or older.

What types of designations can the Commission make?

There are three types of landmarks: individual (exterior) landmarks, interior landmarks, and scenic landmarks. The Landmarks Preservation Commission may also designate areas of the city as historic districts.

1. An *individual landmark* is a property, object, or building that has been designated by the Landmarks Commission. These properties or objects are also referred to as "exterior" landmarks because only their exterior features have been designated. The Roo-

sevelt Island Lighthouse, the Edgewater Village Hall on Staten Island, Grand Central Terminal, and Old West Farms Soldiers' Cemetery in the Bronx are examples of individual landmarks.

2. An *interior landmark* is an interior space that has been designated by the Landmarks Commission. Interior landmarks must be customarily accessible to the public. The lobby of the Woolworth Building, the dining room of the Gage & Tollner restaurant in Brooklyn, and the waiting room of the Marine Air Terminal at LaGuardia Airport are examples of interior landmarks.

3. A *scenic landmark* is a landscape feature or group of features that has been designated by the Landmarks Commission. Scenic landmarks must be situated on city-owned property. Prospect Park and Ocean Parkway in Brooklyn, Verdi Square at Broadway and 73rd Street, and Central Park are examples of scenic landmarks.

4. An *historic district* is an area of the city designated by the Landmarks Commission that represents at least one period or style of architecture typical of one or more eras in the city's history; as a result, the district has a distinct "sense of place." Greenwich Village and SoHo, Mott Haven in the Bronx, Jackson Heights in Queens, Saint George in Staten Island and Fort Greene in Brooklyn, are examples of sections of the city that contain historic districts.

How many buildings has the Commission designated?

Between 1965 and December 2002, the Commission designated 1,093 individual landmarks, 79 historic districts (containing over 22,000 properties), 9 scenic landmarks, and 104 interior landmarks. These buildings are a small percentage of New York City's 850,000 building lots, but they are most important to the city's historic, aesthetic, and cultural heritage.

How can I learn more about the Landmarks Preservation Commission?

Public hearings are held on the ninth floor of the Municipal Building on most Tuesdays. Hearing dates are posted on our website and in the City Record. If you would like more information, call or write the Landmarks Commission at 1 Centre Street, 9th floor north, New York, NY 10007; telephone: 212-669-7817. Our web address is www.nyc.gov/landmarks.

Index

Page numbers in *italic* type indicate a full entry on the landmarked property or interior, historic district, or scenic landmark. Page numbers in **bold** type indicate a photograph of the building. Street addresses are listed as follows: named streets alphabetically; East and West streets numerically under "East and West"; other numbered streets and avenues alphabetically as if spelled out.

Aarons, Alex, 125
Aberdeen Hotel, *78*
Abyssinian Baptist Church and Community House, *205–206*
Ackerman, Frederick L., 62
Actors Studio (Seventh Associate Presbyterian Church), *90*
Adams, Abigail, 167
Adams, Herbert, 99, 120
Adams, John, 167, 363, 368
Adams, Robert, 177
Thatcher and Frances Adams House (63 East 79th Street House), *177*
Adams & Warren, 177
Adams & Woodbridge, 11
Administration Building of Parks and Recreation (The Arsenal), *159*
Admiral's House (Commanding Officer's Quarters, Governors Island), *369*
Jacob Adriance Farmhouse (Queens County Farm Museum, Creedmoor (Cornell) Farmhouse), *293*
Advertising Club, 114
Aeolian Building, *110*
African Burial Ground, *20, 374*
Aguilar, Grace, 207
Aguilar Branch, New York Public Library, *207*
Ahlschlager, Walter W., 142, 202
Ahrens Building, *31*
Aiken, William M., 52
airports, 278, 279
Aitkin, John, 260
Ajello, Gaetan, 148
Akerly, Samuel, 358
L. Alavoine & Company, 111
Albee, E. F., 96
Albemarle-Kenmore Terraces Historic District, 255, *260*
Albemarle Road (Brooklyn) No. 1510, 260
Albers, Josef, 124
Albro & Lindeberg, 122
Alden, Hugo, 304
Aldrich, Chester H., 372
Alexander, William, 335
Algonquin Hotel, 88, *103*
Alhambra Apartments, *244*, 245
Allen, Collens & Willis, 214
Allen, Harry R., 17
Allen, Ingalls & Hoffman, 94
Allen & Collens, 157, 196, 261
Benjamin P. Allen House (Allen-Beville

House), *292–293*
Jonathan W. Allen Stable, *115*
Allmendinger, Louis, 221, 301
Allmendinger & Schlendorf, 295
All Saints' Chapel (Trinity Church), 11
All Saints' Free Church ((Episcopal) Saint Augustine's Episcopal Church), *44*
Almirall, Raymond F., 28, 258, 259, 351
B. Altman & Company Department Store (B. Altman Advanced Learning Super Block), *67–68*, *98*
Alumni House (Fordham University), *318*
Alvin Theater (Neil Simon Theater), *125*
Alvord, Dean, 260
Alwyn Court Apartments, **130**, *131*, 159
Amalgamated Clothing Workers Union, 44
Amax Building (RKO Building, Rockefeller Center), *104*
Ambassador Theater, *93*
American Academy and Institute of Arts and Letters, 194
American Academy of Arts and Letters, 194
American Academy of Dramatic Arts (Colony Club), *77*, *78*, 157
American Bank Note Company Office Building, *18*
American Express Company Building, *11*
American Female Guardian Society and Home for the Friendless, Woody Crest Home, **307**, *307–308*
American Fine Arts Society (Art Students League), *127*, 128, **129**
American Geographical Society (Boricua College), 194
American Horse Exchange, 124
American Methodist Episcopal Church, 351
American Museum of Natural History, 139, *140*, 159
American Numismatic Society, 194
American Radiator Building (Bryant Park Hotel), *99*, 107, 308
American Seamen's Friend Society Sailors' Home and Institute, *53*
American Surety Company Building, *12*
American Telephone and Telegraph Company Long Distance Building, *33*
American Tract Society Building, *24*, 88
American Trust Company, 103
Americas Society (Percy and Maud H. Pyne House), **160**, *160*
Ames, Winthrop, 89

Ammann & Whitney, 370
Amoroux, George L., 166
Amster, James, 120
Amster Yard (Instituto Cervantes), *120*
Andersen, Henry, 191
Anderson, Abraham, 99
Anderson, Peirce, 12
Anderson, William, 330
Anderson Associates, 71, 243
Andrews, Julie, 92
Androvette, Peter, 362
Annunciation Greek Orthodox Church (Fourth Presbyterian Church), 148
Anshe Chesed Synagogue, *45*
Ansonia Hotel, 110, *142*, **143**, 275
ANTA Theater (Guild Theater, Virginia Theater), *125*
Anthony, Wilfred E., 162
Antioch Baptist Church (Greene Avenue Baptist Church and Church House), *242–243*
APA-Phoenix Theater, 95
apartment houses, 231
Apollo Theater, *202*, **203**, 204
Appellate Division Courthouse (New York State Supreme Court), *75*, 314
Apple Bank for Savings (Central Savings Bank), *142*, 232
Appleton, William Henry, 325
D. Appleton & Company, 55, 88
Apthorp Apartments, *144*, 201
Architectural Bureau of the National Council of the YMCA, 205
Architectural Iron Works, 30, 31, 35, 37
Architectural League, 110
Archives Apartments (U.S. Federal Building, United States Appraisers' Store), *51–52*
Ardea apartments, 48
Elizabeth Arden Red Door Salon, 110
Arlington Apartments, 226
Armory Show of 1913, 128
Armstrong, D. Maitland, 51
Armstrong, Henry, 179
Armstrong, Lucille, 283
Louis Armstrong House, *283*, **284**
The Arsenal (Administration Building of Parks and Recreation), *159*
Art Deco, 107
artists, 128
Artman & Fechteler, 334
Art Students League (American Fine Arts Society), *127*, 128, **129**

INDEX